Managing Energy Risk

For other titles in the Wiley Finance Series
please see www.wiley.com/finance

Managing Energy Risk

An Integrated View on Power and Other Energy Markets

Markus Burger
Bernhard Graeber
Gero Schindlmayr

BICENTENNIAL
BICENTENNIAL
1807
⊗WILEY
2007
BICENTENNIAL
BICENTENNIAL

John Wiley & Sons, Ltd

Other Wiley Editorial Offices

John Wiley & Sons Inc., 111 River Street, Hoboken, NJ 07030, USA

Jossey-Bass, 989 Market Street, San Francisco, CA 94103-1741, USA

Wiley-VCH Verlag GmbH, Boschstr. 12, D-69469 Weinheim, Germany

John Wiley & Sons Australia Ltd, 42 McDougall Street, Milton, Queensland 4064, Australia

John Wiley & Sons (Asia) Pte Ltd, 2 Clementi Loop #02-01, Jin Xing Distripark, Singapore 129809

John Wiley & Sons Canada Ltd, 6045 Freemont Blvd, Mississauga, ONT, L5R 4J3, Canada

Wiley also publishes its books in a variety of electronic formats. Some content that appears in print may not be
available in electronic books.

Anniversary Logo Design: Richard J. Pacifico

British Library Cataloguing in Publication Data

A catalogue record for this book is available from the British Library

ISBN-13 978-0-470-02962-6 (HB)

Typeset in 10/12pt Times by Integra Software Services Pvt. Ltd, Pondicherry, India
Printed and bound in Great Britain by Antony Rowe Ltd, Chippenham, Wiltshire
This book is printed on acid-free paper responsibly manufactured from sustainable forestry
in which at least two trees are planted for each one used for paper production.

Contents

Foreword

Around the world, liberalisation of the energy sector has changed the business model of utilities significantly. Before the liberalisation, integrated utilities were not exposed to significant financial risks. Regulated, cost-based tariffs for electricity and gas allowed utilities to pass on all costs incurred to their end customers. Liberalisation has created competition in the energy sector and end user prices have become market based instead of cost based. As a consequence, utilities' revenues generated outside the regulated transmission and distribution business are no longer automatically in line with their costs. Competition has created both strong incentives for improving operational effciency and the need for effective risk management.

In liberalised markets, utilities are exposed to a variety of risks on the cost side as well as on the revenue side: volatile fuel (especially gas, oil, and coal) and CO_2 emission certificate prices, fluctuating wholesale electricity market prices, customers changing their supplier, and uncertain customer demand. Further risks include uncertainty in power plant availability and volatile hydro power generation, depending on river flow rates and reservoir inflows. In this environment, risk management has become a key challenge for every energy company. Liquid markets for physical and financial products for electricity, fuels, and CO_2, provide the opportunity to control and manage risks, but can also create additional risks including credit risks. Not only do energy companies face new challenges but also banks and other financial institutions participating in these markets have to manage risks that differ significantly from those in financial markets.

In energy markets, many risks are fundamentally related to underlying cost structures. For example, electricity prices are not independent of fuel and CO_2 prices. Therefore, an integrated risk management approach is required. This involves the application of methods different from those applied as a standard in financial markets. In particular, market participants must have a deep understanding of the fundamental structure of energy markets.

This book provides a comprehensive overview of the energy markets and their products. It explains models for pricing, portfolio optimisation, risk measurement, and market analysis. Furthermore, it describes risk management methods covering the whole value chain from fuel procurement through wholesale trading to end customer sales. However, it is not limited to the utility perspective. With its focus on both methodological concepts and on their practical application, this book provides a valuable resource for academic researchers and analysts as well as other professionals in the whole energy sector.

The authors, Dr Burger, Dr Graeber, and Dr Schindlmayr, are leading figures of EnBW's energy trading company. Their achievements include the implementation of a modern, full-scale, integrated risk management for EnBW, the development of comprehensive modelling methodologies, and the implementation of various tools and models for the analysis of European energy markets. Therefore, their book integrates both energy economics and financial worlds and is well balanced between theory and practice.

Pierre Lederer
Chief Operating Officer, EnBW Energie Baden-Württemberg AG

Preface

Energy utilisation is crucial for modern society and world energy demand is growing constantly. In recent years, public interest in the energy sector has risen sharply with rapidly increasing oil prices, the liberalisation of energy markets, and the first noticeable effects of climate change caused by the burning of fossil fuels. Securing a reliable and sustainable energy supply in light of declining resources and climate change mitigation will be a key challenge of the 21st century.

Until the mid-20th century, energy demand was almost exclusively met by domestic energy sources. Since then, fossil fuels have become traded internationally and for electricity, regional interconnected markets have evolved. Liberalisation of energy markets in many regions of the world has led to new electricity and gas markets and to significantly increased trading volumes. With the introduction of emissions trading for sulphur dioxide (SO_2) in the United States and for carbon dioxide (CO_2) in Europe, completely new markets with highly specific characteristics have been created. These markets for fossil fuels, electricity, and emission allowances improve macroeconomic effciency with respect to the utilisation of limited resources. However, to achieve effciency at an international level, fair market rules not biased by national or other political interests have to be established and maintained.

Besides the energy companies and besides large consumers and emitters, banks and other speculative traders participate in these growing markets. In recent years, commodities have been increasingly recognised as an important asset class in fund management which can improve a portfolio's risk profile. Energy and emissions markets are often described as unstable and erratic. They are characterised by a multitude of complex products, by high price volatility, and by fundamental interactions between each other. For example, gas prices will not develop independently of oil prices in the long run, as these fuels can be used as substitutes for each other in many applications. Electricity prices depend on electricity generation costs, which are directly impacted by prices for fuels and emission allowances.

For market participants, risk management is essential and has to reflect these specifics adequately. For this purpose, this book pursues a multi-commodity view on the energy markets. In addition to electricity, it also addresses oil, gas, coal, and CO_2 emissions and explains fundamental relations between these commodities.

One specific achievement of this book is the fusion of energy economics approaches, including fundamental market models, with the financial engineering approaches commonly used in banks and other trading companies. In contrast to financial markets, energy markets are significantly influenced by fundamental cost structures, which are covered by energy economics. Effective risk management relies on both aspects. One example of the achieved blend of these approaches is the SMaPs electricity price model described in Chapter 3. It builds on stochastic price models similar to models used for financial markets but it reflects the specific characteristics of electricity markets by using a merit order approach commonly used in fundamental electricity market models.

This book is intended for both academic researchers and professionals either from a technical background in energy economics or from a finance or trading background. The topics covered by this book are not only relevant for risk management but also for structuring, pricing, market analysis, and model development. The main focus is not theoretical scientific concepts but rather methods that have proven successful for real-life application in business. Advantages and disadvantages of different modelling and risk management approaches are discussed.

Chapter 1 provides an introduction to energy markets in general. Different sections describe products, marketplaces and market characteristics for oil, gas, coal, electricity, and emission allowances.

Chapter 2 covers the most important types of energy derivatives with a focus on their mathematical description, pricing models and trading strategies.

Chapter 3 is dedicated to stochastic commodity price models. Topics covered in this chapter are forward curve models, spot price models and forward price models. Special sections focus on electricity price models and multi-commodity modelling approaches.

Chapter 4 focuses on fundamental price mechanisms in electricity markets. It explains the concept of economic power plant dispatch and its application in fundamental market models. In addition, this chapter addresses gas portfolio optimisation and gas market models. Practical examples illustrate the different modelling approaches.

Chapter 5 discusses different types of electricity retail products. Important topics covered in this chapter are the specific risks of retail products, such as volume risk, the calculation of risk premiums, and implications for risk management.

Chapter 6 focuses on the risk management process and addresses market and credit risk. Different risk measures and hedging strategies are discussed.

The chapters are to a large degree self-contained. The reader can start with later chapters and follow references to other chapters where necessary. In particular, Chapters 5 and 6 focus on practical applications and can be read without the mathematical and technical background from Chapters 2 to 4. As an aid for readers with mathematical skills but without specific background in financial mathematics, the appendix resumes the main concepts from econometrics and stochastic analysis used in this book.

1
Energy Markets

Worldwide energy consumption will continue to grow over the next decades. Depending on the economic growth scenario, the average annual growth rate of energy consumption is estimated between 1.5% and 2.6% (Energy Information Administration 2006) with significant differences among the countries. In the reference scenario of 2% worldwide growth rate, non-OECD Asia (including China and India) grows at a rate of 3.7% per year whereas the OECD countries grow only at a rate of 1% per year. The projections for the reference scenario are shown in Figure 1.1.

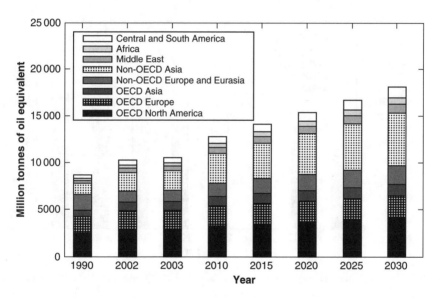

Figure 1.1 World energy consumption outlook by regions (reference scenario). Source: Energy Information Administration (2006)

The main primary energy source worldwide is oil covering 39% of worldwide energy consumption (see Figure 1.2). Second are coal and natural gas each covering 24% of energy consumption. Nuclear energy (6%) and others (8%) have a much smaller share. To meet the growing worldwide demand for energy, there will be an increase in energy consumption from all primary energy sources (Figure 1.3). However, the growth rates for natural gas and coal are expected to be larger than for oil, such that in the year 2030 oil will have a reduced share of only 33%. The shares of coal and natural gas will increase to 27% and 26% respectively.

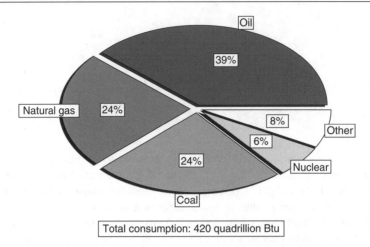

Figure 1.2   World primary energy sources outlook. Source: Energy Information Administration (2006)

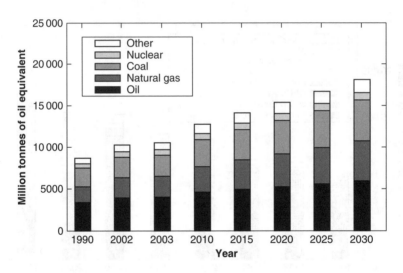

Figure 1.3   World primary energy sources outlook. Source: Energy Information Administration (2006)

The following list gives an overview of energy consumption by end user sectors (Energy Information Administration 2006):

- *Residential sector*: The residential sector (households) uses energy for heating, air conditioning, lighting and power consumption. This sector accounts for 16% of total energy consumption. The energy is delivered mainly in the form of gas, oil and electricity. In the residential sector, there is a strong growth of energy consumption in the non-OECD countries due to growing populations and economic development.
- *Commercial sector*: Consumption in the commercial sector (services and institutions) accounts for 8% of total energy consumption. Within this sector, electricity has the largest share among the different forms of energy.

- *Industrial sector*: The industrial sector includes manufacturing, agriculture, mining and construction. This sector accounts for 49% of total energy consumption and has the highest growth rate of 2.4% mainly driven by economic growth in the non-OECD countries. The most important energy sources in this sector are oil, gas, coal and electricity.
- *Transportation sector:* Consumption in the transportation sector accounts for 27% of total energy consumption and is dominated by oil with a share of 97%.

With the development of a global oil market in the 1980s, energy has become a tradable commodity. In the early 1990s, the deregulation of the natural gas market in the United States led to a liquid and competitive gas market. In Europe, a developed natural gas market exists so far only in the UK, but the process of market liberalisation has also started in continental Europe. The deregulation of the electricity markets in the United States and in several European countries started during the late 1990s and is still continuing (see section 1.4).

The subsequent market overviews use a number of trading terms, some of which will be defined in more detail in the later chapters. The basic trading products mentioned in this chapter are

- *Spot transaction*: Physical transaction with nearby delivery of the commodity.
- *Forward contract*: Bilateral agreement to purchase or sell a certain amount of commodity on a fixed future date (delivery date) at a predetermined contract price.
- *Futures contract*: Exchange traded standardised agreement to purchase or sell a certain amount of a commodity on a fixed future date (delivery date) at a predetermined contract price. Often, there is a financial settlement paying only the value of the commodity at the delivery date instead of a physical delivery.
- *Commodity swap*: A fixed cash flow specified by a fixed commodity price is exchanged against a varying cash flow calculated from a published commodity price index at the respective fixing dates.
- *Option*: An option holder has the right but not the obligation to purchase or sell a certain commodity at a predetermined strike price.

A detailed description of the different trading products is given in Chapter 2.

Bilateral agreements are said to be traded *over-the-counter* (OTC). Such trades are concluded mostly on the phone or through Internet-based broker platforms. For trades concluded at a commodity exchange, the exchange serves as a central counterparty for all transactions. Meanwhile, a number of futures exchanges for energy related commodities exist. The exchanges with global significance are listed below:

- *New York Mercantile Exchange (NYMEX)*: NYMEX is the world's largest physical commodity futures exchange. The wide array of products offered by NYMEX includes futures and options contracts for energy (electricity, oil products, coal, natural gas) and metals (gold, silver, copper, aluminum and platinum). NYMEX light sweet crude oil futures contract introduced in 1983 and NYMEX Henry Hub natural gas futures contract introduced in 1990 have become the most popular energy benchmarks in the United States.
- *Intercontinental Exchange (ICE)*: ICE was founded in May 2000 with the objective of providing an electronic trading platform for OTC energy commodity trading. ICE expanded its business into futures trading by acquiring the International Petroleum Exchange (IPE)

in 2001. ICE's products include derivative contracts based on the key energy commodities: crude oil, refined oil products, natural gas, and electricity. Recently, ICE introduced emissions futures contracts in conjunction with the European Climate Exchange in Amsterdam (see section 1.5). The ICE Brent futures contract serves as an important international benchmark for pricing oil cargos (see section 1.1) in Europe.

There are several other energy exchanges with a focus on specific local markets for electricity or natural gas. Descriptions of those exchanges are included in the subsequent sections.

Unlike in financial markets, the point of delivery plays an important role in commodity trading, since transportation can be costly (coal, oil) or dependent on access to a grid (power, gas). Therefore commodity prices are usually quoted with a reference to the delivery point. Typical delivery points depend on the type of commodity, e.g. Richards Bay in South Africa for coal or Amsterdam–Rotterdam–Antwerp (ARA) for oil or coal. Another important specification for physical commodity trades are the *Incoterms* (international commerce terms) dealing with the clearance responsibilities and transaction costs. The most important Incoterms for energy markets are:

- *Free On Board (FOB)*: The seller pays for transportation of the goods to the port of shipment and for loading costs. The buyer pays for freight, insurance, unloading costs and further transportation to the destination. The transfer of risk is at the ship's rail.
- *Cost, Insurance and Freight (CIF)*: The selling price includes the cost of the goods, the freight or transport costs and also the cost of marine insurance. However, the transfer of risk takes place at the ship's rail.

1.1 THE OIL MARKET

The oil market is certainly the most prominent among the energy markets. *Crude oil* (or *petroleum*) is found in reserves spread across particular regions of the earth's crust, where it can be accessed from the surface. Even though petroleum has been known and used for thousands of years, it became increasingly important during the second half of the 19th century as a primary energy source and as a raw material for chemical products. Today, crude oil is still the predominant source of energy in the transportation sector and is often taken as a benchmark for the price of energy in general. In Europe, for example, prices of natural gas are typically derived from oil prices. Therefore oil prices also have an impact on electricity prices, even though oil plays a minor role as a primary energy source for electricity generation.

Because of oil's great economic importance, oil markets have always been subject to political regulations and interventions. Figure 1.4 shows the historical spot prices for Brent crude oil. Clearly, the oil price is influenced by political events, which explains, for example, the price spike during the First Gulf War 1990/91. In addition, there are long-term economic developments, such as the increase of oil demand in Asia or decreasing reserves/production ratios in some areas of the world.

1.1.1 Consumption, Production and Reserves

Oil consumption and oil production are unevenly distributed across the world. The majority of the world's oil consumption is located in the developed countries in North America,

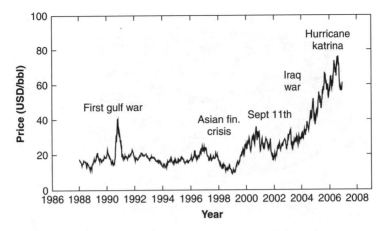

Figure 1.4   Brent historical spot prices. Source: http://www.econstats.com

Europe and Asia (see Figure 1.5), whereas the majority of production is located in developing or transition countries (see Figure 1.6). This imbalance is even more pronounced for oil reserves: 66% of the oil reserves are located in countries in the Middle East (see Figure 1.7). The OPEC member countries control over 40% of the world's oil production and 80% of all known conventional oil reserves. Apart from the known reserves, which can be accessed by conventional methods, there is an increase in known reserves due to improvements in production technology and there are unknown reserves still to be explored.

The *reserves-to-production ratio* describes the number of years that known reserves are estimated to last at the current rate of production. The worldwide reserves-to-production ratio 2005 was approximately 37 years with great differences among the regions (see Figure 1.8). For OPEC members, the reserves-to-production ratio was 73 years, whereas for non-OPEC countries the ratio was only 13 years. As mentioned earlier, reserves are expected to grow over the next decades. On the other hand, oil consumption and therefore oil production are also expected to grow over the next decades. Different scenarios for the world's economic

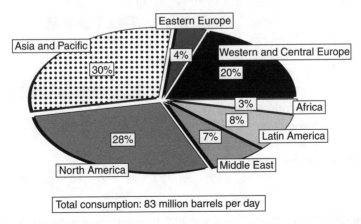

Figure 1.5   World oil consumption 2005 by region. Source: Eni S.p.A. (2006)

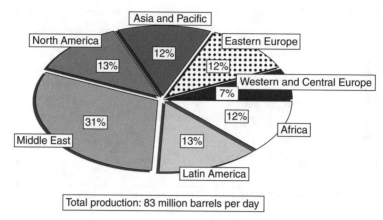

Figure 1.6   World oil production 2005 by region. Source: Eni S.p.A. (2006)

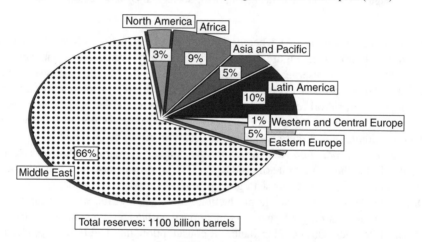

Figure 1.7   World oil reserves 2005 by region. Source: Eni S.p.A. (2006)

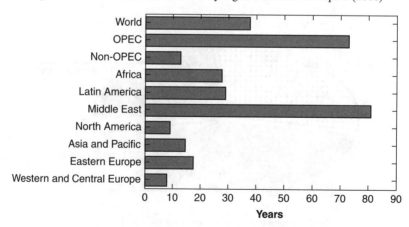

Figure 1.8   Reserves-to-production ratio 2005 by regions. Source: Eni S.p.A. (2006)

growth (see Energy Information Administration 2006) assume an average annual growth rate of 0.9% to 2.0% for the world's oil consumption. This means that in 2030, global oil consumption is estimated to be between 103 and 137 million barrels per day compared to 83 million barrels in 2005.

Depending on its origin, oil can be of different quality. The main characteristics are viscosity and sulphur content. Fluid crude oils with low viscosity have a lower specific weight and are called *light* crudes. With increasing viscosity and specific weight the crudes are called *intermediate* and then *heavy*. Lighter crude oils are more valuable, since they yield more marketable products. Crude oils with a sulphur content of less than 1% are called *sweet*, otherwise they are called *sour*. Since a high sulphur content causes additional costs in the refinery process, sweet crude oils are priced at a premium.

1.1.2 Crude Oil Trading

The physical crude oil market has to deal with a large variety of different oil qualities (viscosity, sulphur content) and with different means of transportation (pipeline, shipping). All of these characteristics influence the oil price. Nevertheless, a liquid oil market has developed, using few reference oil qualities as benchmarks for pricing an individual oil quality. The most popular benchmark oils are:

- *West Texas Intermediate (WTI)*: Reference for the US market. Sulphur content: 0.3%.
- *Brent*: Reference for the North Sea oil market with a similar quality as WTI. Sulphur content: 0.3%.
- *Dubai*: Reference for the Middle East and Far East markets. Sulphur content: 2%.

As the original Brent crude stream has declined over the last decades, the *Brent BFO* index has been created combining Brent, Forties and Oseberg streams. Besides WTI, the Brent BFO index has become the most popular benchmark index for crude oil transactions. Typical physical transactions for BFO crude oil are specified as FOB Sullom Voe (Shetland Islands, UK).

The structure of the physical market for BFO crude oil is connected with its nomination procedure. The sellers are obliged to tell their counterparts 21 days in advance of the first day of the three-day loading window when the cargo will actually be loaded. The final loading schedule is then published by the terminal operator. A contract with an already nominated loading window less than 21 days ahead is called *dated Brent*. The *21-day forward market* trades contracts for delivery up to multiple months ahead where the exact loading window is not yet known and will be nominated 21 days in advance. A typical crude oil cargo has a size of about 500 000 bbl.

The need for producers and consumers to financially hedge oil price risks and the growing importance of oil derivatives for asset managers and speculators gave rise to a very large market of financial instruments connected to oil. The most important commodity exchanges offering oil futures and options are NYMEX for WTI contracts and ICE for Brent contracts. Both WTI and Brent contracts are monthly futures contracts quoted in USD per barrel with a contract size of 1000 bbl. Typically, only the next few months are traded liquidly. For longer-term maturities, there is a liquid OTC market for WTI or Brent swaps.

The ICE Brent Crude Futures Contract was launched 1988 by the former IPE (International Petroleum Exchange). It allows for physical settlement (exchange-for-physical) and for cash settlement. Delivery periods are monthly. Highest liquidity is in the first three delivery months. The last trading day for a specific delivery month is the day before the 15th of the month preceding the delivery month. In case of cash settlement, the underlying price is the ICE Futures Brent Index on the day after the last trading day for this contract. It represents the average price in the 21-day market for the delivery month and is calculated from the appropriate 21-day BFO deals.

The hedging instruments for the 21-day market do not cover the most volatile short-term end of the Brent forward cuve for dated Brent. For this purpose, the *contract for differences* (CFD) has been introduced. A CFD is an over-the-counter swap. The swap buyer receives the weekly mean price for dated Brent and pays the weekly mean price for the front month 21-day Brent contract. In this way, a buyer of a physical Brent cargo priced at dated Brent plus a premium or discount of x USD/bbl can hedge his price risk by entering into a CFD contract converting the dated Brent price into a 21-day forward price. For the 21-day forward price there are standard hedging instruments available.

The long-term forward market for crude oil is dominated by Brent and WTI swaps exchanging a fixed monthly payment against a floating payment, which is the monthly average of the front month futures price. The swap market covers a time period of up to 10 years.

1.1.3 Refined Oil Products

As described earlier, crude oil can be of various qualities concerning its density and sulphur content. To become marketable, *refineries* convert crude oil into various products. The refining process in its basic form is a distillation process, where crude oil is heated in a distillation column. The lightest components can now be extracted at the top of the column whereas the heaviest components are taken out of the bottom of the column. To increase the yield of the more valuable lighter products, a *cracking* process is used, breaking up the longer hydrocarbon molecules. Other processes are needed to remove the sulphur content. Ordered by increasing density, the most important oil products are:

- *Liquefied petroleum gases (LPG)*: Propane or butane.
- *Naphta*: Mainly used in chemical industry.
- *Gasoline*: Mainly used for transportation.
- *Middle distillates*: Kerosine, heating oil and diesel.
- *Fuel oil*: Used in thermal power plants and large combustion engines (factories, ships).

Worldwide there are approximately 700 refineries to match the demand for the different oil distillates (see Figure 1.9). Since building new refineries is a complex project involving very large investments, refining capacities react slowly to changes in demand. Owing to the combined production process, prices of different oil products are usually tightly related to each other and can be expressed in terms of price spreads against crude oil. The lighter and more valuable products have higher spreads against crude oil than the heavier products. In special circumstances, such as a military crisis, prices for certain products (e.g. jet fuel) can spike upwards in relation to crude oil because of the limited refining capacities and the limited flexibility of refineries to change the production ratios among the different products.

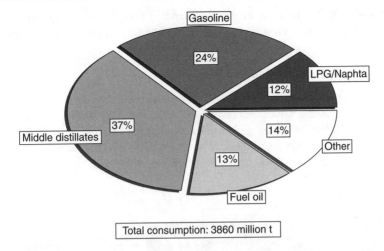

Figure 1.9   Refined oil products: consumption in 2005. Source: Eni S.p.A. (2006)

The European market for refined oil products is divided into ARA (Amsterdam–Rotterdam–Antwerp) and Mediterranean (Genoa). Typical lot sizes for these contracts are barges that correspond to 1000 to 5000 (metric) tonnes.

The most important refined product in Europe is gasoil, which is used for domestic heating and for transportation (diesel). Improvements in diesel engine technology and tax incentives have led to a strong growth of diesel consumption in Europe. Fuel oil plays a limited role, but is still frequently used as a price reference for natural gas contracts.

Typical financial instruments for European gasoil are:

1. *Gasoil swaps*: Gasoil swaps are traded OTC and typically refer to the monthly average gasoil price (ARA or Mediterranean) as published by Platts for setting the floating payments.
2. *ICE gasoil futures*: ICE offers monthly gasoil futures contracts FOB Rotterdam.

In Germany, typical reference prices for HEL (gasoil) and HSL (fuel oil) are published monthly by the "Statistisches Bundesamt". They include certain taxes and transportation costs down the river Rhine. Those *Rheinschiene* prices are often referred to in German natural gas contracts.

1.2   THE NATURAL GAS MARKET

Next to oil and coal, natural gas is one of the most important primary energy sources covering about 25% of worldwide energy consumption. It is primarily used as a fuel for electricity generation, for transportation and for domestic heating. Natural gas consists mainly of methane (CH_4), which is the shortest and lightest in the family of the hydrocarbon molecules. Other components are heavier hydrocarbons, such as ethane, propane and butane, and contaminants, such as sulphur. Natural gas is usually measured in cubic metres. The combustion heat stored in one cubic metre of natural gas at normal atmospheric pressure is about 10.8 kWh (36 850 Btu), but can vary depending on the specific quality. This section gives a general market overview. For economical modelling approaches see section 4.6.

1.2.1 Consumption, Production and Reserves

Worldwide natural gas consumption has a higher growth rate than oil consumption. Between 1994 and 2004 worldwide natural gas consumption increased by 30%, whereas oil consumption increased only by 20%. The global gas consumption in 2004 was 2760 billion cubic metres, which has an energy equivalent of about 30 000 TWh. Figure 1.10 shows how gas consumption is distributed across the different areas of the world.

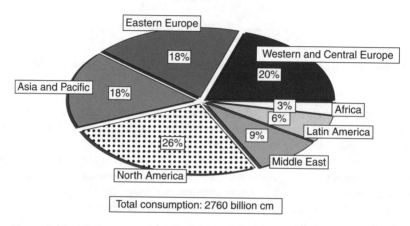

Figure 1.10 World gas consumption 2004 by regions. Source: Eni S.p.A. (2006)

Natural gas is found in the earth's crust mostly in gas or oil fields. Unlike oil, because of its low density, gas is difficult to store and transport. In the past, gas found in oil fields was therefore simply burned without any economic use. With growing demand for primary energy sources, gas prices have risen and large investments have been made to build up an infrastructure for gas transportation, either in the form of pipelines or in the form of liquefied natural gas LNG terminals (see section 1.2.4). The countries with the highest gas production are Russia, the United States and Canada selling most of their gas via pipelines. LNG exports, however, are becoming more and more important with rising gas prices and new investments in LNG terminals. Figures 1.11 and 1.12 give an overview of production volumes and reserves for natural gas.

The proven natural gas reserves amount to about 184 000 billion cubic metres (see Eni S.p.A. 2006). At the current production rate, those reserves are estimated to last for 66 years with large differences for the different areas (see Figure 1.13). In the Middle East the reserves-to-production rate exceeds 200 years, whereas in North America or in Western and Central Europe the reserves-to-production rate is about 20 years or below. Those countries will depend more and more on gas imports. Besides the proven reserves there are still undiscovered reserves estimated at more than 100 000 billion cubic metres (see Energy Information Administration 2006).

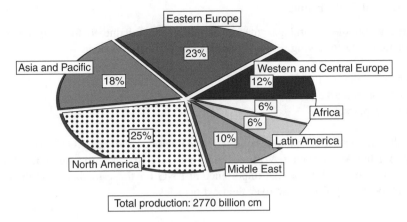

Figure 1.11   World gas production 2004 by regions. Source: Eni S.p.A. (2006)

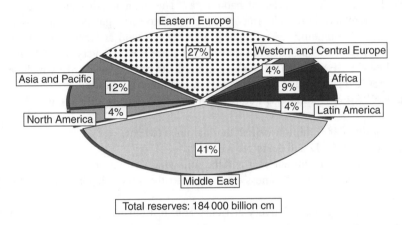

Figure 1.12   World gas reserves 2004 by regions. Source: Eni S.p.A. (2006)

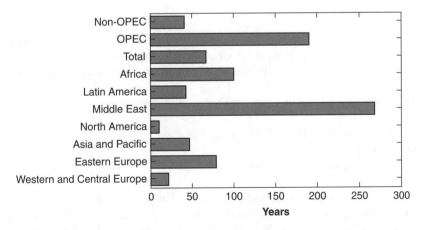

Figure 1.13   Reserves/Production ratio 2004 by regions. Source: Eni S.p.A. (2006)

1.2.2   Natural Gas Trading

Compared to oil the natural gas market is more regional due to the high costs of gas transportation. The following regional markets can be distinguished:

- The North American market.
- The European market.
- The Asian market.

Historically, those regional markets have had little interaction, since LNG played a significant role only for the Asian market. With declining gas reserves and growing demand in North America and Western Europe, the importance of LNG for those markets, and therefore the market interaction, will increase over the next decades.

The North American Market

The United States is an importer of natural gas. The main imports are via pipeline from Canada, but more and more LNG imports are needed to serve gas demand. The gas market is liberalised and competitive. The highest liquidity is found at Henry Hub (Louisiana) in the Gulf of Mexico. Besides a liquid spot market there is also a very liquid futures market introduced by NYMEX in 1990. The range of products offered by NYMEX includes options on gas futures and spreads between Henry Hub and other US gas hubs.

Monthly NYMEX Natural Gas Futures have the following specification:

- *Trading unit*: 10 000 million British thermal units (MBtu).
- *Price quotation*: USD and cents per MBtu
- *Trading months*: The current year and the following five years.
- *Last trading day*: Three business days prior to the first calendar day of the delivery month.
- *Settlement type*: Physical delivery at Henry Hub in Louisiana at a uniform rate over the delivery month.

The European Market

The main exporters to serve Western European demand are Russia, Norway, the Netherlands and Algeria via pipelines. Opposed to the UK, where a liberalised market for gas exists, the market in continental Europe is still dominated by long-term contracts indexed to oil prices (see section 1.2.3).

The most important gas trading hubs in Europe are listed below:

- The National Balancing Point (NBP) in the UK.
- Zeebrugge in Belgium.
- Title Transfer Facility (TTF) in Netherlands.

The continental European market and the UK market are linked by the *Interconnector* pipeline that began operation in 1998. The Interconnector has a length of 230 km and connects Bacton, UK, with Zeebrugge, Belgium. The pipline has a capacity of 20 billion cubic metres of gas per year to transport gas from Bacton to Zeebrugge (forward flow) and a capacity of 23.5 billion cubic metres in the reverse direction (reverse flow). The Interconnector is owned by BG Group (25%), E.ON Ruhrgas (23.59%), Distrigas (16.41%), ConocoPhillips (10%), Gazprom (10%), Total (10%) and ENI (5%). The historical monthly net gas flows are shown in Figure 1.14. Due to decreasing gas production in the UK, the Interconnector is increasingly used in reverse flow direction.

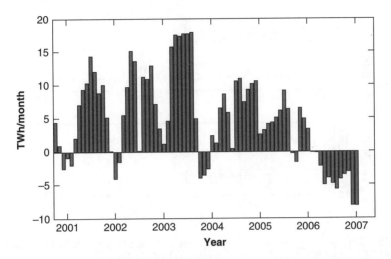

Figure 1.14 Monthly Interconnector gas flows between the UK and continental Europe. Positive values denote net exports from the UK to continental Europe. Source: http://www.interconnector.com

Since the Interconnector makes arbitrage trading possible between the UK and continental Europe (within the technical restrictions of the Interconnector), the gas spot prices at NBP and Zeebrugge are closely connected. Therefore the spread between NBP and Zeebrugge (see Figure 1.15) is most of the time near zero. However, there are short periods of time where the spread is significantly different from zero. Historically, this was regularly the case when the Interconnector was shut down due to maintenance work.

The hubs TTF and Zeebrugge are linked by a network of pipelines within continental Europe. Most of the time the spread between those hubs is therefore close to zero. In extreme situations when pipeline capacity is not sufficient to allow for further arbitrage trading between those hubs, significant spreads are observed. This was, for example, the case during the winter of the gas year 2005/2006 (see Figure 1.15). Price quotations at NBP and Zeebrugge are usually in GB pence per therm, price quotations at TTF in EUR/MWh.

The most liquid futures exchange for natural gas in Europe is ICE. ICE UK Natural Gas Futures have the following specifications:

- *Trading period*: 10–12 consecutive months, 11–12 quarters and six seasons.
- *Contract size*: Five lots of 1000 therms of natural gas per day.
- *Price quotation*: GB pence per therm.
- *Last trading day*: Two business days prior to the first calendar day of the delivery month, quarter or season.

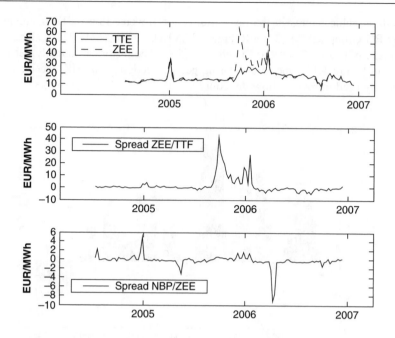

Figure 1.15 Weekly average natural gas spot prices and spreads at the main European hubs TTF, Zeebrugge (ZEE) and NBP. All prices are converted to EUR/MWh

- *Settlement type*: Physical delivery at NBP, equal delivery during each day throughout the delivery period

Besides the ICE there is a futures market for TTF natural gas at the ENDEX exchange in Amsterdam.

The Asian Market

Japan and South Korea cover most of the gas demand through LNG mainly from Indonesia, Malaysia, Australia and the Middle East. This market is dominated by long-term contracts linked to crude oil prices (see section 1.2.3). A typical formula, used in Japan, is $P = A + B \times JCC$, where A and B are constants and JCC is the *Japan Crude Cocktail*, a particular basket of crudes.

1.2.3   Price Formulas with Oil Indexation

Prior to trading natural gas in continental Europe as a commodity of its own, prices for long-term contracts were usually negotiated based on an oil price index formula. Since large investments were needed to build up a gas infrastructure, long-term contracts linked to oil prices guaranteed a long-term supply at a competitive pricing compared to oil. A typical pricing formula for natural gas in continental Europe is of the form

$$P = P_0 + A(X - X_0) + B(Y - Y_0) \tag{1.1}$$

where A and B are constants and X and Y are monthly oil quotations such as gasoil or fuel oil. Similar pricing formulas apply to the Asian market. Typically, such formulas are characterised by a triple (n, l, m):

- n is the averaging period, e.g. six months $(n = 6)$.
- l is the time lag of the price fixing, e.g. $l = 1$ means that to set a price for October the averaging period ends with August.
- m is the recalculation frequency, e.g. $m = 3$ means that the oil price formula is applied every three months to set a new price for the following quarter.

An example for a scheme of type $(6,1,3)$ is shown in Figure 1.16. The new gas price is calculated on the recalculation date and is valid for a three month period.

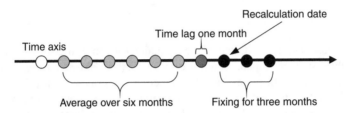

Figure 1.16   Calculation scheme of an oil price formula of type $(6,1,3)$. On the recalculation date, the oil price is averaged over a period of six months ending one month prior to the recalculation date

Hedging the price risk of a gas contract with an oil price formula amounts to hedging an oil price risk. For this purpose the gas position can be translated into an oil position of total magnitude A times the total gas volume. The structure of the oil position over time can be rather complicated depending on the calculation scheme. An example for hedging a gas contract linked to oil prices is given in section 6.1.1.

1.2.4   Liquefied Natural Gas

To transport natural gas over long distances where pipelines are not available, liquefied natural gas (LNG) can be used. LNG is natural gas condensed into a liquid at less than $-161°C$. The density is thereby increased by a factor of about 610 to approximately 0.46 kg/l. Conversly, one (metric) tonne of LNG has a volume of 2.19 cubic metres representing 1336 cubic metres of natural gas with a heating value of 14.4 MWh. With a higher heating value of about 24 MJ/l, the energy density of LNG is comparable to the energy density of crude oil (35 MJ/l). The LNG value chain is shown in Figure 1.17. In the *LNG plant*, the natural gas is cooled down until it becomes liquid. The liquefaction plants, which consist of one or more production units, cause the largest costs in the LNG value chain. A typical modern production unit has a capacity of 5 to 8 million tonnes of LNG per year. After the liquefaction process, the LNG can be loaded onto special insulated *LNG vessels*. A typical LNG vessel has a capacity of about 135 000 cubic metres, but much larger vessels are under consideration. The next step in the value chain is the *regasification terminal*, where the LNG is unloaded, regasified and injected into pipelines. The main exporters for LNG are listed in Table 1.1. Total LNG exports in 2005 amounted to 189 billion cubic metres.

The infrastructure needed for production, transport and regasification is capital intensive and the value chain is costly. Therefore LNG usually cannot compete with gas transported

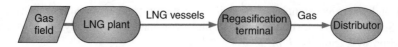

Figure 1.17   LNG value chain

Table 1.1   Main export countries for LNG in 2005. Source: Eni S.p.A. (2006)

Country	LNG exports in billion cm
Indonesia	31.5
Malaysia	28.7
Qatar	27.0
Algeria	25.7

via pipelines. Consequently, LNG has played a major role only in countries were pipelines are not available, such as Japan, South Korea or Taiwan. Most current LNG contracts are long-term contracts with prices linked to pipeline gas prices or oil prices. Take-or-pay clauses typically reduce the volume risk for the seller. Only recently, an increasing number of short-term transactions could be observed. As the currently installed global capacity for regasification terminals is much larger than the global capacity of liquefication plants, short-term transactions can exploit arbitrage opportunities by redirecting LNG vessels to those markets with the most attractive spot prices.

In the future, more and more LNG is needed to serve the growing worldwide gas demand and to replace the decreasing regional gas production in North America or Western Europe. Therefore, many new regasification terminals and LNG plants are planned or are already under construction.

1.3   THE COAL MARKET

Coal is a fossil fuel, usually with the physical appearance of a black or brown rock, consisting of carbonised vegetal matter. It is formed from plant remains that have been compacted, hardened, chemically altered, and metamorphosed by heat and pressure over geological time. It is used as a main source of fuel for the generation of electricity worldwide and for steel production. Coal is a heterogeneous source of energy, with a significantly varying quality. Coal types are distinguished by their physical and chemical characteristics. Characteristics defining coal quality are, for example, carbon, energy, sulphur, and ash content. The higher the carbon content of a coal, the higher its rank or quality. These characteristics determine the coal's price and suitability for various uses.

There are three main categories of coal. These are *hard coal, sub-bituminous coal* and *lignite* (also called brown coal).

Hard coal has a high gross calorific value (GCV) greater than 23 865 kJ/kg (5700 kcal/kg) and can be categorised as follows:

- *Coking coal* is a premium-grade bituminous coal at the top end of the quality spectrum used to manufacture coke for the steelmaking process.

- *Steam coal* is coal used for steam raising and space heating purposes. It includes all anthracite coals and bituminous coals not classified as coking coal. As primary fuel for hard coal fired power plants, steam coal with a calorific value greater than 23 865 kJ/kg (6000 kcal/kg) and with low moisture, ash and sulphur (less than 1%) is used.

Lignite refers to non-agglomerating coal with a GCV less than 17 435 kJ/kg (4165 kcal/kg). Sub-bituminous coal includes non-agglomerating coal with a GCV between those of hard coal and lignite. Shipping of lower quality coals is uneconomical implying that they are not trading products. These low rank coals are therefore not considered in this book.

Since coal may be classified differently, there is sometimes confusion in its classification. Some international agencies classify sub-bituminous coals as hard coal if the energy content is above 18 600 kJ/kg (4440 kcal/kg) and otherwise as lignite (cf. International Energy Agency 2004).

1.3.1   Consumption, Production and Reserves

In 2003 coal accounted for 24% of total world energy consumption. Sixty seven per cent of the produced coal was used for electricity production and 30% for industrial purposes (mainly steel production). In their International Energy Outlook 2006 (see Energy Information Administration 2006), the Energy Information Administration forecasts an increase of coal's share of total world energy consumption to 27% in 2030, while the share as primary fuel in the electric power sector remains at 41%, the same as 2003.

The total reserves of coal around the world are estimated at 909 billion tonnes. At the current consumption level total coal reserves should last approximately 180 years. Based on the consumption forecast of the International Energy Outlook 2006, and assuming that world coal consumption would continue to increase at a rate of 2.0% per year after 2030, current estimated recoverable world coal reserves should last about 70 years.[1]

Unlike oil and gas, coal reserves are more uniformly geographically distributed. The main reserves are in the United States, Russia and China. There are also significant reserves in India, Australia, South Africa, Ukraine and Kazakhstan. The geographic distribution of the total coal reserves with the differentiation between hard coal and sub-bituminous coal/lignite are shown in Figure 1.18.

Coal production is highest in China with 1107 millions tonnes oil equivalent (Mtoe) in 2005. The growing share of coal in world energy consumption can be traced back to increasing production and consumption in China.

Coal production in the United States in 2005 was 576 Mtoe, followed by Australia, India, South Africa, Russia and Indonesia. Figure 1.19 shows coal production in 2005 by region in million tonnes oil equivalent.

Coal consumption is often located in the surrounding area of its production. Because of its lower energy content compared to oil and gas, long distance overland transportation is uneconomical. In general, countries with high coal production also have high coal consumption. Consumption in China in 2005 was 1081 Mtoe. China needs coal not only for producing electricity, but also uses nearly one-half of its 2003 consumption in the industrial sector as the world's leading producer of steel and pig iron.

---

[1] EIA has forecasted the growing rate of coal consumption until 2015 by 3.0% and between 2015 and 2030 by 2%.

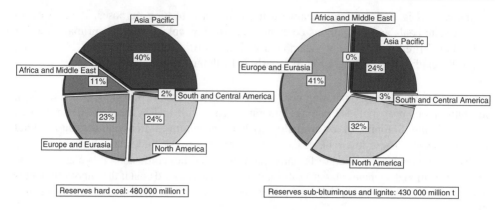

Figure 1.18   Total world coal reserves 2005 by regions. Source: BP (2006)

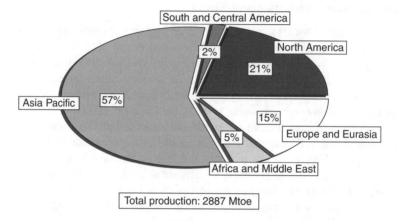

Figure 1.19   Total world coal production 2005 by regions. Source: BP (2006)

In the United States 2005 consumption was 575 Mtoe, followed by India with 212 Mtoe. Japan (212 Mtoe) and at significantly lower rates European countries like Germany and the United Kingdom have consumption exceeding their production. Australia, Indonesia, South Africa, Columbia and Russia are countries where production exceeds consumption and are net exporting nations. Coal consumption in 2005 by region is illustrated in Figure 1.20.

1.3.2   Coal Trading

The volume of international physical coal trading in 2004 was 693 million tonnes (source: EIA). In 2005, this increased to 775 million tonnes with around 90% of this being seaborne trade. Figure 1.21 shows the volume and sea routes for hard coal. There are two main trading regions, the Atlantic and the Pacific region. South Africa, Columbia and Russia are the main coal suppliers for the Atlantic region and Indonesia, Australia and China for the Pacific region. There is also a small interexchange with Australia and Indonesia supplying both the Pacific and the Atlantic region.

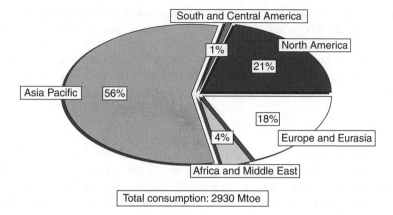

Figure 1.20 Total world coal consumption 2005 by regions. Source: BP (2006)

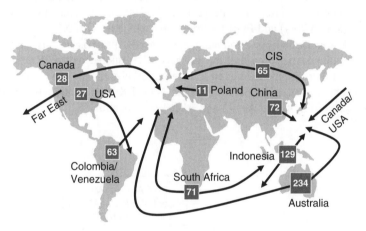

Figure 1.21 Sea routes for hard coal with transported volume. Source: Verein der Kohleimporteure (German Coal Importers Association), 2006

Producers

In the steam coal market, mergers have resulted in high market shares of some companies. The largest privately owned companies, known as the "Big Four", with a market share of approximately 35%, are:

- BHP Billiton, which was formed from a merger between BHP Ltd, Melbourne and Billiton plc, London. In 2006, BHP Billiton generated a turnover of USD 39.1 billion. BHP Billiton has investments in coal mining operations in Australia, South Africa, and Colombia.
- Rio Tinto, which is a combination of two companies: Rio Tinto plc, based in the UK, and Rio Tinto Ltd, based in Australia. Their activities span the world but are strongly represented in Australia and North America.

- Anglo American, which was formed through the combination of Anglo American Corporation of South Africa and Minorco. Anglo American has investments in coal mining operations in South Africa, Australia, and South America.
- Glencore, which also holds approximately 35% in Xstrata. Glencore has investments in coal mining operations in Colombia and South Africa. Xstrata has interests in coal mining operations in Australia, South Africa, Canada, and Colombia.

Physical Coal Prices

Because coal transportation can be expensive, in some instances it accounts for up to 70% of the delivered cost of coal, coal prices depend on the point of delivery. Standard delivery points in international coal trading are, for example, Richards Bay in South Africa, Newcastle in Australia, ARA for Central Europe or the Central Appalachian in the United States.

The characteristics defining the quality of coal also determine its price. Energy content is the most price relevant characteristic, and quoted prices per tonne (or per short ton in the USA) always refer to a specified quality and in particular to a specified energy content.

Figure 1.22 shows coal prices for the years 2004–2006 for delivery FOB Richards Bay (API#2), CIF ARA (API#4) and FOB Central Appalachian (NYMEX).[2] Both Richards Bay and the Central Appalachian are producing areas, so the price is usually quoted Free On Board. ARA is a consumer area and the price is often quoted as a CIF price. The price FOB ARA for further shipment is approximately 2 EUR/t higher. The energy content of Central Appalachian Coal corresponding to the NYMEX specification is higher than the energy content according to the API#2 and API#4 specification.

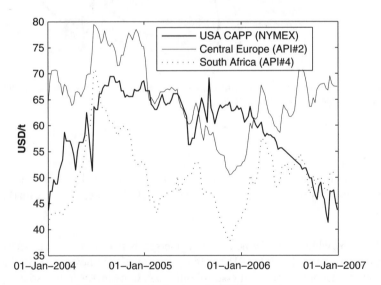

Figure 1.22 Coal prices for different regions

---

[2] CAPP futures contract with the nearest expiration.

Price Indices

Price information for hard coal can be obtained either from exchanges, from brokers or from independent information service providers. These include Argus Media Ltd, which offers price information, market data and business intelligence for the global petroleum, natural gas, electricity and coal industries, and the McCloskey Group, which offers data, news, and analysis focused solely on the coal industry. Price information published by the information services is typically generated via telephone or e-mail survey covering sellers of physical coal, utility buyers, trading companies and broking companies. Market analysts then assess the price of the standard specified coal that conforms to the required specification. The mechanism of price assessment must eliminate the opportunity for gaming the mechanics of the index. In contrast to an exchange, an information service has no secured information about the concluded trades.

Tradition Financial Services (TFS), a broker of OTC physical and derivative products, averages prices originally published by Argus Media and McCloskey (McCloskey's NW European steam coal marker) and has generated the well-accepted All Publications Index (API). The TFS API indices are published in the Argus/McCloskey Coal Price Index Report. There are the following API indices:

- API#2 is the index for the ARA region quoted as CIF ARA and is an important benchmark for Central Europe.[3] Delivery must be within the next 90 days, the energy content is specified at 6000 kcal/kg and the sulphur content must be less than 1%.
- API#3 is the index for FOB Newcastle, Australia. It is also a benchmark for CIF Japan prices by adding a Panamax freight assessment. Delivery must be within the next 90 days, the energy content is specified at 6700 kcal/kg and the sulphur content must be less than 1%.
- API#4 is the index for the FOB Richards Bay, South Africa, physical market. Delivery must be within the next 90 days, the energy content is specified at 6000 kcal/kg and the sulphur content must be less than 1%.

Financial Swaps

Financial swaps are the most common product for risk management for both coal producers and consumers. Because physical coal always has specific characteristics, physical coal trading is not as straightforward as trading financial swaps. The swap market is therefore particularly interesting for financial institutions, which are active market players. Financial swaps are traded usually up to three years in the future, while the time period for physical coal trading is usually shorter.

Marketplaces

Most coal trades are OTC trades. There are several exchanges that offer coal as a trading product, but the traded volume at some smaller exchanges is low.

At *NYMEX*, coal futures for the months of the current year plus the months in the next two calendar years are traded. These Central Appalachian (CAPP) coal futures are a benchmark

---

[3] The former API#1 index (CIF ARA) has been replaced by the more accepted API#2.

for coal prices in the United States. Delivery is to be made FOB buyer's barge at seller's delivery facility on the Ohio and Big Sandy River District, with all duties, entitlements, taxes, fees, and other charges imposed prior to delivery paid by the seller. The specified energy content is 12 000 Btu/pound (approximately 6700 kcal/kg) with a sulphur content of less than 1%.

The *Intercontinental Exchange* (ICE) offers Rotterdam coal futures contracts, which are financially settled, based on delivery to Rotterdam in the Netherlands. It is cash settled against API#2. ICE also offers Richards Bay coal futures, financially settled against API#4. Both are offered for six consecutive months, six consecutive quarters, five consecutive seasons and two consecutive calendar years. The traded volume for some of these products is low.

GlobalCOAL is a broker platform for physical coal for the important markets like Richards Bay, ARA, Newcastle and Puerto Bolivar in Colombia. It is also a marketplace for swaps on API#2 and API#4. A specified master agreement, the Standard Coal Trading Agreement (SCoTA), has to be used.

1.3.3   Freight

The delivery price of coal is determined in part by ocean freight rates. They are an important factor for the price of coal in different regions and the competitiveness of coal against other fuels. The main factor that will affect the future movement of freight rates is the overall development of dry bulk trade.

Mainly Cape and Panama sized vessels are employed in international coal trading. Cape sized vessels, used, for example, for the route Richards Bay to ARA, are also employed in the iron ore trade. As the shipping capacity is limited, the activity of the world's steel industry has an impact on coal freight rates. The other trade that can have an impact on coal freight rates is grain shipment, which is carried out predominantly in Panamax vessels. For both the export of grain and the import of iron ore, China's economy is an important factor. Figure 1.23 shows the volatility of ocean freight costs.

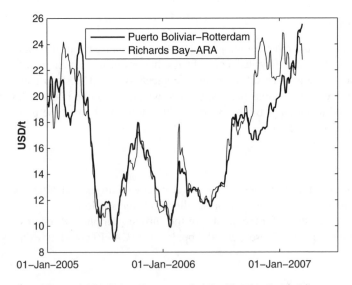

Figure 1.23   Prices for ocean freight (Capsized vessels)

1.3.4   Coal Subsidies in Germany: BAFA-Indexed Prices

In Germany the Federal Office of Economics and Export Control (Bundesamt für Wirtschaft und Ausfuhrkontrolle, BAFA) grants subsidies for German coal mining, promoting the sale of German hard coal to power stations and the steel industry. The aim of these grants is to compensate for the difference between the production costs in Germany and the coal prices of third countries. BAFA fixes the parameter for grants after checking the production costs and publishes the prices of third countries for steam coal and coking coal free German border in the BAFA index. The BAFA index may differ from the spot price (e.g. measured as API#2 price) because the import prices used for determining the BAFA index are reported when the coal is passing the German border. Since most of the contracts are concluded long before delivery, these coal import prices are a mix of forward contract prices concluded at different points of time but with the same delivery date. Imported coal is usually priced in USD, and the foreign exchange rate used for translation in Euros by BAFA is the average spot rate at the month of delivery to the German border. Hedging of BAFA-indexed contracts is difficult. While API#2 swaps are a common trading product, there is no liquid market for BAFA swaps.

1.4   THE ELECTRICITY MARKET

Electricity is a form of energy used for a very wide range of applications. It is easy to control, non-polluting at the location of its usage and convenient; it is used in the application of heat, light and power. As a secondary energy source electricity is generated from the conversion of other energy sources, like coal, natural gas, oil, nuclear power, hydro power and other renewable sources. This implies that electricity markets and electricity prices are fundamentally linked to markets for primary fuels and environmental conditions. To understand the electricity market and price mechanisms it is essential to consider the electricity generation process as well as the fuel markets. This section gives an introduction to the electricity market, to main market places and to wholesale products. Technical background information as well as energy economical modelling approaches can be found in Chapter 4.

1.4.1   Consumption and Production

Electricity is a growing market, even in proportion to the world energy markets. In 1973 electricity consumption accounted for 11% of the total world energy demand and has grown to 18% today. The absolute growth rate of electricity consumption in the future is estimated at an average of 2.7% per year. In the year 2003, world energy consumption was 14 781 TWh[4] and the financial volume of the world's physical consumption can be valued at more than USD 1000 billion per year. The projected growth in electricity consumption published by the Energy Information Administration (EIA)[5] is shown in Figure 1.24. Projected growth in net electricity consumption is most rapid among the non-OECD economies of the world. China leads the absolute growth in annual net electricity consumption with projected increases of 4300 TWh until 2030 followed by the United States with an increase of 1983 TWh.

---

[4] 1 terawatthour = 1 billion kilowatthour.
[5] Source: EIA, System for the Analysis of Global Energy Markets (2006).

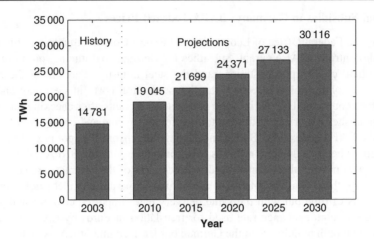

Figure 1.24 World net electricity consumption. Source: EIA

Today's electricity demand and mode of generation for different countries is illustrated in Table 1.2. Demand is highest in the United States with 3640 TWh in 2004 and per capita consumption is twice as high as in comparable European countries. Only in a few small countries with a particular type of generation and demand structure is the per capita consumption higher than in the United States. For example, in Norway 99% of the electricity generation capacity is hydro power, which results in competitive prices while the aluminium

Table 1.2 Net consumption and generation by fuel type in 2004

Country	Net Consumption (TWh)	Production according to primary fuels				
		Coal and lignite (%)	Nuclear (%)	Gas and oil (%)	Hydro (%)	Others (%)
Australia	199	79	0	13	7	1
Austria	58	14	0	20	61	5
Belgium	81	13	55	27	2	2
Canada	503	17	15	9	57	2
Czech Republic	54	60	31	5	3	1
Denmark	33	46	0	29	0	25
Finland	83	27	26	16	18	13
France	416	5	78	4	11	1
Germany	513	44	24	23	4	6
Ireland	23	30	0	63	4	3
Italy	296	17	0	58	16	8
Japan	966	27	26	35	10	2
Mexico	170	11	4	70	11	4
Netherlands	103	26	4	63	0	7
New Zealand	35	10	0	17	65	9
Norway	110	0	0	0	99	1

Poland	100	93	0	4	2	1
South Africa	197	92	5	0	2	0
Spain	231	29	23	28	12	8
Switzerland	56	0	41	2	54	3
Turkey	120	23	0	46	31	0
United Kingdom	340	34	20	42	2	2
United States	3640	50	19	21	7	2

Source: EIA.

industry and use of electricity for heating yields the highest per capita consumption of 24 000 kWh/p.a.

Prices for Electricity

The price for electricity is determined mainly by the fuels used for generation. Price drivers and the market equilibrium price are analysed in Chapter 4. The mix of primary fuels varies from country to country, which means that the variable operation costs also differ. Table 1.3 shows the electricity prices for a yearly baseload contract, which is a common trading product and a price benchmark for retail customers.

Table 1.3 Comparison of wholesale electricity prices

Country	Price for baseload 2008 in the middle of February 2007 (EUR/MWh)
Belgium	51.44
France	48.23
Germany	50.40
Netherlands	53.17
Scandinavia (Nord Pool)	39.10
United Kingdom	47.38
United States (PJM)	45.35

Figure 1.25 illustrates the development of the yearly baseload contract prices.

Prices for industrial customers are illustrated in Table 1.4 and are close to wholesale prices for the underlying load profile. Differences are mainly due to taxes and further state caused costs. At production, variable operation costs are lowest for hydro power plants. Usually marginal costs and not full costs determine electricity prices and therefore countries like Norway with a high percentage of hydro generation have low electricity prices.

In the United Kingdom, coal and gas are the usual primary fuels, implying that the price for electricity is gas price sensitive. It also depends on the price for CO_2 emission allowances. If the price for emission allowances rises there will be a fuel switch to gas fired plants, because a coal fired plant emits more CO_2 per MWh than a gas fired one. With 78% production from nuclear plants, France has also a specific mix of primary fuels. France exports to Germany, Italy, the United Kingdom, Switzerland, Belgium and Spain. These exports influence the electricity prices to these countries.

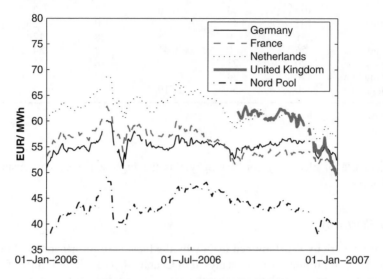

Figure 1.25   Comparison forward contract price for baseload 2008

Table 1.4   Electricity prices for industry

Country	Electricity prices for industry (EUR/MWh)		
	2000	2004	2005
Australia	45.20	60.90	*n.a.*
Austria	38.20	95.80	101.70
Belgium	47.70	*n.a.*	*n.a.*
Canada	38.50	49.00	*n.a.*
Czech Republic	43.00	66.20	80.60
Denmark	57.70	95.90	*n.a.*
Finland	38.60	72.00	70.40
France	35.80	49.80	49.80
Germany	40.60	76.90	*n.a.*
Ireland	48.90	95.70	99.40
Italy	88.90	161.50	*n.a.*
Japan	143.20	127.20	*n.a.*
Mexico	50.90	77.50	87.80
Netherlands	57.10	*n.a.*	*n.a.*
New Zealand	28.00	51.00	54.70
Norway	19.40	43.30	43.40
Poland	36.90	60.10	69.90
South Africa	17.20	*n.a.*	*n.a.*
Spain	42.60	59.90	83.30
Switzerland	69.10	85.40	83.30
Turkey	80.00	100.10	106.60
United Kingdom	55.40	66.70	86.00
United States	46.40	52.50	57.30

Energy end-use prices including taxes, converted in Euros.
Source: EIA November 2006.

1.4.2 Electricity Trading

For many commodities there is an intuitive answer to the question "What is the real trading product?" But for electricity the answer to this question requires further understanding of the technical background.

Among all commodities electricity has the unique feature that it is not storable. An exception are hydro pumped storage power plants, but in most countries their capacity is small compared to total consumption. The second main feature is the necessity for a transmission network, which prevents a global market. These characteristics of electricity shown in Figure 1.26 have strong implications on the trading products and their prices. An often discussed characteristic resulting from the non-storability is the high volatility of power prices, but these high price movements refer to products with a nearby delivery. In the absence of sufficient economical generation capacity, non-storability causes high price movements on the spot market. In the forward market with delivery dates in the far future the price movements are much smaller, because the availability of power plants and weather dependent demand are still unknown.

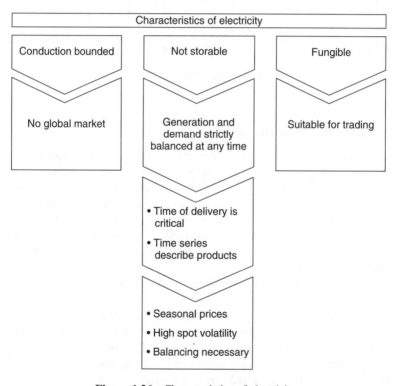

Figure 1.26 Characteristics of electricity

The lack of storability requires an exact matching of supply and demand at all times. Because a merchant cannot forecast the demand of his customers exactly there must be someone responsible for balancing supply and demand. This is a task of the transmission system operator (TSO), who charges the merchant directly or the retail customers via transmission fees for this service. The TSO defines a balancing period (e.g. 30 minutes in the UK, 15 minutes in Germany), which is the granularity of the measured electric energy supply. The continuously varying power requirements of retail customers is integrated over the balancing period and the average power is the size which is forecast and should be delivered by the supplying merchant. As a result, the merchant delivers energy as a discrete time series with time steps according to the balancing period and constant power during these time periods. Figure 1.27 illustrates the continuously varying power requirement (load profile) and the piecewise constant delivery of power during the balancing period.

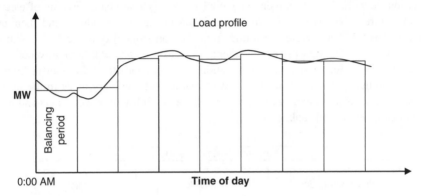

Figure 1.27   Balancing period

1.4.3   Products in the Electricity Markets

The principal products in the electricity markets are delivery time series in a granularity not finer than the balancing period. The usual granularity is one hour and in this book this granularity is assumed if not stated otherwise. Power balancing during the balancing period itself is the task of the TSO. Since the TSO usually has no personal generation capacities he has to purchase products that allow an increase or decrease in production (including import and export) in his transmission system. In this section the main features of products in the electricity market are described. As there is no global market for electricity, the products in regional markets may differ.

The electricity market can be divided into the following categories:

- *Forward and futures market*: The forward and futures market is the relevant market for risk management and serves the participants to hedge their positions. It is also the relevant market for speculation and pure trading purposes. The agreed delivery or acceptance period of these products includes dates later than the next trading day.
- *Day ahead market*: In the day ahead market products are traded which are delivered the next day. If the next day is not a trading day the day ahead market also includes products delivered between the next day and the next trading day. Day ahead products are the most common spot products and can be traded either on a power exchange or as a bilateral agreement. Day ahead products are the underlyings of the futures contracts on the power exchange.
- *Intra-day market*: The intra-day market is for products with a delivery on the same day. This market allows the producers a short-term load dependent optimisation of their

generation. Because this market serves the direct physical supply it is not a market for pure trading purposes. Intra-day products are traded either on a power exchange or bilaterally.

- *Balancing and reserve market*: There are different definitions of the terms balancing market and reserve market, because these markets depend on a regulator and are country specific. In the context of this book the *reserve market* is the market allowing the TSO to purchase the products needed for compensating imbalances between supply and demand in the electricity system. The *balancing market* (also referred to as real-time market) denotes the market where a merchant purchases or sells the additional energy for balancing his accounting grid. This is the service of the TSO who charges or reimburses the merchant for the additional energy, and only in some national markets is the merchant able to buy or sell this balancing energy from or to someone else. So the balancing market can be regarded as a market only in a broad sense.

The different market categories and their time flow are described in Figure 1.28.

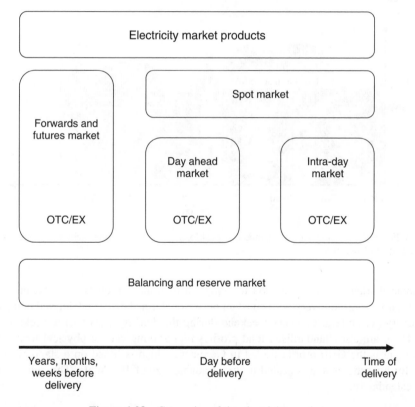

Figure 1.28   Categories of the electricity market

Outside the balancing and reserve market, products in the electricity market can be described by time series. Usually the granularity of the time series is one hour and then each number of the time series specifies the constant power delivered in the corresponding hour. If the delivered power is constant over the delivery period $[T_1, T_2]$ the contract is called a *baseload contract*. If the constant power is delivered only is constant in those predefined hours of the delivery period when the consumption is high the contract is called a *peakload contract*. Peakload hours depend on the particular market. For example, at the New York Mercantile Exchange (NYMEX) peakload hours are the hours 7:00 am to 11:00 pm and in France and Germany the hours are 8:00 am to 8:00 pm on peakload days. Peakload days at NYMEX are Monday–Friday, excluding specified holidays, while in France and Germany they are Monday–Friday including public holidays.

Forward Market

Forwards can be divided into standard forwards and individual power schedules. Standard contracts are baseload or peakload contracts whose delivery period is a day, week, month, quarter or year. Individual schedules are delivery schedules, whose power can vary every hour or even every balancing period (e.g. every 30 minutes in the UK). Figure 1.29 shows a baseload contract, a peakload contract, and an individual schedule, where the delivery period is one week.

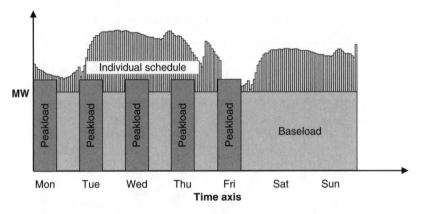

Figure 1.29   Delivery hours of a baseload, a peakload and an individual schedule contract with a delivery period of one week

In some markets there are efforts to standardise further products. These can be block contracts, implying a delivery with constant power on defined dates and defined hours during the delivery period (e.g. on every weekend during the delivery period of a week, month or year). There are also standardised load profiles representing certain physical load patterns. An example is the GH0 profile traded in Germany, which is based on a standardised load profile for households and is scaled up to a tradable size of 10 GWh/a. The delivery period is one calendar year.

Futures Market

As usual for every futures contract (see section 2.1.2) electricity futures are subject to a daily margining. As electricity futures contracts do not have a single delivery date but a delivery period, there must be mechanism to calculate the variation margining during the delivery period. Often contracts with a long delivery period (e.g. a year or a quarter) are split into futures contracts with a shorter delivery period (e.g. a quarter or a month). This procedure is called cascading and is shown in Figure 1.30. In this example the yearly futures contract cascades into three monthly futures contracts and into the three remaining quarterly futures contracts. Later, the quarterly contracts cascade into monthly contracts. The final settlement price of a monthly future is then established from the average of the associated spot market prices.

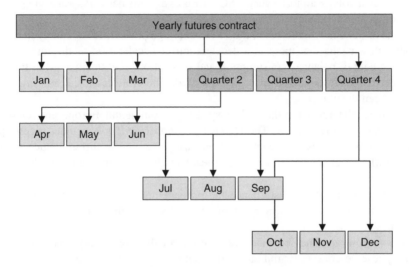

Figure 1.30   Cascading of a yearly futures contract

Spot Market (Day Ahead and Intra-Day Market)

Spot products are traded OTC as well as on power exchanges. The term of payment on an exchange is often shorter than for OTC contracts. Standard products are baseload and peakload contracts with a delivery period of one day. In addition there are hourly contracts and block contracts. Hourly products are traded on the spot market only and are the basis for the pricing of many other products. In the case of block contracts the delivery of electricity with a constant power over several delivery hours is traded. The spot market is the underlying for the forward and futures market.

Balancing and Reserve Market

While forwards and futures markets have a comparable structure in different regions, the balancing and reserve markets are affected by national regulation, which defines the role of the TSO. In the United States the system operators are public utilities regulated by the individual states and FERC.[6]

There are also international associations that secure the interconnected power systems. In Europe the European Transmission System Operators (ETSO) was created in 1999, as an association with the following founding members:

---

[6] Federal Energy Regulatory Commission.

- UCTE, the Union for the Coordination of Transmission of Electricity, TSOs of the continental countries of Western and Central Europe.
- NORDEL, the association of Nordic TSOs.
- UKTSOA, the United Kingdom TSO Association.
- ATSOI, the association of TSOs in Ireland.

Today, ETSO involves almost every TSO in Europe, with networks supplying more than 490 million people with electricity.

A change in frequency indicates to the TSO a shortage or a surplus of energy in the system. Physically, this means that there is a deceleration or acceleration of the turbines because their kinetic energy balances consumption and generation. For stabilising the transmission system this frequency deviation must be equalised. Therefore technical and organisational rules have been developed.

For example, the rules for the UCTE system in continental Europe are referred to in the *UCTE Operation Handbook*. The *UCTE Operation Handbook* includes a description of generation control actions. The control actions are performed in different successive steps, each with different characteristics and qualities, and all depending on each other.

- *Primary reserve*: After a disturbance the primary reserve (also called primary control) starts within seconds as a joint action of all TSOs in the synchronised transmission system.
- *Secondary reserve*: The secondary reserve (also called secondary control) replaces the primary reserve after a few minutes and is put into action by the responsible TSOs only.
- *Tertiary reserve*: The tertiary reserve (also called tertiary control or minute reserve) frees the secondary reserve by rescheduling generation and is put into action by the responsible TSOs.

The sequence of the different control actions is displayed in Figure 1.31.

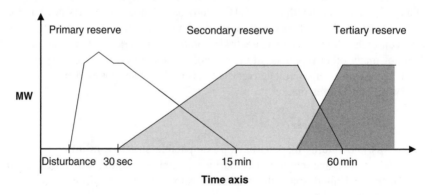

Figure 1.31   Control actions in the UCTE system

The products in the reserve market are derived from these control actions. The TSO tenders the products it needs for fulfilling these functions. In contrast to forwards, futures or spot products, the reserve market products are more technical and refer to specified plants. These plants must be able to reduce or increase production at short notice. While for most other electricity products only energy delivered is payed for, reserve energy products involve often an additional payment of the reserved capacity.

The prices for balancing power are usually prices for the delivered energy only. For the merchant this is often additional cost which is analysed in section 5.5. Prices for balancing power differ widely and are only sometimes related to spot or futures market prices. The relation of the balancing and the spot market in the Netherlands is studied in Boogert and Dupont (2005).

1.4.4 Energy Exchanges

Energy exchanges are major marketplaces for electricity. In recent years more and more countries have founded exchanges for electricity. Some of them are only a marketplace for spot products, but the major exchanges are characterised by the existence of a derivative market with a high trading volume. Most electricity exchanges are located in Europe and North America. The map in Figure 1.32 shows the location of some electricity exchanges worldwide.

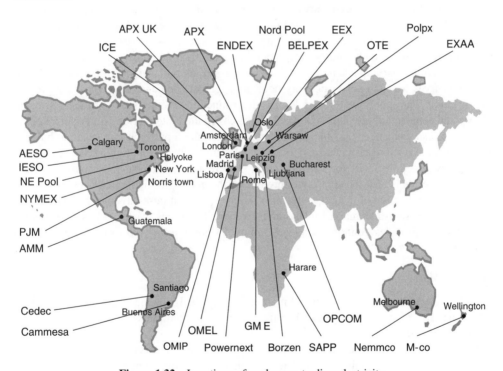

Figure 1.32 Locations of exchanges trading electricity

In this section some of the major exchanges are discussed in more detail.

Nord Pool

Nord Pool is a multinational exchange for trading electricity in Northern Europe. It was founded in 1993 initially as the Norwegian market for physical contracts, as a result of the deregulation of the Norwegian electricity market in 1991. In 1996 the joint Norwegian–Swedish power exchange commenced, the world's first multinational exchange for trade in power contracts. Subsequently Finland and Denmark joined the Nordic power exchange market area. In 2006 the traded volume in the physical market (Elspot) was 250 TWh and there were 294 registered participants. The volume in the financial market was 766 TWh and together with the clearing volume of the OTC market there is a total volume of 2160 TWh with a value of approximately 79 billion Euros. This total trading volume exceeds by far the generation of approximately 370 TWh in Norway, Sweden, Finland and Denmark.

At the Nord Pool there are three product groups:

- Physical market.
- Financial market.
- Clearing service.

Physical Market – Nord Pool Spot AS

Nordic market participants trade power contracts for next day physical delivery at the Elspot market. This day ahead trading is based on an auction trade system. Bids for purchase and sale of power contracts of one-hour duration cover all 24 hours of the next day. Three bidding types are available, namely hourly bids, block bids, and flexible hourly bids. As soon as the noon deadline for participants to submit bids has passed, all buy and sell orders are gathered into two curves for each power-delivery hour: an aggregate demand curve and an aggregate supply curve. The spot price for each hour is determined by the intersection of the aggregate supply and demand curves. This spot price is also called the system price. Since Nord Pool is a multinational exchange, possible grid congestions require a partition into separate bidding areas. Separate price areas occur if the contractual flow between bidding areas exceeds the capacity allocated by TSOs for spot contracts. If there are no such capacity constraints, the spot system price is also the spot price throughout the entire Nordic Power Exchange Area.

After the publication of the Elspot results there is a physical intra-day market called *Elbas* for the areas Eastern Denmark, Finland and Sweden. The Elbas market is based on hourly contracts and provides continuous power trading 24 hours a day, up to one hour prior to delivery.

Financial Market

The Nord Pool offers a liquid financial market for price hedging and risk management with a time horizon of up to four years. The market consists of futures, forwards, options and contracts for differences.

Futures contracts consist of standardised day and week contracts. Weeks are listed in a continuous cycle of eight weeks. The settlement of futures contracts involves a daily marked-to-market settlement and a final spot reference cash settlement after the contract reaches its due date.

Nord Pool uses a slightly modified definition for the term *forward contract*. In the context of this book and consistent with the definition in many publications (e.g. Hull 2005) the term forward is used for OTC trades, which implies that there is no marked-to-market settlement. Nord Pool uses the term forward for their particular exchange products with no marked-to-market settlement in the trading period prior to the due date. The marked-to-market is accumulated as daily loss or profit but not realised throughout the trading period.

During the delivery period the difference between the price when the contract was entered into and the spot reference price will be cleared.

Nord Pool's forward contracts consist of monthly, quarterly, seasonal and yearly contracts. Months are listed in a continuous cycle of six months. Seasons (winter, summer) are replaced by quarters. Years cascade into either seasons or quarters, and quarters cascade into months.

Market participants who use financial market derivatives to hedge spot market prices remain exposed to the risk that the system price will differ from the actual area price of their spot purchases or sales. To overcome this potential price differential risk Nord Pool offers a forward contract product named *Contracts for Difference*. The liquidity of these contracts is sometimes insufficient.

Options contracts traded at Nord Pool use standard forwards as the underlying contract. The option contracts are European style, i.e. they can only be exercised at the exercise date. Options with new strike prices are automatically generated to reflect price movements of the underlying forward instrument.

Nord Pool Clearing also clears contracts traded in the bilateral financial markets that are registered for clearing. To be accepted for clearing a bilateral market electricity contract must conform to the standardised products traded at Nord Pool. This clearing service reduces clearing members' counterparty risk.

European Energy Exchange

The European Energy Exchange (EEX) is located in Leipzig, Germany, and is the leading exchange for electricity in Central Europe. Preceding companies were Leipzig Power Exchange started in 2000 and European Energy Exchange started in 2001. Both exchanges and their supporting associations merged in 2002. In 2006 the total traded volume in the physical spot market was 89 TWh and in the futures market, including OTC clearing, was 1044 TWh. The traded volume clearly exceeds the total consumption in Germany of approximately 540 TWh. At the EEX the product groups are:

- Power spot market.
- Power futures and options.
- Coal futures and EU emission allowances.
- Clearing service.

Power Spot Market

The spot market at the EEX includes a day ahead and an intra-day market. At the day ahead market there is a continuous trading of baseload, peakload and weekend baseload contracts and an auction for single hours and blocks of contiguous hours. Besides a delivery in the grid of the four German TSOs there is also an auction for delivery in the Austrian Power Grid and in the Swissgrid. In the intra-day market full hours and blocks of contiguous hours can be traded with physical delivery in the four German TSO areas. This service offers continuous trading 24 hours a day, seven days a week.

Power Futures and Options

At the EEX futures contracts with financial and physical settlement are traded. The underlying of the financially settled futures contracts is the EEX spot market index Phelix. The settlement of futures contracts involves a daily marked-to-market settlement. Yearly and quarterly futures are fulfilled by cascading, this process is displayed in Figure 1.30. Traded products are baseload and peakload futures for the next six calendar years, the next seven quarters, the current and six following months.

At the end of a month the last payment for monthly futures is established on the basis of the difference between the final settlement price and the settlement price of the previous exchange trading day. The final settlement price is established from the average of the associated EEX spot market prices.

Additionally there are futures contracts with a physical settlement available both in Germany and in France. These contracts are also subject to a daily marked-to-market settlement. The traded volume of these futures is much smaller than those for the financially settled futures.

EEX offers European-style options, i.e. the options can only be exercised on the last day of trading. The underlyings are the financially settled futures. More specifically, options on the respective next five baseload monthly futures, the respective next six baseload quarterly futures and the respective next three baseload yearly futures can be traded. The liquidity of the EEX options market has so far been very low.

EEX offers a well-accepted *clearing service* for OTC trades. The volume of OTC clearing is comparable to the volume of the traded futures. OTC transactions corresponding to available EEX futures or options can be registered by means of a so-called EFP (Exchange Futures for Physical) trade for OTC clearing.

New York Mercantile Exchange

After a delisting in 2002 NYMEX takes a novel approach to the relaunch of electricity futures. The new contracts are PJM electricity futures which have the PJM spot market as an underlying. PJM Interconnection LLC administers more than 44 million customers in Delaware, Illinois, Indiana, Kentucky, Maryland, Michigan, New Jersey, Ohio, Pennsylvania, Tennessee, Virginia, West Virginia, and Washington, DC. This generation and distribution network is also tied to the power grids of the Midwest, New York State, and other areas in the mid-Atlantic states.

NYMEX provides financially settled monthly futures contracts for peakload and off-peakload electricity transactions based on the daily floating price for each day of the month at the PJM western hub. The underlying price of these monthly futures is the arithmetic average of the PJM western hub real-time locational marginal price (LMP) for the peak and off-peak hours of each day provided by PJM Interconnection LLC. The PJM western hub consists of 111 delivery points, primarily on the Pennsylvania Electric Co and the Potomac Electric Co utility transmission systems.

There are monthly futures contracts for the current year plus the next five calendar years. A new calendar year will be added following the termination of trading in the December contract of the current year. Further trading products are options on the PJM monthly futures contracts.

Intercontinental Exchange

ICE electricity futures contracts are deliverable contracts where each clearing member with a position open at cessation of trading for a contract month is obliged to make or take delivery of electricity to or from National Grid Transco, United Kingdom. ICE offers UK baseload and peakload electricity futures for the next 12 months, six quarters and four seasons.

1.5   THE EMISSIONS MARKET

Global warming caused by the greenhouse effect is one of the key environmental challenges of the 21st century. The greenhouse effect itself is caused by the property of certain gases in the atmosphere to absorb and reflect thermal radiation of the earth's surface back to the earth. The natural greenhouse effect is mainly caused by water vapour (H_2O), carbon dioxide (CO_2), ozone (O_3), nitrous oxide (N_2O), and methane (CH_4). Without the natural greenhouse effect the average surface air temperature would be $-20°C$ instead of $+15°C$.

Increased concentrations of greenhouse gases in the atmosphere caused by human activities are responsible for the anthropogenic greenhouse effect. Since the beginning of the 20th century the average air surface temperature increased by 0.6°C and the UN Intergovernmental Panel on Climate Change (IPCC) has projected a further increase by 1.4°C to 5.8°C until 2100. Climate change has had a severe impact on the environment including raising sea levels, threatening coastal communities, increasing the frequency of extreme weather events, storms, draughts, floods, and extinction of endangered species (European Commission 2005a).

1.5.1   Kyoto Protocol

Since the 1970s climate change has been on the political agenda. The first World Climate Conference with scientific focus was organised in 1979 in Geneva. It issued a declaration calling on the world's governments "to foresee and prevent potential man-made changes in climate that might be adverse to the well-being of humanity". The declaration also identified increased atmospheric concentrations of carbon dioxide resulting from utilisation of fossil fuels, deforestation, and changes in land use as main causes of global warming. The conference led to the establishment of the World Climate Programme, to a series of intergovernmental climate conferences and in 1988 to the establishment of the International Panel on Climate Change (IPCC) by the United Nations Environment Programme (UNEP) and the World Meteorological Organisation (WMO). Organised in three working groups, the IPCC prepares assessment reports on available scientific information on climate change, environmental and socio-economic impacts of climate change, and formulation of response strategies. Based on the first IPCC reports published in 1990, the United Nations General Assembly decided to initiate negotiations on an effective framework convention on climate change. The United Nations Framework Convention on Climate Change (UNFCCC) was opened for signature at the United Nations Conference on Environment and Development in Rio de Janeiro in 1992 and entered into force in 1994.[7] Signatories of the UNFCCC have different responsibilities:

- *Annex I countries*: Industrialised countries who have agreed to reduce their greenhouse gas emissions.
- *Annex II countries*: Developed countries who are responsible for bearing the costs of climate change mitigation in developing countries. Annex II countries are a subset of Annex I countries.
- *Developing countries*: These countries have no immediate responsibilities.

---

[7] By 2006, the UNFCCC was ratified by 190 countries.

The UNFCCC sets a framework for climate change mitigation but does not contain green-house gas emission limits for individual countries. Since the UNFCCC entered into force, the parties meet annually in Conferences of the Parties (COP) to assess the progress in climate change mitigation and to negotiate legally binding targets.

The Kyoto Protocol to the UNFCCC was adapted at the 1997 COP 3 in Kyoto, Japan and entered into force in 2005. The Kyoto Protocol commits Annex I Parties to individual, legally binding targets to limit or reduce their greenhouse gas emissions. Only Parties to the Convention who have ratified the Kyoto Protocol will be bound by the Protocol's commitments. One hundred and sixty-eight countries and the European Union (EU) had ratified the Protocol by the end of 2006. Of these, 35 countries and the EU are required to reduce greenhouse gas emissions during the period 2008–2012 below levels specified for each of them (Annex B countries, which are almost identical with the Annex I countries of the UNFCCC). In total, the Annex B countries have committed to reduce their emissions by at least 5% from 1990 levels. The global warming potential of different greenhouse gases is expressed in CO_2 equivalents. Annex A specifies which greenhouse gas emissions are subject to the Kyoto Protocol:

- Carbon dioxide (CO_2).
- Methane (CH_4), CO_2 equivalents: 23.
- Nitrous oxide (N_2O), CO_2 equivalents: 310.
- Hydrofluorocarbons (HFCs), CO_2 equivalents: 140–11 700.
- Perfluorocarbons (PFCs), CO_2 equivalents: 6500–9200.
- Sulphur hexafluoride (SF_6), CO_2 equivalents: 23 900.

The CO_2 equivalent figures above refer to the 100 years time horizon (International Panel on Climate Change 2005). Furthermore, Annex A specifies sectors/source categories for emission covered by the Kyoto Protocol. Main categories are: energy, industrial processes, solvent and other product use, agriculture, and waste.

Quantified emission limits for the first commitment period, from 2008 to 2012, are specified in Annex B of the Kyoto Protocol. Base year is the year 1990. Instead of 1990, Parties may use 1995 as base year for HFCs, PFCs, and SF_6. In addition to total emissions, impacts of land-use, land-use change, and forestry (LULUCF) are considered. Emission limits and changes in emissions between 1990 and 2004 are listed in Table 1.5. Out of the Annex I countries, Australia, Croatia, Turkey, and the Unites States had not ratified the Kyoto Protocol by 2006. For Belarus and Turkey, emission limits had not been defined by 2006.

The Kyoto Protocol defines three types of "flexible mechanisms" to lower the overall costs of achieving its emissions targets: joint implementation (Article 6), clean development mechanism (Article 12), and emissions trading (Article 17). These mechanisms enable Parties to access cost-effective opportunities to reduce emissions or to remove CO_2 from the atmosphere (e.g. by afforestation) in other countries. The establishment of these flexible mechanisms acknowledges that marginal emission reduction costs can vary considerably from region to region while the benefits for the atmosphere are the same, wherever the action is taken. Flexible mechanisms are explained in more detail in section 1.5.3.

Table 1.5   Committed emission limits under the Kyoto Protocol

Emission limitation (% of base year or period) and changes in
emissions without LULUCF between 1990 and 2004 (%)

Country	Limit	Change	Country	Limit	Change
Australia	108	+25.1	Liechtenstein	92	+18.5
Austria	92	+15.7	Lithuania	92	−60.4
Belarus		−41.6	Luxembourg	92	+0.3
Belgium	92	+1.4	Monaco	92	−3.1
Bulgaria	92	−49.1	Netherlands	92	+2.4
Canada	94	+26.6	New Zealand	100	+21.3
Croatia	95	−5.4	Norway	101	+10.3
Czech Republic	92	−25.0	Poland	94	−31.2
Denmark	92	−1.1	Portugal	92	+41.0
Estonia	92	−51.0	Romania	92	− −41.0
EU	92	−0.6	Russian Federation	100	−32.0
Finland	92	+14.5	Slovakia	92	−30.4
France	92	−0.8	Slovenia	92	−0.8
Germany	92	−17.2	Spain	92	+49.0
Greece	92	+26.6	Sweden	92	−3.5
Hungary	94	−31.8	Switzerland	92	+0.4
Iceland	110	−5.0	Turkey		+72.6
Ireland	92	+23.1	Ukraine	100	−55.3
Italy	92	+12.1	UK	92	−14.3
Japan	94	+6.5	United States	93	+15.8
Latvia	92	−58.5			

Source: Kyoto Protocol and UNFCCC (2006).

At annual climate conferences (COPs) following Kyoto, implementation rules for the
Kyoto Protocol were negotiated.[8]

1.5.2   EU Emissions Trading Scheme

The member states of the European Union (EU-15) agreed in 1998 on a Burden Sharing
Agreement. It redistributes among them the overall 8% reduction target under the Kyoto
Protocol. The individual quantified emission limitation or reduction commitments for the
Kyoto period 2008–2012 are listed in Table 1.6.

Only a few countries, among them Germany, the United Kingdom, France, and Sweden,
were on a path to achieving their targets while other countries were expected to have
emissions that significantly exceeded these targets. Overall, it was realised by the European
Commission that the EU commitment under the Kyoto Protocol would not be achieved
without additional measures.

The European Commission considered the introduction of an emissions trading scheme
on a company level as an appropriate measure for achieving the Kyoto target. In 2003, the

---

[8] Detailed information on the UNFCCC, the Kyoto Protocol, and the COPs can be found on the UNFCCC Secretariat's homepage:
http://unfccc.int.

Table 1.6 EU Burden Sharing Agreement targets as % of 1990 emissions

Belgium	92.5	Luxembourg	72
Denmark	79	Netherlands	94
Germany	79	Austria	87
Greece	125	Portugal	127
Spain	115	Finland	100
France	100	Sweden	104
Ireland	113	United Kingdom	87.5
Italy	93.5		

European Council formally adopted the Emissions Trading Directive (Directive 2003/87/EC). The directive describes the framework for the European Emissions Trading Scheme (EU ETS). The scheme covers the electricity and heat sector and energy intensive industrial sectors. All installations above certain size limits, e.g. rated thermal input exceeding 20 MW for combustion installations, have to participate. The EU ETS covers approximately 40% of all emissions under the Kyoto Protocol in the EU.

Only CO_2 emissions are covered in the first trading period, 2005–2007. In the second trading period, 2008–2012, other greenhouse gas emissions under the Kyoto Protocol can be covered as well. In the first trading period, the EU ETS covers all 25 member countries of the EU.

Member States are responsible for the allocation of emission allowances by means of National Allocation Plans (NAPs). Besides emissions within the EU ETS, all other emissions under the Kyoto Protocol have to be considered in order to achieve the emission targets under the Burden Sharing Agreement. Emission allowances (EUAs) are distributed to participating installations. The unit of the EUAs is 1 t CO_2. For the first trading period, at least 95% of the EUAs have to be allocated for free, for the second period at least 90%. All installations in the EU ETS have to submit EUAs for their emissions to national emissions registries. EUAs can be traded freely. Therefore, installations with emissions above their allocation can buy EUAs for their demand and installations with emissions below their allocation can sell them. Transfer of certificates from one year to the next (banking) and for one year to the previous year (borrowing) is possible within a trading period. Banking or borrowing is not possible between the first and the second trading period. But banking is possible from the second trading period to a third trading period. If the operator of an installation fails to deliver sufficient EUAs, a penalty of 40 EUR/t CO_2 for the first period and 100 EUR/t CO_2 for the second period applies and, in addition, EUAs of the next trading period have to be submitted (Schiffer 2005).

The NAPs have to be approved by the European Commission. In June 2005, the last of the 25 National Allocation Plans for the first period 2005–2007 was approved. The allocation process for the first period covered more than 10 500 installations. In total, the Commission has approved the allocation of approximately 2.16 billion allowances per year for the first trading period. Almost 80 million allowances have been put aside by Member States in new entrants reserves to allocate allowances to operators entering the market (European Environment Agency 2006). Each Member State has its own national registry containing accounts, which hold the EUAs. These registries interlink with the Community Independent Transaction Log (CITL), operated by the Commission. It records and checks every transaction. Apart from allocated EUAs for every installation, the CITL also

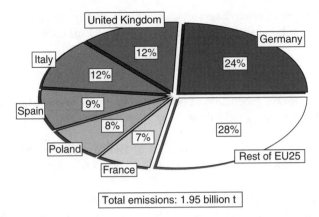

United Kingdom
12%

Germany
24%

Italy
12%

9%

Spain
8%
7%

28%

Poland

France

Rest of EU25

Total emissions: 1.95 billion t

Figure 1.33 CO_2 emissions 2005 in the EU ETS by country. Source: CITL, February 2007

contains information on verified historic emissions for previous years for every installation. Figure 1.33 shows the distribution of historic emissions by country. Four countries, Germany, the United Kingdom, Italy, and Spain, are already responsible for more than 50% of all emissions covered by the EU ETS, and half of the countries are responsible for more than 90%.

CITL emission data allows the classification of emissions by activity. Categories and their total certified emissions 2005 are (CITL, February 2007):

Energy activities

- Combustion installations with a rated thermal input exceeding 20 MW (excepting hazardous or municipal waste installations): 1,380 Mt CO_2 or 71% of all emissions.
- Mineral oil refineries: 150 Mt CO_2 or 8%.
- Coke ovens: 20 Mt CO_2 or 1%.

Production and processing of ferrous metals

- Metal ore (including sulphide ore) roasting or sintering installations: 10 Mt CO_2 or 0.5%.
- Installations for the production of pig iron or steel (primary or secondary fusion) including continuous casting, with a capacity exceeding 2.5 tonnes per hour: 130 Mt CO_2 or 7%.

Mineral industry

- Installations for the production of cement clinker in rotary kilns with a production capacity exceeding 500 tonnes per day or lime in rotary kilns with a production capacity exceeding 50 tonnes per day or in other furnaces with a production capacity exceeding 50 tonnes per day: 170 Mt CO_2 or 9%.
- Installations for the manufacture of glass including glass fibre with a melting capacity exceeding 20 tonnes per day: 20 Mt CO_2 or 1%.
- Installations for the manufacture of ceramic products by firing, in particular roofing tiles, bricks, refractory bricks, tiles, stoneware or porcelain, with a production capacity

exceeding 75 tonnes per day, and/or with a kiln capacity exceeding $4\,m^3$ and with a setting density per kiln exceeding $300\,kg/m^3$: $10\,Mt\ CO_2$ or 0.5%.

Other activities

- Industrial plants for the production of (a) pulp from timber or other fibrous materials and (b) paper and board with a production capacity exceeding 20 tonnes per day: $30\,Mt\ CO_2$ or 1.5%.
- Other activity opted-in pursuant to Article 24 of Directive 2003/87/EC (e.g. installations with capacities below the stated limits above): $30\,Mt\ CO_2$ or 1.5%.

Unfortunately, the categories are not used in a consistent way for all countries.[9] The main category is combustion with more than 70% of total emissions in the EU ETS. Most installations under this category are part of the public heat and electricity sector, which is responsible for approximately 60% of total emissions. Further relevant sectors are cement, steel, and refineries.

1.5.3 Flexible Mechanisms

Under the Kyoto Protocol, countries may meet their emission targets through a combination of domestic activities and the use of flexible mechanisms. Besides allowing countries to meet their targets in a cost-effective way, flexible mechanisms aim to assist developing countries in achieving sustainable development. The Kyoto Protocol includes three flexible mechanisms:

- Joint Implementation (JI).
- Clean Development Mechanism (CDM).
- International Emissions Trading (IET).

JI and CDM are project-based mechanisms. They involve developing and implementing measures that reduce greenhouse gas emissions in another country to generate emission credits. JI projects are carried out in industrialised countries with existing emission targets (Annex B countries under the Kyoto Protocol). CDM projects are carried out in developing countries without targets. JI projects generate Emission Reduction Units (ERUs) and CDM projects generate Certified Emission Reductions (CERs). Not only CO_2, but all greenhouse gases under the Kyoto Protocol are considered for JI and CDM projects. The unit of ERUs and CERs is $t\ CO_2$ equivalents.

JI projects have to be approved by the country in which they are implemented. One criterion is additionality, i.e. the project would not have been implemented without the incentives created by JI. Therefore, measures covered by a company emissions trading scheme like the EU ETS are not eligible as JI projects. The transfer of ERUs generated by JI projects will not begin until 2008.

---

[9] For instance, power plants in France are listed under other activity opted-in while for most other countries they are listed under combustion.

Under the CDM, investors from Annex I countries receive CERs for the actual amount of greenhouse gas emission reductions achieved. The issuing of CERs is subject to host and investor country agreement, third party assessment, and registration by the UNFCCC Clean Development Mechanism Executive Board (CDM EB). A key requirement for CDM projects is additionality: CERs will only be recognised if the reduction of greenhouse gas emissions is additional to any reduction that would occur without the certified project activity. Additional restrictions for projects apply, e.g. nuclear power projects are excluded. Until February 2007, more than 500 CDM projects were registered by the CDM EB. They are expected to create 700 million CERs until the end of 2012. The majority of these CERs are expected from projects in China (41%), India (14%), and Brazil (14%). Main scopes of the CDM project activities are energy industries (50%), waste handling and disposal (20%), and agriculture (10%).[10]

International Emissions Trading (IET) of Assigned Amount Units (AAUs) allows industrialised countries with emission targets (Annex B countries) to exchange emission allowances to meet their national Kyoto targets for the commitment period 2008–2012. Unlike CDM and JI, IET is not project based. Emissions in some countries, especially in Russia and Ukraine, are significantly below their Kyoto targets (see Table 1.5) and more than sufficient AAUs will be available. The question is whether this "hot air" is politically acceptable for meeting Kyoto targets or not.

Besides AAUs, Annex B countries can also use CERs and ERUs for meeting their Kyoto targets. This is what, for instance, the Netherlands is aiming to do through a state purchasing programme. A number of other countries including Japan, Canada, Sweden, Italy, and Spain are also likely to enter the CER market as buyers.

The Linking Directive (Directive 2004/101/EC), adopted by the EU Parliament in 2004, allows emission reduction units generated by project-based flexible mechanisms (JI and CDM) to be utilised for compliance by companies under the EU ETS. The rationale behind this linkage is to create additional potential for cost-efficient measures and to reduce the overall costs for emission compliance for the participating companies in the EU ETS. The Kyoto Protocol states that a significant portion of reductions should be achieved by domestic actions. Therefore, flexible mechanisms are considered supplementary to domestic measures and most National Allocation Plans (NAPs) have implemented limits for the use of JI and CDM. These limits are applied for each installation separately and not on a nationwide level. The Linking Directive allows the use of all ERUs or CERs that comply with the requirements established under the UNFCCC, with a few exceptions. Credits from forestry projects (sinks) are excluded for the first period but might be allowed for the second period after a revision by the European Commission. Hydro power projects greater than 20 MW are required to be in line with criteria from the World Commission on Dams.

ERUs can only be used in the second trading period of the EU ETS. CERs can be used in all periods and unlike EU Allowances (EUAs), they can be banked from the first to the second period. Therefore, the CERs issued during the first period have a higher value than EUAs of the first period in case of a positive price difference between EUAs of the second and of the first period. In the long run, CER and EUA prices can be expected to converge.

---

[10] The UNFCCC Secretariat publishes detailed CDM statistics on the internet under http://cdm.unfccc.int/statistics.

1.5.4   Products and Market Places

Main products on the market are EU Allowances (EUAs) for the first trading period 2005–2007 and for the second trading period 2008–2012. Common are spot, forward, and futures trading of EUAs. In the case of spot trading, the EUAs are transferred from the seller's account at a national registry to the buyer's account directly after the contract is concluded. Forward and futures trades generally have the December of a specified year as settlement date. Physical settlement by transferring EUAs is common, but futures with financial settlement can be found as well. Standardised option contracts for EUAs also exist.

EUA spot and forward contracts as well as options are traded bilaterally (OTC or via brokers). Spot and futures trading is possible at several exchanges. Options are traded at exchanges as well, but the liquidity is very low. Main exchanges are:

- European Climate Exchange (ECX) in Amsterdam.
- European Energy Exchange (EEX) in Leipzig.
- Energy Exchange Austria (EXAA) in Vienna.
- Nord Pool in Oslo.
- PowerNext in Paris.

Figure 1.34 shows the development of CO_2 emission allowance prices since 2005. The development is characterised by high volatility. While futures for the first period (settlement in December 07) and for the second period (settlement in December 08) were priced more or less identically in the beginning, their prices became decoupled. The strong decline in prices for the 2007 futures can be explained by the expected excess of EUAs allocated by the NAPs for the first period.

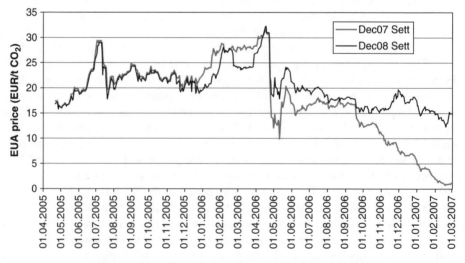

Figure 1.34 CO_2 emissions futures prices. Source: ECX

Fundamentally, the high volatility of CO_2 prices can be explained by the price-inelastic supply of EUAs in the NAPs and by the low demand elasticity in the short term. Most of the short-term demand elasticity exists in the electricity sector where switching from coal fired generation to gas fired generation (fuel switching) is possible. Many other measures for emission reduction require investments with lead times too long for being effective within the first trading period. Further, the demand is uncertain and depends on exogenous influences like wind and hydrological conditions that impact the demand for electricity generation from fossil fuels. On the supply side, CERs have to be considered. As they can be banked from the first to the second period, they will not be available for the first period at prices below the futures prices of the second period EUAs. Figure 1.35 illustrates the fundamental supply and demand situation during the first period. Owing to the very small elasticity of the demand and the inherent demand uncertainty, fundamental prices are very uncertain and may decrease to zero. Assuming sufficient additional supply in the form of CERs, maximum prices will be equal to futures prices for second period EUAs if interest rates are neglected. But as futures prices for second period EUAs are also not stable, a clear upper limit does not exist.

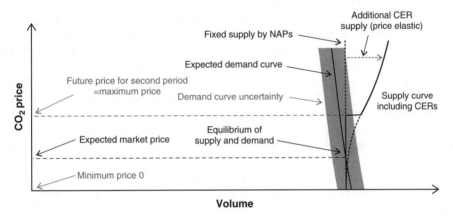

Figure 1.35   Fundamental supply and demand in the European CO_2 market

One additional effect is the allocation in the NAPs. It resulted in most countries in an undersupply in the electricity sector and in an oversupply in all other sectors. Electricity companies were the main actors in the first years. They intended to cover their short position (allocation below expected demand), but only few other actors with a long position (allocation above expected demand) were willing to sell their long position. Further, no consistent and verified historical emission figures for participating installations were available for years before 2005. Based on estimated historical emission figures, a significant shortage in the EU ETS was expected in a business as usual scenario. This led to high certificate prices until April 2006 with peak prices above 30 EUR/t CO_2. At the end of April 2006, certified emission figures for 2005 were published for several countries. They were significantly lower than expected. This led to a price collapse of more than 50% within one week.

CERs and ERUs are traded bilaterally. Unlike EUAs, they are traded internationally and demand is dominated by Annex B countries who buy CERs for achieving their Kyoto targets.

CERs are often bought in the form of bilateral emission reduction purchase agreements (ERPAs). Risks can be distributed differently between buyer and seller. In most cases, the seller commits to delivering all CERs generated from a specific project to the buyer, but the amount of CERs is non-firm. The buyer commits to buying all CERs delivered by the seller for a fixed price.

1.5.5   Emissions Trading in North America

As part of the Acid Rain Program, emissions trading was introduced in the United States in the 1990s for SO_2 emissions from fossil fuel power plants. The so-called "cap-and-trade" method constrains overall emissions and allows certificate trading between participating generation units. In phase I from 1995 to 1999, almost 500 generation units participated. In phase II, which started in the year 2000, the number of participating units exceeds 2000. The Acid Rain Program is regarded as a success, as SO_2 emissions were reduced faster than anticipated.[11]

Regarding CO_2 emissions, the cap-and-trade approach has not been implemented as a mandatory scheme so far. The only greenhouse gas emissions trading scheme operational in the year 2006 in the United Stated is the Chicago Climate Exchange (CCX), a voluntary programme that allows municipal, corporate and other partners to accept a common reduction target for CO_2 and other greenhouse gas emissions under the Kyoto Protocol. It allows full banking flexibility and the use of flexible mechanisms, e.g. in the forestry and agriculture sectors. In 2006, the CCX had approximately 60 members with emission targets.

Mandatory cap-and-trade programmes for CO_2 emissions are considered at state level in the United States. The Regional Greenhouse Gas Initiative (RGGI) was proposed by the Governor of New York in 2003. Targets were defined for the period 2009 to 2015 so far by eight participating states. The establishment of a mandatory trading scheme is also considered in California and Oregon. In Canada, trading schemes might be introduced as well.

Even if these trading schemes will not be linked directly with each other and with the EU ETS, an indirect linkage will exist through flexible mechanisms. Under certain conditions, CERs generated by CDM projects will be accepted in more than one scheme. Therefore, convergence of CO_2 prices in all trading schemes can be expected, at least in the long run.

---

[11] Detailed information on the Acid Rain Program can be found on the US EPA's Acid Rain Program homepage: http://www.epa.gov/airmarkets/progsregs/arp/.

2
Energy Derivatives

An energy derivative is a contract that is derived from an underlying energy related commodity. Such a contract may be an agreement to trade a commodity at some future date or to exchange cash flows based on energy prices at future dates. A basic classification of energy derivatives is given in Figure 2.1. We first distinguish between options and contracts without optionality, such as forwards, futures or swaps. Options in energy markets have a long history. Before the formation of liberalised energy markets optionality was needed to react to fluctuations in consumption, interruptions in transmissions or power plant outages. Power plants or gas storage facilities provided flexibility that was historically used to balance the system load but is presently being used to optimise the profit against market prices (see section 4.2). Many options on a daily or hourly basis can be seen as an abstract model of a certain type of power plant, also referred to as a *virtual power plant*.

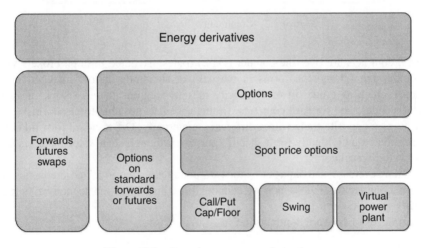

Figure 2.1 Overview on energy derivatives

Besides describing different types of energy derivatives this chapter introduces methods to determine their *fair value*. The fair value of a contract is defined as the price for which a neutral market participant would be willing to buy or sell the contract. When deriving fair values, we make the general assumption that the market is *arbitrage* free, i.e. making a profit without taking any risk is not possible, although there may be such *arbitrage opportunities* in real markets. If a valuation to market prices can be performed on a regular basis one also speaks of a *marked-to-market valuation* of a contract or portfolio. A more theoretical account of derivatives pricing is given in section 3.1.5.

2.1   FORWARDS, FUTURES AND SWAPS

Forwards, futures and swaps are hedging instruments that have no optionality. For a given commodity, they are typically the most liquid type of derivatives. Compared to options, they are much easier to use and to price.

2.1.1   Forward Contracts

Forward contracts are bilateral agreements to purchase or sell a certain amount of a commodity on a fixed future date (delivery date) at a predetermined contract price. The seller of the forward contract has the obligation to deliver the commodity on the delivery date (see Figure 2.2). The payment date specified in the contract is usually also at (or near) the delivery date, so that no cash flow happens until delivery. The current *forward price* $F(t, T)$ at time t for a given delivery date T is the contract price at which forward contracts are currently signed in the market. If a forward contract has been concluded in the past at a different contract price K, the forward contract has a positive or negative fair value.

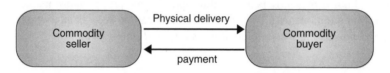

Figure 2.2   Commodity forward contract

Forward contracts are over-the-counter (OTC) trades, executed through brokers via telephone or through Internet platforms in the case of standardised forward contracts.[1] For commodities such as crude oil or electricity in some regions there exists a fairly liquid market of standardised forward contracts. In this case it is possible to close a risk position by executing an opposite trade with a different counterparty. Off-standard forward contracts can be negotiated individually for a specific purpose although such tailor-made trades may be difficult to revise later.

One of the severest disadvantages of forward contracts is the involved credit risk, where one of the counterparties does not, or cannot, fulfil his obligation to deliver or pay the commodity (see section 6.3).

The main uses of forward contracts are to

- hedge the obligation to deliver or purchase a commodity at a future date;
- secure a sales profit from a commodity production;
- speculate on rising or falling commodity prices in case there is no liquid futures market.

If forward contracts are valued against market prices (marked-to-market valuation) then the buyer of the forward contract (holder of the "long" position) makes a profit if the commodity price rises and makes a loss if the commodity price falls. The payoff for a long

---

[1] Different from our definition, the term forward contract is sometimes also used for certain exchange traded products (e.g. at Nord Pool, see section 1.4.3).

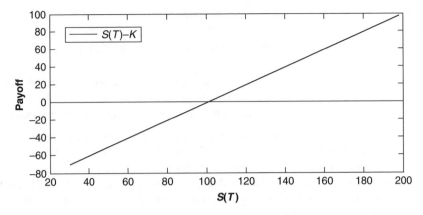

Figure 2.3 Commodity forward contract

forward contract with contract price K is $S(T) - K$, where $S(T)$ is the commodity price at maturity T (see Figure 2.3). Similarly, the payoff for a short position is $K - S(T)$.

Where the forward market is sufficiently liquid, calculating the fair value of a forward contract is model independent and follows immediately from the no-arbitrage assumption. Assume a customer is long on a forward contract for delivery date T at contract price K. By selling another forward contract at the current market price $F = F(t, T)$, the physical deliveries of both forward contracts in the portfolio cancel and there is a fixed net cash flow of $F - K$ at delivery T. The fair value of the forward contract equals the value of this cash flow at today's time t, which is just the discounted value of the difference between the current forward price F and the contract price K, i.e. $e^{-r(T-t)}(F - K)$.

For this example we carry out the arbitrage argument to determine the fair value explicitly. Let $U_{K,T}$ denote the fair value of a forward contract with contract price K and delivery date T. If $U_{K,T}$ were less than $e^{-r(T-t)}(F - K)$, a market participant could purchase the forward contract with contract price K (paying $U_{K,T}$ as a premium) and at the same time sell another forward contract at the current market price $F(t, T)$. Both contracts together yield a fixed cash flow with a higher value $e^{-r(T-t)}(F - K)$ compared to the premium paid, i.e. an arbitrage profit is generated. Conversely, if $U_{K,T}$ were larger than $e^{-r(T-t)}(F - K)$, the process would be to sell the forward contract with contract price K (receiving $U_{K,T}$ as a premium), and to buy another forward contract at the current market price $F(t, T)$ and again gain an arbitrage profit. This shows that the fair value of a forward contract with contract price K is uniquely given by

$$U_{K,T} = e^{-r(T-t)}(F - K),\tag{2.1}$$

where $e^{-r(T-t)}$ is the discount factor to the delivery date T. If we have $K = F$, then the value of the forward contract is exactly zero.

Example: An electricity producer buys $10\,000\,\mathrm{t}$ coal at time t_0 to be delivered two years later at time $T = t_0 + 2$ at a price $K = 60\,\mathrm{USD/t}$. One year later at time $t_1 = t_0 + 1$ the forward price for coal to be delivered at time T has risen to $F(t_1, T) = 70\,\mathrm{USD/t}$. The interest rate for one year at time t_1 is assumed as $R = 4\%$ which gives a discount factor of

$1/(1+R) = 0.96154$. The fair value of the forward contract is

$$U_{K,T} = \frac{1}{1+R} \times 10\,000 \times (70 - 60) \ \text{USD} = 96\,154\,\text{USD}.$$

This value $U_{K,T}$ is the price a neutral market participant would be willing to pay for entering into this contract as the buyer. If the seller counterparty defaults now, this is also the loss the buyer suffers having to buy the coal at the current market price from a different counterparty.

Forward contracts for some commodities do not usually have a single delivery date but either a sequence of deliveries (e.g. coal) or a continuous delivery schedule (e.g. gas or electricity). If we have a sequence of delivery dates $T_1, \ldots, T_n$, we can decompose the forward contract into n forward contracts that each have a single delivery date. Let K be the fixed price of the forward contract with delivery dates $T_1, \ldots, T_n$. Then the present fair value of the contract is given by

$$U_{K,\{T_1,\ldots,T_n\}} = \sum_{i=1}^{n} e^{-r(T_i - t)} \left(F(t, T_i) - K \right). \tag{2.2}$$

The fair price of the forward contract is the price K for which the fair value of the contract is zero. Setting the expression above to zero, we can solve for K:

$$K = \frac{\sum_{i=1}^{n} e^{-r(T_i - t)} F(t, T_i)}{\sum_{i=1}^{n} e^{-r(T_i - t)}}. \tag{2.3}$$

Example: The example forward contract for coal specifies four quarterly deliveries of coal for a given year each with a volume of $30\,000\,\text{t}$. The forward curve and discount factors ($r = 4.5\%$) for the four quarters are given by

Date	Price (USD/t)	Discount Factor
Q1	69.50	0.956
Q2	69.70	0.945
Q3	70.40	0.935
Q4	71.20	0.924

The fair foward price from equation (2.3) is $K = 70.19\,\text{USD/t}$. In this case the fair forward price is very close to the arithmetic average of the quarterly prices $70.20\,\text{USD/t}$.

For delivery over a continuous period $T_1 \le t \le T_2$ the value of a forward contract at fixed price K is given by the integral expression

$$U_{K,T_1,T_2} = \int_{T_1}^{T_2} e^{-r(T-t)} \left(F(t, T) - K \right) dT.$$

Solving $U_{K,T_1,T_2} = 0$ for K we get the fair price of the forward contract as

$$K = \frac{\int_{T_1}^{T_2} e^{-r(T-t)} F(t, T) dT}{\int_{T_1}^{T_2} e^{-r(T-t)} dT}.$$

We will denote the fair price of a forward contract with delivery period $T_1 \le t \le T_2$ as $F(t, T_1, T_2)$.

2.1.2   Futures Contracts

Futures contracts can be defined as standardised forward contracts traded at commodity exchanges where a clearing house serves as a *central counterparty* for all transactions (see Figure 2.4). This eliminates the counterparty risk present in OTC forward contracts. The commodity exchange sets rules to protect the clearinghouse from possible losses. Trading participants usually pay an initial margin as a guarantee. Each trading day a settlement price for the futures contract is determined and gains or losses are immediately realised at a margin account. In this way, no unrealised losses may occur that could impose a substantial credit risk.

Figure 2.4   Commodity futures contract

Futures contracts often do not lead to physical delivery but are settled financially. This is especially in favour of speculators who neither have the capability nor the interest to handle a physical delivery of the commodity. A market participant using a financially settled futures contract to hedge a planned physical buy or sell bears a "basis risk" that the actual price for the physical transaction differs from the final settlement price for the contract. Since futures contracts are standardised and traded against a central counterparty it is easy to close out a futures position by executing a trade opposite to the first one. In this case, those two trades cancel out each other. Most futures contracts are not held until maturity but closed out in advance.

Example: On January 14 a trader enters a long yearly baseload futures contract for electricity at a price of 54.20 EUR/MWh. The contract size is 1 MW giving a contract volume of 8760 MWh since the delivery year has 8760 hours. On January 19 the trader closes his long position at a price of 52.97 EUR/MWh. His total loss is 1.23 EUR/MWh or 10 775 EUR in total. Leaving aside the initial margin payment and interest payments, the market price dependent daily cash flows (*variation margin*) are as follows:

Date	Settlement price	Cash flow (EUR/MWh)	Total cash flow (EUR)
Jan 14	54.25	0.05	438
Jan 15	54.70	0.45	3942
Jan 16	53.53	−1.17	−10 249
Jan 17	53.20	−0.33	−2891
Jan 18	53.25	0.05	438
Jan 19	52.97	−0.28	−2453
Total		**−1.23**	**−10 775**

The immediate realisation of daily profits and losses via a margin account lead to subtle differences of forward and futures prices. However, the theoretical prices of forward and futures contracts do not differ if interest rates are independent of the underlying price, in particular if interest rates are considered as deterministic. For practical purposes, in commodity markets both prices can often be considered as equivalent.

If used for hedging purposes, there is indeed an important difference between forward and futures contracts concerning the hedge ratio, i.e. the optimal number of contracts needed to offset a certain market price risk. Suppose the underlying forward price F changes by ΔF. Then the change in fair value of a forward contract is given by the discounted price shift

$$\Delta U_{K,T} = e^{-r(T-t)} \Delta F.$$

From a futures position we immediately get ΔF as a margin payment, which we can put to a riskless money market account and get interest until expiry. That means that even though forward and futures prices coincide, we have different sensitivities with respect to changes of the underlying forward price (section 6.1.1).

2.1.3 Swaps

Commodity swaps are mid- and long-term risk management instruments used to lock in a fixed price for a commodity over a specific time period. Most swaps are OTC traded and financially settled and for that purpose refer to a commodity index. A swap agreement defines a number of fixing dates and on each of the fixing dates one counterparty (payer) pays the fixed price whereas the other counterparty (receiver) pays the variable price given by the commodity index (Figure 2.5). In practice, only net amounts are paid. If the fixed price exceeds the variable price the payer pays the difference; in the opposite case the payer receives the difference.

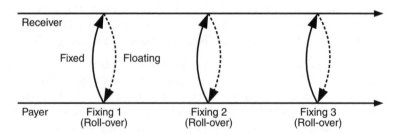

Figure 2.5 Commodity swap agreement

Consider a swap contract with fixing dates $T_1, \ldots, T_n$ where at each fixing date T_i the holder pays a fixed payment K and receives a floating payment $S(T_i)$, where $S(T_i)$ is a given commodity (spot) price index. Receiving a payment $S(T_i)$ at time T_i has the same value as receiving the commodity at time T_i. This swap contract is equivalent to a forward contract with delivery dates $T_1, \ldots, T_n$, except that the settlement is purely financial. The fair value of a swap is given by equation (2.2). The fair swap rate (*par rate*) K that leads to a present value of zero is the same as for the forward contract:

$$K = \frac{\sum_{i=1}^{n} e^{-r(T_i-t)} F(t, T_i)}{\sum_{i=1}^{n} e^{-r(T_i-t)}}. \tag{2.4}$$

A swap holder paying the fixed and receiving the floating cash flows is said to hold a *payer swap*, in the opposite case the swap holder is said to hold a *receiver swap*. The swap contract can be decomposed into two *legs*: the fixed payments and the floating payments. The fixed payments are called the *fixed leg* of the swap, the floating payments are called the *floating leg* of the swap.

2.2   "PLAIN VANILLA" OPTIONS

A *call (put) option* contract gives the option holder the right, but not the obligation, to purchase (sell) a certain commodity at a predetermined strike price. The option seller has the obligation to deliver (purchase) the commodity upon exercise by the option holder. The option seller commonly receives an option premium at the time the contract is signed (up-front). Options can be traded as OTC products or through commodity exchanges. Exchange traded options often do not give the right to physical delivery of the commodity but are financially settled with the option holder receiving a cash payment as a compensation to less favourable market prices than the strike price. In some cases the option holder receives a futures contract on exercise that finally will be financially settled. If $S(T)$ denotes the underlying commodity price at the option's maturity date and K the strike price, the payoff for the option holder will be $\max(S(T) - K, 0)$ for a call option and $\max(K - S(T), 0)$ in the case of a put option. Analogous to financial markets, options can be *European* style (i.e. exercisable only at the maturity date) or *American* style (i.e. exercisable any time until maturity).

Figure 2.6 shows the financial results for the holder of a call option as a function of the underlying price at maturity. The maximum loss for the option holder is the premium paid. For the option seller, however, the maximum loss may be unlimited if he is not in possession of the commodity.

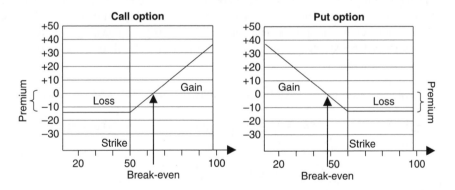

Figure 2.6   Gains and losses for an option holder

2.2.1   The Put–Call Parity and Option Strategies

Options together with futures and forward contracts can be used as hedging instruments or to implement more sophisticated trading strategies. One important relation between the different instruments is the *put–call parity*. Let $C_{K,T}$ and $P_{K,T}$ denote the fair value of a call and a put option, respectively, with strike K and maturity T and let F denote the current underlying forward price for maturity T. Then regardless of any assumptions on stochastic models the following identity holds in an arbitrage-free market:

$$C_{K,T} - P_{K,T} = e^{-r(T-t)} (F - K). \tag{2.5}$$

To prove the identity consider a portfolio consisting of a long call option and a short put option. At maturity T, the following cases can occur

1. $S(T) \geq K$: The call option is exercised and the put option expires worthless. The total payoff is $S(T) - K$.
2. $S(T) < K$: The put option is exercised by the counterparty and the call option expires worthless. The payoff of the short put is $-(K - S(T)) = S(T) - K$.

In both cases the payoff is $S(T) - K$ which is also the payoff of a forward contract with strike K and by equation (2.1) the value is equal to the right-hand side of the identity.

An important consequence of the put–call parity is that a call option can be replicated by a put option and a forward contract as

$$C_{K,T} = P_{K,T} + e^{-r(T-t)} (F - K).$$

Therefore, knowing the price of a put option implies knowing the price of the corresponding call option and vice versa.

Two examples of useful trading strategies involving options are shown in Figure 2.7. A holder of a long forward or futures position can buy a put option (*protective put*) as an insurance against declining commodity prices. If the commodity price falls below the strike price, the put option can be exercised and the commodity is sold at the strike price. Therefore the put option secures a minimum price for selling the commodity without losing the upside potential of rising commodity prices. The *covered call* strategy can be employed to increase profits if the market is expected to stay near the current price level. If a market participant

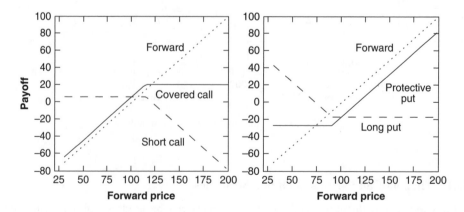

Figure 2.7   Typical option strategies

with a long futures or forward position sells a (out-of-the-money) call option they receive the option premium and in return lose the upside potential above the strike level.

2.2.2 Black's Futures Price Model

The Black model (Black 1976) defines the "market standard" for pricing options on futures contracts. It models a single futures contract for a given maturity in a similar way to the Black–Scholes model for a stock option (Black and Scholes 1973). For a single futures contract with a given fixed maturity date, we denote the futures price by $F(t)$ instead of $F(t, T)$, leaving out explicit reference to the maturity date. By making no distinction between the forward price and the futures price, the model can also be used to model a forward price. The Black model assumes that the futures price $F(t)$ follows a geometric Brownian motion. Since the Black model is primarily used for option pricing, we are here only interested in the risk-neutral parameters (discussed further in section 3.1.5). From equation (3.3) we know that, under the risk-neutral measure, $F(t)$ must be a martingale:

$$F(t) = \mathbb{E}_t[F(T)].$$

In other words this means that the futures price at any time equals the expected futures price at expiry. Therefore, the futures price cannot have any drift term and we get the model equation

$$dF(t) = \sigma(t)F(t)dW(t) \tag{2.6}$$

with deterministic volatility function $\sigma(t)$.

2.2.3 Option Pricing Formulas

To derive analytical formulas for European-style options on futures, let $F(t) = F(t, T_1)$ denote a futures price for expiration date T_1 and let $C_{K,T}(t, F)$ and $P_{K,T}(t, F)$ denote the fair value of a call and respectively a put option with strike K and maturity T. The option maturity T may be earlier or equal to the futures expiry T_1. At maturity of the option, the payoffs are

$$C_{K,T}(T, F) = \max(F(T) - K, 0)$$
$$P_{K,T}(T, F) = \max(K - F(T), 0).$$

Evaluated at time t, the payoff formulas $\max(F(t) - K, 0)$ for the call option and $\max(K - F(t), 0)$ for the put option are also called the *inner value* of the options. They define the payoff received if the option were exercised now. Figure 2.8 shows an example of option prices for a call and a put option as a function of the futures price F.

For a futures contract with the same expiry date as the option $T = T_1$, the payoffs are $\max(S(T) - K, 0)$ and $\max(K - S(T), 0)$, since at expiry the futures price is equal to the spot price $(F(T, T) = S(T))$. In this way, options can be priced on the spot price rather than the futures price.

By general option pricing theory (see section 3.1.5), the fair option price is the expectation of the discounted payoff under the risk-neutral parameters (2.6):

$$C_{K,T}(t, F) = e^{-r(T-t)}\mathbb{E}_t[\max(F(T) - K, 0)]$$
$$P_{K,T}(t, F) = e^{-r(T-t)}\mathbb{E}_t[\max(K - F(T), 0)].$$

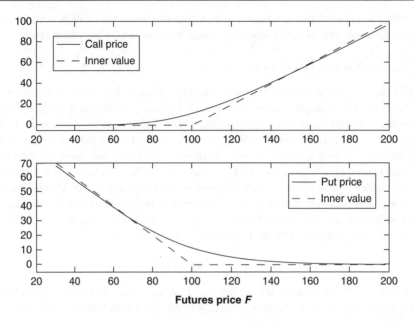

Figure 2.8   European-style option prices for $K = 100$, $T = 1$, $\sigma = 0.3$ and $r = 0.03$

For the model assumptions (2.6) the expectation values can be analytically calculated. Since $F(t)$ has the same dynamics as a stock price under the Black–Scholes model when the dividend yield d is equal to the risk-free rate r, the analytical formulas available for the Black–Scholes model can be used by setting $d = r$. This gives the following results for European – style call and put options:

$$C_{K,T}(t, F) = e^{-r(T-t)} \left(FN(d_1) - KN(d_2) \right) \tag{2.7}$$

$$P_{K,T}(t, F) = e^{-r(T-t)} \left(KN(-d_2) - FN(-d_1) \right) \tag{2.8}$$

evaluated at the current futures price $F = F(t)$, where

$$d_1 = \frac{\ln(F/K) + V/2}{\sqrt{V}}, \quad d_2 = d_1 - \sqrt{V}.$$

The expression $e^{-r(T-t)}$ is the discount factor until maturity and $N(x)$ denotes the *cumulative normal distribution function*

$$N(x) = \frac{1}{\sqrt{2\pi}} \int_{-\infty}^{x} e^{-u^2/2} du.$$

V denotes the variance

$$V = \text{Var}_t[\ln F(T)] = \int_{t}^{T} \sigma^2(s) ds.$$

If the volatility σ is constant, the variance is given simply by $V = \sigma^2(T - t)$.

The numerical implementation of Black's formula involves only standard mathematical operations once the numerical approximation of the cumulative normal distribution function $N(x)$ is available. The function $N(x)$ can be expressed in terms of the *complementary error function*

$$\text{erfc}(x) = \frac{2}{\sqrt{\pi}} \int_x^\infty e^{-u^2} du$$

which is available in many numerical libraries (see, e.g. Press *et al.* 1992). In fact, we get

$$N(x) = 1 - \frac{1}{2} \text{erfc}\left(\frac{x}{\sqrt{2}}\right).$$

2.2.4 Hedging Options: The "Greeks"

The option price within the Black–Scholes theory is an *arbitrage price*, meaning that any other price for which the option can be traded leads to an arbitrage opportunity by replicating the option with a dynamic portfolio strategy of the underlying commodity. The replicating strategy can be used to eliminate (*hedge*) the market price risk of the option. From the derivation of the Black–Scholes formulas, the hedging strategy can be explicitly constructed. For this purpose it is important to look at the sensitivities of an option or portfolio value with respect to changes in the market parameters. These sensitivities of an option or portfolio are traditionally denoted by Greek letters and are called the "Greeks".

Delta Hedging

Let $U(t, F)$ be the price of a European option on a futures price. By Itô's formula (discussed further in section A.2.3) we get

$$dU = \left(\frac{\partial U}{\partial t} + \frac{1}{2}\sigma^2 \frac{\partial^2 U}{\partial F^2}\right) dt + \sigma \frac{\partial U}{\partial F} dW(t).$$

Consider a portfolio consisting of a written option with value $-U(t, F)$ and a number ϕ of futures contracts F. If in a small time period dt the futures price changes by dF, the portfolio value Π will change by

$$d\Pi = -dU + \phi dF.$$

$$= -\left(\frac{\partial U}{\partial t} + \frac{1}{2}\sigma^2 \frac{\partial^2 U}{\partial F^2}\right) dt + \left(\phi - \frac{\partial U}{\partial F}\right) \sigma dW(t).$$

Choosing exactly $\phi = \partial U / \partial F$ at each point of time, the random term involving $W(t)$ can be eliminated and the portfolio evolves deterministically. In an efficient market, any riskless portfolio cannot have a profit greater than the risk-free rate r. Since a reverse portfolio can be constructed buying the option and holding $-\phi$ futures contracts, one can show that the profit of Π cannot be less than the risk-free rate. Hence, we conclude that $d\Pi = r\Pi\, dt$ which leads to the partial differential equation

$$\frac{\partial U}{\partial t} + \frac{1}{2}\sigma^2 \frac{\partial^2 U}{\partial F^2} = rU. \tag{2.9}$$

We have seen that the hedging strategy is defined by the number $\partial U/\partial F$, specifying the number of futures contracts in the hedging portfolio. This number is called the *delta* of the option,

$$\Delta = \frac{\partial U}{\partial F},$$

and the hedging strategy is called *delta hedging*. The delta can be defined for any security as the first derivative of its value with respect to the underlying price. It measures the sensitivity of the portfolio value with respect to small changes in the underlying price F. The delta can either be calculated analytically as a derivative or it can be calculated numerically as

$$\Delta \approx \frac{U(t, F + \Delta F) - U(t, F - \Delta F)}{2\Delta F},$$

where ΔF is a small change of F.

Example: Let $F = 100$ EUR be the price of an electricity futures contract. Let the portfolio value be $U = 5$ million EUR with a delta $\Delta = 1\,000\,000$. If F changes by $\Delta F = 0.05$ EUR to 100.5 EUR, then the portfolio value will change to $\tilde{U} \approx U + \Delta \times \Delta F = 5.5$ million EUR. The change of the portfolio value per 0.01 EUR change of F is $100\,000$ EUR.

A futures contract has a delta of 1, since a price shift of dF in the underlying price leads to exactly the same payoff. A forward contract with strike K and maturity T has a value of $F_{K,T} = e^{-r(T-t)}(F - K)$ and a delta of

$$\frac{\partial \left(e^{-r(T-t)}(F - K) \right)}{\partial F} = e^{-r(T-t)},$$

which is the discount factor until the contract expiry. Therefore although the fair forward and futures prices are the same, the delta is different. In a portfolio consisting of multiple derivatives with the same underlying F, the net delta of the whole portfolio can be considered. The hedging strategy then would be to offset the portfolio delta by an appropriate derivative, such as a futures or forward contract, so that the hedged portfolio has a net delta of zero. In this case the portfolio is said to be *delta neutral*.

For European call and put options the deltas can be computed explicitly as

$$\Delta_C = e^{-r(T-t)} N(d_1)$$

$$\Delta_P = e^{-r(T-t)} \left(N(d_1) - 1 \right).$$

The European-style call and put options as deltas of functions of the futures price are shown in Figure 2.9.

The Theta

The difference between the option price and the inner value is often called the *time value* of the option and measures the value of the optionality in addition to the payoff if the option were exercised immediately. The time value decreases when approaching the expiry of the

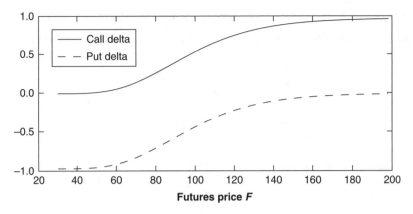

Figure 2.9 European option deltas ($K = 100$, $T = 1$, $\sigma = 0.3$ and $r = 0.03$)

option. This is described by the *theta* (Θ) of an option, defined as the derivative of the option price with respect to time, keeping the futures price and all other parameters fixed:

$$\Theta = \frac{\partial U}{\partial t}.$$

Figure 2.10 shows theta as a function of the futures price. The theta measures the sensitivity of the option price (or more generally of a portfolio) with respect to time if market prices are constant.

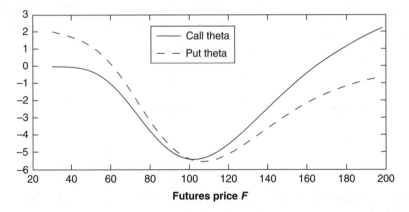

Figure 2.10 European option theta ($K = 100$, $T = 1$, $\sigma = 0.3$ and $r = 0.03$).

Example: For the call option in Figures 2.8 and 2.10 the loss in value per trading day shall be derived if market prices do not change. For the given market prices, let $\Theta = -5$ EUR. Since t was measured in years, a trading day is given by $\Delta t = 1/252$ assuming 252 trading days per year. Then the change in value per trading day is

$$\Delta U = \Theta \times \Delta t \approx 0.02\,\text{EUR}.$$

This loss is caused by the decreased lifetime of the option reducing the optionality.

The analytical formulas for the theta of European-style call and put options are

$$\Theta_C = e^{-r(T-t)}\left(-\frac{FN'(d_1)\sqrt{V}}{2(T-t)} + rFN(d_1) - rKN(d_2)\right)$$

$$\Theta_P = e^{-r(T-t)}\left(-\frac{FN'(d_1)\sqrt{V}}{2(T-t)} - rFN(-d_1) + rKN(-d_2)\right).$$

In these equations N' denotes the derivative of the cumulative normal distribution N, which is the normal density

$$N'(x) = \frac{1}{\sqrt{2\pi}}e^{-x^2/2}.$$

Often, when used in reports, the theta is already normalised to the change in value per one trading day. It can then be calculated numerically as

$$\Theta_{1d} = U(t + \Delta t, F) - U(t, F).$$

The Gamma

Since the delta of an option is dependent on the futures price, the delta hedging strategy is a *dynamic hedging strategy*. Each time the futures price moves up or down, the hedge must be rebalanced by the amount the delta has changed. The measure of how much the delta changes according to a change in the underlying futures price is the *gamma* of the option. It is defined as the first derivative of the option delta or the second derivative of the option price with respect to the futures price:

$$\Gamma = \frac{\partial \Delta}{\partial F} = \frac{\partial^2 U}{\partial F^2}.$$

European-style call and put options with the same strike and maturity have the same gamma given by

$$\Gamma_C = \Gamma_P = \frac{N'(d_1)e^{-r(T-t)}}{F\sqrt{V}}.$$

The gamma as a function of the underlying price is shown in Figure 2.11. The gamma is highest if the futures price is near the strike (*at the money*).

Example: Assume we have a delta neutral electricity option portfolio with a gamma value of $\Gamma = 100\,000$. If the underlying price changes by $\Delta F = 1$, then the new delta value will be

$$\Delta(t, F + \Delta F) \approx \Gamma \times \Delta F = 100\,000.$$

To keep the portfolio delta-neutral we have to rebalance the portfolio and sell future contracts with a total delta of $100\,000$. Since a futures contract has a delta of 1, we have to sell futures contracts with an energy amount of $100\,000$ MWh.

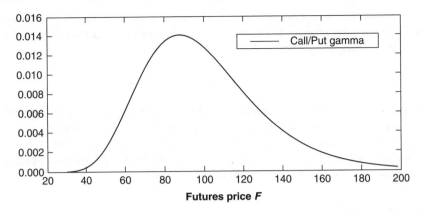

Figure 2.11 European option gamma ($K = 100$, $T = 1$, $\sigma = 0.3$ and $r = 0.03$)

The Vega

Finally, consider the price sensitivity with respect to the option volatility. For European-style call and put options the price increases with increasing volatility. Since estimates about volatility may change over the lifetime of the option, it is important to know the effect a change in volatility has on the option price. The *vega* of an option is defined as the derivative of the option price with respect to the volatility parameter:

$$\mathcal{V} = \frac{\partial U}{\partial \sigma}.$$

As a result of the put–call parity, European-style call and put options with identical strike and maturity have the same vega. The analytical formula is:

$$\mathcal{V}_C = \mathcal{V}_P = FN'(d_1)e^{-r(T-t)}\sqrt{T-t}.$$

An example is shown in Figure 2.12.

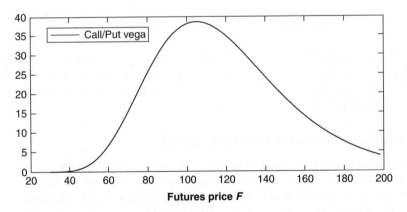

Figure 2.12 European option vega ($K = 100$, $T = 1$, $\sigma = 0.3$ and $r = 0.03$)

Example: Assume the option in Figure 2.12 has a vega of 25 for an underlying price $F = 80$. If the volatility changes from 30% ($\sigma = 0.3$) by one point ($\Delta\sigma = 0.01$) to 31%, then the option price changes by

$$\Delta U \approx \mathcal{V} \times \Delta\sigma = 0.25.$$

Usually the vega is already normalised to the change in value per 1% change in volatility. Then the effect on the portfolio of a change in volatility by 1% is just the vega of the portfolio. A portfolio that only consists of forwards and futures has a vega of zero, which implies that it is not possible to hedge the vega of a portfolio using forwards or futures. The vega can only be reduced using other options.

Hedging the Greeks

The Greeks were defined as the sensitivities of an option value with respect to changes in the market parameters. If the assumptions of Black's model were exactly true, then delta hedging would give a complete hedge. However, there are at least two problems with the model assumptions:

1. The estimate on the model parameters (most importantly the σ) change, altering the valuation of our option or portfolio.
2. A continuous dynamic hedging is not possible. There will always be a finite, but not infinitesimal, change (ΔS) in the underlying price until the hedge can be rebalanced. Rebalancing too often would also lead to unaccaptable transaction costs.

To identify how the option price changes with the market parameters, we use a Taylor series expansion:

$$\Delta U = \frac{\partial U}{\partial F}\Delta F + \frac{\partial U}{\partial \sigma}\Delta\sigma + \frac{\partial U}{\partial t}\Delta t + \frac{1}{2}\frac{\partial^2 U}{\partial F^2}\Delta F^2 + \text{higher order terms}$$

and after replacing the derivatives by the corresponding Greeks, we get

$$\Delta U = \Delta(\Delta F) + \mathcal{V}\Delta\sigma + \Theta\Delta t + \frac{1}{2}\Gamma\Delta F^2 + \text{higher order terms}.$$

By constructing a portfolio that has Δ, Γ and $\mathcal{V}$ close to zero, a portfolio can be properly hedged against changes in the underlying price F and in the volatility parameter σ. Hedging the delta of the portfolio can be done using forward or futures contracts, whereas hedging the gamma or vega involves trading options.

2.2.5   Implied Volatilities and the "Volatility Smile"

The Black model defines the market standard for most futures options and thus plays a similar role as the Black–Scholes model for stock options. Market prices for futures options are often quoted as *implied volatilities* with respect to the Black model. The implied volatility for a given option price is the constant volatility $\hat{\sigma}$ that has to be used in (2.7) or (2.8) to reproduce the given market price. If the market priced options exactly according to the Black model, there would be the same implied volatility for options with different strikes. The market is aware, however, that large price movements are more likely in reality than predicted by a log-normal probability distribution. Therefore, call options with a high strike price to protect against extreme price movements tend to have a higher market price than calculated from Black's model with the same volatility used to price at-the-money options. As a consequence, implied volatility is higher for options with a high strike price.

Figure 2.13 shows an example of the implied volatilities for European Energy Exchange (EEX) baseload electricity options on two underlyings with different strikes. A non-constant implied volatility curve, as shown in the figure, is also called *volatility smile*. The term refers to the convex shape of the implied volatility curve. In one-sided sloped curves, the term *volatility skew* is frequently used.

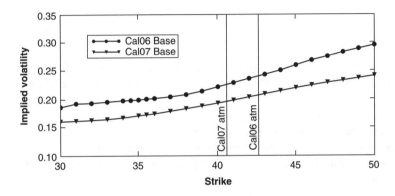

Figure 2.13   Volatility smile of EEX baseload options as of July 2005. The vertical lines indicate the at-the-money level

The Black model used with one set of parameters is insufficient to explain the volatility smile, consequently various extensions of the model have been developed. One possibility is to include jumps of random size in the underlying dynamics. This *jump-diffusion model* approach has been identified by Merton (1976). The additional parameters included in the model, jump size and jump frequency, can be calibrated so that option prices give a close fit to the market price and reproduce the volatility smile. Modelling volatility as a stochastic process rather than as a constant is a second approach. Heston (1993) introduces a *stochastic-volatility model* with mean-reverting volatility which leads to option pricing formulas that are analytically treatable. Additional parameters for the volatility process (e.g. volatility of volatility, mean-reversion speed, mean-reversion constant, correlation of volatility to underlying) can be fitted to the volatility smile observed in the market.

Implied volatilities typically increase with proximity to expiry of the underlying futures contract. Futures contracts with a short time to expiry are more volatile since they are traded more liquidly and market participants receive more information concerning demand and availability of the commodity during the delivery period. An example of such a term structure of implied volatilities for gasoil is shown in Figure 2.14.

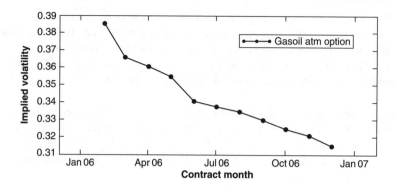

Figure 2.14   Gasoil implied volatility term structure as of January 2006

2.2.6   Swaptions

A *swaption* is an option to enter into a swap contract (see section 2.1.3) at a pre-fixed price (strike) for the fixed payments. The following data specifies a swaption (see Figure 2.15):

- The swap fixing dates $T_1, \ldots, T_n$.
- The swap type, i.e. payer swap or receiver swap.
- The strike K_0 of the swaption, i.e. the fixed price of the swap.
- The option's maturity date T_S, where $T_S < T_1$, i.e. the option is exercised before the swap payments.

A swaption granting the right to enter into a payer swap is called a *call swaption* or *payer swaption*; in the other case the swaption is called a *put swaption* or *receiver swaption*.

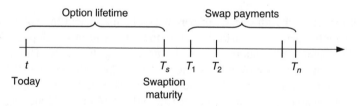

Figure 2.15   Scheme of a swaption. At T_S the swaption holder can exercise the option to enter into the swap

Concerning the pricing formulas many commodity options with physical delivery can be treated as swaptions. The floating leg is then interpreted as the physical delivery of the option. An option on a yearly baseload electricity delivery can be seen as a swaption where the swap has 12 monthly fixing dates. At each fixing date the fixed payment is the monthly energy times the strike price and the floating payment is the value of the delivered electricity.

To derive the payoff of the swaption, let $K(t)$ be the fair swap rate at time t given by equation (2.4). At maturity T_S the value of the swaption is either the value of the underlying swap at time T_S if the value is positive or zero otherwise. The value of the swap at time T_S is

$$U_{\text{swap}}(T_S) = \sum_{i=1}^{n} e^{-r(T_i - T_S)} \left(F(T_S, T_i) - K_0 \right).$$

Since for the fair swap rate $K(T_S)$ at time T_S by definition the value of the fixed leg is equal to the value of the floating leg we have

$$\sum_{i=1}^{n} e^{-r(T_i - T_S)} K(T_S) = \sum_{i=1}^{n} e^{-r(T_i - T_S)} F(T_S, T_i).$$

Substituting the last equation into the expression for $U_{\text{swap}}(T_S)$, the swap value can be expressed as

$$U_{\text{swap}}(T_S) = \sum_{i=1}^{n} e^{-r(T_i - T_S)} \left(K(T_S) - K_0 \right).$$

Using the definition $P = \sum_{i=1}^{n} e^{-r(T_i - T_S)}$ we get the swaption payoff

$$U_{\text{swaption}}(T_S) = P \times \max \left(K(T_S) - K_0, 0 \right). \tag{2.10}$$

Black's Formula for Swaptions

Making additional assumptions on the stochastics of the fair swap rate $K(t)$, a variant of Black's formula (2.7) can be used to price European-style swaptions. By general option pricing theory, the option price is given as the expectation of the discounted payoff (2.10) under the risk-neutral measure

$$U_{\text{swaption}}(t) = e^{-r(T_S - t)} \mathbb{E}_t \left[P \times \max \left(K(T_S) - K_0, 0 \right) \right].$$

Now we make the assumption that the fair swap rate $K(t)$ follows a geometric Brownian motion with volatility σ. Then we are in the same situation as in section 2.2.3 where option price formulas for Black's futures price model were given, only that there is an additional discount factor P. The option price formula for a payer swaption is

$$U_{\text{swaption}}(t, F) = e^{-r(T - t)} P \times \left(K(t) N(d_1) - K_0 N(d_2) \right) \tag{2.11}$$

where

$$d_1 = \frac{\ln(K(t)/K_0) + V/2}{\sqrt{V}}$$

$$d_2 = d_1 - \sqrt{V}$$

$$V = \sigma^2 (T_S - t).$$

2.3 AMERICAN AND ASIAN OPTIONS

American and Asian options belong to the class of *path-dependent options*. Unlike European options, their payoff does not only depend on the underlying price at maturity but on their whole price path from purchase date until maturity. Since analytical formulas for path-dependent options are often not available, option prices have to be calculated using numerical methods, such as Monte Carlo simulation, trinomial trees or PDE solvers. Throughout this section, let the underlying price be denoted by $S(t)$, which could be a spot price of a commodity or a futures price.

2.3.1 American Options

An American-style option grants the holder the right to exercise the option any time τ during the lifetime $[t, T]$ of the option. At the exercise time τ, the option holder receives the payoff $S(\tau) - K$ for a call option or $K - S(\tau)$ for a put option. In case of a physical settlement of the option, the price $S(\tau)$ represents the value of the commodity being delivered. Calculating the fair price for an American option requires finding the optimal *exercise strategy*, i.e. finding the optimal decision for each market price situation whether to exercise or not to exercise.

The standard methods to calculate American option prices are:

- *Binomial/trinomial trees*: The continuous-time model for $S(t)$ based on a Brownian motion is approximated by a discrete-time model and a backwards iteration similar to a dynamic-programming approach can be used.
- *Finite-difference methods*: Finite-difference methods are used to calculate numerical approximations of the partial differential equation satisfied by the option price (see section A.2.4)

Details about these numerical methods can be found in standard textbooks on option pricing (e.g. Wilmott 1998). Standard Monte Carlo methods are not suitable for American options, since they give no solution to the optimal exercise strategy. An extension to the Monte Carlo approach for American options is given in Longstaff and Schwartz (2001).

2.3.2 Asian Options

The Asian option differs from a European option in that the payoff is not a function of the underlying price at maturity but a function of the arithmetic mean of the underlying price over a period of time. An Asian call with fixing dates $T_1, \ldots, T_n$ has the payoff at time $T \geq T_n$

$$\text{payoff} = \max\left(A(T) - K, 0\right),$$

where $A(T)$ is the arithmetic mean

$$A(T) = \frac{1}{n} \sum_{i=1}^{n} S(T_i).$$

Asian options are less expensive than European options because the arithmetic mean has a lower volatility compared to the underlying at a single point in time. Asian options are common in energy markets, since energy is usually delivered over a period of time and the price risk for the whole period needs to be hedged.

If a Black–Scholes framework is assumed, i.e. $S(T_i)$ is log-normally distributed for each fixing date T_i, then the arithmetic mean $A(T)$ is no longer log-normally distributed and there is no simple option price formula similar to the Black–Scholes formula available. One possibility to price Asian options is by means of a Monte–Carlo simulation (see section A.2.5), where each simulation path needs to contain the prices at the fixing dates. Such a Monte Carlo simulation can be used for all types of stochastic models that can be simulated, but often the computations are very slow. There are, however, several approximations to the option price available that can be evaluated very efficiently. Two popular methods, the *Vorst method* and the *log-normal approximation*, are described in the following sections. Example results are shown in Table 2.1. When using Monte Carlo simulations it is advisable to use the geometric-mean approximation (2.12) as a control variate.

Table 2.1 Approximation results for an Asian option with 12 monthly fixings $T_1 = 1, T_2 = 1 + 1/12, \ldots, T_{12} = 1 + 11/12$ and parameters $S(t) = 100$, $K = 100$, $\sigma = 0.3$, $\mu = r = 0.03$

Pricing method	Result
Exact price	15.30
Vorst method	15.19
Log-normal approximation	15.32

The Vorst Method

We assume that $S(t)$ is a geometric Brownian motion (see section 3.2.1) of the form

$$dS(t) = \mu S(t)\, dt + \sigma S(t) dW(t),$$

with respect to the risk-neutral measure. For the logarithm the process equation is

$$d \ln S(t) = \left(\mu - \tfrac{1}{2}\sigma^2\right) dt + \sigma dW(t).$$

The Vorst method (see Vorst 1992) approximates the arithmetic mean by a geometric mean

$$G(T) = \sqrt[n]{\prod_{i=1}^{n} S(T_i)}, \qquad (2.12)$$

which is again log-normally distributed. This can be seen by looking at the logarithm of $G(T)$

$$\ln G(T) = \frac{1}{n} \sum_{i=1}^{n} \ln S(T_i),$$

which is a sum of normally distributed random variables and is therefore also normally distributed. To simplify the notation, let $T_0 = t$ and we get

$$\ln G(T) = \frac{1}{n} \sum_{i=1}^{n} \ln S(T_i)$$

$$= \ln S(t) + \frac{1}{n} \sum_{i=1}^{n} \sum_{j=1}^{i} \left(\ln S(T_j) - \ln S(T_{j-1}) \right)$$

$$= \ln S(t) + \sum_{i=1}^{n} \frac{n-i+1}{n} \left(\ln S(T_i) - \ln S(T_{i-1}) \right).$$

Since the increments $(\ln S(T_i) - \ln S(T_{i-1}))$ are independent, the mean and variance of $\ln G(T)$ are given by

$$\mathbb{E}[\ln G] = \ln S(t) + \left(\mu - \tfrac{1}{2}\sigma^2 \right) \sum_{i=1}^{n} \frac{n-i+1}{n} (T_i - T_{i-1})$$

$$\mathrm{Var}[\ln G] = \sigma^2 \sum_{i=1}^{n} \left(\frac{n-i+1}{n} \right)^2 (T_i - T_{i-1}).$$

To price Asian call or put options, one can now use Black's option price formulas (2.7) and (2.8) setting $F = \mathbb{E}[G] = \exp \left(\mathbb{E}[\ln G] + \tfrac{1}{2}\mathrm{Var}[\ln G] \right)$ and $V = \mathrm{Var}[\ln G]$. However, there is a systematic bias in the option price since the geometric mean is always lower than the arithmetic mean:

$$G(T) \le A(T).$$

In the Vorst approximation this bias is compensated by lowering the strike of the option to

$$K' = K - (\mathbb{E}[A(T)] - \mathbb{E}[G(T)]).$$

The Log-Normal Approximation

Another approach is to approximate the arithmetic average $A(T)$ by a log-normal distribution $\tilde{A}(T)$ which coincides in the first two moments. Since the approximation $\tilde{A}(T)$ must have mean

$$F_A = \mathbb{E}[A(T)] = \frac{1}{n} \sum_{i=1}^{n} F(t, T_i) \tag{2.13}$$

it must be of the form

$$\tilde{A}(T) = F_A \exp \left(-\tfrac{1}{2}\beta^2 + \beta N \right),$$

where N is a standard Gaussian random variable. The second moment of $\tilde{A}(T)$ is given by

$$\mathbb{E}[\tilde{A}^2(T)] = F_A^2 \, \mathbb{E}\left[\exp \left(-\beta^2 + 2\beta N \right) \right] = F_A^2 \, \exp \left(\beta^2 \right).$$

Since by the definition of the variance $\text{Var}[A(T)] = \mathbb{E}[A^2(T)] - \mathbb{E}[A(T)]^2$ and by definition $\mathbb{E}[A(T)] = F_A$, the moment matching condition is

$$F_A^2 \exp(\beta^2) = \mathbb{E}[A^2(T)] = \text{Var}[A(T)] + F_A^2.$$

Solving for β^2 yields

$$\beta^2 = \ln\left(\frac{\mathbb{E}[A^2(T)]}{F_A^2}\right) = \ln\left(1 + \frac{\text{Var}[A(T)]}{F_A^2}\right).$$

Thus, to calculate a value for β, either $\mathbb{E}[A^2(T)]$ or $\text{Var}[A(T)]$ has to be known. An explicit calculation of $\mathbb{E}[A^2(T)]$ yields

$$\mathbb{E}[A^2(T)] = \frac{1}{n^2} \sum_{i,j=1}^{n} F(t, T_i)F(t, T_j) \exp\left(\sigma^2(\min(T_i, T_j) - t)\right).$$

Knowing F_A and β, Black's option pricing formulas (2.7) and (2.8) can again be used with $F = F_A$ and $V = \beta^2$.

2.4 COMMODITY BONDS AND LOANS

Commodity bonds and loans are special kinds of bonds or loans where the interest payment and/or the redemption value are linked to a commodity or commodity index. The purpose of commodity bonds and loans is to have easier or cheaper access to new capital while reducing the risk that interest payments or redemption amounts cannot be paid.

As an example consider an oil company that needs USD 15 million to invest in new production facilities. If it took an ordinary loan it would face the risk that oil prices would decline and not earn enough money to pay back its loan. Instead it could take a commodity loan with the principal linked to the oil price paying 5% interest per year and at maturity pay back the value of 200 000 bbl of oil. Alternatively one could fix a maximum amount for the principal, say USD 17 million, giving the oil company more profit from very high oil prices. As a compensation it might have to pay a higher interest rate. More realistic examples and case studies are given in United Nations Conference on Trade and Development (1998).

2.5 MULTI-UNDERLYING OPTIONS

Often market participants have a risk exposure not with respect to a single underlying, but with respect to a combination of multiple underlyings. As an example, the owner of a coal fired power plant has a risk exposure to the price spread between coal and power (*dark spread*). To hedge such risk exposures, options with multiple underlyings can be constructed. The price of such options depends not only on the volatilities of the underlyings, but also on the correlation structure.

Let $S_1(t), \ldots, S_n(t)$ denote the different underlyings. The multiple-underlying extension of the Black–Scholes framework is given by the following system of stochastic differential equations:

$$dS_i(t) = \mu_i S_i(t)dt + \sigma_i S_i(t)dW_i(t), \qquad (2.14)$$

where $W_1(t), \ldots, W_n(t)$ are Bownian motions correlated by

$$dW_i(t)dW_j(t) = \rho_{ij}dt.$$

The forward prices of the n underlyings are denoted by

$$F_i(t, T) = \mathbb{E}_t[S_i(T)], \quad i = 1, \ldots, n.$$

2.5.1 Basket Options

A *basket option* is an option with not a single commodity as underlying but a basket (or index) $B(t)$, which is calculated as a weighted sum of multiple commodities

$$B(t) = \sum_{i=1}^{n} w_i S_i(t). \tag{2.15}$$

The payoff of a European basket call option on the basket $B(t)$ is

$$\text{payoff} = \max(B(T) - K, 0). \tag{2.16}$$

Example: A basket of energy prices related to power production could be defined as

$$B(t) = 100 \times \left(30\% \frac{oil(t)}{oil(0)} + 30\% \frac{coal(t)}{coal(0)} + 40\% \frac{co2(t)}{co2(0)} \right).$$

At time 0 the basket value is normalised to 100. If the oil price increases by 100%, the basket value $B(t)$ increases by 30% to a value of 130, if the prices of coal and CO_2 emission allowances are constant.

Pricing basket options in the Black–Scholes framework is not straightforward, since a weighted sum of log-normally distributed random variables is no longer log-normally distributed. The same problem arises when pricing Asian options (see section 2.3.2). Using a similar approach as for Asian options, the price of a basket option can be approximated using a log-normal approximation of the basket underlying (2.15).

Let the log-normal approximation be given by

$$\tilde{B}(T) = F_B \exp\left(-\tfrac{1}{2}\beta^2 + \beta N\right),$$

where N is a standard Gaussian random variable. The first two moments of B are given by

$$\mathbb{E}[B(T)] = \sum_{i=1}^{n} w_i F_i(t, T),$$

$$\mathbb{E}[B^2(T)] = \sum_{i,j=1}^{n} w_i w_j F_i(t, T) F_j(t, T) \exp\left(\rho_{ij}\sigma_i\sigma_j\right)$$

whereas the first two moments of $\tilde{B}$ are given by

$$\mathbb{E}[\tilde{B}] = F_B,$$

$$\mathbb{E}[\tilde{B}^2] = F_B^2 \exp\left(\beta^2\right).$$

Setting the first two moments of B and $\tilde{B}$ equal yields

$$F_B = \sum_{i=1}^{n} w_i F_i(t, T),$$

$$\beta^2 = \ln\left(\frac{\sum_{i,j=1}^{n} w_i w_j F_i(t, T) F_j(t, T) \exp\left(\rho_{ij}\sigma_i\sigma_j\right)}{F_B^2}\right).$$

Now Black's option pricing formulas (2.7) and (2.8) can again be used with $F = F_B$ and $V = \beta^2$.

Example: Continuing the example earlier in this section, consider the following basket of oil, coal and CO_2 allowances, where the forward prices are all normalised to 100:

Commodity	Weight (%)	Forward price	Volatility
Oil	30	100	0.3
Coal	30	100	0.2
CO_2	40	100	0.4

The correlation matrix of these three commodities is assumed as

	Oil	Coal	CO_2
Oil	1.0	0.1	0.6
Coal	0.1	1.0	−0.2
CO_2	0.6	−0.2	1.0

The following table compares the log-normal approximation of a one year at-the-money call option to the exact result calculated via a sufficient number of Monte Carlo simulations:

Computation method	Price	Implied volatility (%)
Monte Carlo	8.81	22.85
Log-normal approximation	8.95	23.16

The approximation error in this example is small but noticable. However, often the uncertainties about correlations and volatility skew are larger than the approximation errors from a log-normal approximation making this method suitable for a day-to-day valuation and for the calculation of Greeks.

As already mentioned in the example, one problem pricing basket options is how to determine the volatility skew and the correlations from given market data. As one approach, one can use the *moneyness* (underlying price divided by the strike price) to infer the volatility of each underlying from the single-underlying volatility skews. If a liquid market for options on a given basket exists, the correlation can be implied from market prices assuming all correlations ρ_{ij} are equal to a constant ρ. In this case, the implied correlation can depend on the strike of the basket option. Such a dependence is called a *correlation skew*. If option prices for a given basket do not exist, correlations have to be estimated from historical time series.

2.5.2 Spread Options

Market participants in energy markets are often not outright exposed to commodity prices but rather to the difference of two or more commodity prices involved in a production or transformation process. Examples are given below:

- The *dark spread* between power and coal, modelling a coal fired power plant.
- The *spark spread* between power and gas, modelling a gas fired power plant.
- The *crack spread* between different refinement levels of oil, modelling a refinement process.

The owner of a power plant can use a spread option model to hedge the market risk of the power plant using futures or he can directly sell a spread option offsetting risks of the power plant.

When exercised, a spread option pays the option holder at maturity T the difference of two underlying prices minus the strike price K. Denoting the underlying prices by $S_1(t)$ and $S_2(t)$, the payoff formula is

$$\text{payoff} = \max\left(S_1(T) - S_2(T) - K, 0\right).$$

Unlike basket options, a log-normal approximation of the spread is usually not recommended since a spread can be positive or negative.

The case $K = 0$ (*exchange option*) is treated analytically in Margrabe (1978). It turns out that the pricing formula is identical to Black's formulas (2.7) and (2.8) setting the strike equal to the second forward price $F_2(t, T)$ and the volatility to $\tilde{\sigma} = \sqrt{\sigma_1^2 - 2\rho\sigma_1\sigma_2 + \sigma_2^2}$, where ρ is the correlation between the two underlyings. For a call option we have the *Margrabe formula*

$$U = e^{-r(T-t)}\left(F_1 N(d_1) - F_2 N(d_2)\right)$$

evaluated at the current futures prices $F_1 = F_1(t, T)$, $F_2 = F_2(t, T)$, where

$$d_1 = \frac{\ln(F_1/F_2) + V/2}{\sqrt{V}}, \quad d_2 = d_1 - \sqrt{V}$$

and $V = \tilde{\sigma}^2(T - t)$.

The value of a spread option depends strongly on the correlation between the two underlyings (see Figure 2.16). The higher the correlation between the two underlyings the lower is the value of the spread option. This is intuitively right, since the volatility of the spread is lower for highly correlated underlyings.

The general case $K \neq 0$ has no easy analytical solution. Option prices can either be calculated using Monte Carlo simulations for the two underlyings or using semi-analytical techniques that involve a numerical integration (Pearson 1995). A simple approximation using the Margrabe formula (see Eydeland and Wolyniec 2003) is to replace F_2 by $F_2 + K$ and σ_2 by $\sigma_2 F_1/(F_2 + K)$.

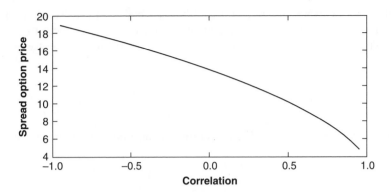

Figure 2.16   Value of a spread option as a function of the correlation for $F_1 = F_2 = 100$, $T = 1$, $\sigma_1 = 0.3$ and $\sigma_2 = 0.2$

2.5.3   Quanto and Composite Options

Often, commodities are traded in a currency different from a market participant's home currency. In the following, let USD be the currency the commodity is traded in (the foreign currency) and EUR be the home currency of the market participant. We call a trader in the USD market the USD trader and a trader in the EUR market a EUR trader. Let $X(t)$ be the exchange rate from EUR to USD, i.e. the value of one EUR in USD. There are three ways to structure an option specifically for EUR traders:

1. *Plain conversion*: Take an ordinary option in USD and convert the payoff into EUR at maturity. The payoff in EUR then is

$$P = \max(S(T) - K, 0)/X(T) \quad \text{(in EUR)}.$$

2. *Composite option*: Construct a synthetic underlying $Z(t) = S(t)/X(t)$ traded in EUR by converting at each time t the underlying price $S(t)$ from USD into EUR. An option written on this synthetic underlying with strike $\tilde{K}$ (in EUR) has the payoff

$$P = \max(S(T)/X(T) - \tilde{K}, 0) \quad \text{(in EUR)}.$$

3. *Quanto option*: Take the USD payoff and convert it at a fixed exchange rate X_0 into EUR without applying the current exchange rate. In contrast to the plain conversion described above, the payoff in EUR does not explicitly depend anymore on the exchange rate $X(t)$:

$$P = \max(S(T) - K, 0)/X_0 \quad \text{(in EUR)}.$$

In case 1 (plain conversion) the value of the option at time t is just the usual option price in USD converted to EUR at the current exchange rate. In fact, buying the option in USD in the foreign market and converting the payoff at maturity yields the same payoff.

The other two cases are more complicated but can both be treated analytically. To fix some notation, let r_{USD} and r_{EUR} be the (continuously compounded) interest rates for USD and EUR. The model for $S(t)$ (in USD) with respect to the risk-neutral measure is assumed as

$$\frac{dS(t)}{S(t)} = (r_{USD} - y) \; dt + \sigma_S \; dW_S(t),$$

where y is the convenience yield. The model for the corresponding futures price $F(t)$ is

$$\frac{dF(t)}{F(t)} = \sigma_S \; dW_S(t).$$

The stochastic differential equation for the exchange rate $X(t)$ with respect to the risk-neutral measure is

$$\frac{dX(t)}{X(t)} = (r_{USD} - r_{EUR}) \; dt + \sigma_X \; dW_X(t).$$

The risk-neutral drift must be $r_{USD} - r_{EUR}$ since one EUR can be seen as a traded asset in the USD-based market, where the interest rate r_{EUR} plays the role of the (dividend) yield. The forward price for one EUR is

$$F_X(t) = F_X(t, T) = e^{(r_{USD} - r_{EUR})(T-t)}.$$

Let ρ be the correlation between the two risk factors $W_S(t)$ and $W_X(t)$. The dependence of quanto and composite options on ρ is shown in Figure 2.17.

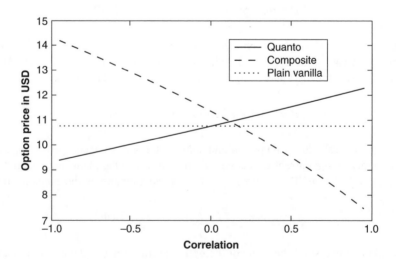

Figure 2.17 Value of quanto and composite options as a function of the correlation for $F = K = 100$, $T = 1$, $\sigma = 0.3$ and $\sigma_X = 0.1$.

Composite Options

A composite option can be priced using the Black–Scholes framework applied to the synthetic underlying $Z(t) = S(t)/X(t)$. Using Itô's formula (see section A.2.3), one gets

$$\frac{dZ(t)}{Z} = \left(r_{EUR} - y + \sigma_x^2 - \rho\sigma_S\sigma_X\right)dt + \sigma_S dW_S(t) - \sigma_X dW_X(t).$$

From the perspective of the EUR market, the underlying Z is a tradable asset (it is just the value of $S(t)$ converted to EUR). Therefore, with respect to the risk-neutral measure in the EUR market the drift must be $r_{EUR} - y$ and a change of measure yields the stochastic differential equation

$$\frac{dZ(t)}{Z} = (r_{EUR} - y)\,dt + \sigma_S dW_S(t) - \sigma_X dW_X(t).$$

The stochastic term $\sigma_S dW_S(t) + \sigma_X dW_X(t)$ can be written as $\sigma_Z dW_Z(t)$ using a single Brownian motion $W_Z(t)$ and the volatility

$$\sigma_Z = \sqrt{\sigma_S^2 - 2\rho\sigma_S\sigma_X + \sigma_X^2}.$$

Now the Black–Scholes formula can be applied to the underlying Z:

$$U = e^{-r_{EUR}(T-t)}\left(F_Z N(d_1) - \tilde{K} N(d_2)\right)$$

evaluated at the synthetic futures price for Z

$$F_Z(t) = F_S(t)/F_X(t)$$

with

$$d_1 = \frac{\ln(F_Z/\tilde{K}) + V/2}{\sqrt{V}}, \quad d_2 = d_1 - \sqrt{V} \quad \text{and} \quad V = \sigma_Z^2(T-t).$$

Quanto Options

The payoff of the quanto option for the USD trader is

$$P_{USD} = \max(S(T) - K, 0)X(T)/X_0 \quad \text{(in USD)}.$$

To price the option, a *change of numeraire* technique can be used. Details about this technique can be found in Musiela and Rutkowski (2004). As numeraire we use the USD value of one EUR including the accumulated interest payments

$$\beta(t) = e^{r_{EUR}t}X(t).$$

Now we consider all values relative to the numeraire $\beta(t)$, in particular $Z(t) = S(t)/\beta(t)$. Instead of the usual risk-neutral measure one now chooses a measure $\tilde{Q}$ under which all prices of non-dividend paying assets relative to the numeraire $\beta(t)$ are martingales. Then the option price (in USD) is given by

$$U = \beta(t)\mathbb{E}_t^{\tilde{Q}}\left[\frac{P_{USD}}{\beta(T)}\right] = e^{-r_{EUR}(T-t)}(X(t)/X_0)\mathbb{E}_t^{\tilde{Q}}\left[\max(S(T) - K, 0)\right].$$

It can be shown that under $\tilde{Q}$ the stochastic differential equation for $S(t)$ has an additional drift term $\rho\sigma_X\sigma_S\,dt$:

$$\frac{dS(t)}{S(t)} = (r_{USD} - y + \rho\sigma_X\sigma_S)\,dt + \sigma_S dW_S(t),$$

Applying the Black–Scholes formula, the option price formula is

$$U = e^{-r_{EUR}(T-t)}\,(X(t)/X_0)\left(\tilde{F}_S N(d_1) - KN(d_2)\right)$$

evaluated at the quanto forward price under $\tilde{Q}$

$$\tilde{F}_S(t) = \exp\left(\rho\sigma_X\sigma_S(T - t)\right)F_S(t)$$

with

$$d_1 = \frac{\ln(\tilde{F}_S/K) + V/2}{\sqrt{V}}, \quad d_2 = d_1 - \sqrt{V} \quad \text{and} \quad V = \sigma_S^2(T - t).$$

2.6   SPOT PRICE OPTIONS

In section 2.2 we considered options on forwards or futures contracts, where we have one exercise opportunity before the start of delivery. For flow commodities, such as power or gas, there is a demand for optionality on a short-term basis, since storage capacities are limited and demand varies from day to day due to weather conditions not known much in advance.

Consider a power distribution company that procures its energy demand partly via standard forward contracts and partly on the spot market. The delivery obligation from the company's full service contracts is an hourly load schedule that depends on weather conditions and the customer's behaviour. The company needs to rely on the spot market for two reasons:

1. There is no liquid forward market for hourly load schedules and the distribution company does not want to pay a high premium for such individual products. The distribution company therefore buys baseload and peakload products on the forward market. The exact hourly profile is then bought on the spot market.
2. The weather conditions determining the load can be forecasted reliably only shortly before the delivery day, so matching the forecasted load has to be done on the spot market.

Since spot market prices are extremely volatile, the company wants to secure a certain price for additional energy it may need. One possible product that serves this purpose is a strip of call options for a certain capacity on an hourly basis. Whenever the spot price is high (above the option's strike level) the distribution company can exercise the option and pays only the strike price. Since the strike price can be seen as the maximum price paid for the energy, the product is also called a *cap* on the electricity price.

There are variants to the simple strip of call options, such as swing options, with additional restrictions on the optionality and thus may lead to reduced option premiums or give a better match to optionalities granted by physical assets.

2.6.1 Pricing Spot Price Options

The statistical properties of spot prices for energy are much different from underlyings considered in standard option pricing theory. The assumptions of the Black–Scholes or Black's model (see section 2.2.2), that prices follow a geometric Brownian motion, is in most cases not appropriate. Therefore, one can use either one of the mean-reverting models described in section 3.2 or, to take into account price spikes and seasonalities, a model following the ideas in section 3.4.

Let an option be given by payoffs $h_1(S(t_1)), \ldots, h_N(S(t_N))$ at times $t_1, \ldots, t_N$. An exercise strategy $\phi_i \in \{0, 1\}$ indicates whether to exercise or not exercise the option. The exercise strategy ϕ_i can be based only on information up to t_i, the time of decision. Given an appropriate model for the spot price $S(t)$, the option price is given as the discounted expectation of the option's payoff under the risk-neutral measure (see section 3.2) and with an optimal exercise strategy:

$$U(t) = \max_{\phi} \mathbb{E}_t^Q \left[\sum_{i=1}^{N} e^{-r(t_i - t)} \phi_i h_i(S(t_i)) \right], \tag{2.17}$$

where the optimisation is done over all exercise strategies $\phi = (\phi_1, \ldots, \phi_N)$. There may be additional restrictions on the number of exercise opportunities:

$$E_{min} \leq \sum_{i=1}^{N} \phi_i \leq E_{max}.$$

Since, for the more complicated models, analytical formulas are no longer available, one has to employ numerical methods to evaluate the option price. In many cases, Monte Carlo schemes have to be used. A Monte Carlo technique for dealing with exercise strategies can be found in Longstaff and Schwartz (2001), where American options are studied.

To interpret the theoretical option value given by equation (2.17) the following remarks may be helpful:

- The price is not strictly an arbitrage price in the sense that there exists a complete hedging strategy. One reason is a market *incompleteness* due to a lacking forward market for all single delivery times t_i.
- The option price is model dependent. For options getting their value from few extreme market events (e.g. spikes) the values derived from two stochastic models may differ substantially.
- In equation (2.17) it is assumed that the option can be exercised optimally against spot prices. In real-world examples, one often has to nominate the exercise before the spot auction where the spot prices are determined.

- An optimal exercise strategy is often very complicated to calculate and may be difficult to implement in daily business.

Because of those uncertainties it is useful to calculate the *intrinsic value* of an option. This is defined as the value against the forward curve instead of the stochastic paths:

$$IV(t) = \max_{\phi} \sum_{i=1}^{N} e^{-r(t_i-t)} \phi_i \, h_i(F(t, t_i)). \tag{2.18}$$

Since today's forward prices are used, the problem is deterministic and the expectation operator is not needed. Equation (2.18) describes a deterministic linear optimisation problem. The intrinsic value reflects the option value if one had to nominate the complete exercise schedule today based on the information in today's forward curve. Thus, the intrinsic value gives a lower bound on the option value.

An upper bound to the option price is found by dropping the restriction that the exercise decision can only be based on the information up to the time of decision. Then the decisions can use all the information on the future spot prices and optimise the value *ex post* over the whole spot price path. Under this assumption the optimisation is done pathwise and the pricing equation can be reformulated as

$$U^*(t) = \mathbb{E}_t^Q \left[\max_{\phi} \sum_{i=1}^{N} e^{-r(t_i-t)} \phi_i h_i(S(t_i)) \right]. \tag{2.19}$$

If $S^k(t)$ for $k = 1, \ldots, n$ are simulation paths, the Monte Carlo approximation of the upper option value is

$$U^*(t) = \frac{1}{n} \sum_{k=1}^{n} U_k^*$$

where

$$U_k^* = \max_{\phi} \sum_{i=1}^{N} e^{-r(t_i-t)} \phi_i h_i(S^k(t_i)).$$

For each path a linear optimisation problem needs to be solved.

2.6.2 Caps and Floors

Buying a *cap*, the option holder has the right (but not the obligation) to buy a certain amount of energy at stipulated times $t_1, \ldots, t_N$ during the delivery period at a fixed strike price K. The option exercise typically has to be nominated a certain time in advance. The strike price K secures a maximum price for buying the energy, since in all cases where the spot price is above the strike price, the option holder can exercise the option and buys the energy at price K. In this way, the cap is used to protect a short position against increasing market prices (see Figure 2.18). Since the cap can be considered as a strip of independent call options, the option is exercised at any given t_i if the market price $S(t_i)$ is above the strike price K, in which case the profit (compared to market prices) is $S(t_i) - K$ (see section 2.2).

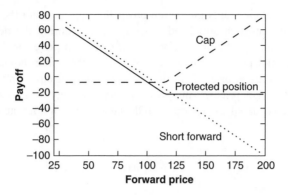

Figure 2.18   Protecting a short position with a cap

As described in section 2.6.1, the fair value of the option is given by the discounted expected payoffs under the (risk-neutral) stochastic model. The cap price may be divided by the number of delivery hours to make different delivery periods comparable. In this case we get a price per MWh. The formula for the cap is

$$U(t) = \frac{1}{N} \sum_{i=1}^{N} e^{-r(t_i - t)} \mathbb{E}\left[\max(S(t_i) - K, 0)\right].$$

Figure 2.19 shows the price per MWh of a one-year cap as a function of the strike price. For high strike prices there are few opportunities to exercise the option and the value is determinded more and more by the price spikes within the delivery period. In the example for strike prices greater than about 140 EUR/MWh, the intrinsic value is zero, i.e. all forward prices are below the strike price. The average number of exercised hours over all simulation paths is given in Figure 2.20. For a strike price of 140 EUR/MWh there are on average still about 200 exercises per year that generate an average profit of about 1 EUR/MWh or about 8760 EUR per year.

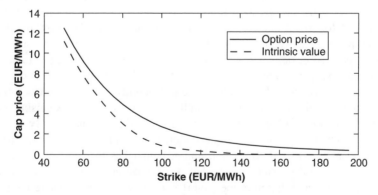

Figure 2.19   Price and intrinsic value of a cap as a function of the strike price. The delivery period is one year

Similar to a cap, a *floor* grants the option buyer the right (but not the obligation) to sell a certain amount of energy at stipulated times $t_1, \ldots, t_N$ during the delivery period at a fixed strike price K. The strike price K secures a minimum price for the energy, since in all cases where the spot price is below the strike price, the option holder can exercise the option and sell the energy at price K. In this way, the cap is used to protect a long position against decreasing market prices. This *protective put* strategy was shown in Figure 2.7. The floor can be considered as a strip of independent put options and the fair value is given by

$$U(t) = \sum_{i=1}^{N} e^{-r(t_i - t)} \mathbb{E}\left[\max(K - S(t_i), 0)\right].$$

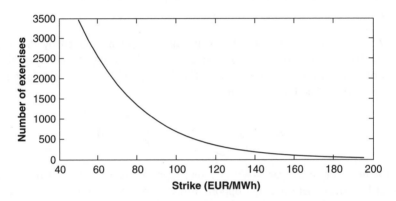

Figure 2.20   Average number of hours the cap is exercised for a given strike price (one year delivery period $= 8760$ hours)

2.6.3   Swing Options

A *swing* option is similar to a cap or floor except that we have additional restrictions on the number of option exercises. Let $\phi_i \in \{0, 1\}$ be the decision whether to exercise ($\phi_i = 1$) or not to exercise ($\phi_i = 0$) the option at time t_i. The option's payoff at time t_i then is given by $\phi_i (S(t_i) - K)$ for a call and $\phi_i (K - S(t_i))$ for a put option. We now require that the number of exercises is between E_{min} and E_{max}. This restriction imposes a constraint on the energy that is received or delivered by exercising the option. Figure 2.21 graphically shows the possible exercise paths over time. If the option holder exercises all hours right from the start of the exercise period, he follows the left boundary of the exercise region. If he delays exercising he follows the time axis until he is forced to start exercising all hours at time $T - E_{min}$ to end up with E_{min} exercises at time T (right boundary). By deciding from time to time which hours to exercise, the option holder might follow some path similar to the example in Figure 2.21. Since the option holder has to exercise a certain number of hours, it is in general possible that he has to exercise at times where the spot price is below the strike price and therefore the payoff is negative. In cases where the strike price is high, it may even happen that the value of the swing option is negative for the option holder.

To determine the option value, we have to find an optimal exercise strategy $\Phi = (\phi_1, \ldots, \phi_N)$ maximising the expected payoff (see section 2.6.1)

$$\sum_{i=1}^{N} e^{-r(t_i - t)} \mathbb{E}\left[\phi_i(S(t_i) - K)\right] \to \max \qquad (2.20)$$

subject to the restrictions

$$E_{min} \leq \sum_{i=1}^{N} \phi_i \leq E_{max}.$$

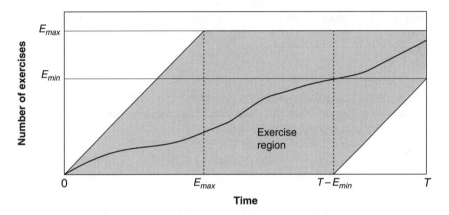

Figure 2.21 Example exercise path for a swing option

If the spot prices were deterministic and known in advance, we would have a linear optimisation problem. It can easily be seen that the condition $\phi_i \in \{0, 1\}$ can be relaxed to $0 \leq \phi_i \leq 1$ without changing the solution, such that we have no integer conditions. The steps to solve the deterministic case are:

1. Calculate the discounted payoffs $P(t_i) = e^{-r(t_i - t)}(S(t_i) - K)$.
2. Sort the discounted payoffs $P(t_i)$ in descending order.
3. Take the first E_{min} payoffs regardless of their value and subsequent payoffs up to E_{max} until their sign becomes negative.

The exercise strategy for stochastic spot prices is more complicated than in the deterministic case. The decision at time t_i, whether to exercise or not, can only be based on the history of spot prices $S(t_1), \ldots, S(t_i)$ and on the assumptions of the stochastic properties of the future spot prices $S(t_{i+1}), \ldots, S(t_N)$. Without regarding the complexity of finding an optimal exercise strategy we can calculate lower and upper bounds on the swing value. As a lower bound we can take the intrinsic value of the option. As an upper bound we can calculate the expected value assuming that we knew each spot price path in advance (see section 2.6.1).

Using a Monte Carlo approach we generate n simulation paths $S^k(t_1), \ldots, S^k(t_N)$ for $k = 1, \ldots, n$. For each path S^k we solve the linear optimisation problem for $\phi_1, \ldots, \phi_n$

$$\sum_{i=1}^{N} e^{-r(t_i - t)} \phi_i (S^k(t_i) - K) \to \max$$

subject to the energy constraints

$$E_{min} \leq \sum_{i=1}^{N} \phi_i \leq E_{max}.$$

Since the path $S^k(t_i)$ is assumed to be known in advance, the algorithm based on sorting the payoffs can be used here. Let the maximum be attained at U_k^*, which then is the optimal value from path S^k. The expected value over all paths is given by the average

$$U^* = \frac{1}{n} \sum_{k=1}^{n} U_k^*.$$

A strategy based only on the available information at the time of the decision cannot in general attain the maximum value for each path. Therefore, the true option value must fall between the intrinsic value and the upper bound U^*:

$$IV(t) \leq U(t) \leq U^*(t)$$

Figure 2.22 shows intrinsic value, option price and upper bound for an example swing option as a function of the strike price. For high strike prices above 120 EUR/MWh the option value becomes negative. The average number of exercises for a given strike price is shown in Figure 2.23. Below a strike price of around 50 EUR/MWh it is optimal to exercise the maximum number of 2000 hours because there are enough hours available above the strike price. Increasing the strike price there are on average not enough hours with prices above

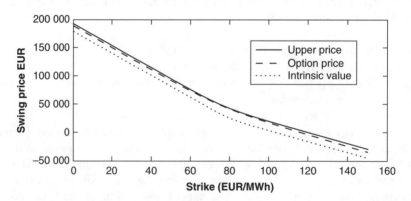

Figure 2.22   Price and intrinsic value of a swing option as a function of the strike price. The delivery period is one year and $E_{min} = 1000$, $E_{max} = 2000$

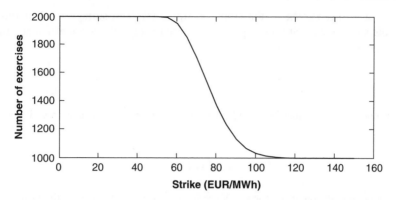

Figure 2.23 Average number of hours the swing option is exercised for a given strike price. $E_{min} = 1000$, $E_{max} = 2000$

the strike price available, so the number of exercises decreases. Above a strike price of around 110 EUR/MWh the average number of exercises approaches the minimum number of 1000 hours, since most paths then contain fewer than 1000 hours with prices above the strike level.

2.6.4 Virtual Storage

A *virtual storage* contract allows the option holder to inject and to withdraw energy. It can be seen as an abstract model of a physical storage, such as gas storage (e.g. depleted natural gas field or salt cavern) or power storage (e.g. hydro pump storage plant, see section 4.2.2). Often a virtual storage contract simplifies the technical restrictions of a physical plant. In this section we consider such a simplified storage contract and focus on the option pricing techniques.

The optionality of a virtual storage is subject to a number of operational constraints:

- A maximum injection rate R_i.
- A maximum withdrawal rate R_w.
- A storage capacity C.
- An injection efficiency λ, i.e. the percentage of the injected energy that becomes available in the storage.

To find a mathematical description of the option, we let $\phi(t)$ denote the withdrawal rate ($\phi(t) > 0$) and $\psi(t)$ the injection rate ($\psi(t) > 0$). Both $\phi(t)$ and $\psi(t)$ define the exercise decision at time t. The discounted payoff is given by the value of the withdrawn energy $\phi(t)S(t)$ and by the costs of the injected energy $\psi(t)S(t)$:

$$\text{payoff} = \sum_{i=1}^{N} e^{-r(t_i - t)}(\phi(t_i) - \psi(t_i))S(t_i).$$

The restrictions on the maximum injection and withdrawal rates are

$$0 \leq \phi(t_i) \leq R_w$$
$$0 \leq \psi(t_i) \leq R_i.$$

Next, one has to keep track of the stored energy $L(t)$. The storage level at time t_{i+1} is given by the storage level at time t_i plus the injected energy times the efficiency minus the withdrawn energy:

$$L(t_{i+1}) = L(t_i) + \lambda \psi(t_i) - \phi(t_i).$$

The initial energy $L(t_1)$ must be specified in the contract. The storage capacity restrictions are

$$0 \leq L(t_i) \leq C.$$

The constraints are all linear, so for a given price path one has to solve a linear programming problem. Solving the problem for the forward curve yields the intrinsic value. Proceeding in the same way as in section 2.6.3 for swing options, an upper bound on the price is found by solving the problem for a large number of simulation paths and taking the average. A least-squares Monte Carlo approach (Longstaff and Schwartz 2001) for the option value is studied in Boogert and de Jong (2006).

Example: We consider two different virtual storage contracts with injection and withdrawal rate equal to 10 MW. The first storage has a capacity of 1000 MWh, whereas the second storage has a capacity of 120 MWh. Figure 2.24 shows the optimal exercise against the forward curve over a two week period. The results are the following:

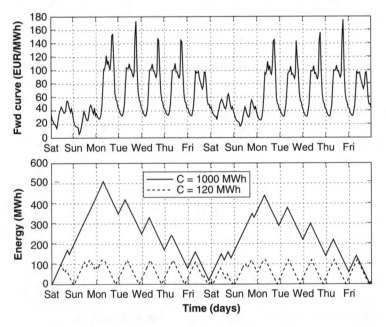

Figure 2.24   Optimal exercise of a virtual storage contract (lower graph) with respect to the forward curve (upper graph) for different storage capacities C. Injection rate and withdrawal rate are both 10 MW.

- $C = 1000\,$MWh: Starting with a weekend, the low prices are used to store energy at the maximum injection rate. Then over the weekdays, energy is retrieved at peak hours and partly injected again at offpeak hours, such that the stored energy is again at zero before the next weekend. The second week has a similar pattern. The maximum storage capacity of 1000 MWh is not attained. The intrinsic value is EUR 93 000.
- $C = 120\,$MWh: The storage capacity allows only to inject energy for 12 hours at the maximum injection rate, therefore energy is injected over night and withdrawn during the peak hours. The intrinsic value now is EUR 81 000.

Solving the linear optimisation problem can be done using either a general linear programming solver or a dynamic programming implementation tailored to the specific problem.

The linear optimisation problem: The optimisation problem for one price path for the variables $\phi(t_i)$, $\psi(t_i)$ and $L(t_i)$ $(i = 1, \ldots, N)$ is

$$\sum_{i=1}^{N} e^{-r(t_i - t)} S(t_i) \phi(t_i) - e^{-r(t_i - t)} S(t_i) \psi(t_i) \to \max \tag{2.21}$$

such that

$$\begin{aligned}
0 &\le \phi(t_i) \le R_w \quad (i = 1, \ldots, N) \\
0 &\le \psi(t_i) \le R_i \quad (i = 1, \ldots, N) \\
0 &\le L(t_i) \le C \quad (i = 1, \ldots, N) \\
L(t_1) &= L_0
\end{aligned} \tag{2.22}$$

$$L(t_{i+1}) - L(t_i) - \lambda \psi(t_i) + \phi(t_i) = 0, \quad (i = 1, \ldots, N - 1)$$

The problem consists of $3N$ variables, $6N$ linear inequality constraints and $N - 1$ linear equation constraints. In the case of electricity virtual storage contracts over a full year with exercise opportunities on an hourly basis the number of variables exceeds 25 000. Depending on the type of storage, a good approximation is to impose monthly target storage levels (which can also be optimised in a second step) and to optimise on a monthly basis.

Dynamic programming approach: Let $U(i, L)$ be the value of the virtual storage at time t_i with storage level L. The dynamic programming approach, explained in more detail in section 4.2.3, leads to the following backward iteration:

$\underline{i = N + 1:}$

$$U(N + 1, L) = 0, \quad \text{for all} \quad L.$$

The time t_{N+1} is after the last exercise.

$\underline{i \le N:}$ We assume that the values $U(i + 1, L)$ are known for all states (storage levels) L. Then for a given strategy ϕ, ψ at time t_i the next state $L(t_{i+1}, L, \phi, \psi)$ is given by the transition equation

$$L(t_{i+1}, L, \phi, \psi) = L + \lambda \psi - \phi.$$

To find the optimal strategy for a given state L, one has to solve

$$U(i, L) = \max_{\substack{0 \leq \phi \leq R_w \\ 0 \leq \psi \leq R_i}} U(i+1, L(t_{i+1}, L, \phi, \psi)) + (\phi - \psi)\tilde{S}(t_i),$$

where $\tilde{S}(t_i) = e^{-rt_i} S(t_i)$ is the discounted spot price. Usually, it is enough to consider the three cases:

1. Do nothing ($\phi = \psi = 0$).
2. Maximum injection ($\phi = 0$, $\psi = \min(R_i, (C - L)/\lambda)$).
3. Maximum withdrawal ($\psi = 0$, $\phi = \min(R_w, L)$).

The optimal injection ψ and withdrawal ϕ, denoted by $\phi^*(i, L)$ and $\psi^*(i, L)$, define the exercise strategy.

After completion of the backward iteration, the value at time t_1 for a current storage level L is $U(t_1, L)$. The optimal storage level and exercise schedule over time are calculated by forward iteration starting with the initial storage level $L(t_1)$. At each time t_i, we apply the optimal exercise strategy $\phi(t_i) = \phi^*(t_i, L(t_i))$ and $\psi(t_i) = \psi^*(t_i, L(t_i))$. The iteration to the next time step is

$$L(t_{i+1}) = L(t_i) + \lambda\psi - \phi.$$

3
Commodity Price Models

Financial and commodity markets have converged in many ways. Availability of commodity exchanges and the standardisation of commodity contracts have made it possible to construct derivative products similar to those known from financial markets and to use similar mathematical approaches to price them and quantify their risks. So what makes modelling commodity prices different from modelling financial markets? The differences are a result of the following market characteristics:

- *Storability*: Some commodities, such as gold, are easily storable at low costs, while others are hardly storable at all, such as electricity. Storability is a major factor determining the relation between spot price and forward price.
- *Consumption*: Most commodities are primarily held for consumption and not for investment. This is related to the limited or costly storability of many commodities.
- *Delivery*: Energy, in form of electricity or gas, is not usually delivered at one point of time, but over a delivery period. Electricity and gas also need special infrastructure to be delivered.
- *Market regulation*: Energy markets traditionally were highly regulated and are still often dominated by few players. Changes of legal regulations and trading decisions of dominant players may have an impact on market prices.

Fundamental market characteristics have a strong impact on the behaviour of commodity and energy prices. There are two different approaches to stochastic modelling of commodity prices. First, one can try to model the fundamental price drivers and use fundamental market models similar to those described in Chapter 4. The disadvantage of such an approach is that the model may become very complicated and calibration of model parameters difficult. Where the focus is not on understanding the market mechanisms but on using the model for simulation or pricing applications, direct calibration of an appropriate stochastic model to market prices is used. This second approach is described here, although ideas from the fundamental approach are also used (see the SMaPS model in section 3.4.2).

To choose an appropriate stochastic model for a commodity, typical features of commodity prices must be identified. The following statistical features are often found in commodity prices, where the importance depends strongly on the particular commodity:

- *Mean-reversion*: In many commodity markets prices fluctuate around some equilibrium price that is stable on a medium term. In the long term, the equilibrium price may also change.
- *Seasonality*: For many commodities, including energy, the demand follows a seasonal pattern. Due to storage limitations seasonality is also seen in the prices.

- *Price spikes*: The demand for commodities is often inelastic to prices. If there is limited storage capacity available, constraints in availability may lead to extremely high spot prices.

Since the focus of the chapter is on applications in the context of energy derivatives, other commodity markets are not explicitly mentioned. For applications in other commodity markets see, e.g. Geman (2005). Other books covering energy price modelling are Pilipovic (1997), Clewlow and Strickland (2000), and Eydeland and Wolyniec (2003).

3.1   FORWARD CURVES AND THE MARKET PRICE OF RISK

The *forward price* $F(t, T)$ at time t of a commodity for delivery date T is defined as the price of a forward contract that yields a contract fair value of zero (see section 2.1.1). Typically, the forward price of a commodity at time t depends on the delivery date T. This dependence is called the *forward curve* at time t. In practice, a liquid market exists only for forward contracts with a set of standardised expiry dates, e.g. monthly delivery dates for the next 12 calendar months. By interpolating between those expiry dates we often assume that the full forward curve $F(t, T)$ for all $t < T < T_{max}$ is known. Given the forward curve $F(t, T)$, the spot price can be interpreted as the limit case $T \to t$, i.e.

$$S(t) = F(t, t) = \lim_{T \to t} F(t, T).$$

For commodities like gas or electricity, traded contracts do not have single delivery dates, but delivery periods. The forward price at time t for a delivery period $[T_1, T_2]$ is denoted by $F(t, T_1, T_2)$.

Figures 3.1 and 3.2 show example forward curves for Brent oil and natural gas. The gas forward curve has a pronounced seasonality, since demand is seasonal and storage capacity is limited. Depending on the commodity, forward curves can have a different structure and also may change their shape over time. Possible shapes of forward curves will be discussed further in section 3.1.3.

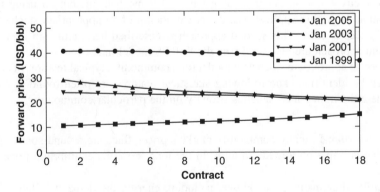

Figure 3.1   Brent crude oil monthly forward curve (ICE)

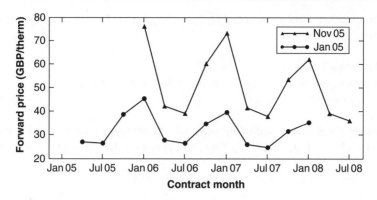

Figure 3.2 Natural gas monthly forward curve (ICE)

3.1.1　Investment Assets

Investment assets, such as gold, are assets mainly held for investment purposes. As such, they have to be easily storable and standardised. Pricing models for such commodities come closest to those of financial assets. The relationship between spot price $S(t)$ and forward price $F(t, T)$ can be derived from cash-and-carry arbitrage arguments. Let $C(t, T)$ denote the present value of the storage costs to store one unit of the commodity from today (time t) until the forward expiry T. Then the arbitrage-free forward price is given by

$$F(t, T) = (S(t) + C(t, T)) \, e^{r(T-t)},$$

where r is the (instantaneous) continuously compounded interest rate (Hull 2005). If there is an income from storing the commodity, it can be included in $C(t, T)$ with a negative value. The methodology is completely analogous when calculating forward prices for financial assets, such as foreign currencies or stocks, where $C(t, T)$ represents the interest payments of the foreign currency or the dividend payments of the stock. If storage costs in any time period are proportional to the asset price, they can be considered as an additional negative yield and added to the financing costs:

$$F(t, T) = S(t) e^{(r+c)(T-t)},$$

where c is the continuously compounded rate for storage costs.

3.1.2　Consumption Assets and Convenience Yield

Many commodities, such as oil or gas, are not primarily traded for investment purposes but for consumption. There is a steady flow from sources (production or exploration) to sinks (consumption). Often, there are limited storage facilities to balance differences between production and consumption over a period of time. This behaviour has strong effects on forward prices. For longer time horizons it is too costly to hedge a short forward position by storing the commodity up to the forward expiration date. To understand where the usual arbitrage argument fails a closer investigation is made of the hedge strategy. In a market situation where $F(t, T) > (S(t) + C(t, T)) e^{r(T-t)}$ an arbitrage strategy would be to

- short the forward contract;
- borrow the amount of $S(t) + C(t, T)$ at the risk-free rate; and
- buy the commodity at price $S(t)$.

The risk-less profit at time T including accumulated interest payments would be the difference $F(t, T) - (S(t) + C(t, T)) e^{r(T-t)}$. Thus, an upper limit for the forward price is

$$F(t, T) \leq (S(t) + C(t, T)) e^{r(T-t)}.$$

The inverse inequality, however, does not necessarily hold in this case. In a market situation where $F(t, T) < (S(t) + C(t, T)) e^{r(T-t)}$ (strict inequality) a possible strategy for a holder long on the commodity would be to buy the forward contract and sell one unit of the commodity at price $S(t)$. At the forward expiry date the holder gets back the commodity and makes more money than anyone holding the commodity until the expiry date and pays the storage costs for the whole period. However, this is in most cases not an attractive alternative for a holder of the commodity as they require the commodity for consumption and do not plan to hold the commodity until expiry of the forward contract. The purpose of storage facilities is primarily to balance offer and demand and to guarantee supply on a limited time horizon.

Let $Y(t, T)$ be the sum of the additional benefits owners of a commodity have from owning the commodity from time t to time T compared to being long a forward contract. Then the forward price inequality can be replaced by the equality

$$F(t, T) = (S(t) + C(t, T) - Y(t, T)) e^{r(T-t)}.$$

If those benefits and the storage costs are written as yields y and c, this equation becomes

$$F(t, T) = S(t) e^{(r+c-y)(T-t)}.$$

The yield y is then called the *convenience yield*. The convenience yield plays the same role dividends play for stocks. Often, the storage cost is by convention included in the convenience yield, such that the convenience yield is the benefit from holding the commodity minus the storage costs. In this case, the forward price formula simply becomes

$$F(t, T) = S(t) e^{(r-y)(T-t)}, \tag{3.1}$$

where the convenience yield can be positive or negative.

The value of the forward price depends to a large extent on market expectations about the future availability of the commodity. It may change over time even if storage costs do not change. The convenience yield is responsible for the fact that the forward prices of commodities have an independent stochastic behaviour that is not explained by spot prices. Using a more fundamental approach, commodity price dynamics can be understood by taking into account inventories and the market for storage (Pindyck 2001, 2002). Electricity prices can be seen as a limit case. Since electricity is hardly storable, forward prices are completely determined by the expectations about future availability and production costs and not by the current spot price.

3.1.3   Contango, Backwardation and Seasonality

Forward prices depend on the convenience yield (see equation (3.1)). In particular, the convenience yield (including storage costs) determines whether the forward curve is upward or downward sloping. Since convenience yield can change over time, forward curves for a commodity can take different shapes at different times. Pindyck (2001) distinguishes the following cases:

- A downward sloping forward curve is called a *backwardation*. A *strong backwardation* occurs where $S(t) > F(t, T)$ and a *weak backwardation* occurs where $e^{-r(T-t)}F(t, T) < S(t) < F(t, T)$. By equation (3.1) a strong backwardation occurs for a large convenience yield that overcompensates for storage costs and financing costs. For a weak backwardation, convenience yield compensates for storage costs but not for financing costs.
- An upward sloping forward curve (i.e. $S(t) < F(t, T)$) is called *contango*.

As pointed out by Pindyck (2001), there is an economic reason for backwardation for commodities that are produced from limited natural reserves. Such a natural reserve can be considered as an American-style option to extract and sell the commodity at the spot market. High spot prices are an incentive to exercise the option. In a contango situation, owners of a commodity reserve would prefer to reduce the extraction of commodity and instead sell it on the forward market. This would lead to rising spot prices and declining forward prices.

For commodities such as oil, gas and electricity, consumption and therefore demand follow strong seasonal patterns. Seasonal patterns can be observed statistically in historical spot prices and are also reflected in the shape of the forward curve. The seasonality is less pronounced where sufficient storage capacity is available.

3.1.4   The Market Price of Risk

For commodities with limited storage capacities the relationship between spot and forward prices depends on the convenience yield and on expectations on the future availability of the commodity (see section 3.1.2). Thus, there is a relationship between forward prices $F(t, T)$ and the expected spot price $\mathbb{E}_t[S_T]$ at the forward expiry date. A systematic difference between forward prices and expected spot prices does not lead to arbitrage opportunities, but may generate profits on average. For example, if $F(t, T) > \mathbb{E}_t[S(T)]$ a speculator could sell a forward contract at price $F = F(t, T)$ in the hope that the spot price at maturity will be below F, which it is on average. The profit or loss at time T then is $F - S(T)$. However, such a trading strategy is risky and speculators will use it if they expect enough profit as compensation for the risk taken. But how can a situation, such as $F(t, T) > \mathbb{E}_t[S(T)]$, occur in first place? No other speculator would be willing to buy a forward contract above the expected spot price, unless he needs those forward contracts to offset risk he already has in his portfolio. However, apart from speculators there may also be hedgers as a group of market participants, who are prepared to buy forward contracts at a premium price to reduce the market risk of their company. There may also be other hedgers who need to sell forward contracts to reduce their market risk and therefore would drive forward prices down. Since this may equally be true, there is no general rule for the relation between forward prices and expected spot prices. Whether the risk premium is positive or negative depends very much on the structure of the market participants and their particular interests. Only when the risk premium in either direction becomes too large is there an incentive for speculators to take the risk in exchange for the premium. In equilibrium conditions the premium paid for a given "unit" of risk is called the *market price of risk* . For an analysis of risk premia in the US electricity market see Geman and Vasicek (2001) or Bessembinder and Lemmon (2002).

3.1.5   Derivatives Pricing and the Risk-Neutral Measure

It is beyond the scope of this book to give a rigorous account of the mathematical theory of derivatives pricing. There are many specialised books on this subject available (e.g. Baxter and Rennie 1996, Bingham and Kiesel 2004, Hull 2005, and Lamberton and Lapeyre 1996). Here we resume only basic principles.

In option pricing theory, one assumes that the market is governed by a number of risk factors $Z_1(t), \ldots, Z_n(t)$. Those risk factors do not need to be tradable assets but can be rather general. Examples of the types of risk factors for energy markets are the environmental temperature or the total system load, or future electricity prices for a given future delivery period. By assumption, the risk factors follow a stochastic model of the form:

$$dZ_i(t) = m_i(t)dt + s_i(t)dW_i(t)$$

where $W_1(t), \ldots, W_n(t)$ are Brownian motions and $m_i(t)$ and $s_i(t)$ can be rather general (depending on $W_i(t)$) allowing mean-reverting or fat-tail behaviour. Thus, one can think of $W_1(t), \ldots, W_n(t)$ as true, but non-observable, risk factors. Classical option pricing theory assumes a *complete market* meaning that there are enough tradable contracts available to hedge each risk factor separately. In this case there would be at least n tradable contracts $X_1(t), \ldots, X_n(t)$ depending on the corresponding risk factors. From Itô's lemma, the tradable contract prices also follow some stochastic differential equation of the form

$$dX_i(t) = \mu_i(t)dt + \sum_{j=1}^{n} \sigma_{i,j}(t)dW_j(t), \quad i = 1, \ldots, n.$$

It is assumed that tradable contracts have no yield or cash flow up to the expiry date. Because of convenience yield and storage costs, the commodity itself does not qualify as such a contract, although forward contracts do. Assume that a derivative at its maturity date T has a payoff of the form $h(Z_1(T), \ldots, Z_n(T))$. Mathematical theory identifies a replicating hedge portfolio consisting only of the tradable contracts that have the same payoff as the derivative and therefore can be used to hedge all risk. Under those assumptions the value of the derivative is independent of any risk preferences in the market and the derivative price (*fair value*) is uniquely determined by the hedging costs. Any other derivative price would lead to an arbitrage opportunity. As the derivative price does not depend on the risk preferences it should be the same in a totally risk indifferent (*risk neutral*) world. In such a world there should on average be no excess return of a risky tradable contract relative to a riskless money market account. The value of a riskless money market account is given by $\beta(t) = e^{rt}$ and for non-constant interest rates, by $\beta(t) = \exp\left(\int_0^t r(s)ds\right)$. We have the following rule:

In the risk-neutral world (denoted by Q), the discounted price process $\tilde{X}(t) = X(t)/\beta(t)$ of a tradable contract X is a *martingale*, i.e. the following holds for all $t \leq T$:

$$\tilde{X}(t) = \mathbb{E}_t^Q\left[\tilde{X}(T)\right].$$

For constant interest rates this is equivalent to

$$X(t) = e^{-r(T-t)}\mathbb{E}_t^Q[X(T)].$$

Since the discounted prices of tradable contracts $X_1, \ldots, X_n$ are martingales and the derivative can be exactly replicated by a portfolio of tradable contracts, the discounted value of the derivative must also be a martingale. This argument leads to the option pricing formula

$$U(t) = e^{-r(T-t)}\mathbb{E}_t^Q[h(Z_1(T), \ldots, Z_n(T))].$$

Switching from the "true" world to the "risk-neutral" world means choosing an appropriate equivalent probability measure, which leaves the possible paths for the risk factors $W_i(t)$ the same but assigns different probabilities. An equivalent probability measure, under which the discounted price processes of all tradable contracts are martingales (in particular of $X_1, \ldots, X_n$), is called the *risk-neutral measure* or the *equivalent martingale measure*. We denote the risk-neutral measure by Q and the original statistical measure by P. Under Q, the processes $W_i(t)$ are no longer standard Brownian motions but, by *Girsanov's theorem*, the processes

$$\tilde{W}_i(t) = W_i(t) + \int_0^t \gamma_i(s)ds$$

are standard Brownian motions under Q for some function γ_i. Taking the differential, we get (under Q)

$$dW_i(t) = d\tilde{W}_i(t) - \gamma_i(t)dt.$$

Substituting $\tilde{W}_t$ back into the equations for $Z_i(t)$ and $X_i(t)$ we get under Q:

$$dZ_i(t) = \tilde{m}_i(t)dt + s_i(t)d\tilde{W}_i(t)$$

$$dX_i(t) = \tilde{\mu}_i(t)dt + \sum_{j=1}^n \sigma_{i,j}(t)d\tilde{W}_j(t)$$

with new drift constants $\tilde{m}_i = m_i - s_i\gamma_i$ and $\tilde{\mu}_i = \mu_i - \sum_{j=1}^n \sigma_{i,j}(t)\gamma_j$.

To price derivatives, we have the following steps:

1. Take a stochastic model for the risk factors $Z_1(t), \ldots, Z_n(t)$.
2. Identify the risk-neutral measure Q, under which the discounted price processes of the tradable contracts $X_1(t), \ldots, X_n(t)$ are martingales. This changes the drift coefficients in the model equations for the risk factors.

3. Calculate the derivative price from the discounted expected value of the derivatives payoff under the risk-neutral measure as

$$U(t) = e^{-r(T-t)} \mathbb{E}_t^Q \left[h(Z_1(T), \ldots, Z_n(T)) \right]. \tag{3.2}$$

The *fundamental theorem of asset pricing* gives some more information about the risk-neutral measure:

1. If a market admits no arbitrage (riskless gains above the riskless money market rate), then there always exists a risk-neutral measure (equivalent martingale measure).
2. If a market is complete (all relevant risk factors can be hedged by tradable contracts), then the risk-neutral measure is unique.

As a consequence, option prices in a complete arbitrage-free market are uniquely determined and do not depend on risk preferences of the market participants. However, in typical energy markets the assumptions of no arbitrage and a complete market can be far from true in reality. Since many markets are not yet fully transparent to market participants there may be more arbitrage opportunities available than in classical financial markets. Market incompleteness arises in situations where for some risks there are no tradable hedge contracts available. In incomplete markets not all risk can be hedged and risk-minimising hedging strategies can be considered instead (Carr *et al.* 2001). An example from electricity markets is the risk of a change in the hourly shape of the forward curve when selling or buying an individual load schedule. Hedging instruments typically are standardised products such as baseload or peakload contracts that do not hedge all risk on an hourly granularity. Compared to many financial markets, the classical derivative pricing theory in complete markets may be less accurate, but is nevertheless of value to find a basis for trading decisions and to make adjustments to take into account individual risk preferences.

Let us identify what the risk-neutral measure means in the context of commodity spot prices. As the commodity itself often has a convenience yield and storage costs, the discounted spot price process itself does not have to be a martingale under the risk-neutral measure. For forward prices this is different: they do not have any cash flows or yields up to the expiry date and thus their discounted price processes have to be martingales. Let $K = F(t, T)$ be the forward price (not the value of the forward contract) and $S(t)$ be the spot price at time t. By definition of the forward price, the fair value at time t of a forward contract with contract price K and expiry date T is zero. The discounted value of the forward contract at expiry date T is given by

$$e^{-r(T-t)} (S(T) - K).$$

From its property as a martingale under the risk-neutral measure Q, the discounted value of the forward contract at time t (which is zero) must be equal to the expectation of the discounted value of the forward contract at time T. Assuming constant interest rates, we get

$$0 = e^{-r(T-t)} \mathbb{E}_t^Q [S(T) - K].$$

Substituting $F(t, T)$ for the solution K of the last equation we arrive at the important formula for the forward price

$$F(t, T) = \mathbb{E}_t^Q[S(T)].$$
(3.3)

The forward price is the expected spot price under the risk-neutral measure. This implies that the process $F(t, T)$ as a function of t, is also a martingale since $S(T) = F(T, T)$. Note that (3.3) does not hold in general if interest rates are considered as stochastic.

3.2 COMMODITY SPOT PRICE MODELS

For many commodities the forward and futures markets are more liquid than the actual physical spot market. However, it is the spot market, that is the underlying of the forward market, that determines much of the characteristics of a particular commodity market. Modelling spot prices is important in two different contexts:

1. *Risk analysis*: If a portfolio value depends on future spot prices, a stochastic model can simulate price scenarios to evaluate the corresponding profits and losses for the portfolio. For this application we need the stochastic process under the statistical probability measure and a model which closely represents the actual spot price behaviour.
2. *Derivatives pricing*: In section 3.1.5 we concluded that the stochastic process is needed under the risk-neutral measure. The process parameters can be inferred from market prices of traded options or estimated statistically from historical spot prices. In the latter case the process has to be adjusted to the risk-neutral drift.

In the following sections we introduce three important stochastic models for commodity prices. One of the models, geometric Brownian motion, is well known from financial markets while the other two, the one-factor Schwartz model and the Schwartz–Smith model, have their main applications within commodity markets.

3.2.1 Geometric Brownian motion

Geometric Brownian motion (GBM) with drift is widely used for modelling financial assets and is the basis for the Black–Scholes formula for European-style option prices (Black and Scholes 1973).

GBM is described by the following stochastic differential equation:

$$\frac{dS(t)}{S(t)} = \mu \, dt + \sigma \, dW(t),$$
(3.4)

where μ and σ are constant. As usual, $W(t)$ denotes a standard Brownian motion. Using Itô's lemma it is easily shown that the natural logarithm of $S(t)$ satisfies the equation

$$d \ln S(t) = \left(\mu - \tfrac{1}{2}\sigma^2\right) dt + \sigma \, dW(t).$$

Integrating this equation yields

$$S(t) = S(0) \exp \left(\left(\mu - \tfrac{1}{2}\sigma^2\right) t + \sigma W(t)\right).$$
(3.5)

Model Characteristics

The most important characteristics of GBM are:

- The asset price $S(t)$ is positive for all t.
- For $t_1 < t_2 < t_3$ the asset returns $S(t_2) - S(t_1)/S(t_1)$ and $S(t_3) - S(t_2)/S(t_2)$, or equivalently the logarithmic increments $\ln S(t_2) - \ln S(t_1)$ and $\ln S(t_3) - \ln S(t_2)$, are independent.
- At today's spot price $S(0)$, the logarithm of the spot price $\ln S(t)$ is normally distributed with mean $\ln S(0) + \mu t - \frac{1}{2}\sigma^2 t$ and variance $\sigma^2 t$.
- At today's spot price $S(0)$ the expectation of $S(t)$ is given by

$$\mathbb{E}[S(t)] = S(0)e^{\mu t}.$$

GBM is applicable for price processes without mean reversion. Typical sample paths are shown in Figure 3.3. Numerical calculation is discussed later in this section. The dashed line indicates the corridor of one standard deviation

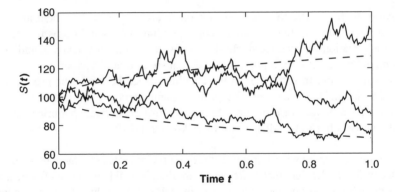

Figure 3.3   GBM sample paths for one year ($\sigma = 0.3, \mu = 0$)

$$S(0)\exp\left((\mu - \sigma^2/2)t - \sigma\sqrt{t}\right) < S(t) < S(0)\exp\left((\mu - \sigma^2/2)t + \sigma\sqrt{t}\right).$$

The corridor of one standard deviation of $\ln S(t)$ increases with $\sigma\sqrt{t}$ and the variance $\mathrm{Var}[\ln S(t)] = \sigma^2 t$ increases linearly with t. This means that the longer the time horizon the larger the price uncertainty.

A straightforward generalisation of the model in equation (3.4) is obtained using time dependent but deterministic functions for μ and σ. Then the logarithm $\ln S(t)$ is still normally distributed with mean $\int_0^t \mu(s) - \frac{1}{2}\sigma^2(s)\, ds$ and variance $\int_0^t \sigma^2(s)\, ds$.

Forward and Option Price Formulas

In section 3.1.5 the forward price was given by the expectation under the risk-neutral measure Q. Under Q, the process follows the stochastic model equation

$$\frac{dS(t)}{S(t)} = \mu^* dt + \sigma d\tilde{W}(t), \qquad (3.6)$$

Using risk-neutral parameters we derive the forward prices as

$$F(t, T) = \mathbb{E}_t^Q[S(T)] = S(t)e^{\mu^*(T-t)}. \tag{3.7}$$

For non-constant risk-neutral drift μ^* this generalises to $F(t, T) = S(t) \exp\left(\int_t^T \mu^*(s)ds\right)$.

Depending on the sign of μ^*, the forward curve can be in contango or backwardation. Note that, in contrast to modelling stock prices, the risk-neutral μ^* is not given *a priori* as it contains the convenience yield. Figure 3.4 shows the possible forward curve shapes for the GBM model with constant μ^*. More general shapes can be obtained using non-constant values for the drift parameter μ^*.

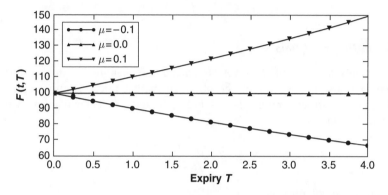

Figure 3.4   GBM forward curves for different constant values of μ

In equation (3.7) the forward curve changes stochastically with $S(t)$. The dynamics of the forward curve are easily calculated using Itô's lemma:

$$dF(t, T) = e^{\mu^*(T-t)}dS(t) - \mu^* S(t)e^{\mu^*(T-t)}\, dt$$

$$= \sigma e^{\mu^*(T-t)}dS(t)d\tilde{W}(t)$$

$$= \sigma F(t, T)d\tilde{W}(t),$$

giving Black's model for futures prices (cf. section 2.2.2)

$$\frac{dF(t, T)}{F(t, T)} = \sigma d\tilde{W}(t). \tag{3.8}$$

For European-style call and put options on the spot price index $S(t)$ we use the Black–Scholes formula

$$C_{K,T}(t, F) = e^{-r(T-t)}\mathbb{E}_t^Q\left[\max(S(T) - K, 0)\right]$$

$$= e^{-r(T-t)}\left(FN(d_1) - KN(d_2)\right)$$

$$P_{K,T}(t, F) = e^{-r(T-t)}\mathbb{E}_t^Q\left[\max(K - S(T), 0)\right]$$

$$= e^{-r(T-t)}\left(KN(-d_2) - FN(-d_1)\right)$$

where

$$F = F(t, T) = S(t)e^{\mu^*(T-t)}$$

$$d_1 = \frac{\ln(F/K) + \frac{1}{2}\sigma^2(T-t)}{\sigma\sqrt{T-t}}$$

$$d_2 = d_1 - \sigma\sqrt{T-t}.$$

For non-constant volatility $\sigma(t)$, the same formulas can be used if σ is replaced by $\bar{\sigma}$, which is defined as

$$\bar{\sigma}^2 = \frac{1}{T-t}\int_t^T \sigma^2(s)ds.$$

Calibration to Historical Data

Model parameters are commonly given as annualised quantities with the time variable t measured in years. Let $S_0, \ldots, S_N$ be observed market prices at times $t_0, \ldots, t_N$. As discussed earlier, logarithmic returns $\ln S_{t_i} - \ln S_{t_{i-1}}$ are independent and normally distributed with standard deviation $\sigma\sqrt{t_i - t_{i-1}}$. Setting

$$X_i = \frac{\ln S(t_i) - \ln S(t_{i-1})}{\sqrt{t_i - t_{i-1}}}$$

we can estimate the volatility as

$$\hat{\sigma}^2 = \frac{1}{N-1}\sum_{i=1}^N (X_i - \bar{X})^2$$

where $\bar{X} = \frac{1}{N}\sum_{i=1}^N X_i$. To evaluate $t_i - t_{i-1}$ as a year fraction in the formulas above we can either take the actual number of days and divide by 365 or we can take the number of trading days between t_i and t_{i-1} and divide by the total number of trading days per year, which may be about 250. In market practice, total annual trading days is usually set by convention to a certain number, regardless of the actual number of trading days in that year.

Using historical price data, volatility is not constant but depends on the time period and granularity of the data used for the parameter estimation. A moving time window of a certain period length, e.g. 20 trading days, can be used to obtain a graphical representation of historical volatility behaviour. An example is shown in Figure 3.5. The longer the moving time window for the volatility calculation, the smoother the curve.

Calibration under the Risk-Neutral Measure

Historical spot market prices do not reveal any information about the market price of risk. Additional market information is used to calibrate the risk-neutral parameters. Such additional market data can be futures or forward price data which is available for most commodities. Assuming known market prices for a number of futures contracts $F(t, T_1), \cdots, F(t, T_n)$ with maturities $t \equiv T_0 < T_1 < T_2 < \cdots < T_n$ we must have under the risk-neutral measure Q

$$\mathbb{E}_t^Q[S(T_i)] = F(t, T_i), \quad i = 1, \ldots, n.$$

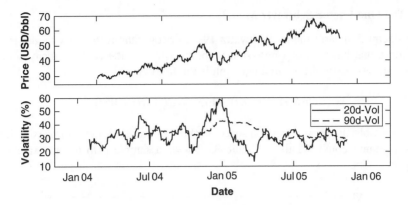

Figure 3.5 Historical volatility for Brent frontmonth prices

We can choose a piecewise constant risk-neutral drift μ^* such that the above identities hold and that all given futures prices are correctly priced. Let

$$\mu^*(t) = \sum_{i=1}^{n} \mu_i^* \mathbf{1}_{[T_{i-1},T_i)}(t).$$

Then formula (3.7) for the forward price becomes

$$F(t, T_k) = S(t) \exp\left(\sum_{i=1}^{k} \mu_i^*(T_i - T_{i-1})\right).$$

Given the market prices $F(t, T_i)$ we can extract all μ_i^* iteratively as

$$\mu_1^* = \frac{1}{T_1 - t}\left(\ln \frac{F(t, T_1)}{S(t)}\right)$$

$$\mu_i^* = \frac{1}{T_i - T_{i-1}}\left(\ln \frac{F(t, T_i)}{F(t, T_{i-1})}\right), \quad i = 2, \dots, k.$$

The volatility is not changed under the risk-neutral measure, therefore it can be estimated from historical data. If market prices for options are available one can use implied volatilities as a model parameter. This is explained in more detail in section 2.2.5.

Generating Simulation Paths

For option pricing via Monte Carlo techniques or for risk analysis there is a need to numerically generate simulation paths according to the stochastic model. Simulating GBM follows immediately from equation (3.5). Letting $t_1, \dots, t_n$ be the points of time and $\Delta t_i = t_i - t_{i-1}$ we generate a path taking the following steps:

1. Generate standard normally distributed random numbers $\epsilon_1, \dots, \epsilon_n$.
2. Starting with today's spot price $S(t_0)$ we iteratively calculate

$$S(t_i) = S(t_{i-1}) \exp\left((\mu - \sigma^2/2)\Delta t_i + \sigma\sqrt{\Delta t_i}\epsilon_i\right).$$

3.2.2   The One-Factor Schwartz Model

The one-factor Schwartz model (Schwartz 1997) or logarithmic Vasicek model is used to model prices that have a mean-reversion property, which is the case for many commodity markets. The stochastic differential equation is the following:

$$d \ln S(t) = \kappa \left(\theta(t) - \ln S(t) \right) dt + \sigma(t) dW(t), \tag{3.9}$$

where κ describes the mean reversion speed, $\theta(t)$ the (logarithmic) mean reversion level and $\sigma(t)$ the (instantaneous) volatility. Figure 3.6 shows a sample path for an example set of model parameters.

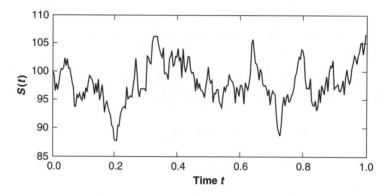

Figure 3.6   Schwartz model sample path for one year ($\sigma = 0.3$, $\theta = \ln 100$, $\kappa = 12$)

Using Itô's formula, the model equation (3.9) can alternatively be written in the following form:

$$\frac{dS(t)}{S(t)} = \kappa \left(\tilde{\theta}(t) - \ln S(t) \right) dt + \sigma(t) dW(t),$$

with $\tilde{\theta}(t) = \theta(t) + \frac{\sigma^2}{4\kappa}$.

In the general case, all parameters may be deterministic functions of time. However, for notational convenience, we assume κ is always constant. If constancy is not assumed the term $e^{-\kappa(T-t)}$ is replaced by $\exp\left(-\int_t^T \kappa(s) ds \right)$ in all formulas. In the following discussion θ and σ are assumed to be constant to get explicit formulas.

Model Characteristics

GBM (see section 3.2.1) has no "mean" level around which the price fluctuates. Regardless of how high or low the price is the probabilities for the price to increase or decrease in the next time period do not change. Commodity prices often have a mean reversion property so that if prices are already above or below a long-term mean level they tend to be drawn back towards the mean. In a chart (e.g. Figure 3.6), we see fluctuations around a mean level. In financial markets a similar behaviour can be observed for interest rates. The Vasicek model

$$dX(t) = \kappa \left(\theta - X(t) \right) dt + \sigma dW(t)$$

is popular and well studied for the short-term interest rate. It incorporates mean reversion to a long-term mean level while allowing for efficient numerical methods. Using the Vasicek model directly for commodity prices has the disadvantage that, with a certain probability, prices may become negative. For modelling commodity prices the Vasicek model is typically applied to the logarithm of the price instead of the price itself.

Mean-reversion speed κ can be evaluated as follows. If there were no stochastic fluctuations ($\sigma = 0$) then instead of the stochastic differential equation (3.9) we have an ordinary differential equation for $y(t) = \ln S(t)$ of the form

$$\frac{dy(t)}{dt} = \kappa \left(\theta - y(t) \right)$$

where the solution can easily be calculated as

$$y(t) = y(0)e^{-\kappa t} + \theta \left(1 - e^{-\kappa t} \right),$$

so that an exponential convergence occurs from $y(0)$ to θ with a "half-life" of $\tau = \ln 2/\kappa$.

Applying Itô's lemma, the solution to the stochastic differential equation (3.9) can be derived as

$$S(t) = \exp\left(e^{-\kappa t} \ln S(0) + \int_0^t \kappa \theta e^{-\kappa(t-s)} ds + \int_0^t \sigma(s) e^{-\kappa(t-s)} dW(s) \right). \tag{3.10}$$

For the special case of constant parameters the first integral can be computed explicitly as

$$S(t) = \exp\left(e^{-\kappa t} \ln S(0) + \theta \left(1 - e^{-\kappa t} \right) + \sigma \int_0^t e^{-\kappa(t-s)} dW(s) \right).$$

From equation (3.10) and theorem A.1 it can be seen that $\ln S(t)$ is normally distributed with

$$\mathbb{E}[\ln S(t)] = e^{-\kappa t} \ln S(0) + \int_0^t \kappa \theta e^{-\kappa(t-s)} ds \quad \text{and}$$

$$\mathrm{Var}[\ln S(t)] = \int_0^t \sigma^2(s) e^{-2\kappa(t-s)} ds.$$

Thus the spot price $S(t)$ is log-normally distributed. Using the general identity

$$\mathbb{E}\left[e^X \right] = e^{\mathbb{E}[X] + \mathrm{Var}[X]/2}$$

for an arbitrary normally distributed random variable X applied to $X = \ln S(t)$, the expectation of $S(t)$ can be calculated as

$$\mathbb{E}[S(t)] = \exp\left(\mathbb{E}[\ln S(t)] + \frac{1}{2} \mathrm{Var}[\ln S(t)] \right). \tag{3.11}$$

Forward and Option Price Formulas

To calculate forward and option prices we need the price process under the risk-neutral measure. Previously it was identified that switching to the risk-neutral measure changes the drift of the process. Therefore the risk-neutral process can be written as

$$d \ln S(t) = \kappa \left(\theta^* - \ln S_t \right) dt + \sigma d\tilde{W}_t, \tag{3.12}$$

where $\theta^* = \theta - \lambda/\kappa$ and λ is the market price of risk. To simplify the notation we now assume that all parameters are constant. The integrals in equation (3.11) applied to the risk-neutral process can be computed explicitly to derive the following expression for the forward price $F(t, T)$:

$$F(t, T) = \exp\left(e^{-\kappa(T-t)}\ln S(t) + \theta^*\left(1 - e^{-\kappa(T-t)}\right) + \frac{\sigma^2}{4\kappa}\left(1 - e^{-2\kappa(T-t)}\right)\right). \qquad (3.13)$$

Regardless of the current spot price, for the long-term limit as $T \to \infty$ the forward price devolves to $F(t, T) \to \exp(\theta^* + \frac{\sigma^2}{4\kappa})$. The mean-reversion constant κ determines the convergence speed. If the current spot price $S(0)$ is below the long-term limit the forward curve is upward sloping (contango) and if the current spot price is above the long-term limit the forward curve is downward sloping (backwardation). Figure 3.7 shows these different cases and can be compared to the forward curve shapes for GBM previously shown in Figure 3.4.

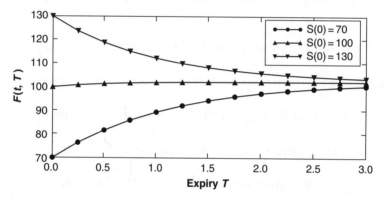

Figure 3.7   Schwartz model forward curves ($\kappa = 1$, $\theta = \ln 100$) for different values of $S(0)$.

For option prices, since $S(t)$ is log-normally distributed, the prices for European-style call and put options can be calculated analytically via the Black–Scholes formula:

$$C_{K,T}(t, F) = e^{-r(T-t)}\left(FN(d_1) - KN(d_2)\right)$$
$$P_{K,T}(t, F) = e^{-r(T-t)}\left(KN(-d_2) - FN(-d_1)\right)$$

where

$$F = F(t, T)$$
$$V = \frac{\sigma^2}{2\kappa}\left(1 - e^{-2\kappa(T-t)}\right)$$
$$d_1 = \frac{\ln(F/K) + \frac{1}{2}V}{\sqrt{V}} \qquad d_2 = d_1 - \sqrt{V}.$$

Calibration to Historical Data

The simplest method for calibrating the one-factor Schwartz model to historical data is by linear regression. Let $S_0, \ldots, S_N$ be a series of historical prices and Δt the time between two observations. The Euler discretisation of the model equation (3.9) is

$$\ln S_i - \ln S_{i-1} = \kappa(\theta - \ln S_{i-1})\Delta t + \epsilon_i,$$

where ϵ_i are independent normally distributed random numbers with mean zero and standard deviation $\sigma\sqrt{\Delta t}$. Substituting $a = 1 - \kappa\Delta t$, $b = \kappa\theta\Delta t$ and $y_i = \ln S_i$ this is equivalent to

$$y_i = ay_{i-1} + b + \epsilon_i.$$

Thus a least squares algorithm yields values for a and b minimising the variance of ϵ_i. The model parameters then can be recovered as

$$\theta = \frac{b}{1-a}, \quad \kappa = \frac{1-a}{\Delta t}, \quad \sigma^2 = \frac{\mathrm{Var}[\epsilon_i]}{\Delta t}.$$

For a more accurate calibration one can use a maximum likelihood method.

Generating Simulation Paths

Let $t_0, \ldots, t_N$ be the path dates, $\Delta t_i = t_i - t_{i-1}$ and assume constant parameters. Using equation (3.10) with $S(t_{i-1})$ instead of $S(0)$ and $S(t_i)$ instead of $S(t)$ we get

$$S(t_i) = \exp\left(e^{-\kappa\Delta t_i}\ln S(t_{i-1}) + \theta\left(1 - e^{-\kappa\Delta t_i}\right) + \sigma\int_{t_{i-1}}^{t_i} e^{-\kappa(t_i-s)}dW(s)\right).$$

The integral $\sigma\int_{t_{i-1}}^{t_i} e^{-\kappa(t_i-s)}dW(s)$ is normally distributed with mean zero and variance

$$V_i = \frac{\sigma^2}{2\kappa}\left(1 - e^{-2\kappa\Delta t_i}\right).$$

Therefore, we can proceed similarly as in section 3.2.1 for GBM:

1. Generate standard normally distributed random numbers $\epsilon_1, \ldots, \epsilon_N$.
2. Starting with today's spot price $S(t_0)$ iteratively calculate

$$S(t_i) = \exp\left(e^{-\kappa\Delta t_i}\ln S(t_{i-1}) + \theta\left(1 - e^{-\kappa\Delta t_i}\right) + \sqrt{V_i}\epsilon_i\right).$$

3.2.3   The Schwartz–Smith Model

Even though mean-reverting behaviour is observable in many commodity markets, simple mean-reverting models such as the one-factor Schwartz model (3.9) have the drawback that they require a predefined fixed mean-reverting level that is not known and may change in the long term. Schwartz and Smith (2000) propose a model combining mean-reverting behaviour on a short time scale with a non-mean-reverting behaviour on a long time scale. The commodity price $S(t)$ is modelled by:

$$\ln S(t) = \chi(t) + \xi(t). \tag{3.14}$$

The first factor $\chi(t)$ represents the short-term variations and follows a mean-reverting (*Ornstein–Uhlenbeck*) process

$$d\chi(t) = -\kappa\chi(t)dt + \sigma_\chi dW_\chi(t). \tag{3.15}$$

The second factor $\xi(t)$ represents the long-term dynamics and is given by a Brownian motion with drift

$$d\xi(t) = \mu_\xi dt + \sigma_\xi dW_\xi(t), \tag{3.16}$$

where $dW_\chi(t)$ and $dW_\xi(t)$ are standard Brownian motions with correlation ρ. Two sample paths from a Schwartz–Smith model are shown in Figure 3.8.

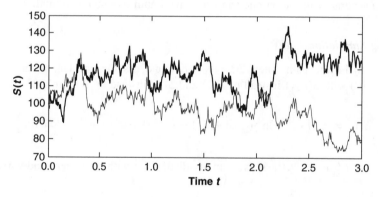

Figure 3.8 Sample paths for the Schwartz–Smith model ($\sigma_\chi = 0.3$, $\sigma_\xi = 0.1$, $\kappa = 4$, $\mu_\xi = 0.02$, $\rho = 0$)

Model Characteristics

This two-factor model can be seen as an extension to the mean-reverting model (3.9) so that the "mean" level is also stochastic. Setting $X(t) = \ln S(t)$, $\theta(t) = \xi(t) + \mu_\xi/\kappa$, $\sigma_X^2 = \sigma_\chi^2 + \sigma_\xi^2 + 2\rho\sigma_\chi\sigma_\xi$ and $W_X(t) = \sigma_X^{-1}\left(\sigma_\chi W_\chi(t) + \sigma_\xi W_\xi(t)\right)$ gives

$$dX(t) = \kappa\left(\theta(t) - X(t)\right)dt + \sigma_X dW_X(t)$$
$$d\theta(t) = \mu_\xi dt + \sigma_\xi dW_\xi(t),$$

The first equation defines a mean-reverting process for $X(t)$ to the mean level $\theta(t)$. In the second equation $\theta(t)$ follows a Brownian motion with drift.

Integrating the stochastic differential equation for $\ln S(t)$ we get, compared to equation (3.10) for the one-factor Schwartz model,

$$\ln S(t) = \xi(0) + \mu t + e^{-\kappa t}\chi(0) + \sigma_\chi \int_0^t e^{-\kappa(t-s)}\,dW_\chi(s) + \sigma_\xi W_\xi(t).$$

From this identity we see that $\ln S(t)$ is normally distributed with mean

$$\mathbb{E}[\ln S(t)] = \xi(0) + \mu t + e^{-\kappa t}\chi(0) \tag{3.17}$$

and variance

$$\mathrm{Var}[\ln S(t)] = \frac{\sigma_\chi^2}{2\kappa}\left(1 - e^{-2\kappa t}\right) + \sigma_\xi^2 t + \frac{2\rho\sigma_\chi\sigma_\xi}{\kappa}\left(1 - e^{-\kappa t}\right). \tag{3.18}$$

The spot price $S(t)$ itself is log-normally distributed with

$$\mathbb{E}[S(t)] = \exp\left(\mathbb{E}[X(t)] + \frac{1}{2}\mathrm{Var}[X(t)]\right).$$

Forward and Option Price Formulas

To derive a formula for futures prices we need to switch to the risk-neutral measure. From section 3.1.5 the futures price is given by

$$F(t, T) = \mathbb{E}_t^Q[S(T)],$$

where Q is the risk-neutral measure. The processes $\chi(t)$ and $\xi(t)$ under Q follow the stochastic differential equations

$$d\chi(t) = \left(-\kappa\chi(t) - \lambda_\chi\right)dt + \sigma_\chi d\tilde{W}_\chi(t)$$
$$d\xi(t) = \mu_\xi^* dt + \sigma_\xi d\tilde{W}_\xi(t),$$

where $\mu^* = \mu_\xi - \lambda_\xi$ and λ_χ and λ_ξ represent the market prices of risk corresponding to the respective risk factors which are assumed to be constant. The futures prices can be calculated as follows:

$$\ln F(t, T) = \mathbb{E}_t^Q[X(T)] + \frac{1}{2}\mathrm{Var}^Q[X(T)]$$

$$= e^{-\kappa(T-t)}\chi(t) + \xi(t) + \left(\mu_\xi^* + \sigma_\xi^2/2\right)(T - t) - \left(1 - e^{-\kappa(T-t)}\right)\frac{\lambda_\chi}{\kappa} \tag{3.19}$$

$$+ \frac{\sigma_\chi^2}{4\kappa}\left(1 - e^{-2\kappa(T-t)}\right) + \frac{\rho\sigma_\chi\sigma_\xi}{\kappa}\left(1 - e^{-\kappa(T-t)}\right).$$

Compared to the one-factor Schwartz model, the additional parameters give more flexibility to the possible shapes of forward curves that can be modelled. A range of curve shapes are shown in Figure 3.9. The asymptotics of $\ln F(t, T)$ for large T are determined by the

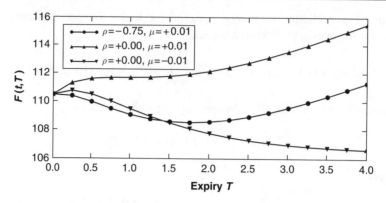

Figure 3.9 Different forward curves for the Schwartz–Smith model with $\kappa = 1, \sigma_\chi = 0.5, \sigma_\xi = 0.1, \chi(0) = 0.1, \xi(0) = \ln 100$ and variations of ρ and μ_ξ^*

long-term process $\xi(t)$, which is a GBM. If we have $T - t \gg 1/\kappa$, such that $e^{-\kappa(T-t)} \approx 0$, we derive

$$\ln F(t, T) \sim \xi(t) + C + \left(\mu_\xi^* + \sigma_\xi^2/2\right)(T - t) \qquad \text{for} \quad T \to \infty$$

with

$$C = -\frac{\lambda_\chi}{\kappa} + \frac{\sigma_\chi^2}{4\kappa} + \frac{\rho\sigma_\chi\sigma_\xi}{\kappa}.$$

As it was the case for the one-factor Schwartz model, we still have the property that $S(t)$ is log-normally distributed. Prices for European-style call and put options can be calculated analytically via the Black–Scholes formula:

$$C_{K,T}(t, F) = e^{-r(T-t)}\left(FN(d_1) - KN(d_2)\right)$$
$$P_{K,T}(t, F) = e^{-r(T-t)}\left(KN(-d_2) - FN(-d_1)\right)$$

where

$$F = F(t, T)$$
$$V = \frac{\sigma_\chi^2}{2\kappa}\left(1 - e^{-2\kappa(T-t)}\right) + \sigma_\xi^2(T - t) + \frac{2\rho\sigma_\chi\sigma_\xi}{\kappa}\left(1 - e^{-\kappa(T-t)}\right)$$
$$d_1 = \frac{\ln(F/K) + \frac{1}{2}V}{\sqrt{V}} \qquad d_2 = d_1 - \sqrt{V}.$$

Calibration to Historical Data

Calibrating the Schwartz two-factor model to historical data is more difficult than calibrating the one-factor models since the stochastic factors $\chi(t)$ and $\xi(t)$ are not directly observable. Observable data usually consists of:

- spot prices $S_i = S(t_i) = \exp(\chi(t_i) + \xi(t_i))$, $i = 0, \ldots, N$; and
- forward prices $F_{i,j} = F(t_i, T_j)$ for different maturity dates T_j, $j = 1, \ldots, n$.

To overcome the problem that the stochastic process is not observable we make use of the Kalman filter described later in section A.1.4. To derive a state space representation, integrate the model differential equations (3.15) and (3.16) to get

$$\chi_{i+1} = e^{-\kappa\Delta t}\chi_i + \epsilon_i^\chi$$

$$\xi_{i+1} = \xi_i + \mu\Delta t + \epsilon_i^\xi$$

where $\chi_i = \chi(t_i)$, $\xi_i = \xi(t_i)$ and ϵ_i^χ, ϵ_i^ξ are normally distributed random numbers with covariance matrix

$$\text{Cov}[(\epsilon_i^\chi, \epsilon_i^\xi)] = \begin{pmatrix} \frac{\sigma_\chi^2}{2\kappa}\left(1 - e^{-2\kappa\Delta t}\right) & \frac{\rho\sigma_\chi\sigma_\xi}{\kappa}\left(1 - e^{-\kappa\Delta t}\right) \\ \frac{\rho\sigma_\chi\sigma_\xi}{\kappa}\left(1 - e^{-\kappa\Delta t}\right) & \sigma_\xi^2\Delta t \end{pmatrix}. \tag{3.20}$$

In matrix notation the discretised equations become

$$\begin{pmatrix} \chi_{i+1} \\ \xi_{i+1} \end{pmatrix} = \begin{pmatrix} e^{-\kappa\Delta t} & 0 \\ 0 & 1 \end{pmatrix} \begin{pmatrix} \chi_i \\ \xi_i \end{pmatrix} + \begin{pmatrix} 0 \\ \mu_\xi \end{pmatrix} + \begin{pmatrix} \epsilon_i^\chi \\ \epsilon_i^\xi \end{pmatrix}. \tag{3.21}$$

The observable factors include the logarithm of the spot price

$$\ln S_i = \chi_i + \xi_i$$

and logarithms of futures prices $f_{i,j} = \ln F(t_i, T_j)$. Note that the state space representation is taken with respect to the statistical measure and not the risk-neutral measure, since the model is calibrated to historical spot price data. The risk-neutral measure is only needed to derive futures prices. From the futures price formula (3.19), the measuremen equations are

$$\begin{pmatrix} \ln S_i \\ f_{i,1} \\ \vdots \\ f_{i,n} \end{pmatrix} = \begin{pmatrix} 1 & 1 \\ e^{-\kappa(T_1-t)} & 1 \\ \vdots & \vdots \\ e^{-\kappa(T_n-t)} & 1 \end{pmatrix} \cdot \begin{pmatrix} \chi_i \\ \xi_i \end{pmatrix} + \begin{pmatrix} 0 \\ A(T_1) \\ \vdots \\ A(T_n) \end{pmatrix} \tag{3.22}$$

with

$$A(T) = \left(\mu_\xi^* + \sigma_\xi^2/2\right)(T - t) - \left(1 - e^{-\kappa(T-t)}\right)\frac{\lambda_\chi}{\kappa}$$

$$+ \frac{\sigma_\chi^2}{4\kappa}\left(1 - e^{-2\kappa(T-t)}\right) + \frac{\rho\sigma_\chi\sigma_\xi}{\kappa}\left(1 - e^{-\kappa(T-t)}\right).$$

Generating Simulation Paths

For simulation, let $t_0, \ldots, t_N$ be the path dates, $\Delta t = t_i - t_{i-1}$, and assume constant parameters. The sample path values $S_i = S(t_i)$ can be generated using the iteration scheme from equation (3.21) as follows:

1. Generate two-dimensional random vectors $(\epsilon_0^\chi, \epsilon_0^\xi), \ldots, (\epsilon_N^\chi, \epsilon_N^\xi)$ where each random vector $(\epsilon_i^\chi, \epsilon_i^\xi)$ is drawn from a bivariate normal distribution with mean zero and covariance matrix given by equation (3.20).

2. Starting with today's state variables χ_0 and ξ_0 iteratively calculate χ_{i+1} and ξ_{i+1} from equation (3.21).
3. Calculate $S(t_i) = \exp(\chi_i + \xi_i)$.

3.3   STOCHASTIC FORWARD CURVE MODELS

In section 2.2.2 a single futures price was modelled by a geometric Brownian motion. Looking at implied volatilities of different futures contracts of the same commodity it was shown (Figure 2.14) that the implied volatility depends on the time to expiry of the futures contract. Typically, implied volatility decreases with time to expiry, explained by futures with longer time to expiry having less new information available. Often, the dynamics of not only single futures contracts but of the whole forward or futures curves $F(t, T)$ are modelled. In this case, regard must be given to the volatility structure of the forward curve and the covariance structure of futures contracts with different expiry dates. The situation is similar to the Heath–Jarrow–Morton (HJM) theory for interest rates (Heath *et al.* 1992), where the dynamics of the interest rate term structure are modelled.

A general model for the dynamics of the forward curve is

$$dF(t, T) = \alpha(t, T)dt + \sum_{i=1}^{n} \sigma_i(t, T)dW_i(t) \tag{3.23}$$

where $W_1, \ldots, W_n$ are standard Brownian motion processes and $\sigma_1(t, T), \ldots, \sigma_n(t, T)$ are the volatilities. In its general form, the volatility functions $\sigma_i(t, T)$ can be stochastic processes. This section considers special cases for this general multidimensional model and examines its specific characteristics.

Assuming that the market allows no arbitrage there exists an equivalent martingale (risk-neutral) measure Q under which all forward prices are martingales. If the process in equation (3.23) is written with respect to Q the drift term $\alpha(t, T)$ becomes zero for all t and T. Since we are interested in the dynamics under the risk-neutral measure, we assume zero drift:

$$dF(t, T) = \sum_{i=1}^{n} \sigma_i(t, T)dW_i(t). \tag{3.24}$$

Using the identity $S(t) = F(t, t)$, each model for the forward curve $F(t, T)$ also contains a model for the spot price $S(t)$ that can be derived as follows:

$$dS(t) = \left. \frac{\partial F(t, T)}{\partial T} \right|_{T=t} dt + dF(t, T)|_{T=t}. \tag{3.25}$$

The first term can be calculated more explicitly using the integration of equation (3.24) and taking the derivative with respect to T. In this way we get the following model equation for the spot price:

$$dS(t) = \int_0^t \left(\sum_{i=1}^{n} \frac{\partial \sigma_i(s, t)}{\partial T} dW_i(s) \right) dt + \sum_{i=1}^{n} \sigma_i(t, t)dW_i(t). \tag{3.26}$$

Since the drift term depends on the realised path of the Brownian motion, the process $S(t)$ is in general non-Markovian.

The model equations (3.24) and (3.26) so far are general and rather theoretical. In the followings, examples of models that can be fitted to real market data are presented.

3.3.1   One-Factor Forward Curve Models

The simplest case of model (3.24) occurs where $n = 1$ and the forward curve dynamic depends on only one Brownian motion. With a volatility specification

$$\sigma_1(t, T) = e^{-\kappa(T-t)}\sigma,$$

where κ is a positive constant modelling the volatility dependence on the time to expiry, the model equation becomes

$$\frac{dF(t, T)}{F(t, T)} = e^{-\kappa(T-t)}\sigma dW(t). \tag{3.27}$$

An explicit solution is given by

$$F(t, T) = F(0, T) \exp\left(-\int_0^t \tfrac{1}{2}\sigma^2 e^{-2\kappa(T-s)} ds + \int_0^t \sigma e^{-\kappa(T-s)} dW(s)\right). \tag{3.28}$$

The implied spot price model can be calculated using equation (3.26) by applying the simple chain rule to get

$$\frac{\partial F(t, T)}{\partial T} = F(t, T)\frac{\partial \ln F(t, T)}{\partial T}$$

and by taking the derivative of the logarithm of (3.28) with respect to T

$$\frac{\partial \ln F(t, T)}{\partial T} = \frac{\partial \ln F(0, T)}{\partial T} + \kappa\left(\ln F(0, T) - \ln F(t, T) + \frac{\sigma^2}{2}\int_0^t e^{-2\kappa(T-s)} ds\right).$$

Setting $T = t$ and applying the result to equation (3.26) we derive

$$\frac{dS(t)}{S(t)} = \kappa\left(\mu(t) - \ln S(t)\right) dt + \sigma dW(t) \tag{3.29}$$

where

$$\mu(t) = \frac{1}{\kappa}\frac{\partial \ln F(0, t)}{\partial t} + \ln F(0, T) + \frac{\sigma^2}{4\kappa}\left(1 - e^{-2\kappa t}\right).$$

The forward curve model applied to a particular futures contract is a special case of the Black model (section 2.2.2) and all option pricing formulas derived for the Black model can be employed. The implied volatility $\bar{\sigma}_{t,T_1,T}$ for an option expiring in T_1 written on a futures contract $F_{t,T}$ is

$$\bar{\sigma}_{t,T_1,T}^2 = \frac{1}{T_1 - t}\int_t^{T_1} e^{-2\kappa(T-s)}\sigma^2 ds$$

$$= \frac{\sigma^2}{2\kappa(T_1 - t)} \left(e^{-2\kappa(T-T_1)} - e^{-2\kappa(T-t)} \right). \tag{3.30}$$

This identity can also be used to calibrate the forward curve model to a given implied volatility term structure observed in the market. The calibration works as follows: let T_1^i, T^i, $\bar{\sigma}^i$ $(i = 1, \ldots, N)$ be a set of option expiries, the underlying futures expiries and the corresponding market implied volatilities. For each set of model parameters $\Phi = (\kappa, \sigma)$ we can calculate the model implied volatilities $\bar{\sigma}_\Phi^i = \bar{\sigma}_{t,T_1^i,T^i}$ by substitution. The optimal parameters are found by solving an optimisation problem

$$\min_\Phi \sum_{i=1}^{N} \left| \bar{\sigma}^i - \bar{\sigma}_\Phi^i \right|^2.$$

Calibration of a model to implied volatility data is shown in Figure 3.10.

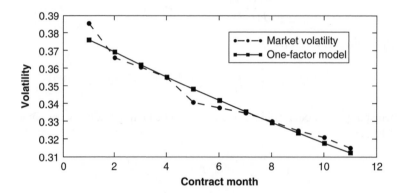

Figure 3.10   Model calibration to implied volatility data ($\kappa = 0.48$, $\sigma = 0.38$)

A second example of a one-factor forward curve model corresponds to the Cox–Ingersoll–Ross model for interest short rates (Cox *et al.* 1985). The model equation is

$$dF(t, T) = e^{-\kappa(T-t)} \sigma \sqrt{F(t, t)} \, dW(t). \tag{3.31}$$

Heath and Jara (2000) note that the futures curve dynamic depends only on the current spot price $S(t) = F(t, t)$ and that futures prices can become negative. Integrating yields

$$F(t, T) = F(0, T) + \int_0^t e^{-\kappa(T-s)} \sigma \sqrt{F(s, s)} dW(s)$$

and one can derive the implied spot price dynamics as:

$$dS(t) = \left(\frac{\partial F(0, t)}{\partial t} - \kappa S(t) \right) dt + \sigma_t \sqrt{S(t)} dW(t).$$

In most cases the model (3.27) seems more appropriate for commodity prices than model (3.31).

3.3.2 A Two-Factor Forward Curve Model

The one-factor model equation (3.27) has the disadvantage that with only a single source of randomness, futures contracts of different expiry dates are all perfectly correlated and cannot explain changes in the shape of the forward curve. Further, the volatility exponentially approaches zero for increasing time to expiry. For modelling a more realistic dynamic of the forward curve multiple sources of randomness are considered. As previously stated, not all volatility functions $\sigma(t, T)$ yield a simple Markovian spot price dynamic.

A two-factor model with good analytical tractability is given by:

$$\frac{dF(t, T)}{F(t, T)} = e^{-\kappa(T-t)}\sigma_1 dW_1(t) + \sigma_2 dW_2(t), \tag{3.32}$$

where $W_1(t)$ and $W_2(t)$ are Brownian motions with correlation $dW_1(t)dW_2(t) = \rho dt$.

The implied spot price model $S(t) = F(t, t)$ is derived as in section 3.3.1

$$\frac{dS(t)}{S(t)} = \kappa\left(\alpha(t) + \xi(t) - \ln S(t)\right) dt + \sigma_1 dW_1(t) + \sigma_2 dW_2(t) \tag{3.33}$$

where $\alpha(t)$ is the deterministic function

$$\alpha(t) = \frac{\partial F(0, t)}{\partial t} + \kappa \ln F(0, t) - \frac{1}{2}\int_0^t \frac{\partial \sigma^2(s, t)}{\partial t} + \kappa\sigma^2(s, t)ds,$$

$$\sigma^2(s, t) = \sigma_1^2 e^{-2\kappa(t-s)} + 2\rho\sigma_1\sigma_2 e^{-\kappa(t-s)} + \sigma_2^2$$

and $\xi(t)$ is a Brownian motion given by the stochastic differential equation

$$d\xi(t) = \sigma_2 dW_2(t).$$

The calculation uses the integrated logarithmic forward price

$$\ln F(t, T) = \ln F(0, T) - \frac{1}{2}\int_0^t \sigma^2(s, T)ds + \chi(t, T) + \xi(t), \tag{3.34}$$

where $\chi(t, T) = \int_0^t e^{-\kappa(T-s)}\sigma_1 dW_1(s)$ and $\xi(t) = \int_0^t \sigma_2 dW_2(s)$.

The model gives back the two-factor Schwartz spot price model presented in (3.14)–(3.16) with time dependent parameters. Setting $T = t$ in (3.34) and $\chi(t) = \chi(t, t)$, we get

$$\ln S(t) = A(t) + \chi(t) + \xi(t),$$

where

$$A(t) = \ln F(0, t) - \frac{1}{2}\int_0^t \sigma^2(s, t)ds$$

$$= \ln F(0, t) - \left(\frac{\sigma_1^2}{4\kappa}\left(1 - e^{-2\kappa t}\right) + \frac{\rho\sigma_1\sigma_2}{\kappa}\left(1 - e^{\kappa t}\right) + \frac{\sigma_2^2 t}{2}\right).$$

The processes $\chi(t)$ and $\xi(t)$ satisfy the stochastic differential equations

$$d\chi(t) = -\kappa\chi(t) + \sigma_1 dW_1(t)$$
$$d\xi(t) = \sigma_2 dW_2(t).$$

As for the one-factor model, the implied volatility $\bar{\sigma}(t, T_1, T)$ for an option expiring in T_1 written on a futures contract $F(t, T)$ is calculated as

$$\bar{\sigma}^2(t, T_1, T) = \frac{\sigma_1^2}{2\kappa(T_1 - t)} \left(e^{-2\kappa(T-T_1)} - e^{-2\kappa(T-t)}\right) + \sigma_2^2$$

$$+ \frac{2\rho\sigma_1\sigma_2}{\kappa(T_1 - t)} \left(e^{-\kappa(T-T_1)} - e^{-\kappa(T-t)}\right). \tag{3.35}$$

This formula can be used to price European-style options. Figure 3.11 shows calibration results for the two-factor model using the same data set as for the one-factor model in Figure 3.10. The two-factor model fits closer to the shape of the market implied volatility curve. There is additional complexity if the implied volatilities refer to futures contracts with different time periods, e.g. months, quarters and years. For more details about the model calibration see Kiesel *et al.* (2006).

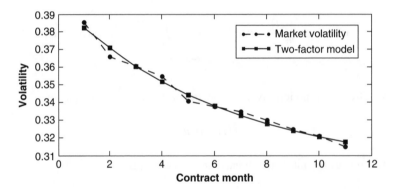

Figure 3.11 Two-factor model calibration to implied volatility data ($\kappa = 1.87$, $\sigma_1 = 0.26$, $\sigma_2 = 0.28$, $\rho = 0$)

3.3.3 A Multi-Factor Exponential Model

Heath and Jara (2000) describe an analytically tractable n-factor model. Taking the general forward curve model from equation (3.24) with the volatility functions

$$\sigma_i(t, T) = F(t, T) \sum_{j=1}^{m} \beta_{i,j} \exp\left(-\lambda_j(T - t)\right), \quad \lambda_j \geq 0$$

we derive the model equation

$$\frac{dF(t, T)}{F(t, T)} = \sum_{i=1}^{n} \sum_{j=1}^{m} \beta_{i,j} e^{-\lambda_j(T-t)} dW_i(t).$$

This stochastic differential equation is solved explicitly by assuming the technical condition $\lambda_j + \lambda_k \neq 0$ for all pairs j, k, to give

$$F(t, T) = F(0, T) \exp \left\{ \int_0^t \sum_{i=1}^n \sum_{j=1}^m \beta_{i,j} e^{-\lambda_j(T-s)} dW_i(s) - \frac{1}{2} \int_0^t \sum_{i=1}^n \left(\sum_{j=1}^m \beta_{i,j} e^{-\lambda_j(T-s)} \right)^2 ds \right\}$$

$$= F(0, T) \exp \left\{ \sum_{j=1}^m e^{-\lambda_j(T-t)} Z_j(t) - \frac{1}{2} \sum_{i=1}^n \sum_{j,k=1}^m \frac{\beta_{i,j} \beta_{i,k}}{\lambda_j + \lambda_k} \left(e^{-(\lambda_j + \lambda_k)(T-t)} - e^{-(\lambda_j + \lambda_k)T} \right) \right\},$$

where

$$Z_j(t) = \int_0^t \sum_{i=1}^n \beta_{i,j} e^{-\lambda_j(t-s)} dW_i(s).$$

The auxiliary processes $Z_j(t)$ are Ornstein–Uhlenbeck processes satisfying

$$dZ_j(t) = -\lambda_j Z_j(t) dt + \sum_{i=1}^n \beta_{i,j} \, dW_i(t).$$

From here we get the derived spot price $S(t) = F(t, t)$ as

$$S(t) = F(0, t) \exp \left\{ \sum_{j=1}^m Z_j(t) - \frac{1}{2} \sum_{i=1}^n \sum_{j,k=1}^m \frac{\beta_{i,j} \beta_{i,k}}{\lambda_j + \lambda_k} \left(1 - e^{-(\lambda_j + \lambda_k)t} \right) \right\}.$$

3.4   ELECTRICITY PRICE MODELS

Electricity is a particular case among commodities because it is hardly storable. In most countries there is a limited capacity of reservoir power plants, and the use of pumps for increasing storage results in a loss of a substantial part of the stored energy. An implication of non-storability is that the relationship between spot prices and futures prices cannot be described with cost of carry and thus we have a limiting case of the considerations in section 3.1.2. An equilibrium model for the electricity forward market is studied in Bessembinder and Lemmon (2002). There are enormous price fluctuations observed in all electricity spot markets. As shown in Figure 3.12, price fluctuations have a strong daily and weekly pattern with pronounced annual periodicity. As described in Chapter 4, this can be explained from a microeconomic viewpoint by looking at the market price of electricity as an equilibrium price based on supply and demand curves. Since the demand is very inelastic, marginal costs of the supply side as described in the so-called merit order curve determine the price to a large extent. If total load is low, plants with the lowest variable production costs are used as a priority. When the total load is high, gas or oil fired plants with high fuel costs are utilised. The periodicity of the total load is responsible for the periodicity of the electricity prices.

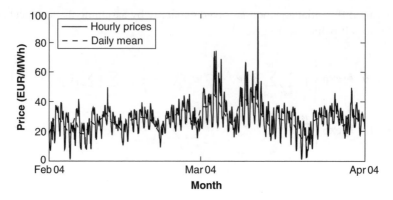

Figure 3.12   EEX spot prices (Month weekly and daily seasonality)

The following features have been observed in all known electricity markets (see Johnson and Barz (1999) for a comparative study of several markets):

- *Seasonal patterns and periodicities*: All markets show seasonal patterns of electricity demand and prices over the course of the day, week and year. Seasonality is more pronounced than in other commodity markets where more storage capacity is available.
- *Price spikes*: Electricity spot prices exhibit extreme spikes that are not observed in other commodity markets. Usual diffusion processes with normal or log-normal marginal distributions are not appropriate to reproduce this behaviour.
- *Mean reversion*: Prices have the tendency to revert rapidly from price spikes to a mean level. Characteristic times of mean reversion have a magnitude of days or at most weeks and can be explained by changes in weather conditions or recovery from power plant outages. Mean-reversion times in electricity markets are much shorter than mean-reversion times in other commodity markets.
- *Price dependent volatilities*: In all markets there is a strong correlation between price levels and levels of volatility.
- *Long-term non-stationarity*: Due to increasing uncertainty about factors such as supply and demand or fuel costs in the long term, a non-stationary model is more appropriate on the longer time horizon. Non-stationarity is needed for a model to be consistent with the observed dynamics of futures prices.

3.4.1   The Hourly Forward Curve

In most electricity markets there is a liquid market for a set of standardised contracts with certain delivery periods (monthly, quarterly and yearly) and certain delivery structures (baseload and peakload). For the near future there is finer granularity of traded contracts (e.g. monthly contracts) than for the future far ahead, where often only yearly contracts are traded. Figure 3.13 shows the futures prices at the European Energy Exchange (EEX) as an example of the European market.

In the OTC market and in the retail market many contracts involve individual delivery structures on an hourly or finer time granularity. To price hourly structures, a forward curve on an hourly basis is required. Take the case of a continuous spot price $S(T)$ and a continuous

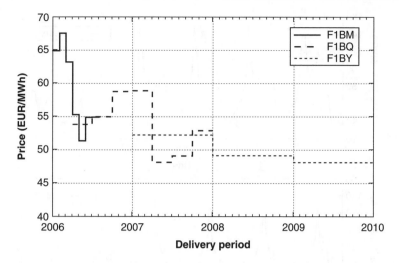

Figure 3.13 EEX prices for monthly (F1BM), quarterly (F1BQ) and yearly (F1BY) baseload futures contracts

fixed delivery schedule $L(T)$ for $T_0 \leq T \leq T_N$, where N denotes the number of hours of the delivery period. The present value at time t of the actual delivery is given by

$$V(t) = \mathbb{E}_t \left[\int_{T_0}^{T_N} e^{-r(T-t)} L(T) S(T) dT \right].$$

If $L(t)$ is a deterministic function we derive

$$V(t) = \int_{T_0}^{T_1} e^{-r(T-t)} L(T) \mathbb{E}_t[S(T)] dT = \int_{T_0}^{T_1} e^{-r(T-t)} L(T) F(t, T) dT.$$

$L(T)$ may be specified on an hourly basis with a number of discrete delivery times T_i for each start of an hourly period and load values $L(T_i)$. In this case, we can approximate the integral expression by a discrete sum

$$V(t) = \sum_{i=0}^{N-1} e^{-r(T_i-t)} L(T_i) F(t, T_i).$$

To value such an electricity delivery schedule, one has to know the forward curve $F(t, T)$ on at least an hourly basis over the time of delivery. Since there are no direct market prices available for single hours beyond the spot market, market participants require a model to break down quoted forward prices to a finer granularity. A typical approach is to evaluate historical hourly spot prices and use historical daily and weekly patterns as weights to break down the quoted forward prices. An example result for the German market is shown in Figure 3.14. The calculation consists of two steps:

1. Calculate hourly weights $s_i = s(T_i)$ from historical spot prices using forecasting methods, similar to those for load forecasting (section 5.4).
2. Break down the quoted forward prices to hourly prices.

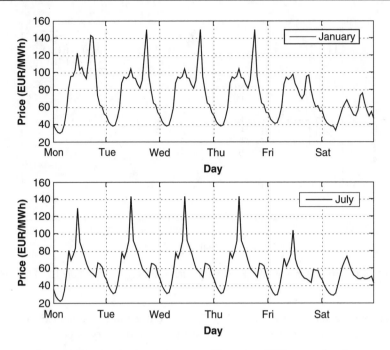

Figure 3.14   Hourly forward curve calibrated to EEX spot price data

For the second step we assume that hourly prices scale linearly with the traded forward prices for peak and base. Let J_k^b denote the set of hours corresponding to the delivery period of a traded baseload forward F_k^b. Let $|J_k^b|$ denote the number of hours contained in J_k^b, i.e. the energy of the forward contract F_k^b. The mean of all hourly forward prices within the delivery period equals the price of the traded forward contract:

$$\frac{1}{|J_k^b|} \sum_{i \in J_k^b} F(t, T_i) = F_k^b \quad \text{for all } k = 1, \ldots, N_b. \tag{3.36}$$

Similarly, delivery hours for peakload contract F_k^p are denoted by J_k^p and we derive:

$$\frac{1}{|J_k^p|} \sum_{i \in J_k^p} F(t, T_i) = F_k^p \quad \text{for all } k = 1, \ldots, N_p. \tag{3.37}$$

For example, if F_k^p is an EEX peakload contract for July 2008, then J_k^p would contain the hours 8:00 to 20:00 for Monday to Friday.

Now the assumption for the hourly forward prices is

$$F(t, T_i) = \left(\sum_{m=1}^{N_b} \alpha_m e_{mi} + \sum_{m=1}^{N_p} \beta_m f_{mi} \right) s_i,$$

where

$$e_{mi} = \begin{cases} 1 & \text{for } i \in J_m^b \\ 0 & \text{otherwise} \end{cases}, \qquad f_{mi} = \begin{cases} 1 & \text{for } i \in J_m^p \\ 0 & \text{otherwise} \end{cases}$$

The coefficients α_m and β_m are scaling factors which are effective on the delivery period of the traded forward contract F_l^b or F_l^p respectively. Substituting this assumption we derive

$$\frac{1}{|J_k^b|} \sum_{i \in J_k^b} \left(\sum_{m=1}^{N_b} \alpha_m e_{mi} + \sum_{m=1}^{N_p} \beta_m f_{mi} \right) s_i = F_k^b \quad \text{for all } k = 1, \ldots, N_b.$$

Rearranging terms these equations can be written as

$$\sum_{m=1}^{N_b} A_{km}^b \alpha_m + \sum_{m=1}^{N_p} B_{km}^b \beta_m = F_k^b |J_k^b| \quad \text{for all } k = 1, \ldots, N_b, \tag{3.38}$$

where

$$A_{km}^b = \sum_{i \in J_k^b} e_{mi} s_i = \sum_{i \in J_k^b \cap J_m^b} s_i \quad \text{and} \quad B_{km}^b = \sum_{i \in J_k^b} f_{mi} s_i = \sum_{i \in J_k^b \cap J_m^p} s_i.$$

The analogous equations for the peakload contracts are

$$\sum_{m=1}^{N_b} A_{km}^p \alpha_m + \sum_{m=1}^{N_p} B_{km}^p \beta_m = F_k^p |J_k^p| \quad \text{for all } k = 1, \ldots, N_p, \tag{3.39}$$

where

$$A_{km}^p = \sum_{i \in J_k^p \cap J_m^b} s_i \quad \text{and} \quad B_{km}^p = \sum_{i \in J_k^p \cap J_m^p} s_i.$$

Equations (3.38) and (3.39) define a linear system of $N_b + N_p$ equations for the same number of variables α_m and β_m. If there are no arbitrage opportunities in the forward prices then there is a unique solution for the scaling factors α_m and β_m. Sometimes forward prices are not totally arbitrage- free, for example where a yearly contract is slightly inconsistent with the quarterly contracts covering the same delivery year. In these situations, we can remove redundant forward prices or solve a least squares problem instead of trying to solve a linear system exactly.

3.4.2 The SMaPS Model

The Spot Market Price Simulation (SMaPS) model (Burger *et al.* 2004) uses ideas from the fundamental market models (see Chapter 4) and stochastic time-series theory to model electricity spot prices. As one stochastic factor explaining electricity spot prices it models the total system load. The model can be used in situations where load and prices are considered as stochastic, e.g. full service electricity contracts (discussed further in section 5.5).

Model overview

In the SMaPS model the spot market price is described by a discrete stochastic process S_t, $t = 0, 1, \ldots$ with hours as time units. The full model can be considered as a three-factor model, based on the following stochastic processes:

- total system load (electricity demand) L_t, $t \geq 0$;
- short-term price variations X_t, $t \geq 0$;
- long-term price variations Y_t, $t \geq 0$;

as well as the following additional quantities:

- (logarithmic) empirical merit order curve $f(t, L)$;
- average relative availability of power plants v_t.

The fundamental equation of the SMaPS model is

$$S_t = \exp(f(t, L_t/v_t) + X_t + Y_t). \tag{3.40}$$

The two stochastic factors L_t and X_t produce the short-term price variations, while factor Y_t is responsible for the long-term stochastic behaviour. All three factors are assumed to be stochastically independent. The process L_t describes the total system (grid) load. In many markets the total system load is published on a regular basis, so the process parameters can be estimated directly from load data, independent of the spot market prices. To eliminate the seasonality of the system load, we set

$$L_t = l_t + \hat{L}_t,$$

where $\hat{L}_t$ is a deterministic load forecast and l_t is a SARIMA time series model with a 24h seasonality. The deterministic function v_t specifies the expected relative availability of power plants in the system. In Germany, maintenance of power plants is mainly done in summer when the average load is lower and consequently the availability of power plants is higher in winter than summer. The highest availability is normalised to one and the expression L_t/v_t will be called the adjusted load.

For technical reasons there is a nonlinear relationship between price and load described by the so-called *merit order curve* (see section 4.3.1). However, the merit order curve at a future point in time t depends on uncertain parameters such as fuel costs, economic situation and availability of power plants. Accordingly, in the model a physical merit order curve is substituted by an empirical function estimated from hourly price and load data, called the *empirical merit order curve*. The empirical merit order curve depends to some extent on weekday and daytime such that f is time dependent. Different empirical curves are used for different weekdays and daytimes. In practice, only a few different curves are used, differentiating between workdays and holidays and between peak hours and off-peak hours (Figure 3.15).

Model selection and calibration

Since electricity prices may show different behaviour in different markets, the model chosen depends on the market considered. We look here at EEX spot prices, but similar results

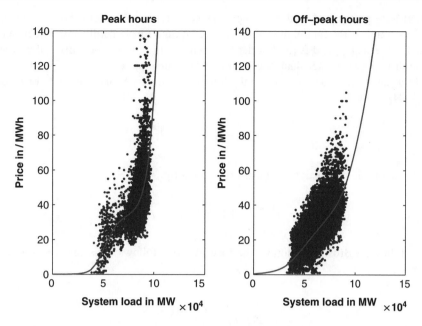

Figure 3.15 SMaPS empirical merit order curve, calibrated to EEX prices January 2003–December 2005

hold for other markets. The analysis of the load process uses only load data. To build the residual process $l_t = L_t - \hat{L}_t$ we need the deterministic component $\hat{L}_t$ which can be found by regression methods using techniques from section 5.4. Statistical analysis of the load residual l_t reveals a strong auto-correlation for a 24-hour time lag. A family of stochastic time series models that models such a seasonal behaviour is the family of SARIMA processes. The simplest model that gives a satisfactory fit is a SARIMA$(1, 0, 1) \times (1, 0, 1)_{24}$ model. It is defined by composing an ARMA(1,1) rule to differences with a 24h time lag. The model equation is

$$(l_t - \Phi_1 l_{t-24}) - \phi_1 (l_{t-1} - \Phi_1 l_{t-25}) = (\epsilon_t - \Theta_1 \epsilon_{t-24}) - \theta_1 (\epsilon_{t-1} - \Theta_1 \epsilon_{t-25}).$$

Multiplying out the coefficients, we get the iterative rule

$$l_t = \phi_1 l_{t-1} + \Phi_1 l_{t-24} - \Phi_1 \phi_1 l_{t-25} + \epsilon_t - \theta_1 \epsilon_{t-1} - \Theta_1 \epsilon_{t-24} + \Theta_1 \theta_1 \epsilon_{t-25}.$$

It is beyond the scope of this book to study the calibration and properties of these processes in detail and interested readers are directed to the standard literature on time series models, e.g. Brockwell and Davis (2002). Numerical algorithms for parameter calibration can be found in many mathematical software packages (e.g. Matlab, S-PLUS) and numerical libraries (e.g. NAG).

The short-term price process X_t explains market fluctuations that are not explained by the load. A significant auto-correlation for a 24-hour time lag can be observed also leading to the choice of a SARIMA$(1, 0, 1) \times (1, 0, 1)_{24}$ model with different parameters.

The long-term price process Y_t is modelled by a random walk, which can be seen as the discrete version of a Brownian motion. The model equation is

$$Y_{t+1} = Y_t + \left(\mu_t - \tfrac{1}{2}\sigma_Y^2\right) + \sigma_Y \epsilon_t^Y.$$

The short-term processes l_t and X_t model very short-term fluctuations. For a point in time $T \gg t$ far enough in the future, the values l_t or X_t at time t have hardly any influence on the expected values $\mathbb{E}_t[l_T]$ and $\mathbb{E}_t[X_T]$ at the later time T. In typical cases this will be the case for time differences greater than one month. The futures price $F(t, T) = \mathbb{E}_t[S_T]$ for $T \gg t$ depends, as an approximation, only on the long-term process Y_t and not on X_t or l_t. Burger et al. (2004) show that

$$F(t, T) = \hat{S}_T e^{Y_t + \mu(T - t)},$$

where $\hat{S}_T$ is a (non-stochastic) technical price given by

$$\hat{S}_T = e^{\mathrm{Var}[X_T]/2} \mathbb{E}\left[\exp\left(f(T, L_T / v_T)\right)\right].$$

Since Y_t follows a Brownian motion, the forward price follows a discrete version of GBM of the form

$$\frac{dF(t, T)}{F(t, T)} = \sigma^Y dW(t).$$

In the long-term approximation the model reduces to Black's model for futures prices. To calibrate the model parameters, we can choose forward or futures prices with a long time to expiry and calibrate the parameters of Black's model using the methods in section 2.2.2.

3.4.3   Regime-Switching Model

In the SMaPS model introduced in section 3.4.2 the electricity spot price is modelled as a time series with an hourly granularity and a seasonality of time lag 24. Another approach, regime switching, uses a daily 24-dimensional vector process instead of the 24h seasonality (Schindlmayr 2005). Using a principal component analysis (PCA) the vector process can be decomposed into independent stochastic factors. A similar PCA approach is also used in Skantze et al. (2000), but is first applied to the load process, which is considered as a fundamental driver for the spot price. Here, the PCA is applied directly to the hourly spot price profiles. Besides decomposing the vector process into independent factors, the PCA can also be used to reduce the number of stochastic factors by taking into account only the most significant factors. This reduction of dimension speeds up computations and reduces memory usage. Modelling the spot process on a daily basis is also closer to the actual trading process, where spot prices are usually the result of an auction for the day (or weekend) ahead. A regime switching approach in a continuous time setup with applications to option pricing is considered in Deng (2000).

The following notation is used:

- $\mathbf{S}_t = (S_t^1, \ldots, S_t^{24})$ Vector of hourly spot prices on day t.
- $\mathbf{s}_t = \ln \mathbf{S}_t$ Vector of logarithmic hourly spot prices.
- $s_t = \frac{1}{24} \sum_{i=1}^{24} s_t^i$ Mean logarithmic price.

Hourly spot prices are modelled at a logarithmic scale decomposed into the mean level and the hourly profile:

$$\mathbf{s}_t = s_t + \mathbf{h}_t, \quad \sum_{i=1}^{24} h_t^i = 0. \tag{3.41}$$

For the scalar process s_t and the vector process $\mathbf{h}_t$ the following time series models are used:

1. The non-seasonal component of s_t is an AR(1) model with regime-switching.
2. The stochastic component of $\mathbf{h}_t$ is decomposed via a principal component analysis (PCA) into factor loads u_t^i ($i = 1, \ldots, 24$) which are then modelled as independent ARMA processes.

It is often advisable to treat business days and non-business days as separate processes since they have a different behaviour regarding volatility and spikes. Fitting a single process to both business and non-business days generally gives poor results. In the simplest case, one can neglect the correlation between price on business and non-business days and take independent processes.

The daily price process

The (logarithmic) daily price process s_t has a yearly seasonality and is sensitive to weekdays and holidays. To account for price spikes in the daily prices a regime-switching approach is used.

First, the seasonal component of s_t is identified using a regression model:

$$s_t = \sum_{d=1}^{N_d} \mathbf{1}_{J_d^{DT}}(t)\beta_d^A + \mathbf{1}_{J_d^{DT}}(t)\cos(2\pi t/365)\beta_d^B + \mathbf{1}_{J_d^{DT}}(t)\sin(2\pi t/365)\beta_d^C + \mathbf{1}_{J_d^{DT}}(t)t\beta_d^D + y_t,$$

where y_t is the residual and $\mathbf{1}_J(t)$ the indicator function

$$\mathbf{1}_J(t) = \begin{cases} 1 & t \in J \\ 0 & \text{otherwise} \end{cases}.$$

The sets J_d^{DT}, $d = 1, \ldots, N_d$ define a partition into day types (e.g. Mo, Tu–Th, Fr, Sa, Su, Holidays). The regression coefficients $\beta_d^A, \ldots, \beta_d^E$ have the following meaning:

Coefficient	Description
β_d^A	mean level
β_d^B, β_d^C	amplitudes for yearly seasonality
β_d^D	deterministic drift

Next, a regime switching ARMA process is calibrated to the y_t data with the process divided into business and non-business days:

$$y_t = \mathbf{1}_{J^B}(t)y_t^B + \mathbf{1}_{J^H}(t)y_t^H,$$

where J^B denote the business and J^H the non-business days.

The following description of model and calibration for either of the processes y_t^B or y_t^H is simplified by leaving out the superscript and working with a time series y_k, $k = 1, \ldots, N$ observed at times t_k.

To account for price spikes, an AR(1) model with regime switching is chosen, where the regime change is modelled via a discrete Markov chain. The model equation is given by

$$y_k - \mu_{r_k} = \phi_{r_k}\left(y_{k-1} - \mu_{r_{k-1}}\right) + \sigma_{r_k}\epsilon_k, \tag{3.42}$$

where $r_k \in \{1, 2\}$ denotes the current regime at time t_k and $\epsilon_k \sim N(0, 1)$. The Markov chain is characterised by the transition probability matrix

$$P = \begin{pmatrix} p_{11} & p_{21} \\ p_{12} & p_{22} \end{pmatrix}.$$

with $p_{ij} = P(r_k = j | r_{k-1} = i)$.

Since the regime state is not observable we use a Hamilton filter (see section A.1.5). The Hamilton filter requires that transition probabilities depend only on the current state. The two-state model is transformed into a four-state model (Hamilton (1994), p. 691) with states $\tilde{r}_k \in \{1, 2, 3, 4\}$, such that

$$\begin{aligned}
\tilde{r}_k &= 1 \quad \text{if } r_k = 1 \text{ and } r_{k-1} = 1 \\
\tilde{r}_k &= 2 \quad \text{if } r_k = 2 \text{ and } r_{k-1} = 1 \\
\tilde{r}_k &= 3 \quad \text{if } r_k = 1 \text{ and } r_{k-1} = 2 \\
\tilde{r}_k &= 4 \quad \text{if } r_k = 2 \text{ and } r_{k-1} = 2.
\end{aligned}$$

The transition probability matrix becomes

$$\tilde{P} = \begin{pmatrix} p_{11} & 0 & p_{11} & 0 \\ p_{12} & 0 & p_{12} & 0 \\ 0 & p_{21} & 0 & p_{21} \\ 0 & p_{22} & 0 & p_{22} \end{pmatrix}.$$

The conditional probability densities are

$$f(y_k|y_{k-1}, \tilde{r}_k = 1) = \frac{1}{\sqrt{2\pi}\sigma_1} \exp\left(\frac{-[(y_k - \mu_1) - \phi_1(y_{k-1} - \mu_1)]^2}{2\sigma_1^2}\right)$$

$$f(y_k|y_{k-1}, \tilde{r}_k = 2) = \frac{1}{\sqrt{2\pi}\sigma_2} \exp\left(\frac{-[(y_k - \mu_2) - \phi_2(y_{k-1} - \mu_1)]^2}{2\sigma_2^2}\right)$$

$$f(y_k|y_{k-1}, \tilde{r}_k = 3) = \frac{1}{\sqrt{2\pi}\sigma_1} \exp\left(\frac{-[(y_k - \mu_1) - \phi_1(y_{k-1} - \mu_2)]^2}{2\sigma_1^2}\right)$$

$$f(y_k|y_{k-1}, \tilde{r}_k = 4) = \frac{1}{\sqrt{2\pi}\sigma_2} \exp\left(\frac{-[(y_k - \mu_2) - \phi_2(y_{k-1} - \mu_2)]^2}{2\sigma_2^2}\right).$$

In this way, the model is of the general form

$$y_k = \tilde{\mu}_{\tilde{r}_k} + \tilde{\phi}_{\tilde{r}_k} y_{k-1} + \tilde{\sigma}_{\tilde{r}_k} \epsilon_k. \tag{3.43}$$

The Hamilton filter produces estimates $\hat{\xi}^i_{k|k}$ for the probability $P(\tilde{r}_k = i | y_k, y_{k-1}, \dots)$ that the observation was generated by regime i based on observations up to time k. The vector of all those estimates is denoted by $\hat{\xi}_{k|k}$. The forecast of the probability that the process is in a certain regime at the next time step, $P(\tilde{r}_{k+1} = i | y_k, y_{k-1}, \dots)$, is denoted by $\hat{\xi}^i_{k+1|k}$ or $\hat{\xi}_{k+1|k}$ for the vector. Adapting the general Hamilton iteration equations to the current situation we get the following algorithm:

1. *Start*: For $\hat{\xi}_{1|0}$ choose the unconditional probabilities of the Markov chain generated by P.
2. *Calculate* $\hat{\xi}_{k|k}$:

$$\hat{\xi}^i_{k|k} = \frac{\hat{\xi}^i_{k|k-1} \eta^i_k}{\sum_{i=1}^4 \hat{\xi}^i_{k|k-1} \eta^i_k}, \tag{3.44}$$

where $\eta^i_k = f(y_k | y_{k-1}, \tilde{r}_k = i)$ denotes the conditional probability density.
3. *Calculate* $\hat{\xi}_{k+1|k}$:

$$\hat{\xi}^i_{k+1|k} = P \cdot \hat{\xi}^i_{k|k}. \tag{3.45}$$

4. *Iterate*: Repeat from step 2 with k increased by one.

Figure 3.16 shows the regime probability $\hat{\xi}^i_{k|k}$ for the spike regime, for example spot price data. In periods of high volatility the probability for the spike regime increases.

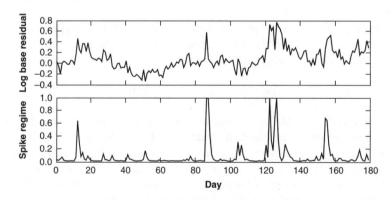

Figure 3.16   Regime inspection returned by the Hamilton filter

A byproduct of the Hamilton filter is the log maximum likelihood function, calculated as

$$L = \sum_{k=1}^{N_k} \ln \left(\sum_{i=1}^4 \hat{\xi}^i_{k|k} \eta^i_k \right). \tag{3.46}$$

The optimal parameters can be found by numerically maximising the function L. Example calibration results for EEX spot price data from January 2001 to May 2005 are the following:

	μ	ϕ	σ	
regime 1	−0.004	0.74	0.11	$P = \begin{pmatrix} 0.94 & 0.28 \\ 0.06 & 0.72 \end{pmatrix}.$
regime 2	−0.02	0.68	0.30	

The hourly profile process

The hourly profile process is defined as the logarithmic spot process normalised to mean zero:

$$\mathbf{h}_t = \mathbf{s}_t - s_t.$$

The steps for modelling the profile dynamics are:

1. De-seasonalise the profile for each hour.
2. Use PCA to decompose the vector process into factor loads.
3. Model each factor load as an ARMA process.

Daily spot price profiles have a pronounced yearly and weekly seasonality due to different temperature and light conditions. De-seasonalising the profiles for each single hour utilises a similar technique to that for the daily process s_t. The profiles can be written as

$$\mathbf{h}_t = \hat{\mathbf{h}}_t + \Delta\mathbf{h}_t,$$

where $\hat{\mathbf{h}}_t$ is the deterministic seasonal component and $\Delta\mathbf{h}_t$ is the stochastic residual from the regression.

The residuals $\Delta\mathbf{h}_t$ form a vector process with a covariance structure reflecting the different volatilities of each single hour and the correlations between the hourly profile values. As before, the process $\Delta\mathbf{h}_t$ is divided into business days and non-business days:

$$\Delta\mathbf{h}_t = \mathbf{1}_{J^H}(t)\Delta\mathbf{h}_t^B + \mathbf{1}_{J^H}(t)\Delta\mathbf{h}_t^H.$$

The two processes $\Delta\mathbf{h}_t^B$ and $\Delta\mathbf{h}_t^H$ are treated separately. For notational convenience we regard only one of these processes and denote it by $\Delta\mathbf{h}_k$, $k = 1, \ldots, N$. By PCA the vector process $\Delta\mathbf{h}_k$ is now decomposed into independent factor loads (see section A.1.3). Let $\mathbf{p}_1, \ldots, \mathbf{p}_{24}$ be the principal component factors of $\Delta\mathbf{h}_k$ after column-wise normalisation to standard deviation 1, i.e. the eigenvectors of the matrix $(\Delta\mathbf{h})^T\Delta\mathbf{h}/N$, where $\Delta\mathbf{h}$ is an $N \times 24$-matrix. It is assumed that the corresponding eigenvalues are in descending order $\lambda_1 > \ldots > \lambda_{24}$. The 24×24-matrix $(\mathbf{p}_1, \ldots, \mathbf{p}_{24})$ containing the eigenvectors as columns is denoted by Q. The $N \times 24$-matrix of factor loads is then given by $W = (\Delta\mathbf{h})Q$. An example of the principal components is shown in Figure 3.17.

The ith eigenvalue λ_i represents the variance contributed by the ith principal component. In typical cases, a large number of principal components is needed to explain most of the variance.

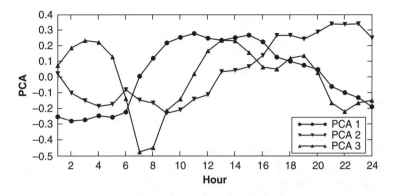

Figure 3.17   First three principal components (EEX spot data, business days).

For stochastic modelling of the factor loads, let $w_k^i = W_{ki}$, $i = i, \ldots, 24$, $k = 1, \ldots, N$ be the time series of the ith factor load, which is the ith column of the matrix W. The series w_k^i are modelled as independent ARMA processes. From the simulated factor loads W the process $\Delta \mathbf{h}_t$ can be calculated as $\Delta \mathbf{h}_t = WQ^T$.

A more careful study of the profile dynamics reveals that on days with extremely high daily price the profiles behave differently, since those prices often are the result of spikes at single hours. To get a more realistic price behaviour on days where the regime is in a volatile state, we can randomly draw historical profiles according to the day type, season and regime state.

3.5   MULTI-COMMODITY MODELS

Modelling the joint dynamics of multiple commodities is a great challenge, since the interdependencies among the commodity prices often have a very complex structure. On the one hand, there are price dependencies caused by fundamental economic relations. Electricity spot prices usually will not fall below the marginal variable costs of generation determined by fuel prices and the prices of emission allowances. On the other hand, there are many factors influencing commodities prices that are difficult to quantify such as strategic behaviour of market participants. Often data about fundamental drivers of the market are not exactly known and must be estimated by the market participants. Those estimates change over time and cause further price fluctuations that to a casual observer appear as stochastic.

In this section we first take a statistical view of the joint price dynamics using the concepts of regression analysis, correlation and cointegration. On the basis of these statistical findings a strategy for model building can be defined (see section 3.5.4).

3.5.1   Regression Analysis

To analyse the relation between electricity, coal, oil and carbon emission prices, a linear regression can be used of the form

$$P_{el} = a_0 + a_1 t + a_{coal} P_{coal} + a_{oil} P_{oil} + a_{co2} P_{co2} + \epsilon,$$

where

$$P_{el} = \text{electricity price}$$

$$P_{coal} = \text{coal price}$$

$$P_{oil} = \text{Brent oil price}$$

$$P_{co2} = \text{EU emission allowances (EUA)}$$

The linear regression can be applied for spot prices and for forward prices. Since spot prices are much more volatile than forward prices, the relation is more pronounced for forward prices. As an example we take the forward prices for year 2007 (see Figure 3.18). The regression results are shown in Table 3.1. A graph of the original data and the prediction given by the regression model is shown in Figure 3.19. For an explanation of the regression results see section A.1.1. The most significant regressors in this time period are time (trend) and EUAs. In this example, the critical t-ratios for a 99% and a 95% confidence level are 2.65 and 2.00 respectively. The trend and EUAs are significant at all reasonable confidence levels. Oil is still significant at a 99% confidence level, whereas coal is significant only at a 95% confidence level. A more detailed regression analysis of peak and off-peak prices reveals that the oil dependence is due to oil dependence of the peak prices ($a_{oil} = 0.565$, t-ratio 8.71) whereas for the off-peak prices oil has no significance ($a_{oil} = 0.016$, t-ratio 0.40). EUAs are highly significant for peak ($a_{co_2} = 0.662$, t-ratio 12.91) and even more for off-peak ($a_{co_2} = 0.704$, t-ratio 22.68) with similar values.

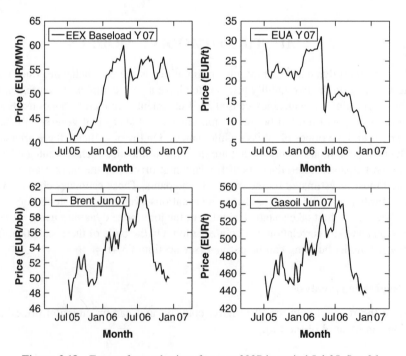

Figure 3.18   Energy forward prices for year 2007 in period Jul 05–Sep 06

Table 3.1 Regression results for EEX baseload on forward prices year-2007 based on average weekly prices quotes between July 2005 and December 2006

Commodity	Coeff.	Range	t-ratio	Significant (99%)
Intercept	−3.124	(−9.210, 2.962)	−1.02	no
Trend	0.048	(0.045, 0.051)	31.30	yes
Coal	0.146	(0.019, 0.273)	2.30	no
Oil	0.212	(0.128, 0.296)	5.02	yes
EUA	0.689	(0.622, 0.755)	20.62	yes

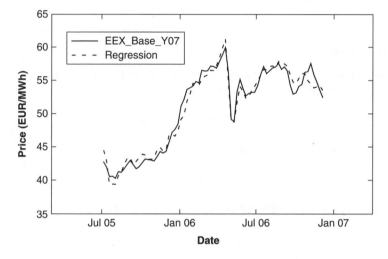

Figure 3.19   Regression of electricity forward prices on coal, oil and CO_2 forward prices.

The high significance of a linear trend may seem surprising, since there is no apparent fundamental reason. Apart from fuel prices, prices for electricity are in the long term influenced by the availability of generation and transmission capacities, which change over time. Those effects, however, are not a sufficient explanation for such changes within a year. Here we also have to consider changes in the market expectations and changes in the risk premium paid in the forward market. The example time period also does not reveal enough data for complex statistical analysis. Considering longer time periods becomes problematic when the market structure changes, e.g. the introduction of a market for carbon emissions or changes in the cross border transmission rules. When building such a regression model, tests on parameter stability and observations of structural changes are necessary.

Regression models can become the starting point of a stochastic multi-commodity model. For this purpose, the regressors and the residuals ϵ_t have to be modelled stochastically. The autocorrelation function of the residuals ϵ_t shown in Figure 3.20 reveals a pronounced autocorrelation that has to be reflected by an appropriate model for ϵ_t.

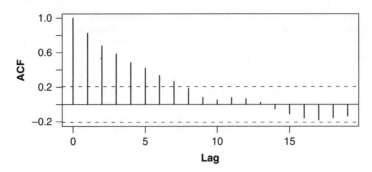

Figure 3.20   Autocorrelation function of residual ϵ_t

3.5.2   Correlation Analysis

Many analytic option pricing formulas for multi-underlying options assume a multidimensional log-normal process of the form (see section 2.5)

$$dS_i(t) = \mu_i S_i(t)dt + \sigma_i S_i(t)dW_i(t),\qquad(3.47)$$

where $W_1(t), \ldots, W_n(t)$ are Bownian motions correlated by

$$dW_i(t)dW_j(t) = \rho_{ij}dt.$$

The correlations ρ_{ij} can be estimated as the correlations of the log-returns,

$$\rho_{ij} = \mathrm{Corr}[r_i, r_j],$$

where the log-returns $r_{i,k}$ at times $k = t_1, \ldots, t_N$ are defined as

$$r_{i,k} = \ln S_i(t_k) - \ln S_i(t_{k-1}).$$

By the model assumptions, the log-returns $r_{i,k}$ are normally distributed with variance $\sigma_i^2 \Delta t$. An estimator for the correlation is given by

$$\hat{\rho}_{ij} = \frac{\sum_{k=1}^{N} r_{i,k} r_{j,k}}{\sqrt{\sum_{k=1}^{N} r_{i,k}^2 \sum_{k=1}^{N} r_{j,k}^2}}.$$

For the example commodities in Figure 3.18 the estimated volatilites and correlations are shown in Table 3.2. Not surprisingly after the regression results, there is a high correlation between electricity weekly returns and EUA weekly returns.

3.5.3   Cointegration

In the multi-factor model (3.47) each single asset $S_i(t)$ follows a non-stationary process. On the logarithmic scale the model is a multidimensional Brownian motion with drift

$$d \ln S_i(t) = \left(\mu_i - \sigma_i^2/2\right) dt + \sigma_i dW_i(t).$$

Table 3.2 Correlation matrix and historical volatility for forward prices Year-2007 based on average weekly prices quotes between July 2005 and December 2006

Correlation	Electricity	EUA	Brent Crude	Coal
Electricity	1	0.87	0.23	0.13
EUA	0.87	1	0.17	0.10
Brent crude	0.23	0.17	1	0.10
Coal	0.13	0.10	0.10	1
Volatility	19%	72%	16%	12%

The dependence between the assets is characterised by the correlations ρ_{ij} between the risk factors $W_i(t)$, but even if the correlation is very high, the single assets will eventually diverge from each other. Spreads between the assets are not mean reverting to some long-term average spread.

The regression analysis of section 3.5.1 shows that in commodity markets due to fundamental reasons the dependence is stronger, such that certain linear combinations of the commodities appear to be stationary, at least over certain time periods. In such cases the time series is called *cointegrated*. More precisely, the non-stationary time series $S_i(t)$ of class $I(1)$ are called cointegrated if there is a *cointegration vector* $(1, -\beta_1, -\beta_2, \ldots, -\beta_n)$ such that the linear combination

$$S_n(t) - \beta_1 S_1(t) - \beta_2 S_2(t) - \cdots - \beta_n S_n(t)$$

is of class $I(0)$, i.e. stationary. Figure 3.21 shows the residuals of the regression in Figure 3.19. Even though the data is not sufficient for rigorous statistical tests, the residuals have a stationary character.

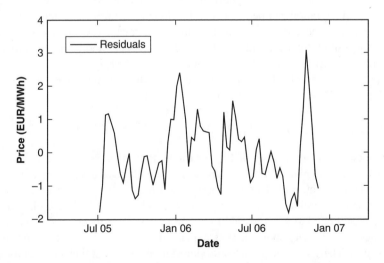

Figure 3.21 Regression residuals of electricity forwards on coal, oil and CO_2 forward prices (from Figure 3.19)

3.5.4   Model Building

The starting point for a multi-commodity model is a statistical analysis of the single commodities and of their joint dynamics to get an idea of the general model structure. The model decision also depends strongly on the intended application of the model:

- Should the model be used for quantifying risk or for option pricing?
- Which risk factors need to be explicitly considered?
- What market data is available (spot prices, forward prices, volatilities)?

If the model is intended to be used for option pricing the model is usually written in risk-neutral parameters (see section 3.2) and consistency with available market prices and availability of fast numerical methods for option pricing may be more important than statistical accuracy. If the model is intended to be used for measuring risk (e.g. Value-at-Risk calculation) then statistical properties, such as tails of the distribution, become more important.

As a simple example, the analysis of the single commodities may result in the following choice of models for spot prices:

Commodity	Model choice
Electricity	Regime switching (section 3.4.3)
EUA	GBM (section 3.2.1)
Brent crude	GBM
Coal	GBM

More realistic examples use a Schwartz–Smith model (section 3.2.3) for oil or coal prices.

Next, the dependency structure needs to be analysed. One important question is whether there are any cointegration vectors present. At this point the time horizon for the model has to be taken into account. Often, for short time horizons (e.g. when calculating market risk over 10 days) cointegration can be neglected. For long time horizons cointegration becomes much more important because it prevents fundamentally related commodity prices to diverge too much. An example focusing on the short-term multi-commodity risk of forward prices using hyperbolic distributions is studied in Boerger *et al.* (2007).

In the spot price example above, a cointegration vector relating the electricity spot price to the fuel and EUA prices can be assumed of the form

$$S_{el}(t) = a_0 + f(t) + a_{coal}S_{coal}(t) + a_{oil}S_{oil}(t) + a_{co_2}S_{co_2}(t) + \epsilon(t),$$

where $f(t)$ models the seasonality of the electricity spot prices and ϵ is the deviation from the "fundamentally" explained price. If there is no cointegration vector relating EUAs, oil and coal, a multi-variate GBM of the form (3.47) for these three prices is chosen, with a correlation matrix similar to the lower left 3×3 submatrix of the correlation matrix in Table 3.2, but calibrated to spot instead of forward prices. The process $\epsilon(t)$ still reflects many characteristics of electricity spot prices as explained in section 3.4, such as mean-reversion and price spikes. Therefore, the models introduced in 3.4 are natural candidates for $\epsilon(t)$, only that the stochastic components due to changes in fuel prices and EUA prices have already been taken out.

4
Fundamental Market Models

Market prices can be understood as clearing (or equilibrium) prices at the intersection of cumulative bid (demand) and offer (supply) curves (see Figure 4.1). Fundamental market models use cost-based bid and offer curves to derive estimations (or indications) of market prices. They do not necessarily allow forecasting of market prices. These models give insight into fundamental price drivers and market mechanisms. Therefore, fundamental market models can be used for the development of trading strategies as well as for decision support for investments or acquisitions.

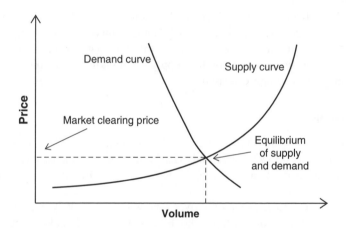

Figure 4.1 Cumulative supply and demand curves

This chapter concentrates on fundamental market models for electricity markets. We first describe the most important fundamental price drivers for electricity prices in section 4.1. The principles of economic power plant dispatch discussed in section 4.2 are crucial for describing and understanding the supply side of electricity markets. Different methodological modelling approaches are discussed in section 4.3.

Data quality is critical for high quality description of electricity markets. A general overview on data required for modelling as well as on information sources can be found in section 4.4. Finally, we present examples for the application of fundamental electricity market models in section 4.5 and shortly describe in sections 4.6 and 4.7 how fundamental market modelling approaches can be applied to gas markets, other fuel markets, and to the market for CO_2 emissions certificates.

4.1 FUNDAMENTAL PRICE DRIVERS IN ELECTRICITY MARKETS

In contrast to other commodities, large quantities of electricity cannot be stored directly.[1] Power generation and demand within an interconnected electric power system has to be in balance at all times. Spot markets have short delivery intervals, commonly 60 or 30 minutes (see section 1.4.3). Scheduling periods for physical power delivery are even shorter with periods as low as 15 minutes in most transmission areas. Deviations of scheduled generation from real time demand are compensated by balancing power (see section 1.4.3).

In power markets, spot prices are published for every delivery interval. Each of these interval prices can be understood as an equilibrium price of bid and offer curves for the specific time interval (see Figure 4.1). In most real markets, only part of the total physical demand and supply is traded in the spot market. An exception are compulsory pool markets, as in Spain. Most fundamental market models represent the equilibrium price of the whole system considering total physical demand and supply, which are not identical to the bid and offer side in the spot market. The equilibrium prices derived with fundamental market models can explain spot market prices well if economic power plant dispatch for the whole system can be assumed.[2]

Figure 4.2 shows the main price drivers on the demand side and on the supply side. Due to limited interconnection capacities between different transmission areas of the power system, price differences between market regions occur. Interregional transmission flows can have an impact on the demand as well as on the supply situation in any region. The main drivers are analysed in the following subsections.

4.1.1 Demand Side

A sectoral breakdown of the European electricity demand is given in Table 4.1. The main consumers are industry (37%), households (26%), the services industry (22%), and others (5%). The regional distribution of electricity demand within Europe is shown in Figure 4.8 on page 144.

Electricity demand fluctuates strongly over time with typical daily, weekly, and seasonal patterns and significant regional differences. Electricity demand is also strongly influenced by consumer behaviour. Figure 4.3 depicts the demand or load curves for summer and winter Wednesdays in Germany and France. Differences between these curves are caused by differing consumption patterns and different intensities of activities responsible for electricity demand, such as air-conditioning or electric heating.

Two different approaches are possible for explaining and forecasting electricity demand (see section 5.4): a bottom-up approach that analyses load curves on the level of sectors or even single consumers or a top-down approach that analyses aggregated load curves on a country or regional level. As aggregated load curves exhibit a very regular pattern, load

---

[1] For small-scale applications, indirect storage is possible with capacitors, batteries, fly wheels, etc. For large-scale applications, storage is achieved with hydroelectric storage schemes (see sections 4.1.2 and 4.2.2). With increasing quantities of fluctuating wind energy in Europe new storage technologies are currently under consideration. Compressed air energy storage (CAES) is the only proven large-scale technology (Crotogino *et al.* 2001). The main components of a CAES system are an open cycle gas turbine with separated turbine and air compressor and underground caverns for storing compressed air.

[2] Fundamental market models based on short run marginal costs can explain observed spot market prices well in competitive markets, as in Germany. In other markets, it might be necessary to consider strategic behaviour of market participants (see section 4.3.4).

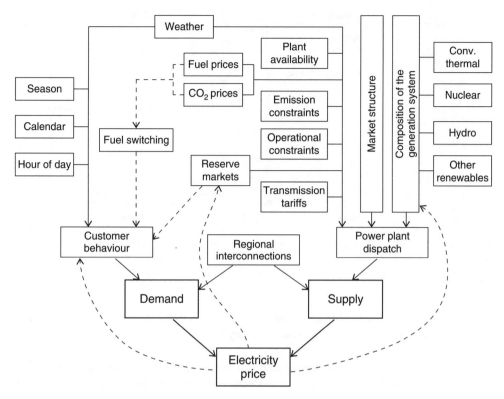

Figure 4.2 Fundamental price drivers in power markets

Table 4.1 Sectoral breakdown of electricity demand in Europe (EU25) 2003

Sector			TWh
Energy sector (without electricity generation sector)		4%	122
Transmission and distribution losses		7%	201
Industry		37%	1074
Iron and steel industry	4.2%		122
Chemical industry	6.5%		192
Food, drink, and tobacco industry	3.5%		102
Paper and printing industry	4.6%		136
Engineering and other metal industry	5.0%		147
Other industries	12.7%		374
Households		26%	752
Services		22%	650
Rail transport		2%	70
Agriculture		2%	47
Other sectors		1%	18
Total consumption (without electricity generation sector)		100%	2935

Source: Eurostat and own calculations; partly provisional values.

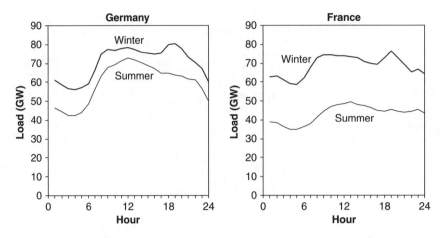

Figure 4.3 Seasonal differences in daily load curves (Wednesday 19 January and Wednesday 17 August 2005). Source: UCTE.

forecasting is preferably performed on this level. Hourly electricity demand of a country or region can be explained well by the following key factors:

1. *Season*: Load patterns show typical seasonal behaviour. This can be explained by the varying duration of day light, seasonal production patterns of some industries, and demand for heating and cooling.
2. *Day of the week*: There are strong differences in the sectoral activities between different weekdays and weekend days.
3. *Irregular sectoral non-work or limited activity days*: These include public holidays, school holidays, days between public holidays and weekends. On these days, the demand of industry and services is generally lower while household demand might increase.
4. *Hour of the day*: Electricity demand follows typical daily patterns with characteristic differences between different day types (working days, weekends, holidays, etc.).
5. *Weather*: Electricity demand for heating and cooling depends on environmental temperatures and, to a smaller extent, on wind speeds. Buildings buffer temperatures to a certain degree and therefore time lags between temperature change and the ensuing electricity demand response can occur. Electricity demand for lighting in most sectors depends on global irradiance.

Using combinations of categories 1 to 3, it is possible to form clusters of days (day types) with distinct load characteristics. Examples for France are shown in Figure 4.4. The differentiation of day types can be used in load forecasting algorithms (see section 5.4).

As demand patterns directly impact electricity prices, variables 1 to 4 are generally used for constructing hourly price forward curves (see section 3.4.1).

Besides these exogenous influences, electricity prices also have some impact on electricity demand in the longer term. Electricity prices will have an impact on the penetration of energy efficient technologies, the extent of substitution by other energy carriers, or the relocation of energy intensive industries to countries with lower electricity costs. In most cases, these

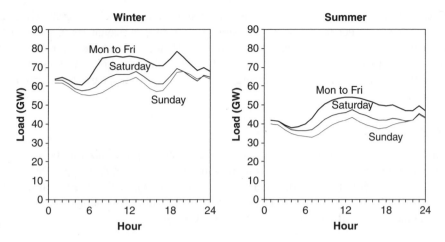

Figure 4.4 Characteristic daily load curves for typical days in France. Source: RTE, own calculations

longer-term impacts cannot be separated from general consumption trends due to limited availability of disaggregated demand data.

In the short term, the impact of wholesale prices on demand strongly depends on pricing signals in electricity contracts with final customers. Up-to-date real-time pricing is not common in the electricity sector in Europe. There are, however, a large variety of contracts that impact customer behaviour to a certain degree and cause demand elasticity. Main types include:

- *Interruptible contracts*: The supplier can interrupt the contract for a certain number of hours each year with or without the payment of a compensation for electricity not supplied.
- *Capacity payments*: Contracts containing a price component that depends on the customer's peak load within a defined time interval (e.g. one year). As a statistical correlation between individual customer load, total system load, and prices exists, these contracts may cause a slight price elasticity of demand.
- *Spot market indexed contracts*: Contracts with a variable price component indexed to spot market prices in the wholesale market. These types of contracts are common in some sectors in Scandinavia (Bye 2003).
- *Short-term price adjustments*: Most Scandinavian utilities have standard contracts that allow price adjustments with two weeks, notice. These standard contracts are the most common type of contracts in the residential sector. In combination with spot indexed contracts, they did have a significant demand impact during a period of high prices in the Nord Pool in 2003 (von der Fehr *et al.* 2005). Price adjustments with short notice can also be found in the UK.
- *Flexible price tariffs*: With one or two days notice, the supply company can increase electricity tariffs for a limited number of days during the winter period to a pre-defined higher level. Peak day prices generally exceed normal prices by more than 200%. This pricing element is common for industrial as well as residential consumers in France. Load reduction of up to 20% can be achieved at peak load times (International Energy Agency 2003).

In spite of these measures, the extent of demand responses to prices is generally considered small. It is strongly dependent on pricing strategies in different countries. Clear statistical quantification of the impact is generally not possible. Hence, in fundamental market models the price elasticity of demand is usually only reflected by the use of observed historical load patterns that already contain price responses of the demand. In this case, the demand curve is a vertical line.

4.1.2 Supply Side

Electricity is generated by a wide variety of different technologies. This variety is caused by regional differences in availability of resources, different or changing political preferences, and incentive patterns for specific technologies. A breakdown of the generation in Europe is listed in Table 4.2. As a uniform classification of generation technologies does not exist, statistical data from different sources is often inconsistent.[3]

Table 4.2 Breakdown of electricity generation in Europe (EU25) 2003

Technology			TWh
Conventional thermal		54.8%	1669
Coal	17.9%		546
Natural gas	17.1%		520
Lignite	7.0%		212
Oil	4.9%		149
Other conv. thermal or multi-fuel	7.9%		242
Nuclear		30.4%	925
Renewables		12.9%	394
Hydro power (non-pumped storage)	9.4%		287
Biomass	1.9%		58
Solar	0.01%		0.4
Geothermal	0.2%		5
Wind	1.4%		44
Hydro power (pumped storage)		1.0%	31
Derived gas		0.9%	28
Total net electricity generation including pumped storage hydro		100.0%	3047

Source: Eurostat, European Commission (2005b), and own calculations. Partly provisional values.

Figure 4.5 shows a typical demand curve and the corresponding generation (or dispatch) pattern for different plant types. Nuclear power plants are operated in base load with constant output. Conventional thermal plants are operated at more or less constant power. For meeting the variable changes in demand, conventional thermal, hydro storage, and hydro pumped storage plants are used. During the night when demand is low, the pumps of hydro storage schemes are operated to raise water from lower into upper reservoirs. This creates additional

---

[3] Reasons for inconsistencies include: thermal power plants using more than one fuel, generation from waste sometimes counted as renewable and sometimes not, and statistics not differentiating between generation in hydro plants from natural inflow (renewable) and from pumped storage (not renewable).

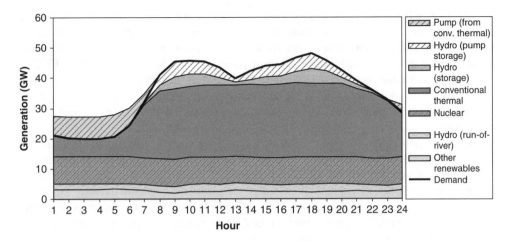

Figure 4.5 Typical daily dispatch patterns for different generation technologies

demand. During the day changes in demand are compensated using storage and pumped storage plants. Run-of-river hydro plants, geothermal, wind, and solar power plants produce in correspondence to the current resource availability (water flow rates, sunshine, wind etc.). The actual dispatch pattern varies from country to country due to different load patterns and generation system configurations. It is generally a result of economic power plant dispatch. The mathematical description for modelling power plant dispatch will be discussed in section 4.2. The following sections give a short overview over the main characteristics of the technologies that have relevance for electricity markets.

Conventional Thermal Power Plants

Conventional thermal power plants have the largest share in electricity generation in Europe. Their energy sources are fossil fuels or in some cases biomass. Conversion to electricity occurs by means of a steam turbine (Rankine cycle), a gas turbine (Joules cycle) or an internal combustion engine (Diesel cycle). The main fuels are listed below:

- *Coal*: Coal fired power plants have a long tradition in electricity systems due to the availability of indigenous resources in Europe. The share of coal in electricity generation has been declining due to fuel costs. Coal mining in Europe is no longer competitive on the world market and is highly subsidised. Increasing quantities of imported coal are used in European power stations; however, transportation costs for imported coal can be high. Other reasons for the declining generation share of coal power plants are environmental constraints and associated costs. European countries have introduced limits for dust, SO_2, and NO_x emissions. For compliance, coal power plant operators either have to invest in flue gas cleaning technologies or have to reduce the generation output. Coal composition varies from source to source and not all coal qualities are suitable for use in all power stations.
- *Natural gas*: stations have gained an increasing share in electricity generation over the last decades. The main reasons are the development of combined cycle gas turbines (CCGT)

with high efficiencies, the expansion of the gas pipeline system, relative environmental friendliness, and low investment costs in comparison with other power generation technologies. Other gas power plant technologies include gas fired steam turbines and open cycle gas turbines; however, both of them have lower efficiencies than CCGTs. Open cycle gas turbines (GTs) are mainly used for peak load or as reserve capacity (see section 4.3.1). For small-scale local and industrial applications of combined heat and power (CHP) generation, gas fired combustion engines are often used. In many cases, gas prices are directly or indirectly linked to oil prices (see section 1.2.3).

- *Lignite*: Lignite is a low quality coal with high moisture and ash content and low calorific value, also referred to as *brown coal*. In Europe, lignite resources are predominantly located in Germany, Poland, Greece, Romania, Hungary, and Slovakia. Owing to the low calorific value of lignite, lignite fired power plants are generally located close to the mine to avoid high transport costs. Lignite fired plants have low fuel costs compared to other conventional thermal power stations. Disadvantages are higher investment costs and higher specific CO_2 emissions.

- *Oil*: The role of oil in power generation in Europe is relatively small due to environmental legislation that limits the use of heavy fuel oil. In most countries, only low sulphur gasoil is used. As gasoil prices are generally higher than prices for other fossil fuels, oil fired power plants are primarily used as peak or reserve capacity or in local applications. Italy is the only country in Europe where oil fired power plants play a significant role. Steam turbines, gas turbines as well as combustion engines are common technologies.

- *Other fuels*: A large variety of other fuels are used in conventional thermal power stations either as primary fuel or as auxiliary fuel. Examples are: peat (in Finland and Ireland), derived gas (e.g. coke oven gas or coal-derived synthesis gas), petroleum coke, Orimulsion[4] (an emulsion of natural bitumen suspended in water produced in Venezuela – used in Italy), industrial and municipal waste, and different types of biomass (e.g. wood, straw, olive cake residue or sewage sludge). These fuels play a minor role in power generation and have little impact on wholesale market prices.

Nuclear Power Plants

Nuclear power plants play an important role in electricity generation in Europe. Nuclear power plants are thermal power plants with a Rankine cycle. A nuclear fission reaction in the reactor provides the required heat. Nuclear power plants are characterised by low variable operation costs (fuel costs), zero CO_2 emissions, but high operation and maintenance costs, high investment costs, and long planning and construction times. Nuclear plants are generally used for baseload electricity generation.

The future development of nuclear power in Europe is currently under debate. In several European countries, a nuclear phase-out has been introduced: Sweden (1980), Italy (1987), Belgium (1999), and Germany (2000). The nuclear phase-out limits the remaining operation time or generation of existing nuclear power plants. In Germany, the last nuclear reactor is expected to close in 2021. Austria, the Netherlands, and Spain have enacted laws not to build new nuclear power stations. France and Finland have decided to build a new nuclear reactor and governments in other countries, including the UK, are considering this option as well.

---

[4] Orimulsion is a registered trademark of Petroleos de Venezuela SA.

Hydro Power Plants

The use of hydro power for electricity generation in Europe started in the 19th century. The potential energy of dammed water is converted into electricity by use of a turbine and a generator. Hydro electricity is classified as renewable energy with the exception of pumped storage. Different types of hydro power plants exist and are listed below:

- *Run-of-river power plants*: These hydro electric power plants are located at rivers and utilise height differences at weirs. They can be found all over Europe with a wide range of installed capacities. The turbine flow rate and generation output depends on the natural flow rate of the river. In some cases, generation output can be slightly adjusted on a short-term basis (hours to days) by modulation of the headwater level.
- *Storage power plants*: These hydro power plants consist of a reservoir, a turbine located below the reservoir, and a generator. The turbine is connected to the reservoir by a pipe (see Figure 4.6a). The reservoir is filled by natural inflow. The water is released through the turbine at times of peak demand or peak electricity price.
- *Pumped storage power plants*: These hydro power plants consist of an upper and a lower reservoir connected by a turbine as well as a pump (see Figure 4.6b). The upper reservoir is filled by water pumped uphill from the lower reservoir at times of low electricity demand or price. In addition, there may be natural inflows to the upper reservoir. During times of peak demand or price, the water is released from the upper reservoir. It flows through the turbine, generates electricity, and is received in the lower reservoir.
- *Tidal power plants*: The only large-scale tidal power plant in Europe is located in La Rance, France. It utilises the tidal range. A barrage (dam) blocks the incoming and outgoing tides of a coastal basin. A tidal power plant is operated similar to a run-of-river power plant, but with changing flow directions.

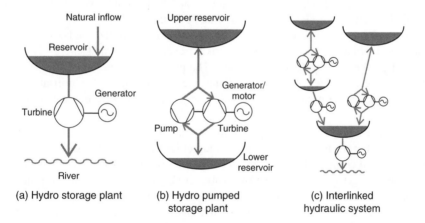

(a) Hydro storage plant (b) Hydro pumped storage plant (c) Interlinked hydraulic system

Figure 4.6 Storage and pumped storage power plants

Storage and pumped storage plants often form complex interlinked hydraulic systems (see Figure 4.6c). Their operation may also impact the generation of run-of-river power plants located on a river below these storage schemes. External constraints such as minimum flow rates in original river beds have to be respected.

Other Renewables

The main characteristics of different sources of renewable energy relevant for fundamental market models are described in the following subsections:

- *Biomass*: Biomass can be categorised into solid, liquid, and gaseous forms. There are several technologies for conversion into electricity: use as auxiliary fuels in conventional thermal power stations, conventional steam turbines (especially for solid biomass) or internal combustion engines (biogas and bioliquids). Combined heat and power (CHP) is possible. With the exception of co-firing the production pattern is generally flat.
- *Photovoltaic (PV)*: In Germany, the installed capacity of PVs has shown huge growth rates in recent years reaching 0.5% of the total installed generation capacity in 2005, but the overall impact is still small. The generation pattern depends on solar radiation (daylight hours only, summer peak) and is characterised by a low annual load factor[5] (approximately 10%).
- *Solar thermal power*: Solar thermal power systems use concentrated solar radiation as a high temperature energy source to produce electrical power. Different technologies are available (e.g. parabolic troughs or power towers), but there have not been any significant commercial applications in Europe so far. The production pattern is comparable to photovoltaic systems.
- *Small hydro*: Generally small hydro power plants are run-of-river power plants located on small rivers. These power plants generate electricity with a typical run-of-river production pattern. The expansion of hydro electricity generation in Europe is limited, as most of the hydro power resources are already utilised.
- *Wind power*: Wind energy is converted into electricity by use of turbines. Wind turbines are grouped into wind farms, which can reach capacities as large as 100 MW or more. Wind energy has the most significant impact on electricity wholesale markets in Europe due to fluctuating production patterns and high cumulative installed capacity. A production pattern for Germany for one month is shown in Figure 4.7.
- *Geothermal energy*: Instead of fossil fuels, hot geothermal fluids can be utilised as a heat source in thermal power plants with Rankine cycle. Geothermal energy is utilised for electricity generation in Iceland and Italy. The production pattern is flat.
- *Ocean energy*: Besides tidal power plants mentioned above, the utilisation of ocean energy is still in the prototype stage with a large variety of different technologies.

The European Union and national governments intend to increase the share of renewable energy sources for electricity generation. The target for the EU15 countries is a share of 22% by the year 2010 compared to 14% in 1997 (European Parliament and the Council 2001). The European target is broken down into national targets for each Member State. Member States have implemented different national support schemes for achieving their target. While the schemes are different, the impact on electricity wholesale markets is generally the same. Electricity generation from renewable power plants is only subject to plant and resource availability and not to market prices as these plants have either negligible variable costs or

---

[5] The load factor LF is defined as $LF = \sum_{t=1}^{T} P_t/(Pmax \cdot T)$, where P_t is the generation output during time interval t, $Pmax$ is the installed peak capacity, and T is the number of time intervals t. A similar measure is the number of full-load hours FLH defined as $FLH = \sum_{t=1}^{T} P_t/Pmax$.

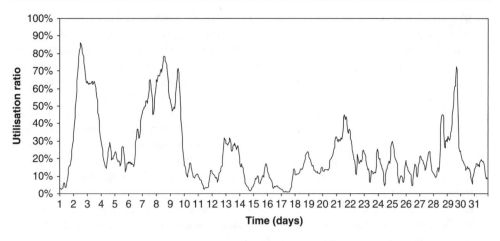

Figure 4.7 Variability in wind production pattern in Germany

they receive feed-in tariffs exceeding their variable costs. Hence, they reduce demand, which would otherwise have to be met by freely dispatchable plants participating in the wholesale electricity market. In most countries, the costs of renewable electricity production is not reflected in wholesale electricity market prices. However, in the United Kingdom, Italy, and Poland, electricity producers are required to have a certain share of renewable energy in their total electricity production, or have to submit an equivalent amount of certificates from renewable energy generation. The extent of these price impacts strongly depend on the details of the national support schemes for renewables and have to be appropriately reflected in fundamental market models. In general, the impact of renewables on electricity markets will gain in importance with increasing production shares of renewable energy in Europe.

Price Drivers on the Supply Side

Figure 4.2 on page 133 shows the main price drivers on the supply side. The most important one is the composition of the generation system. It is not static but changes and develops over time. Old, uneconomic plants are closed and new ones are opened. The long-term development of a generation system is influenced by multiple factors including resource availability, load development, electricity and fuel prices, technological development, development of investment and operational costs, politics, and market structure.

In an existing generation system, the supply curve can be influenced by the market structure and the behaviour of single market participants. In markets with perfect competition, all players will bid on the basis of short run marginal costs. In oligopolic or monopolic markets, a strategic behaviour can be rational instead. This can lead to offers above or below short run marginal costs. Strategic behaviour can have a broad variety of motivations and therefore it is difficult to assess or reflect in a model. Game theory is one approach (see section 4.3.4), but strategic behaviour is only considered on a pure economic basis and assumes more or less perfect information. Another modelling approach that does reflect strategic decisions is system dynamics (see section 4.3.3).

Additional price drivers on the supply side, which have to be considered in fundamental market models, are:

- *Weather*: Weather has several impacts on the available generation output and to a lesser extent on generation costs. The output of photovoltaic systems directly depends on solar radiation. The output of wind turbines depends on wind speeds. The production from run-of-river plants depends on river flow rates, which are influenced by precipitation. The natural inflow into hydro storage plants depends on precipitation as well, but is also influenced by snow and glacier melt and evaporation and seepage rates.

  Conventional thermal and nuclear plants require cooling water. If this water is taken from rivers, maximum generation output as well as efficiency can depend on river flow rates and water temperatures. Where there are environmental restrictions for maximum water withdrawal and heat discharge to the rivers, this can restrict generation output during hot or dry periods. Maximum generation output and efficiency of open cycle gas turbines and CCGTs depend significantly on outside air temperatures and to a lesser degree on air humidity. Lower air temperatures enable higher efficiencies and increase the maximum generation output. Costs for inland transport by barge can depend on river water levels and can influence overall fuel costs.

- *Plant availability*: Besides the environmental conditions mentioned above, plant availability is reduced by planned outages for maintenance and by unplanned outages. Where possible, planned outages are scheduled to occur during times with low electricity demand and low market prices. Unplanned outages are stochastic events distributed uniformly over the year. The probability of unplanned outages is slightly higher after longer shutdowns and might also depend on environmental conditions and authorisation constraints.

- *Fuel prices*: Under the assumption of perfect markets every power plant will offer electricity in the spot market at short run marginal cost. For conventional thermal power plants, fuel costs are the primary factor in these short-run variable costs. Fuel costs can be derived from world market fuel prices (e.g. coal prices in ARA; see section 1.3.2) plus costs for transport to the power station. There are many exceptions. Gas fired power plants may have individual long-term supply contracts including take-or-pay quantities. Lignite or coal mines can be owned by the generation company. In these cases, variable fuel costs can be a result of internal cost calculations.

  Operators of nuclear plants often have long-term fuel contracts lasting several years. Therefore, uranium world market prices might not be relevant for individual operators.

- *CO_2 prices*: Since the introduction of the European Emissions Trading Scheme (EU ETS) in the EU in 2005, CO_2 emission allowances have become a new production factor (see section 1.5). Specific emission factors depend on the fuel type and on plant efficiency. Plant operators receive a certain amount of emission allowances for free. This allocation is regulated by national allocation plans (NAPs), which differ from country to country. As the CO_2 emission allowances from free allocation can be sold, CO_2 prices are considered as opportunity costs for plant dispatch decisions.

- *Emission constraints*: In certain European countries (e.g. the UK, France, and Italy), emission constraints, especially on SO_2 emissions, impact power plant dispatch and therefore wholesale market prices.

- *Operational constraints*: Minimum up- and down times, restrictions on load change rates, start-up costs, and other technical constraints impact plant dispatch (see section 4.2). Further constraints can be imposed by the grid operator. Some plants have to be dispatched for network stability reasons. Another type of plant with operational constraints are combined heat and power plants (CHPs). In this case, commitments for serving heat demands impact electricity generation. Supply alternatives (e.g. heat-only boilers) have to be considered.

- *Reserve markets*: For system stability reasons, generation reserves in different qualities are required to balance short deviations between generation and demand (see section 1.4.3). In many countries, there are markets for these system services. Generation capacity allocated for reserve provision cannot take part in the energy market. This has an important impact on the dispatch of these power plants. Owing to their ability to change generation output with high gradients, hydro power plants are often used for reserve provision, which significantly changes their dispatch pattern. Often, storage and pumped storage hydro power plants are also dispatched at times of low demand to a certain degree for providing negative reserve capacity. In Figure 4.5, these impacts are not depicted.

    Positive tertiary reserve can also be provided by interruptible loads on the demand side, but generally the fraction of reserves provided by the demand side is small compared to those provided by the supply side. In Figure 4.2, the interaction between demand side and reserve markets is indicated by a dotted line.

- *Transmission tariffs*: In some European countries, power plant operators have to pay transmission tariffs for generation or for consumption in hydro storage pumps. These tariffs have in some cases an energy (i.e. production related) component and they might vary over time (ETSO 2005).

4.1.3 Interconnections

The European electricity market is a non-uniform market that is composed of different regional markets with different delivery points or zones for which different prices are recorded (see section 1.4.4). Market regions are physically interconnected by transmission lines. Consequently, market prices in different regions can influence each other. The interconnected European network is divided into regional balancing zones, which cover in most cases the geographical area of individual transmission system operators (TSOs). Physical network constraints within one balancing zone are generally handled by the TSO via redispatching measures and do not affect trading activities. Between some neighbouring balancing zones (e.g. in Germany) there are no transmission limits that would restrict trading activities. In most cases, a transmission restriction occurs at borders between countries. If a transmission restriction between zones exists transmission rights are generally auctioned by the TSOs to the market participants. Capacity limits and the design of capacity allocation procedures impact the demand and supply side and therefore wholesale electricity market prices in affected zones. Physical energy flows between countries in Europe during 2005 are depicted in Figure 4.8.

4.2 ECONOMIC POWER PLANT DISPATCH

For building fundamental market models, it is necessary to understand how power plants are dispatched and which parameters are considered in dispatch decisions. In this section, we will discuss how economic power plant dispatch can be modelled.

Economic power plant dispatch can have two different objectives:

- *Minimisation of total operating costs*: In a situation where a given load has to be met (e.g. after the closure of the spot market to serve the customer load or other electricity sales),

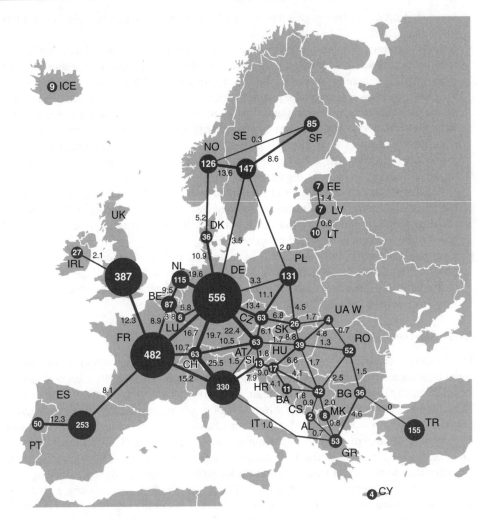

Figure 4.8 Consumption and international electricity exchange in Europe 2005 in TWh. Source: UCTE, NORDEL, VDN

the total variable generation costs have to be minimised. Costs in this sense include all direct costs as well as opportunity costs, e.g. for CO_2 certificates or for the use of water from hydro reservoirs.

- *Maximisation of profit margins in the electricity wholesale market*: This is the normal framework for a producer with a small market share in the mid term where he optimises and hedges his generation revenues by trading on the forward markets for electricity and fuels (see section 6.1.2).

The mathematical depiction of plant characteristics is similar in both cases; however, the objective function is different. In the second situation with profit margin maximisation, units can generally be modelled independently unless there are overall constraints, e.g. emission limits, reserve requirements or connections between generation units in interlinked hydro systems. In the following subsections, we consider both planning objectives and describe appropriate optimisation methods.

Economic dispatch has been the main issue in the electric power industry since the establishment of interconnected networks and is covered by many textbooks and scientific publications (see, e.g., Sheble and Fahd 1994; Sen and Kothari 1998; Bhattacharya *et al.* 2001; Stoft 2002; Weber 2005). In this section, the focus is to give an overview of the most important aspects relevant to understanding electricity market fundamentals.

4.2.1 Thermal Power Plants

In this section, we describe the main constraints for modelling of thermal power plants including load dependent heat rates, variable start-up costs, minimum load, maximum up- and downtimes, maximum load change rates, and reserve requirements. Other restrictions like emission limits, take-or-pay quantities or additional operational constraints for combined heat and power plants (CHPs), will be considered briefly. The formulation below does not cover all technical, operational, and financial constraints at a single plant level, but from a market perspective is sufficient for most practical applications. One further simplification is the (piecewise) linear approximation of non-linear constraints, which is generally sufficient as well. The linear approximation increases problem solvability and allows the use of standard optimisation methods including mixed integer programming (MIP).

Indices, Parameters, and Variables

For the notation of symbols we use the following conventions: parameters and indices are printed in italic font (e.g. parameter $Pmax_g$ or index t). Variables are printed in roman font (e.g. $P_{g,t}$). Discrete variables are printed in overlined roman font (e.g. $\overline{B}_{g,t}$). The index $t^{\leftarrow1}$ refers to the time interval previous to t. We assume hourly time resolution. For simplicity marginal effects at the beginning and at the end of the modelling horizon are neglected.

Thermal power plants are modelled as single generation units g. The smallest element we consider is one unit. A power plant can consist of several units, which might have different characteristics. Sometimes it is possible to depict units with similar characteristics by one modelled unit. The state of one unit g during time interval t is described by the following variables:

- $\overline{B}_{g,t}$ is the binary operation variable. It has the value 1 if the unit g is running and otherwise the value 0.
- $\overline{A}_{g,t}$ is the binary start-up variable. For the time interval t during which the state of a unit changes from off-line to on-line, it has the value 1 and for all other time intervals the value 0.
- $P_{g,t}$ is the electric power output of the unit g during the interval t.

Capacity Constraints and Start-Up Variables

The main constraint of a thermal unit is its capacity constraint (equation (4.1)). It limits the electric power $P_{g,t}$ to the maximum power $Pmax_g$ if the unit is turned on ($\overline{B}_{g,t} = 1$) and otherwise to 0. Thermal units further have a minimum output $Pmin_g$ below which stable operation is not possible. This constraint is reflected by equation (4.2). The unit has to run at least with the electric power $Pmin_g$ or it has to be switched off ($\overline{B}_{g,t} = 0$).

$$P_{g,t} \leq \overline{B}_{g,t} \cdot Pmax_g \qquad \forall(g, t)^6 \tag{4.1}$$

$$P_{g,t} \geq \overline{B}_{g,t} \cdot Pmin_g \qquad \forall(g, t). \tag{4.2}$$

The start-up variable $\overline{A}_{g,t}$ must have the value 1 if the status of a unit g changes from off-line in time interval $t^{\leftarrow 1}$ to on-line in time t as defined in equation (4.3). As in most cases plant start-up is associated with start-up costs (see equation (4.8)) generally no further constraints are required to ensure that $\overline{A}_{g,t}$ has the value 0 in all other time intervals.

$$\overline{A}_{g,t} \geq \overline{B}_{g,t} - \overline{B}_{g,t^{\leftarrow 1}} \qquad \forall(g, t) \tag{4.3}$$

Minimum Up- and Downtimes

Many thermal plants have restrictions on the frequency of start-ups and shut-downs introduced to prevent risks of system failure or damage or for other technological reasons. These restrictions are modelled with minimum uptimes Tup_g and minimum downtimes $Tdown_g$ and the two constraints

$$\overline{A}_{g,t} \cdot Tup_g \leq \sum_{\tau=t}^{t+Tup_g-1} \overline{B}_{g,\tau} \qquad \forall(g, t) \tag{4.4}$$

and

$$\overline{A}_{g,t} \cdot Tdown_g \leq \sum_{\tau=t-Tdown_g}^{t-1} (1 - \overline{B}_{g,\tau}) \qquad \forall(g, t). \tag{4.5}$$

If the start-up variable $\overline{A}_{g,t}$ has the value 1 in time interval t (i.e. the unit was off-line in time interval $t^{\leftarrow 1}$ and changed its status to on-line in time interval t) then the sum of the operations variables $\overline{B}_{g,\tau}$ over the duration of the minimum uptime Tup_g after t has to be equivalent to Tup_g. Corresponding considerations are valid for the minimum downtime: the operation variable $\overline{B}_{g,\tau}$ has to be 0 for the time period of $Tdown_g$ before a start-up.

Maximum Ramp Rates

To avoid wear due to thermal stress, for most thermal power plants, restrictions for load change apply. These restrictions can be different for different operation points between minimum and maximum load $Pmin_g$ and $Pmax_g$ and different for increasing and decreasing of the load. Here we consider one constant maximum ramp rate DP_g. The load $P_{g,t}$ (i.e. the generation output or power) in time interval t cannot differ by more than $\pm DP_g$ from the load $P_{g,t^{\leftarrow 1}}$ in the previous time interval $t^{\leftarrow 1}$ (i.e. $P_{g,t} \leq P_{g,t^{\leftarrow 1}} + DP_g$ and $P_{g,t} \geq P_{g,t^{\leftarrow 1}} - DP_g$).

---

[6] $\forall(g, t)$: for all generation units g that are part of the economic dispatch problem and for all time intervals t in the optimisation period.

It has to be ensured that a unit can be started or switched off even if DP_g is smaller than the minimum power *Pmin*. In these situations where $\overline{B}_{g,t\leftarrow 1}=0$ or $\overline{B}_{g,t}=0$, respectively, the maximum load change is not DP_g but rather $\max(DP_g, Pmin_g)$. This potentially higher load change than DP_g is enabled by the expressions $+(1-\overline{B}_{g,t\leftarrow 1})\cdot\max(0, Pmin_g-DP_g)$ and $-(1-\overline{B}_{g,t})\cdot\max(0, Pmin_g-DP_g)$ in equations (4.6) and (4.7), respectively.

$$P_{g,t}\leq P_{g,t\leftarrow 1}+DP_g+(1-\overline{B}_{g,t\leftarrow 1})\cdot\max(0, Pmin_g-DP_g)\qquad \forall(g,t) \qquad (4.6)$$

$$P_{g,t}\geq P_{g,t\leftarrow 1}-DP_g-(1-\overline{B}_{g,t})\cdot\max(0, Pmin_g-DP_g)\qquad \forall(g,t). \qquad (4.7)$$

In economic dispatch models with high time resolution, it might be necessary to consider generation curves for the start-up process before the minimum stable load $Pmin_g$ is reached as the generation output of a unit in reality does not jump from 0 to $Pmin_g$ instantaneously. The same consideration holds for the shutdown process.

Variable Operation Cost

The aim of economic plant dispatch is the minimisation of operation costs or the maximisation of the profit margin. In both cases, the variable operation costs C have to be determined. In practice, many components and aspects have to be considered for deriving good estimates for variable operation costs and their dependence on plant dispatch. For modelling purposes, we consider two cost components: start-up costs $CA_{g,t}$ and variable operation costs $CP_{g,t}=f_g(P_{g,t})$, which depend on generation output $P_{g,t}$. It is not easy for plant operators to calculate the start-up costs and the operation cost function. It is even more difficult to estimate these costs for generation units of other operators participating in the market for modelling purposes (see section 4.4). The main aspects that have to be considered are fuel and CO_2 costs, heat rate (i.e. efficiency), and variable maintenance costs. Here we assume that variable start-up costs and the operation cost function $f_g(P_{g,t})$ are known.

In the easiest case, start-up costs are considered to have a constant value cA_g. In this case,

$$CA_{g,t}=cA_g\cdot\overline{A}_{g,t}\quad \forall(g,t). \qquad (4.8)$$

Generally, the operation cost function $f_g(P_{g,t})$ is a non-linear curve. In most cases, the approximation by a linear function is possible (see Figure 4.9) with

$$CP_{g,t}=cB_g\cdot\overline{B}_{g,t}+cV_g\cdot P_{g,t}\quad \forall(g,t). \qquad (4.9)$$

The parameter cV_g is the slope of the linear approximation k of the cost function **f** in Figure 4.9. Generally, parameters cA_g, cB_g, and cV_g are time dependent. The time dependency is neglected here.

The total operation cost for the modelling horizon can now be derived as

$$C=\sum_{g,t}(CA_{g,t}+CP_{g,t}) \qquad (4.10)$$

or

$$C=\sum_{g,t}(cA_g\cdot\overline{A}_{g,t}+cB_g\cdot\overline{B}_{g,t}+cV_g\cdot P_{g,t}). \qquad (4.11)$$

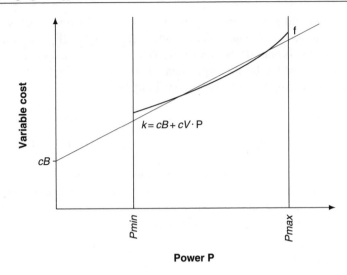

Figure 4.9   Linear approximation of the operation cost function

If the approximation of the operation cost function $f_g(P_{g,t})$ with one single straight line is not sufficient, a piecewise linear approximation is possible to improve accuracy.

Idle Time Dependent Start-Up Costs

Start-up costs may be dependent on the duration of idleness before the start-up. With longer duration of idleness, the start-up costs increase as the boiler cools down further and more heat is required to warm it up again. Therefore, the approximation equation (4.8) might not be adequate but a more precise depiction is possible with only a few additional equations. Figure 4.10 shows a start-up cost curve.

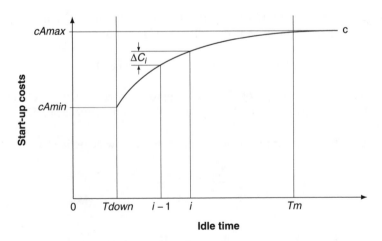

Figure 4.10   Dependence of start-up costs on previous idle time

For every start-up, costs of at least $cAmin$ are incurred. For long idle times prior to the start-up, the start-up costs reach $cAmax$ asymptotically. After an idle time Tm the start-up costs can be considered as constant. If the idle time is increased from $i-1$ to i time intervals, the start-up costs increase by ΔC_i. For an idle time of τ before a start-up ($Tdown + 1 \leq \tau \leq Tm$), the total costs CAn for this start-up are

$$\text{CAn} = cAmin + \sum_{i=Tdown+1}^{\tau} \Delta C_i. \tag{4.12}$$

The fixed component $cAmin$ of the start-up costs is allocated to the time interval in which the start-up takes place, the additional component $\sum_{i=Tdown+1}^{\tau} \Delta C_i$ to time intervals prior to the start-up:

- The variable $CA_{g,t}$ is defined as a positive variable (see equation (4.13)). It does not reflect the total costs for one start-up but only the part of the start-up costs allocated to interval t.
- The minimum start-up cost $cAmin_g$ is allocated to the time interval in which the start-up takes place (see equation (4.14)).
- All remaining start-up costs are allocated to the time intervals of the idle time ($\overline{B}_{g,t} = 0$) prior to the start-up that are more than $Tdown_g$ before the start-up and not more than Tm_g before the start-up (see equation (4.15)).
- If the unit g is idle in time interval t ($\overline{B}_{g,t} = 0$) and τ time intervals later a start-up occurs for the first time ($Tdown_g \leq \tau \leq Tm_g$) the variable $CA_{g,t}$ will have the value $\Delta C_{g,\tau}$ of the incremental start-up costs (see equation (4.15)). The term $-\overline{B}_{g,t} \cdot cAmax_g$ in equation (4.15) ensures that the right part of the equation is negative if the unit g is in operation in time interval t ($\overline{B}_{g,t} = 1$). These equations apply if incremental start-up costs $\Delta C_{g,i}$ are decreasing with increasing idle time (see equation (4.16)).

$$CA_{g,t} \geq 0 \quad \forall(g, t) \tag{4.13}$$

$$CA_{g,t} \geq A_{g,t} \cdot cAmin_g \quad \forall(g, t) \tag{4.14}$$

$$CA_{g,t} \geq \overline{A}_{g,t+i} \cdot \Delta C_{g,i} - \overline{B}_{g,t} \cdot cAmax_g \quad \forall(g, t, i) | Tdown_g < i \leq Tm_g \tag{4.15}$$

$$\Delta C_{g,i+1} \leq \Delta C_{g,i} \quad \forall(g, i) | Tdown_g < i < Tm_g. \tag{4.16}$$

Equation (4.11) for total variable costs is now replaced by

$$C = \sum_{g,t} (CA_{g,t} + cB_g \cdot \overline{B}_{g,t} + cV_g \cdot P_{g,t}). \tag{4.17}$$

Reserve Constraints

For system stability reasons, the provision of positive and negative reserve capacity in different qualities is required (see section 1.4.3). For simplicity reasons, we consider one positive reserve quality with the capacity $Rtotal_t$. An idle unit g ($\overline{B}_{g,t} = 0$) can contribute with a maximum value of RS_g to the reserve. For nuclear power stations and other large thermal power stations, this value is 0. If a unit g is in operation ($\overline{B}_{g,t} = 1$) the maximum reserve contribution is RB_g as ramp rates limit the flexibility. Further, the reserve contribution is limited to the difference between present power $P_{g,t}$ and maximum power $Pmax_g$. Limits for the reserve contribution $R_{g,t}$ of unit g depend on its operation state

$$R_{g,t} \leq Pmax_g - P_{g,t} \quad \forall(g,t) \tag{4.18}$$

and

$$R_{g,t} \leq \overline{B}_{g,t} \cdot RB_g + (1 - \overline{B}_{g,t}) \cdot RS_g \quad \forall(g,t). \tag{4.19}$$

We also ensure that the sum of all reserve contributions is sufficient by

$$\sum_g R_{g,t} \geq Rtotal_t \quad \forall t. \tag{4.20}$$

Time-Integral Constraints

Besides the time-integral constraints imposed by minimum up- and downtimes (equations (4.4) and (4.5)), further time-integral constraints are relevant including annual emission or heat discharge limits to rivers, or take-or-pay contracts for fuels. As an example, we consider upper fuel limits $Fmax_g$ and lower fuel limits $Fmin_g$. We assume that the fuel consumption depends linearly on the number of start-ups, the number of operation hours, and the energy produced. For describing this dependency, we introduce linear parameters fA_g and fB_g and fV_g, respectively, and receive as approximation for the cumulative fuel consumption F_g

$$F_g = \sum_t (fA_g \cdot \overline{A}_{g,t} + fB_g \cdot \overline{B}_{g,t} + fV_g \cdot P_{g,t}) \quad \forall g. \tag{4.21}$$

Upper and lower limits can be formulated as

$$F_g \leq Fmax_g \quad \forall g \tag{4.22}$$

and

$$F_g \geq Fmin_g \quad \forall g. \tag{4.23}$$

CHP Constraints

For economic dispatch of combined heat and power plants (CHPs), not only the electricity generation $P_{g,t}$ but also the heat flow $Q_{g,t}$ have to be considered. In most cases, the ratio between electricity generation and heat flow can be varied to a certain degree. For short-term optimisation, the complete range of possible operation points in a P-Q chart and associated variable costs for each point generally has to be taken into account. Further, there may be a variety of other heat supply and heat storage options that have to be considered. For market models, it is often difficult to find detailed information on CHP systems. The most significant impact of CHP is a reduction of maximum electric power by $PredCHP_{g,t}$, which, in most cases, can be considered dependent on season and weather or, more generally, time dependent (equation (4.24)). Further, a minimum forced generation output might apply, which is also time dependent (equation (4.25)).

$$P_{g,t} \leq Pmax_g - PredCHP_{g,t} \quad \forall(g,t) \tag{4.24}$$

$$P_{g,t} \geq PminCHP_{g,t} \quad \forall(g,t). \tag{4.25}$$

For mid-term planning, these approximations may be sufficient as well. If time-integral fuel or emission restrictions exist, additional fuel consumption or emissions due to heat generation $Q_{g,t}$ have to be taken into account.

Objective Functions

The objective of short-term planning after the closure of the day ahead market is to meet the load L_t at minimum total variable cost C derived by equation (4.11) or (4.17). The load balance equation is

$$\sum_g P_{g,t} \geq L_t \quad \forall t \tag{4.26}$$

and the objective function[7] is

$$C = \sum_{g,t}(CA_{g,t} + cB_g \cdot \overline{B}_{g,t} + cV_g \cdot P_{g,t}) \overset{!}{=} min. \tag{4.27}$$

The load balance equation (4.26) could be formulated as well as an equality constraint, but the formulation as an inequality constraint is more common as it helps to avoid infeasibility. For the mid-term planning in liquid markets, the objective is to maximise profit margins M between variable generation cost and generation revenues at expected spot market prices S_t. In this case, the load balance equation (4.26) does not apply and the objective function is

$$M = \sum_t(S_t \cdot \sum_g P_{g,t}) - C \overset{!}{=} max. \tag{4.28}$$

If no reserve constraints (see equation (4.20)) or other constraints affecting more than one power plant apply, the optimisation problem can be decomposed by plant and formulated and solved for each plant separately. This has implications on the optimisation methods that can be used (see section 4.2.3).

4.2.2 Hydro Power Plants

Hydro storage and hydro pumped storage power plants can be dispatched freely within certain technical constraints.[8] While the dispatch of thermal power plants is mainly influenced by

---

[7] For reflecting the time value of money, a discount factor d_t can be introduced in the objective function. In this case, equation (4.27) has to be modified to:

$$C = \sum_{g,t}(d_t \cdot (CA_{g,t} + cB_g \cdot \overline{B}_{g,t} + cV_g \cdot P_{g,t})) \overset{!}{=} min$$

For simplicity, we neglect the discount factor in all equations in this chapter. If required it can be inserted in the same way into the other objective functions (4.28) and (4.35).

[8] Run-of-river hydro power plants are not considered here as their production patterns are only determined by the river flow rates and are not influenced by economic power plant dispatch.

specific variable generation costs, the main criteria for the dispatch of hydro power plants is the optimal use of limited reservoir contents.

Here we present a general formulation of the economic dispatch problem for interlinked hydraulic systems (see Figure 4.6). This formulation is also applicable for stand-alone hydro storage or pumped storage power plants as they can be interpreted as specific (simple) cases of an interlinked hydraulic system. First, we have to describe the topology of the hydraulic system and the main characteristics of its elements:

- Reservoirs r: for modelling purposes we can describe reservoirs by the following parameters and variables:

  - $Vmax_r$: maximum volume of the reservoir r that can be utilised. For simplicity, we assume that this parameter and most other technical parameters do not depend on time t.
  - $Qin_{r,t}$: natural inflow into reservoir r in time interval t. It is appropriate to use expected values; it may be more appropriate to reflect the stochastic nature of this parameter by the use of scenarios.
  - $V_{r,t}$: reservoir content at the end of time interval t (positive variable).
  - $Qr_{r,t}$: race water flow rate (positive variable). This variable is needed to allow an overflow when the reservoir exceeds the maximum level. There may be restrictions for race water flow rates; however, these restrictions are neglected here.

- Hydro power stations h: These elements in the model can contain pumps as well as turbines. One power station can consist of several separate units, but it is often possible to depict all hydro turbines in one hydro power station as one single model element. Hydro power stations h can be described by:

  - $PTmax_{h,t}$: maximum available cumulative electric power of the turbines in power station h.
  - $PPmax_{h,t}$: maximum available cumulative electric power of the pumps in power station h.
  - QT_h: specific flow rate per electric turbine power output.
  - QP_h: specific flow rate per electric pump power input.
  - $PT_{h,t}$: electric turbine power output (positive variable).
  - $PP_{h,t}$: electric pump power input (positive variable).[9]

- Hydraulic connections between reservoirs r and power stations h: In the following equations, we will use the index $hup(r)$ for all power stations that are located directly above reservoir r and the index $hdown(r)$ for all power stations that are located directly below reservoir r.

Figure 4.11 summarises all variables and parameters for modelling hydro power plants.

---

[9] In most cases, pumps can only be switched on or off but not freely regulated to a certain power input. This restriction can be modelled by the introduction of discrete variables. As this restriction is generally not relevant for market models it is neglected here for simplicity reasons.

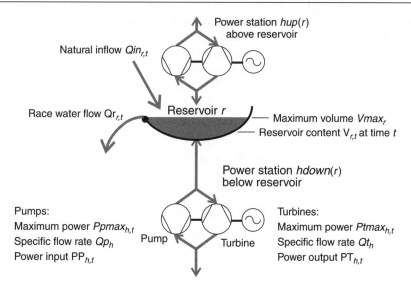

Figure 4.11   Variables and parameters for modelling hydro power plants.

In general, maximum power $PTmax_{h,t}$ and the specific flow rates QT_h and QP_h depend on the reservoir levels $V_{r,t}$ of the upper and the lower reservoir. Further, specific flow rates of turbines QT_h also depend on the power output $PT_{h,t}$ and the number of turbines in operation (i.e. $QT_h = f(PT_{h,t})$). A similar consideration is valid for pumps. For keeping the model formulation linear, we assume constant parameters. While this approximation is generally appropriate for market models, it may be necessary to consider more accurate approximations of these functions (e.g. piecewise linear approximations and operation states of single turbines or pumps) for short-term planning models. Water travel time between reservoirs is also assumed to be negligible. They might be relevant for hydraulic systems with several reservoirs on one river and can be included in a linear model formulation (see Graeber 2002).

Volume units for the reservoir content and the flow rates (e.g. m^3 and m^3/h) are commonly used, although the use of energy units (e.g. MWh and MW) are also common but can be slightly confusing.

Reservoir Balance

The main equation for hydro power plants is the reservoir balance equation

$$
\begin{aligned}
V_{r,t} = {} & V_{r,t-1} + Qin_{r,t} - Qr_{r,t} \\
& + \sum_{hup(r)} (QT_{hup(r)} \cdot PT_{hup(r),t}) + \sum_{hdown(r)} (QP_{hdown(r)} \cdot PP_{hdown(r),t}) \\
& - \sum_{hdown(r)} (QT_{hdown(r)} \cdot PT_{hdown(r),t}) - \sum_{hup(r)} (QP_{hup(r)} \cdot PP_{hup(r),t}) \\
& \forall (r, t).
\end{aligned}
\tag{4.29}
$$

The reservoir content $V_{r,t}$ at the end of time interval t is equivalent to the content at the end of the previous interval $t^{\leftarrow 1}$ plus the natural inflows $Qin_{r,t}$ and inflows from turbines above $\sum_{hup(r)} (QT_{hup(r)} \cdot PT_{hup(r),t})$ as well as pumps below $\sum_{hdown(r)} (QP_{hdown(r)} \cdot PP_{hdown(r),t})$ minus race water flows $Qr_{r,t}$ and outflows to turbines below $\sum_{hdown(r)} (QT_{hdown(r)} \cdot PT_{hdown(r),t})$ as well as to pumps above $\sum_{hup(r)} (QP_{hup(r)} \cdot PP_{hup(r),t})$.

Constraints

Upper limits for the reservoir content $V_{r,t}$ as well as for the turbine power output $PT_{h,t}$ and the pump power input $PP_{h,t}$ are

$$V_{r,t} \leq Vmax_r \quad \forall (r, t), \tag{4.30}$$

$$PT_{h,t} \leq PTmax_{h,t} \quad \forall (h, t) \tag{4.31}$$

and

$$PP_{h,t} \leq PPmax_{h,t} \quad \forall (h, t). \tag{4.32}$$

Further constraints have to be formulated for fixing the reservoir content to its initial and final value at the beginning and end of the modelling period. In the case of daily or weekly reservoir cycles, it is possible to introduce an equation that forces the initial and final reservoir content to be equal instead of fixing it to explicit values. For simplicity reasons, we do not include these constraints for initial and final reservoir contents here.

Not only thermal power plants but also hydro power plants can participate in the provision of positive and negative reserve capacity. Again, for simplicity reasons we consider only one positive reserve quality with the capacity $Rtotal_t$ and assume that all turbines and pumps are flexible enough to contribute to the total free turbine capacity $PTmax_{h,t} - PT_{h,t}$ and the present pump power $PP_{h,t}$ in providing this reserve quality. If thermal as well as hydro units participate in the reserve provision equation (4.20) is enhanced to

$$\sum_g R_{g,t} + \sum_h (PTmax_{h,t} - PT_{h,t} + PP_{h,t}) \geq Rtotal_t \quad \forall t. \tag{4.33}$$

Objective Functions

The objective of short-term planning after the closure of the day ahead market is to meet the load L_t at minimum total variable cost C of the thermal generation units derived in section 4.2.1. In the case of a system with thermal and hydro units, these costs remain the same. Therefore, the objective function (4.27) itself remains unchanged. In the load balance equation of the thermal system (4.26), net hydro generation $\sum_h (PT_{h,t} - PP_{h,t})$ has to be added to receive

$$\sum_g P_{g,t} + \sum_h (PT_{h,t} - PP_{h,t}) \geq L_t \quad \forall t. \tag{4.34}$$

If the objective is to maximise profit margins M, net hydro generation $\sum_h(PT_{h,t} - PP_{h,t})$ has to be added to the objective function (4.28) for the thermal system. We obtain

$$M = \sum_t \left[S_t \cdot \left(\sum_g P_{g,t} + \sum_h (PT_{h,t} - PP_{h,t}) \right) \right] - C \stackrel{!}{=} \max. \qquad (4.35)$$

It is possible to decompose this optimisation problem into several smaller problems representing parts of the generation system that can be optimised independently from the rest of the system if no overlapping constraints exist.

4.2.3 Optimisation Methods

For solving the economic power plant dispatch problem, different optimisation methods can be applied. Here we concentrate on the most common methods including linear and mixed integer programming, dynamic programming, and decomposition approaches. More comprehensive descriptions can be found in standard operations research or optimisation textbooks (e.g. Chong and Zak 2001; Hillier and Lieberman 2004; Winston 2003). Examples of the application of optimisation methods for swing option and virtual storage pricing are described in sections 2.6.3 and 2.6.4.

Linear and Mixed Integer Programming

Linear optimisation problems (LP-problems[10]) consist of a linear objective function and linear constraints. The profit maximisation problem for hydro power plants formulated above is an example of a linear programming problem.

In matrix form with the vector $\mathbf{x}$ of all variables, the parameter vectors $\mathbf{c}$ and $\mathbf{b}$ and the parameter matrix $\mathbf{A}$ the problem can be expressed as:

$$\mathbf{c}^T\mathbf{x} \stackrel{!}{=} \max$$

$$\mathbf{A}\mathbf{x} \le \mathbf{b}$$

$$\mathbf{x} \ge 0.$$

For solving LP-problems, several algorithms have been developed. The most common one is the simplex algorithm. Faster but often less robust methods include interior point algorithms. With these algorithms LP-problems with several millions of variables can be solved efficiently. Generally, the time required for solving a problem can be predicted reasonably well.

If some of the variables $\mathbf{x}$ are required to have integer values the problem is a mixed integer programming (MIP) problem. The problem formulation for our thermal power plants include binary operation and start-up variables and therefore it is an MIP problem.

MIP problems are generally solved with branch and bound or branch and cut algorithms. Large-scale MIP problems with a large number of integer variables are difficult to solve. Solver time can increase almost exponentially with the number of binary variables. Slight

---

[10] LP: linear programming

changes in the data can result in huge changes in required solver time (e.g. a few minutes versus several hours). Therefore, it is very difficult to predict solver times. For this reason, MIP problems are often not solved until a proven optimum is reached. Often, only a feasible solution that is reached within a given time limit or that is within a defined distance from the optimum is generated.

Several commercial development environments are available for the efficiently formulating and solving LP or MIP problems.[11] Within these environments, several optimisation algorithms and solvers can be selected.

Dynamic Programming

Often, it is not possible to solve large-scale optimisation problems within an acceptable time with standard algorithms. If the problem structure allows a decomposition into smaller subproblems which can be solved sequentially solution times can be reduced significantly. One approach that can be used for power plant dispatch problems is dynamic programming.

An optimisation problem can be solved by dynamic programming algorithms if it has the following characteristics:

- The optimisation problem can be divided into several stages n. In economic power plant dispatch problems, for every time interval a new dispatch decision can be taken. Therefore, every time interval can be considered a separate stage.
- In every stage n, a finite number of discrete states s_n can be reached. For example, for thermal power plants there could be three relevant operation states: *switched off, running at minimum power output* and *running at maximum power output*.
- If the system is at state s_n in stage n a discrete number of decisions $x_{n,s}$ is possible. Every decision will transform the system into a new state s_{n+1} in the next stage $n+1$. A transition function T can be introduced for linking the new state s_{n+1} to the previous state s_n and the decision $x_{n,s}$: $s_{n+1} = T(s_n, x_{n,s})$. For example, if a thermal plant is in the state *running at minimum load* and the decision *shut down* is taken then the new state in the next time interval will be *switched off*.
- In all stages n, the optimal sequence of decisions $x_{m,s}$ for this and all later stages $(m \geq n)$ does depend on the state s_n in stage n but not on the sequence of decisions $x_{o,s}$ with $o < m$ that led to the state s_n. This criterion is called the Bellman principle. If we neglect minumum up- and downtimes and if there are no time-integral constraints this criterion is satisfied for our dispatch problem. But if there are, for instance, time-integral upper fuel limits for a power plant, the optimal dispatch decision for future time intervals will depend on the remaining fuel and therefore on the path chosen for reaching a certain operation state. In this case, the Bellman principle would not be satisfied.

If the contribution of decision $x_{n,s}$ to the global objective is $M(s_n, x_{n,s})$ then the global objective function is $f = \sum_n M(s_n, x_{n,s})$. If we are in stage n at state s_n and we consider all further stages as a subproblem then we have a new objective function $f_{n,s} = \sum_m M(s_m, x_{m,s})$ with $m \geq n$. If the Bellman principle is satisfied then the objective value $f_{n,s}^{\star}$ of this objective

---

[11] Common development environments include AIMMS, AMPL, GAMS, Ilog OPL Studio, Lindo, Xpress-MP (Dash).

function and the optimal decision $x_{n,s}^{\star}$ does not depend on decisions in earlier stages. We can formulate

$$f_{n,s}^{\star} = \max_{x_{m,s}} \left[f_{n,s} \right] \quad \text{with} \quad m \geq n$$

$$= \max_{x_{n,s}} \left[M(s_n, x_{n,s}) + f_{n+1,s'}^{\star} \right] \quad \text{with} \quad s' = T(s_n, x_{n,s})$$

$$= M(s_n, x_{n,s}^{\star}) + f_{n+1,s'\star}^{\star} \quad \text{with} \quad s'^{\star} = T(s_n, x_{n,s}^{\star}).$$

This formulation of the Bellman equation can be used for backward recursively solving a dynamic programming problem.

The following adapted travelling salesman example will illustrate the backward recursive approach of dynamic programming algorithms.

Suppose that a salesman has to travel in five days from town A to town J along the road network shown in Figure 4.12. His profit margins M depend on the towns he visits and on the travel expenses to get from one town to the next town. The numbers on the arrows in Figure 4.12 represent the margins he can achieve if he decides to choose one specific path. Owing to the special structure of the problem, we can break it up into five stages n. Stage 1 contains node A, stage 2 contains nodes B, C, and D, stage 3 contains nodes E, F, and G, stage 4 contains nodes H and I, and stage 5 contains node J. The states s in each stage correspond to the names of the nodes. For instance, stage 3 contains states E, F, and G. The decisions $x_{n,s}$ that can be taken are to go to the next town along one of the arrows, e.g. in the first stage *go to B*. The transition matrix $T(s_n, x_{n,s})$, which links a decision $x_{n,s}$ taken in stage n and state s_n with the reached state s_{n+1} in the next stage $n+1$ is straightforward as the name of the decision already contains the state in the next stage.

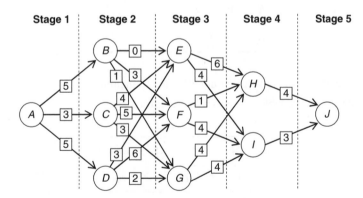

Figure 4.12   Dynamic programming example: road network

If we let s denote a node in stage n and z a node in the next stage $n+1$ and let $f_{n,s}^{\star}$ be the maximum profit that can be obtained on a path from node s to the destination node J, we can write

$$f_{n,s}^{\star} = \max_{z} \left[M_{s,z} + f_{n+1,z}^{\star} \right] \tag{4.36}$$

where $M_{s,z}$ is the profit that can be achieved by the decision to go from s to z. This equation gives us the recursion we need to solve this specific problem. We start at stage 5 where no decision is taken with $f_{5,J}^\star = 0$.

For the other stages, we obtain:

- *Stage 4*: During stage 4, there are no real decisions to make. The salesman has to go to destination J. So we derive:

$$f_{4,H}^\star = 4 \quad \text{by going to } J$$
$$f_{4,I}^\star = 3 \quad \text{by going to } J$$

- *Stage 3*: In this stage, there are more choices. For calculating $f_{3,E}^\star$, we have to make the following considerations. From E it is possible to go to H or I. The immediate profit of going to H is $M_{E,H} = 6$ and the maximum profit in stage 4 at state H is $f_{4,H}^\star = 4$ adding up to a total of 10. The immediate profit of going to I is $M_{E,I} = 4$ and the maximum profit in stage 4 at state I is $f_{4,I}^\star = 3$ adding up to a total of 7. Therefore, from E the best decision is to go to H to obtain a total maximum profit of $f_{3,E}^\star = 10$.
  The following table displays all results:

s_3	$M_{s_3,z_3} + f_{4,z_3}^\star$		$f_{3,s_3}^\star$	Decision:
	H	I		go to
E	10	7	10	H
F	5	7	7	I
G	8	7	8	H

The same calculations have to be done for the remaining stages.

- *Stage 2*: The following table displays all results for stage 2:

s_2	$M_{s_2,z_2} + f_{3,z_2}^\star$			$f_{2,s_2}^\star$	Decision:
	E	F	G		go to
B	10	10	9	10	E or F
C	14	12	11	14	E
D	13	13	10	13	E or F

If we are in node B or D in stage 2 it is possible to take two decisions that lead to the same maximum profit. In many cases, only one best solution is required and therefore most implementations of dynamic programming algorithms record only one of several decisions that lead to identical objective values.

- *Stage 1*: The following table displays all results for stage 1:

s_1	$M_{s_1,z_1} + f^{\star}_{2,z_1}$			$f^{\star}_{1,s_1}$	Decision:
	B	C	D		go to
A	15	17	18	18	D

The optimal value f for this small salesman problem is $f = f^{\star}_{1,A} = 18$ and there are two paths that lead to this result: $A \rightarrow D \rightarrow E \rightarrow H \rightarrow J$ and $A \rightarrow D \rightarrow F \rightarrow I \rightarrow J$.

This small problem could have been solved without more effort by complete enumeration. But for larger problems with discrete decisions, complete enumeration is often not feasible and the benefit of dynamic programming algorithms is significant.

Dynamic programming algorithms can be very efficient for solving economic dispatch problems for single plants with profit maximisation against market prices as objective if they can be formulated without stage-integral constraints. As mentioned above time intervals can be considered as stages. As time-integral constraints exist for thermal as well as for hydro power plants we have to discuss these constraints and have to find an appropriate definition of states that avoids stage-integral constraints violating the Bellman principle.

For applying dynamic programming to a single thermal power plant g, the following constraints have to be considered:

- *Time-integral fuel or emission constraints*: e.g. equation (4.22) or (4.23). If these kinds of constraint exist, the efficient application of dynamic programming algorithms is not straightforward and not necessarily faster than standard LP or MIP algorithms. Therefore, we assume that no such constraints exist.
- *Maximum ramp rates*: Constraints (4.6) and (4.7) introduced by maximum ramp rates can be reflected by defining several reasonable power output levels as separate states but it is not common to consider them in dynamic programming algorithms. If ramp rates are neglected three relevant power output levels have to be considered: no generation $(P = 0)$; generation at minimum load $(P = Pmin)$ and generation at maximum load $(P = Pmax)$. All other power output levels between minimum and maximum load would lead to identical or lower objective values. Identical objective values occur in the case that market prices S_t are identical with incremental variable costs cV.
- *Minimum up- and downtimes*: Constraints (4.4) and (4.5) can be considered by defining states not only by the power output level but as second characteristic also by the time a plant is already in one of the two operation states *on* or *off*.

With these considerations we can define a dynamic programming problem for the profit optimisation of a thermal power plant in the following way:

- *Stages*: Every time interval t is one stage.
- *States*: A state is defined by the power level and the number of time intervals the plant is already in one of the two operation states *on* or *off*. Let's consider a minimum uptime of $Tup = 2$ and a minimum downtime of $Tdown = 3$. If a continuous operation time of Tup is reached or exceeded future decisions do not depend on the duration by which Tup is exceeded. Therefore, all these states can be summarised as one state. Similar

considerations apply to *Tdown*. Therefore, in our example, we have to consider only the following seven states *s* at the end of each time interval:

$s_{0/1}$ the plant is switched off for 1 time interval
$s_{0/2}$ the plant is switched off for 2 time intervals
$s_{0/2+}$ the plant is switched off for 3 or more time intervals
$s_{min/1}$ the plant is running at minimum power and is switched on 1 time interval
$s_{min/1+}$ the plant is running at minimum power and is switched on 2 or more time intervals
$s_{max/1}$ the plant is running at maximum power and is switched on 1 time interval
$s_{max/1+}$ the plant is running at maximum power and is switched on 2 or more time intervals

- *Decision variables*: Generally, in each stage three decisions x have to be considered:

x_0 change to or remain at $P = 0$
x_{min} change to or remain at $P = Pmin$
x_{max} change to or remain at $P = Pmax$

But it has to be ensured that only decisions are possible that do not violate minimum up- or downtime constraints as shown in Table 4.3.

Table 4.3   Dynamic programming transition matrix for thermal power plants

State	Decision x_t					
s_t	x_0		x_{min}		x_{max}	
	$M(t, x_t)$	s_{t+1}	$M(t, x_t)$	s_{t+1}	$M(t, x_t)$	s_{t+1}
$s_{0/1}$	0	$s_{0/2}$	—	—	—	—
$s_{0/2}$	0	$s_{0/2+}$	—	—	—	—
$s_{0/2+}$	0	$s_{0/2+}$	$M1_{t+1} - cA$	$s_{min/1}$	$M2_{t+1} - cA$	$s_{max/1}$
$s_{min/1}$	—	—	$M1_{t+1}+$	$s_{min/1+}$	$M2_{t+1}$	$s_{max/1+}$
$s_{min/1+}$	0	$s_{0/1}$	$M1_{t+1}+$	$s_{min/1+}$	$M2_{t+1}$	$s_{max/1+}$
$s_{max/1}$	—	—	$M1_{t+1}+$	$s_{min/1+}$	$M2_{t+1}$	$s_{max/1+}$
$s_{max/1+}$	0	$s_{0/1}$	$M1_{t+1}+$	$s_{min/1+}$	$M2_{t+1}$	$s_{max/1+}$

- *Profit margins*: The profit $M(t, x_t)$ generated in the stage $t + 1$ depends on decision x taken in stage t and on the current state s_t. The same cost and profit components as in the objective function (4.28) have to be considered here for every stage t.[12] We can

---

[12] The time value of money can be considered by optimising discounted profits $d_t \cdot M(t, x_t)$ with d_t representing the discount factor instead of undiscounted profits $M(t, x_t)$.

summarise these components in the following way: start-up costs cA; profit margin at minimum load $M1_t = Pmin \cdot (S_t - cV) - cB$; profit margin at maximum load $M2_t = Pmax \cdot (S_t - cV) - cB$.

- *Transition matrix*: The transition matrix shown in Table 4.3 describes the new state s_{t+1} in the next stage reached by decision x_t.

Possible decisions x_t (– indicates an infeasible decision), profit margins $M(t, x_t)$ and the new state s_{t+1} reached are shown Table 4.3 and are illustrated by Figure 4.13:

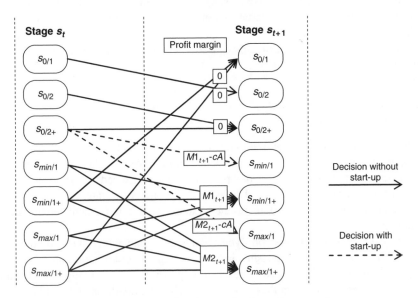

Figure 4.13   Definition of states for thermal power plants

These definitions describe all parameters required for formulating a dynamic programming algorithm for a single thermal power plant.

The economic dispatch problem for single hydro power plants can also be formulated as a dynamic programming problem. In the case of a linear problem formulation as shown in section 4.2.2, only small performance gains compared with LP algorithms can be expected. But in the case of the depiction of non-linearities, dynamic programming algorithms can exhibit significant advantages compared with standard algorithms. The following considerations can be used:

- *Stages*: For hydro power plants operated on a daily or weekly cycle, every time interval t is one stage. For seasonal reservoirs, it might be appropriate to model one day or one week as one stage. In this case, separate subproblems have to be formulated for every stage, which can be solved, e.g., with LP algorithms.
- *States*: Water levels of the upper reservoir can be used to describe states. This continuous variable has to be discretised by identifying relevant discrete levels. For daily or weekly reservoir cycles, it is possible to identify water levels by considering possible changes caused by natural inflow and three reasonable decisions: *no generation, generation at maximum load*, and *pumping at maximum load* (see below). Beginning at the initial

reservoir level it is possible to build a tree to identify all possible states. Upper and lower reservoir levels have to be respected in this process as well as possible race water flows. It is possible to depict the dependency of turbine and pump flow rates on reservoir levels. If a certain number of states (e.g. 20 to 50) are reached in one stage, reservoir levels that are very close to each other are combined to one modelled state to limit the number of states. The resulting approximation is generally small compared to other approximations. The optimal number of modelled states has to be determined by trade-off considerations between computational resources and accuracy. For hydro power plants with seasonal reservoir cycles and daily or weekly stages, states can be formulated by dividing the possible reservoir range into a certain number (e.g. 50 to 100) equidistant stages. Once again this is an approximation.

- *Decision variables*: In the case of daily or weekly reservoir cycles, three decision variables have to be considered:

  - *no generation*
  - *generation at maximum load*
  - *pumping at maximum load*

  In cases where generation or pumping at maximum load would lead to a violation of upper or lower reservoir levels, these decisions have to be interpreted as pumping or generation at maximum possible part-load not to exceed reservoir levels. Maximum generation and pumping load as well as specific flow rates depend on reservoir levels and therefore on the state of the system. This can be depicted in the model formulation.

  In the case of seasonal reservoir cycles, decision variables that have to be considered are to reach each of the states possible in the next stage. Possible stages must be within the range of reservoir levels that can be reached by generating or pumping at maximum load for all time intervals between these stages. In each case, the decision would be to choose the optimal path to reach the specific state in the next stage. This small subproblem could be formulated as an LP-problem and solved with standard solvers.

- *Profit margins*: The profit margins for each decision can be calculated equivalent to the hydro part of equation (4.35) as net electricity generation times wholesale market prices. In the case of several time intervals per stage, this margin has to be optimised.

- *Transition matrix*: For the construction of the decision matrix, approximations in the definition of nodes as discussed above have to be considered.

Decomposition Approaches

As most optimisation algorithms exhibit more than a linear, often almost exponential, increase of solver time with growing size of the optimisation problem, the basic idea of decomposition approaches is to break down the optimisation problem into several smaller subproblems by relaxing all constraints that span more than one subproblem. For meeting these overlapping constraints, additional parameters are introduced in the subproblems, which give incentives to meet these constraints. The most common decomposition approach for economic dispatch problems is the Lagrange relaxation. In this case, a coordinator sends price signals to all subproblems, which can be interpreted as shadow variables for the relaxed constraints (see Figure 4.14). The coordinator adapts these prices until all overlapping constraints are met. While for continuous convex problems this approach leads to a proven optimum, this is not

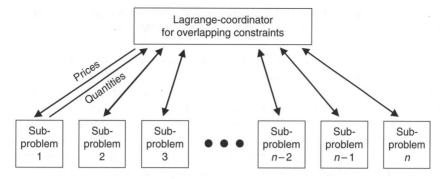

Figure 4.14 Lagrange decomposition approach

the case for problems with integer constraints, which occur in economic dispatch problems including thermal plants. Therefore, the iteration approach has to be designed carefully to avoid suboptimal solutions as well as convergence problems. For decreasing solution time, it is possible to solve subproblems in parallel on several CPUs. But due to the required coordination effort, the performance gains are often less than expected.

For decomposition approaches, it is necessary to decide carefully where the problem can be divided into subproblems most efficiently. For economic dispatch problems, it is often possible to decompose the problem into several subproblems with reduced number of time intervals (e.g. hours or days) or into subproblems considering only single plants.

If a good approximation of the optimal solution is sufficient it is possible in some cases to avoid iterative approaches by applying heuristical approaches for fixing variables affected by overlapping constraints. For example, one could divide the dispatch optimisation problem for one thermal power plant with the aim to optimise market revenues into separate monthly subproblems and neglect the small differences to the optimal solution that might occur at the transition from one month to another.

Heuristics

Heuristics are optimisation algorithms that solve optimisation problems quickly but there is no proof that the solution obtained is the optimal solution or that the solution is within a defined distance from the optimal solution for all possible combinations of parameters. Often, heuristics are based on specific structures of an optimisation problem and have to be adapted or abandoned if the problem structure changes. Most decomposition approaches can be considered as heuristics as well.

Heuristics can often be applied for reducing the problem size by fixing variables for which an easy heuristic solution can be derived. The remaining smaller problem can be solved with standard algorithms. For the economic power plant dispatch problem with cost minimisation as objective, one heuristical approach could be the following:

1. Formulate a linear dispatch problem *LDP* that neglects minimum up- and downtimes (constraints (4.4) and (4.5)) as well as start-up costs cA_g and the minimum output constraint (4.2).

2. Solve the *LDP* with a standard LP algorithm. The result can be considered as approximation of the more complex mixed integer problem *MIDP* without negligence of binary constraints.

3. Analyse the resulting dispatch pattern for every thermal power plant chronologically. If one plant g is continuously in operation for n time intervals before the next shutdown, then if n exceeds the minimum uptime Tup_g by at least x time intervals, one could assume that the power plant would also be dispatched in the precise problem *MIDP* for a number of $n - x$ time intervals in the middle of these n intervals. The operations variables $\bar{B}_{g,t}$ for these $n - x$ time intervals t could be fixed to $\bar{B}_{g,t} = 1$ for step 4. The same consideration could be made for times with continuous power output of 0 that exceeds the minimum downtime $Tdown_g$ by at least y time intervals to fix additional binary variables to $\bar{B}_{g,t} = 0$. The parameters x and y would have to be chosen appropriately in a way that differences between the exact solution of the mixed integer problem *MIDP* and the heuristical results that can be tolerated.

4. Solve the complete mixed integer problem *MIDP* that was simplified by the fixation of binary variables in step 3.

This example algorithm does not result in proven optimal solutions but might be significantly faster than the complete mixed integer problem *MIDP* as the computing times for mixed integer problems strongly depend on the number of binary variables. In section 4.3.1, the calculation of shadow prices or water values for hydro reservoirs based on price duration curves is explained. This is another example of a heuristical approach.

For economic dispatch problems, it is also possible to apply more general heuristical approaches like simulated annealing or generic algorithms. But in any case, methodological approaches have to be adapted to the specific problem structure to exhibit full performance advantages.

Selecting Appropriate Methods

For practical applications, it is very important to consider carefully all requirements before starting to implement one optimisation approach for the economic power plant dispatch problem. Advantages and disadvantages have to be considered against many, often conflicting, aims. The most important aspects are:

- *Level of detail*: It is possible to develop very detailed dispatch models, which consider many features, e.g. non-linear efficiency curves or time dependent start-up costs. Higher levels of detail will result not only in more effort for model development and maintenance as well as longer solution times but also more effort for keeping all parameters accurate and correct when the model is applied. Practical experiences shows that the last aspect limits the value of very detailed models. For example, efficiencies depend on outside temperature and humidity conditions and on fuel quality. Further, the exact marginal fuel costs are very difficult to determine. Considering these uncertainties a linear approximation of the efficiency curve might be adequate.

  Appropriate depiction of stochastic parameters, like reservoir inflows or load, is a challenge for many economic dispatch problems. Scenario analysis, i.e. solving the problem independently for every scenario, can be a first approach. Stochastic programming models, which derive an optimal solution simultaneously considering a large number of scenarios, are more complex. While these approaches are appropriate in some cases, the danger is that certain stochastic aspects are modelled with a very high level of detail while other aspects with similar impacts on the results are modelled with much less detail. Further, uncertainties in the estimation of probability distributions for stochastic parameters have to be considered. As stochastic programming models require more resources for model development and maintenance, and as they are often difficult to solve, it is advisable to analyse potential benefits compared to deterministic approaches carefully. The number of scenarios that can be used for describing stochastic parameters is often very limited due to computational resource limits. Therefore, scenario reduction algorithms are often applied (see Heitsch and Römisch 2003).

- *Optimality of results*: While standard algorithms often guarantee the optimality of the results, heuristics and decomposition approaches often do not allow to find the exact optimum. Keeping the uncertainty of several input parameters in mind the added value of an optimal solution against a good approximation may be minimal in many cases.

- *Solution times*: Decomposition approaches and heuristical approaches can often reduce the solution time dramatically compared with standard algorithms. It is also possible to reduce solution times by using faster commercial solvers, better hardware or by solving several problems in parallel. Heuristical approaches and branch and bound algorithms sometimes have very unpredictable solution times. While a standard algorithm solves a problem predictable within 40 to 60 minutes, a heuristical approach may solve the problem 95% of the time within 15 minutes but requires more than 3 hours in a few cases. In this case, the standard algorithm with good predictability of the solution time might be favourable even if the average solution time is much longer.

- *Robustness*: Some optimisation algorithms, especially decomposition approaches or heuristics, are not very robust, i.e. for certain input parameters the solver does not manage to find a solution although a solution exists that can be found by using another solver. Reasons for this behaviour can be numerical as well as convergency problems. Often, this behaviour is not acceptable. In many cases, even extensive tests with different sets of input parameters do not reveal this behaviour, but in operation it suddenly appears. For critical applications, it may be advisable to develop two different optimisation algorithms to provide a backup for these rare events. Commercial optimisation packages often allow the use of different solvers and can easily provide this kind of algorithmic backup solution.

- *Development resources*: With optimisation packages and standard algorithms it is often possible to implement economic dispatch models within days or weeks by one or two experts. The development resources required for dynamic programming, heuristics, and especially decomposition approaches are much higher. For heuristical approaches, it is very difficult to estimate the time needed for development and to judge if the algorithm will lead to the expected results.

- *Flexibility*: In practical applications, it is often necessary to modify and adapt economic dispatch models to meet new requirements as electricity markets and regulatory requirements change. While models implemented with optimisation packages can be adapted quickly, it requires a longer time with all other approaches. In the case of heuristics or dynamic programming, it is possible that the algorithm cannot be adapted at all and totally new algorithms have to be developed. One example is the use of dynamic programming algorithms for thermal power plants, which cannot handle time-integral fuel constraints. Therefore, the introduction of these kinds of constraints would require new approaches.

In view of all these aspects, it is advisable to discuss operational requirements as well as advantages and disadvantages of different optimisation approaches intensively before starting the development of a model.

4.3 METHODOLOGICAL APPROACHES

Economic power plant dispatch is the main fundamental aspect for understanding the supply side of electricity markets. And under the common assumption of inelastic demand it is all we need to simulate wholesale electricity market prices in a competitive market.

There are two main differences between the economic power plant dispatch problem and market models: data availability and model size. While within a company good information is available about the company's own power plants, this information is only partly available for the whole market being modelled. The number of power plants of one company is generally significantly smaller than the total number of power plants participating in the market. Therefore, building market models can be similar to solving economic power plant dispatch problems but is not identical. In this section, we discuss different methodological approaches that can be applied for electricity market modelling.

4.3.1 Merit Order Curve

A merit order curve is a cost-based description of the fundamental supply curve in a market as depicted in Figure 4.1. We first want to consider the basic principles of applying merit order curves for market models[13] and then we will discuss how additional constraints and influencing factors can be reflected.

Construction Principles

The merit order curve can be constructed and applied for modelling electricity markets in the following six steps:

1. Estimate the variable operation costs c_i for every power plant i available for electricity generation in a specific market.[14]
2. Estimate the maximum available capacity $Pmax_i$ for every power plant i.
3. Rank all power plants i by variable cost c_i and plot the variable costs over the cumulative available capacity (see e.g. in Figure 4.15). This curve is called the *merit order* curve or *supply curve*.
4. Estimate the load (demand) that has to be met in this specific market during a specific time interval.
5. Plot the demand curve as a vertical line at the estimated load on the capacity axis.
6. The position of the intersection of the vertical demand curve with the merit order curve indicates the market equilibrium price, which can be read on the variable cost axis.

---

[13] Market models based on merit order curves are also called *stack models*.

[14] Theoretically it is not the question to estimate variable operation costs but rather to estimate the minimum price at which the dispatcher of a plant is willing to produce electricity for a specific time interval with a specific plant. A dispatcher will have to consider many constraints, although for thermal power plants variable operation costs are a good estimate for this price.

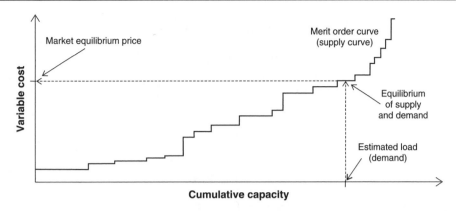

Figure 4.15 Calculation of the market equilibrium price with the merit order curve

This method generates an estimation for the market equilibrium price for one specific time interval. The repeated application allows the calculation of hourly price curves or average prices for longer periods (e.g. annual base and peak prices). In addition to prices, it is also possible to calculate electricity production, fuel consumption and CO_2 emissions for every power plant, by assuming that all plants with variable costs below the equilibrium price are in operation at maximum available capacity $Pmax_h$, that all plants above equilibrium price are not in operation, and that the plant at the equilibrium price is in operation at part load at a level required to meet the remaining gap of the load.

Time Aggregation

Time aggregation is one measure to reduce computation time. Variable costs c_i and available capacity Pmx_i change by time. Therefore, the shape of the merit order curve also changes with time. If no detailed information is available with hourly or daily resolution, the merit order curve can be considered as constant within a longer time period (e.g. one month). In this case, time aggregation based on a load duration curve is possible. The load duration curve is constructed out of a chronological load curve by sorting the load values in descending order. The load duration curve can be approximated by calculating average values for load levels representing several time intervals in the load duration curve (see Figure 4.16). These load levels can all represent an identical number of time intervals or different numbers. In sections where the load duration curve is steeper, more load levels can be introduced to improve the accuracy of results. As a next step all load levels can be intersected with the merit order curve to obtain a price duration curve or an average price for the whole time period. It is also possible to reconstruct chronological load curves by remembering which load level represents which chronological time interval.

The aggregation of time intervals based on the load duration curves allows depiction of the full range of load levels including extreme peaks by a relatively small number of load levels. Capturing the extreme peaks is quite important as the merit order curve usually becomes very steep at high load levels.

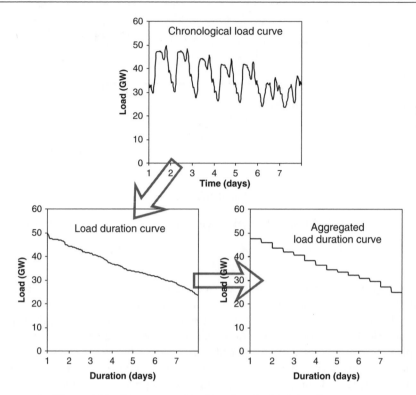

Figure 4.16   Time aggregation based on the load duration curve

Must-Run Power Plants

Not all power plants are freely dispatchable. Run-of-river hydro power plants and wind turbines produce at zero variable cost only depending on resource availability. There are two approaches for modelling these type of plants:

- *Integration into the merit order curve*: The available capacity of run-of-river hydro power plants and wind turbines, which is equivalent to their generation output, can be integrated into merit order curves at zero variable cost. As wind generation is strongly fluctuating, in systems with a substantial amount of wind energy, it is not adequate to use average generation levels for these plants.[15] Therefore, the merit order curve would have to be reconstructed for every individual time interval.
- *Subtraction from the load*: Instead of depicting run-of-river hydro power plants and wind turbines in the merit order curve (supply side), their generation can also be considered as reduction of the demand. In this case, chronological generation patterns can be subtracted from chronological load values. Furthermore, it is possible to apply one merit order curve valid for longer time intervals and to aggregate time intervals based on the duration

---

[15] It is adequate to model average generation levels as long as the merit order curve can be considered as linear in the range of wind generation fluctuations. However, close to the maximum cumulative capacity the merit order curve becomes steep and non-linear, an approximation with average generation levels might result in different, less volatile prices.

curve of the residual load. Figure 4.17 shows the construction of this duration curve for a system with a substantial amount of fluctuating wind energy generation. The shape of the residual load duration curve is significantly different from the load duration curve. Minimum load levels are lower.

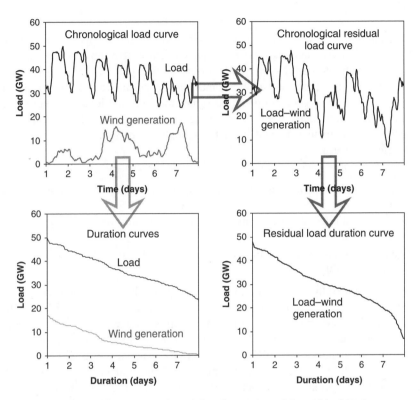

Figure 4.17   Construction of duration curves of the residual load

Solar electricity generation has similar characteristics to wind energy. As the installed solar capacity is still very small in most systems it is adequate to assume a flat production pattern and apply one of two the methods explained above. Plants not participating in the electricity market include other subsidised renewable technologies like biofuel or geothermal generation. They can be depicted in the same way.

A further category of plant are combined heat and power plants (CHPs) and must-run plants for network stability. These plants produce generally at a certain minimum output level, but can increase output up to the full available capacity. They are best depicted by two intervals in the merit order curve: one segment for the must-run part at zero variable cost and one segment for the additional available capacity at variable cost.

Storage and Pumped Storage Hydro Power Plants

Storage and pumped storage hydro power plants have negligible variable costs, but they cannot simply be depicted at the left side of the merit order curve with full capacity due to limited reservoir capacity and natural inflows. Economic power plant dispatch considers these limits. Generation will be allocated to times with high prices and pumping will occur at times of low prices, generally at night or during weekends. Depending on the system being modelled, the reservoir sizes, and the time frame under consideration there are two main approaches for integrating hydro power plants into the merit order approach:

- *Typical generation patterns*: The generation of storage and pumped storage plants has typical daily, weekly, and seasonal patterns. Therefore, it is possible to use historical production patterns to derive expected hydro generation patterns. With these production patterns storage and pumped storage plants can be considered as must-run plants as described above. Their generation can be subtracted from the load or integrated at zero variable cost into the merit order curve. In the case of huge annual differences in hydro production due to meteorological impacts, it might be necessary to consider different hydrological scenarios.

  This simple approach is suitable for the following purposes:

  - Electricity markets with a small amount of hydro generation from storage and pumped storage.
  - Storage and pumped storage plants with small reservoirs, which are operated in daily or weekly cycles.
  - Long-term market models with low time resolution and their application for many years into the future.

- *Water values*: Operators of storage hydro power plants have to decide when to use the limited reservoir content. For this purpose, water values are calculated. Water values can be interpreted as opportunity costs of using reservoir water at a specific time and not at an optimal later point of time. Water values can be calculated for reservoir content but also as opportunity costs $mPT_{h,t}$ for electricity generated in a hydro power station as explained in the next section. These opportunity costs $mPT_{h,t}$ can be compared with variable costs of thermal power plants and determine the prices at which a hydro power plant will bid in a competitive market. Therefore, hydro power plants can be integrated into the merit order curve with their generation capacity $PTmax_{h,t}$ and their opportunity costs $mPT_{h,t}$.

  Pumped storage hydro power plants will pump if market prices are low. For pumping based on reservoir water values, opportunity values $mPP_{h,t}$ for pumping can be calculated. With these opportunity values the maximum pumping capacity $PPmax_{h,t}$ can be integrated into the demand curve. Figure 4.18 depicts the integration of hydro generation capacity into the supply curve as well as the integration of pumping capacity into the demand curve.

  This water value-based approach is suitable for the following purposes:

  - Electricity markets with a large amount of hydro generation from storage and pumped storage.
  - Storage and pumped storage plants with large reservoirs, which are operated in seasonal cycles.
  - Short-term market models, which focus on several months or weeks, as for this modelling horizon electricity prices on the futures market and present reservoir levels can strongly influence water values and therefore opportunity costs of hydro generation.

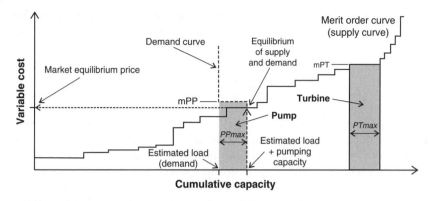

Figure 4.18   Integration of hydro generation capacity into the merit order curve

Water Values for Hydro Power Plants

Water values are important for calculating the prices at which a hydro power plant bids in a competitive market. Therefore, we want to consider in more detail how they can be derived.

Linear optimisation models for economic power plant dispatch can be used for calculating water values. Most commercial solvers calculate not only optimal values for all variables but also marginal values for all constraints.[16] In our case, we use the marginal values $mV_{r,t}$ of the reservoir balance equation (4.29), which are the water values of reservoir r at time t.[17] Water values $mV_{r,t}$ stay constant over time unless the reservoir content reaches upper or lower limits. For market offers, the water values have to be converted into opportunity costs $mPT_{h,t}$ for electricity generated in a power station h[18] as

$$mPT_{h,t} = \frac{mV_{rup(h),t} - mV_{rdown(h),t}}{QT_h} \qquad (4.37)$$

where $rup(h)$ is the reservoir directly above hydro power plant h, $rdown(h)$ is the reservoir directly below hydro power plant h and QT_h is the specific flow rate per electric turbine power output.

For pumped storage hydro power plants, the calculation of an opportunity value $mPT_{h,t}$ for pumping can be calculated as well using the specific pump flow rate QP_h as

$$mPP_{h,t} = \frac{mV_{rup(h),t} - mV_{rdown(h),t}}{QP_h}. \qquad (4.38)$$

For large stand-alone reservoirs with an annual reservoir cycle, it is possible to derive opportunity costs $mPT_{h,t}$ for turbine generation with a heuristical approach using price

---

[16] In the case of mixed integer linear dispatch models, marginal values can be calculated as well. Most solvers fix all integer variables and solve the resulting LP-problem for deriving marginal values. For calculating water values, these marginal values can be used in most cases, while remaining aware of the fact that integer constraints are not reflected.

[17] If a discount factor is used in the objective function the marginal values of the reservoir balance equation are discounted water values.

[18] Often, the opportunity costs $mPT_{h,t}$ for electricity generation are also called water values.

duration curves. Assuming the same reservoir level at the beginning and end of a long time period (e.g. one year), we first calculate the number n_h of full load hours of electricity generation as

$$n_h = \frac{\sum_t Qin_{rup(h),t}}{QT_h \cdot PTmax_h} \tag{4.39}$$

where $Qin_{rup(h),t}$ is the natural inflow and $PTmax_h$ is the maximum generation output.

A price duration curve can be constructed from an hourly price forward curve (see section 3.4.1) or from hourly stochastic price paths (see sections 3.4.2 and 3.4.3) by sorting price values in descending order. The construction principle is the same as for load duration curves shown in Figure 4.16. As shown in Figure 4.19 a hydro power plant with $n_h = 2000$ full load hours per year will aim to produce in the hours with the 2000 highest prices out of the 8760 hourly prices of one year. The lowest of these prices represents the opportunity costs mPT_h for turbine generation. In the remaining price segments with prices below mPT_h, the hydro power plant will not generate.

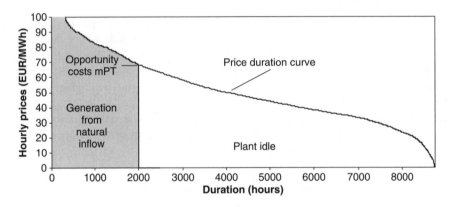

Figure 4.19   Deriving water values from a price duration curve.

The size of the shaded area in Figure 4.19 multiplied by the generation capacity $PTmax_h$ is equivalent to the market revenues M_h of the hydro power plant. We obtain

$$M_h = \sum_{t|S_t > mPT_{h,t}} S_t \cdot PTmax_h. \tag{4.40}$$

This heuristical approach is applicable if the hydro reservoir is large and if no reservoir limits are reached. But it can also be applied for a time period at the end of which a reservoir limit is reached. Most large-scale reservoirs in Europe reach their minimum levels before the snow melt in spring. Therefore, the existing usable reservoir content and the expected inflows before the minimum level is reached determine the quantity of electricity that can be generated in the time before the snow melt.

For pumped storage hydro power plants, it is possible to calculate opportunity costs mPT_h for generating and opportunity values mPP_h for pumping based on price duration curves. Figure 4.20 shows the construction principle under the assumption of identical generation and pumping capacity ($PPmax_h = PTmax_h$), cycle efficiency of $\eta^{\circ} = QP_h/QT_h = 75\%$, and

$n_h = 2000$ full load hours generation from natural inflow as in the example above. In this case, for every 3 additional hours of generation, 4 hours of pumping are required. The price difference between the lowest price hour with generation and the highest price hour with pumping has to be 25% to cover cycle losses ($\mathrm{mPP}_h = \eta^\circ \cdot \mathrm{mPT}_h$).

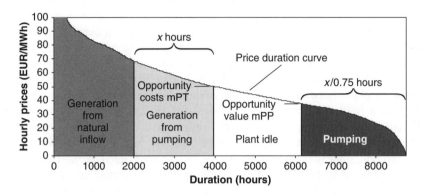

Figure 4.20 Deriving water values from a price duration curve

Market revenues M_h can be calculated, in this case as difference between the size of the two light shades areas for generation in Figure 4.20 multiplied by the generation capacity $PTmax_h$ and the dark shades area for pumping multiplied by the pumping capacity $PPmax_h$. We obtain

$$\mathrm{M}_h = \sum_{t|S_t>\mathrm{mPT}_{h,t}} S_t \cdot PTmax_h - \sum_{t|S_t<\mathrm{mPP}_{h,t}} S_t \cdot PPmax_h. \tag{4.41}$$

Reserve Constraints

Reserve requirements constrain the operation of power plants and therefore impact electricity markets. Quality requirements for reserves vary between grid operators and it is difficult to obtain detailed information on means of reserve provision in different markets. Therefore, we will concentrate here only on the characteristic impacts of reserve provision and differentiate by type:

- *Primary reserve*: This type of reserve has the task of keeping the frequency of the interconnected synchronised AC[19] electricity network at a constant level. As fast reaction times are required it can only be provided by generators in synchronised operation, i.e. as *spinning reserve*. It is shared in the whole interconnected network, e.g. in the UCTE network, 3000 MW positive and 3000 MW negative primary reserves are available. Within UCTE the primary reserve capacity is relatively small compared to other reserves and primary reserve can be provided to a certain degree by some thermal or hydro power plants from technically available short-term reserves without imposing any constraints on the longer-term maximum output level. Therefore, it can be neglected for market

---

[19] Alternating current.

modelling within UCTE. In smaller synchronised networks such as in England, Scotland, and Wales, the primary reserve capacity exceeds the provision potential with no impact and should be considered in the same way as secondary reserve.

- *Secondary reserve*: This type of reserve has the task of keeping the sum of all exchanges of one network control area with all neighboring areas at the planned level. If generation is too low within one control area, net exports of this area would be lower than planned (or net imports higher than planned) and positive secondary reserve will be requested. With too much generation within a control area negative reserve will be called for. Most network operators ask for secondary reserve provision with synchronised generators, i.e. as *spinning reserve* like primary reserve. This means that some of the generating plants cannot operate at full capacity to provide positive reserve and that some of the plants have to operate above minimum generation level to provide negative reserve. If it is known which plants are used for positive secondary reserve provision the available power reflected in the merit order curve of these plants can be reduced by their contribution to the positive reserve capacity. Part of the available capacity of plants providing negative secondary reserve can be considered as must-run. Therefore, it can be depicted at the left-hand side of the merit order curve with zero variable cost. This zero cost part consists of the minimum power plus the negative reserve capacity. Hydro power plants are often used for provision of secondary reserves. If hydro power generation is modelled with typical generation patterns based on historical values as described above one has to consider that they already reflect the impact of reserve provision.

  If no information is available on which plants are used for providing secondary reserve one possible approach is to add the total positive secondary reserve to the load and to neglect the negative secondary reserve.

- *Tertiary reserve*: This type of reserve compensates for deviations from planned exchanges between control areas and assists secondary reserve. It has longer activation times and is not provided as spinning reserve. Positive tertiary reserve is often provided with open cycle gas turbines (GTs). These plants have high variable costs and therefore they can be normally found at the right-hand side of the merit order curve. Part of the positive tertiary reserve can also be provided from the demand side by interruptible load. In both cases, positive tertiary reserve has no direct impact on the merit order approach.

  If supply capacity limits are reached within a system positive tertiary reserve capacity has to be considered as reduction of available generation capacity. If no other information on tertiary reserve provision is available, tertiary reserve provided by thermal power plants and hydro power plants within the merit order curve can be allocated to power plants with the highest variable costs on the right side of the merit order curve. It has to be considered that part of the positive tertiary reserve can be provided by interruptible load or by hydro generation depicted by typical production curves.

  Negative tertiary reserve can be provided by most synchronised power plants by load reduction or by switching on pumps of pumped storage hydro power plants. In some cases, increasing the load on the demand side is also possible to a certain degree. Like negative secondary reserve it is either possible to neglect negative tertiary reserve in the merit order approach or to reflect it as additional must-run generation.

Time-Integral Constraints

Time-integral constraints cannot be directly depicted in the merit order approach. But it is possible to estimate their impact and to adjust variable costs c_i of power plants accordingly. Start-up costs and minimum up- and downtimes have the following effects.

During peak load times, during which marginal thermal plants are dispatched only for a short period of time, these plants are only dispatched if electricity prices are high enough to cover variable costs as well as start-up costs. This can be reflected by estimating relevant variable costs $c_{i_{peak}}$ of thermal peaking power plants i_{peak} as

$$c_{i_{peak}} = cV_{i_{peak}} + \frac{cB_{i_{peak}}}{Pmax_{i_{peak}}} + \frac{cA_{i_{peak}}}{Tup_{i_{peak}} \cdot Pmax_{i_{peak}}}, \tag{4.42}$$

where $cV_{i_{peak}}$ are incremental variable costs, $cB_{i_{peak}}$ are hourly operation costs, $cA_{i_{peak}}$ are start-up costs and $Tup_{i_{peak}}$ is the minimum uptime.

During low load periods thermal plants are only shut off for short times if this is more economic than operating them at minimum load under consideration of required start-up costs in the case of shutting down. Therefore, baseload thermal plants bid into electricity markets during these periods below their incremental variable costs cV_i. This can be reflected by estimating *for low load periods* relevant variable costs $c_{i_{base}}$ of thermal baseload power plants i_{base} as

$$c_{i_{base}} = cV_{i_{base}} + \frac{cB_{i_{base}}}{Pmin_{i_{base}}} - \frac{cA_{i_{base}}}{Tdown_{i_{base}} \cdot Pmin_{i_{base}}}, \tag{4.43}$$

where $Pmin_{i_{base}}$ is the minimum load of power plant i_{base} and $Tdown_{i_{base}}$ is the minimum down time.

Time-integral minimum or maximum fuel or emission constraints (equations (4.22) and (4.23)) can cause thermal power plants to bid below or above variable costs. A common example for this aspect are combined cycle gas turbine (CCGT) power plants with take-or-pay gas contracts. Similar to water values of hydro power plants, opportunity costs for fuel usage are the relevant criteria. They can be derived as marginal values of equation (4.22) or (4.23) or from a price duration curve as described above for hydro power plants.

International Exchange

International exchange can significantly influence electricity prices. It is important to depict them in merit order curve models. The easiest approach is the estimation of chronological net import time series, which are subtracted from the load or integrated into the supply curve with zero variable cost. These approaches are equivalent to the one described above for renewable must-run generation.

A more sophisticated approach would be to estimate bid and offer curves of neighbouring market areas and integrate them into the supply and demand curve.

It is also possible to build multi-regional merit order curve models for calculating regional prices using a market splitting or implicit auction approach similar to the algorithm used at Nord Pool, the Scandinavian electricity exchange. For multi-regional or nodal markets, linear programming optimisation approaches as described in section 4.3.2 should be considered as well. A detailed mathematical description of market splitting can be found in Bompard *et al.* (2003).

Price Peaks Caused by Supply Scarcity

As it is very difficult to estimate available capacity and load exactly, it is also often necessary to extend the merit order curve with virtual capacity to the left to ensure that in the model a match of supply and demand is always possible. For this virtual capacity variable, costs higher than variable costs of the last real power plant in the merit order curve should be assumed.

Variable generation costs even under consideration of start-up costs do not exceed approximately 200 EUR/MWh. But spot market prices in many markets do exceed this level for several hours every year. In these hours, market participants do not offer all available capacity at short run marginal costs. This market behaviour can be reflected in the merit order approach by adding a scarcity premium cS_i to the variable costs c_i. There are two approaches for estimating the level of this scarcity premium:

- *Historical price fit*: By comparing historical price duration curves on the spot market with simulation results based on variable costs it is possible to estimate scarcity premiums cS_i. It is necessary to determine the marginal plant i_d that is responsible for each simulated price S'_d at duration d in the duration curve. With observed historical prices S_d we can estimate a scarcity premium cS_j for every plant j as

$$cS_j = \frac{\sum_{d|i_d=j} (S_d - S'_d)}{\sum_{d|i_d=j} 1}. \qquad (4.44)$$

Figure 4.21 depicts this approach for the 100 highest hours of an annual price duration curve. For obtaining robust results, it is advisable to use several years of historical data. This approach is not only suitable for estimating scarcity premiums but also for adjusting variable costs of the merit order curve in general to historically observed prices.

- *Merit order curve fit to published bid and offer curves at electricity exchanges*: Several electricity exchanges publish hourly cumulative bid and offer curves for the spot market. Figure 4.22a depicts one example for bid and offer curves as they can be observed in the spot market. The elasticity of physical supply and possibly also physical demand is reflected in both cumulative offer and bid curves, as generation companies have commitments for physical delivery (short position) when they enter into the spot market. Therefore, incremental physical generation capacity can be reflected in the bid as well as in the offer curve. With our assumption of inelastic demand we can calculate a residual cumulative offer curve in Figure 4.22b by adding all decremental bids as incremental offers to the offer curve. If all physical supply capacity would enter into the spot market strictly at variable cost this residual cumulative offer curve would have exactly the same shape as the merit order curve. In reality, this is not the case as shown in Figure 4.22c. Differences can have several reasons:

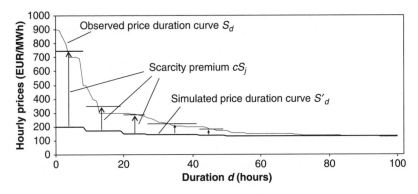

Figure 4.21   Deriving scarcity premiums from historical price duration curves

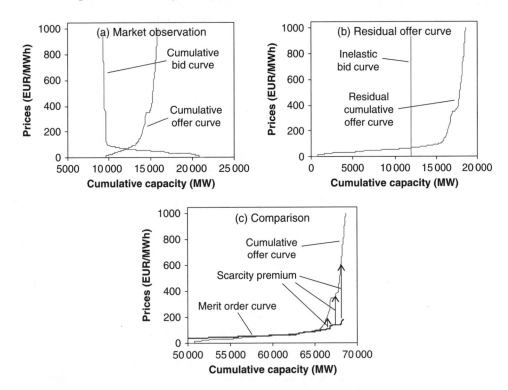

Figure 4.22   Deriving scarcity premiums from observed spot market bid and offer curves

- Inaccuracies and uncertainties regarding data and assumptions when deriving the merit order curve.
- Market players with generation assets generally offer only capacity in the expected price range but not all available capacity. This explains the deviation at the left-hand side of Figure 4.22c.
- Block offers (combined offers for several hours) are not completely reflected in published cumulative bid and offer curves of electricity exchanges.
- Scarcity premiums.

Scarcity premiums can be estimated from differences between the merit order curve and the cumulative residual offer curve in Figure 4.22c. It is advisable to use several observed bid and offer curves of carefully selected hours for which high prices have been expected and for which it can be assumed that all available physical supply capacity is reflected.

4.3.2 Optimisation Models

Optimisation models describe the whole market as an economic power plant dispatch problem (see section 4.2). The optimisation objective is to minimise total system costs for satisfying electricity demand. Market prices can be derived as hourly marginal costs. In this section, we will discuss single and multi-regional approaches, possibilities for reducing computation time and how system expansion can be included for long-term analysis.

Single Region Models

In general, a market model formulated as an optimisation problem for one single region without any transmission constraints is identical to the economic power plant dispatch problem described in section 4.2 with the cost minimising objective function (4.27). The main constraint is to satisfy demand (equation (4.34)). All relevant constraints can be included as far as sufficient data is available and as far as the optimisation problem stays solvable within acceptable computation time. Possible approaches for solving the optimisation problem are described in section 4.2.3.

While for economic power plant dispatch optimal decisions (i.e. optimal values for all variables) are the relevant result, market models try to derive fundamental market prices. In a competitive market, these prices are equivalent to system marginal costs, which are the marginal values of the load balance equation (4.34). Most optimisation algorithms for linear (LP) or mixed integer (MIP) problems compute these values. In the case of MIP models, most solvers fix for this purpose all integer variables and solve the resulting LP-problem for deriving marginal values. For calculating system marginal costs, these marginal values can be used, remaining aware that integer constraints are not reflected. Another approach is to vary the load L_t by $\pm \Delta L$ (e.g. ± 100 MW) for a time period τ (e.g. peak or off-peak periods within one month), and solve the optimisation problem for these two cases to obtain the total cost difference ΔC between the two objective values of the objective function (4.27). Specific marginal costs S'_τ can be derived as

$$S'_\tau = \frac{\Delta C}{2\Delta L}.$$

(4.45)

This approach has to be repeated separately for every period τ for which marginal cost values are required. This approach has the advantage that start-up costs and other integer constraints are reflected.

Multi-Regional Models

Transmission capacity limits within an interconnected network can create different market areas with different market prices.[20] A nodal model topology is suitable to depict interlinked electricity markets with transmission constraints. Figure 4.23 depicts an example with all relevant system elements.

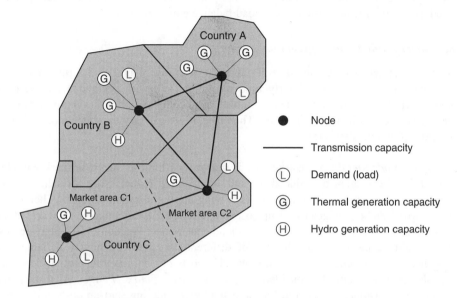

Figure 4.23   Topology example for a multi-regional model

For building a multi-regional market model, the economic dispatch problem has to be enhanced by regional differentiation for load and generation as well by modelling transmission capacities. The load balance equation (4.34) has to be formulated for every node n and has to take into account transmission flows $PF_{n,m,t}$ from node n to node m during time interval t. $PF_{n,m,t}$ is a positive variable ($PF_{n,m,t} \geq 0$). We obtain as the nodal load balance equation

$$\sum_{g(n)} P_{g(n),t} + \sum_{h(n)} (PT_{h(n),t} - PP_{h(n),t}) + \sum_{m} (PF_{m,n,t} - PF_{n,m,t}) \geq L_{n,t} \quad \forall (n,t) \qquad (4.46)$$

where $g(n)$ and $h(n)$ are thermal or hydro power plants located at node n, respectively. $P_{g,t}$ is the power output of a thermal power plant g. $PT_{h,t}$ and $PP_{h,t}$ are the turbine power generation or pumping power consumption of a hydro power plant h, respectively. $L_{n,t}$ is the load at node n during time interval t.

Transmission flows $PF_{n,m,t}$ are constrained to available transmission capacity $PFmax_{n,m}$ by

$$PF_{n,m,t} \leq PFmax_{n,m} \quad \forall (n,m,t). \qquad (4.47)$$

---

[20] Minor transmission constraints within one market area are in many cases solved by redispatching measures paid for by the transmission system operators.

Transmission capacity is published by grid operators as net transfer capacity (*NTC values*). These values depend on the overall load flow situation as well as on the availability of network elements. Therefore, these values vary by time.

All remaining equations of the economic power plant dispatch problem described in section 4.2 remain unchanged including the objective function (4.27). In the same way as for a single regional model, market prices (marginal system costs) at every node n can be derived as marginal values of the nodal load balance equation (4.46).

Model Simplification and Aggregation

Large-scale market models with several hundreds of power plants, with a time horizon of several months or years, with hourly time resolution, and with detailed depiction of all elements including integer constraints resemble a huge complex optimisation problem, which cannot be solved within acceptable time. Therefore, it is necessary to reduce model size and complexity. Possible steps are:

1. *Reducing model detail*: As data quality is generally a limiting factor in market models, model detail can often be reduced without significantly reducing result quality. Integer constraints cause most difficulties while solving the optimisation problem. Therefore, a first step would be to neglect start-up costs (equation (4.3)), minimum up- and downtimes (equations (4.4) and (4.5)) and minimum load constraints (equation (4.2)). Start-up costs cA_g would be neglected and instead of differentiating between hourly variable costs cB_g and output dependent incremental variable costs cV_g only average output-dependent variable costs c_g would be considered: $c_g = cA_g + cV_g \cdot Pmax_g/Pmax_g$. As discussed in section 4.3.1, variable costs could be adjusted by considering start-up costs and scarcity premiums.

   With these simplifications, maximum ramp rates (equations (4.6) and (4.7)) can be neglected as well. This means that all dynamic constraints for thermal power plants except time-integral fuel or emission constraints are neglected. The simplified objective function is

$$C = \sum_{g,t} c_g \cdot P_{g,t} \overset{!}{=} \min. \tag{4.48}$$

   $P_{g,t}$ is the generation output of thermal power plant g during time interval t.
2. *Aggregation of model elements*: In a large system, many thermal power plants linked to one node will have similar characteristics (mainly variable generation costs). Therefore, it is possible to aggregate several power plants to one equivalent power plant with their cumulative capacity and their average variable costs. Often, power plants are differentiated by type of fuel and by efficiency (which is derived from the age of a power plant) and aggregated in the resulting clusters. While this is one possible approach if no detailed data is available, it is more advisable to cluster plants by type of fuel and by variable costs as in many cases fuel transport costs vary significantly by plant location.

   Hydro storage and pumped storage power plants with similar ratios between reservoir size and turbine as well as pump capacity can be aggregated as well to one equivalent hydro power plant with cumulative capacities. For many systems, it is possible to obtain good results with two to three equivalent hydro power plants (e.g. one hydro storage power plant with annual reservoir cycle, one pumped storage hydro power plant with annual reservoir cycle, and one pumped storage hydro power plant with daily or weekly reservoir cycle). Further simplification is possible by depicting hydro generation with typical generation curves, which are derived from historical time series, and by avoiding to optimise hydro power dispatch within the market model.

3. *Time aggregation*: Time aggregation is one means of reducing model size. Instead of modelling a long time period in hourly resolution, it is possible to depict different load levels with typical days. Further, it is possible to aggregate hourly time intervals with similar load levels within one day. In the case of a long-term model of several years, it is also possible to model only key years instead of every year. Figure 4.24 depicts an example of a strong aggregation of the time scale used for a long-term model.

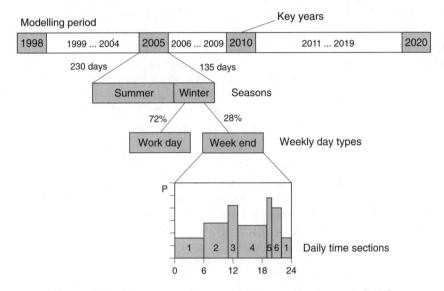

Figure 4.24   Time aggregation example. Source: Graeber *et al.* (2005)

While for long-term modelling strong aggregation of the time scale is adequate, for shorter-term models more detail is required. It is especially important to depict high load situations and not only medium load situations. Therefore, it is not adequate to model only one average working day and one average weekend day per month with average wind energy production levels. Instead, it is advisable to include extreme days, e.g. one cold winter day with low wind energy production levels. It is very important to choose the time structure of the model carefully. Cluster analysis or scenario reduction algorithms can be applied for identifying similar days, which can be combined into one modelled day.

4. *Time separation*: Another possibility for reducing model complexity is to separate the problem into smaller subproblems. Besides classical decomposition approaches and iterative, coordinated solving of subproblems as described in section 4.2.3, it is often possible to estimate for smaller time periods start and end levels for the time-integral constraints such as hydro reservoir levels or emission limits based on historical data. The modelling horizon can be, for instance, divided into separate months or seasons. For each of these shorter time periods, the optimisation model is solved separately.

System Expansion

So far we have only considered an existing electricity system. This is adequate for modelling horizons up to a few years into the future. Owing to long lead times for new power plants and for network capacity expansions, changes in the system can be foreseen for this time period.[21] For long-term models, it is crucial to have realistic assumptions for capacity additions. There are two possible approaches for this aspect:

- *Exogeneous capacity expansion*: In this case, capacity expansion is not part of the opti-misation problem. Scenarios for system expansion are formulated, e.g. based on political aims for the future fuel mix in the generation system. Development of demand, availabil-ity of fuels, availability of sites for new power plants, preferences of single players for different fuels, technological development, investment as well as operation and mainte-nance costs etc. have to be considered. The requirement is that these scenarios are consistent and plausible, but in the end they will be very subjective and possibly hard to justify.
- *Indogeneous capacity expansion*: In this case, capacity expansion decisions are part of the optimisation problem. As explained below, additional investment decision variables have to be introduced. The result is a least cost system expansion plan. This is an objective result but not necessarily a realistic one for the following reasons:
  - The optimisation is based on fixed assumptions about future developments for load, fuel prices, technological development, etc. In reality, expectation for future developments of relevant parameters change over time. For instance, in the year 2000, long-term oil price predictions of $30/bbl would have been considered high. However, in 2005 long-term oil price predictions of $40/bbl would have been considered low.
  - Different players have different expectations regarding future developments but also regarding project profitability.
  - Some players have preferences for some technologies, e.g. small players might prefer combined cycle gas turbine (CCGT) power plants to coal power plants due to smaller unit sizes and lower specific investment costs.
  - Political incentives for specific technologies change over time.
  - Transmission network expansions often require a very long authorisation process with unpredictable outcome.

For obtaining more realistic results, it is common to introduce additional (subjective) constraints that depict minimum requirements for diversity of generation capacity addi-tions.

In the following, we consider basic model enhancements for indogeneous capacity expansion of thermal power plants.[22] For every expansion option, which can be a specific project or just one type of technology with characteristic properties, we introduce as additional model elements new power plants g_{new}. Their installed capacity in year y is described by

---

[21] This section concentrates on capacity additions. Decommissioning of existing capacity also has to be considered. Generally, technical lifetimes can be estimated. When a power plant reaches this lifetime, it is considered as unavailable thereafter. More detailed considerations would include mothballing of power plants that do not earn their fixed operation and maintenance costs or de-mothballing of power plants. In this section, we will not further describe these aspects, but they can be modelled in a similar way.

[22] Expansion of hydro power plants and of transmission capacities can be modelled in a similar way. See Graeber (2002).

$\text{Pinst}_{g_{new},y}.$[23] With the availability factor $fa_{g_{new},t}$ we obtain the maximum available capacity $\text{Pmax}_{g_{new},t}$ as

$$\text{Pmax}_{g_{new},t} = fa_{g_{new},t} \cdot \text{Pinst}_{g_{new},y(t)} \quad \forall(g_{new}, t) \tag{4.49}$$

where $y(t)$ is the year that belongs to time interval t. For new power plants g_{new}, in equation (4.1) variable $\text{Pmax}_{g_{new},t}$ has to be used instead of parameter Pmax_g.

Additional capacity once commissioned is also available in all future years. We introduce

$$\text{Pinst}_{g_{new},t} \geq \text{Pinst}_{g_{new},t'} \quad \forall(g_{new}, t, t' > t). \tag{4.50}$$

Besides variable costs $c_{g_{new}}$ (or for more detailed models cost components $cA_{g_{new}}$, $cB_{g_{new}}$, and $cV_{g_{new}}$ as described in section 4.2.1), we have to consider specific investment costs $cI_{g_{new}}$ as well as specific annual operation and maintenance (O & M) costs $cOM_{g_{new}}$. Both of these parameters are specific values related to installed capacity $\text{Pinst}_{g_{new},t}$. It is important to consider capital costs during the building period and decommissioning costs if they are significant. $cI_{g_{new}}$ has to be calculated as net present value of the total investment and decomissioning costs at the time of the commissioning of a new power plant. Specific investment costs $cI_{g_{new}}$ are converted into specific annuities $cY_{g_{new}}$ of the investment costs

$$cY_{g_{new}} = cI_{g_{new}} \cdot \frac{i \cdot (1+i)^n}{(1+i)^n - 1}. \tag{4.51}$$

In this equation, i is the required rate of return (or capital costs) for the project and n is the technical lifetime of the new power plant. Considering investment costs as annuities $cY_{g_{new}}$ has the advantage that the terminal value at the end of the modelling period for new investments has not to be considered.

Specific annual O & M costs and annuities have to be added to objective function (4.48) without indogeneous capacity additions. We obtain a new objective function

$$C = \sum_{g,t} c_g \cdot P_{g,t} + \sum_{g_{new},y} \text{Pinst}_{g_{new},y} \cdot (cY_{g_{new}} + cOM_{g_{new}}) \overset{!}{=} \min. \tag{4.52}$$

All other equations of the market model without capacity expansion remain unchanged and have to be applied for existing as well as for new power plants.

For long-term models, one has to decide which currency values to use: *nominal* or *real* values. Nominal values reflect the correct time value of the currency. Real values are inflation corrected values. Both approaches are possible, but the use of real values has the advantage that some values (e.g. investment costs, O&M costs or fuel costs) can be considered as constant over time.

System marginal costs obtained by market models with indogeneous capacity expansion reflect full costs of new capacity additions. Theoretically, these system marginal costs are the market prices that have to be expected in a competitive market. In the market model results, expansion costs for new peak capacity are allocated to single peak load hours. This

---

[23] The capacity variable $\text{Pinst}_{g_{new},y}$ can be a discrete variable for given plant sizes or a continuous variable. For reducing model complexity, using continuous variables is recommended.

leads to very high prices in these hours. As expansion decisions have to be taken many years in advance and future load development stays uncertain, these modelling results are not realistic in current market frameworks. In which way electricity markets will further develop to give efficient incentive for least cost capacity expansion, especially regarding peaking capacity, is still an open question. Therefore, the main use of long-term models with indogeneous capacity expansion is to derive consistent system expansion scenarios rather than deriving market prices with high time resolution.

4.3.3   System Dynamics

System dynamics is a modelling approach for analysing the behaviour of complex dynamic systems over time. The basic elements of a system dynamics model are stocks, flows and feedback loops. Within feedback loops time delays can occur. Mathematically, a system dynamics model is a set of non-linear coupled differential equations solved as an approximation with discrete time steps. System dynamics models can be implemented in a spreadsheet program but more convenient is the use of special commercial software tools.[24] The aim of system dynamics models is not to provide precise forecasts of future developments, rather, they provide insight into dynamic interdependencies taking into account socio-economic, environmental, and technical aspects. They are often used for studying possible impacts of political measures.

System dynamics was developed in the 1960s by Jay W. Forrester at the MIT Sloan School of Management. Its application for energy economical studies has a long tradition. One popular example is *The Limits of Growth: a report for the Club of Rome's project on the predicament of mankind* by Donella H. Meadows *et al.*, which was published in 1972 (Meadows *et al.* 1972).

Long-term electricity market models with indogeneous system expansion based on optimisation approaches as described in section 4.3.2 depict a long-term steady state of the system. Dynamics that can cause deviations from this steady state, e.g. overcapacity after a period of high market prices are not reflected. Studying such long-term dynamic behaviours is the strength of market models based on system dynamics. It allows depiction of a decision making process for investments in new power plants, but as it is not possible to estimate all required parameters reliably from historical data, most modelling results strongly rely on subjective estimation of required input parameters.

Figure 4.25 depicts the basic structure of a simplified system dynamics electricity market model. The main elements of a system dynamics model are stocks, which are associated with state variables. In our example, we have on the supply side generation capacity under construction Gc and available installed capacity Ga. The demand side consists of the demand variable L. Further elements are flows, which are characterised by flow rates (decision variables). On the demand side, we have the demand growth Lr. Demand and demand growth rate are linked with one feedback loop in the following way:

$$\text{Lr}_t = \alpha \cdot \text{L}_t \tag{4.53}$$

$$\text{L}_t = \text{L}_{t-1} + \text{Lr}_{t-1} \tag{4.54}$$

---

[24] Commercial system dynamics software packages include AnyLogic, CONSIDEO, MapSys, Powersim Studio, Stella and iThink, and Vansim.

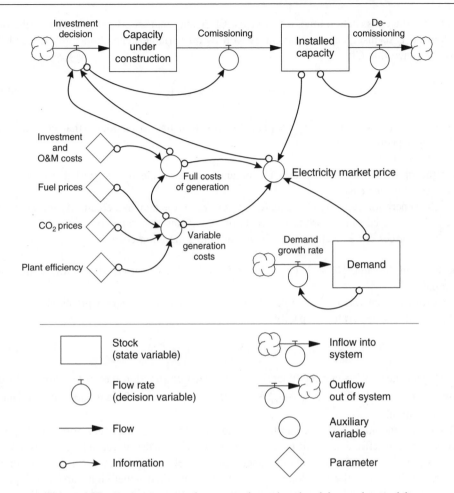

Figure 4.25 Basic structure of a system dynamics electricity market model

where α is the load growth rate (e.g. 3%p.a.). Installed generation capacity Ga changes by generation capacity being comissioned Gs and generation capacity being decomissioned Gx:

$$Ga_t = Ga_{t-1} + Gs_{t-1} - Gx_{t-1} \tag{4.55}$$

$$Gx_t = \beta \cdot Ga_t \tag{4.56}$$

where β is the decomissioning factor (e.g. 3% of the installed capacity p.a.). Capacity under construction Gc is increased by investment decisions Gd and decreased by comissioned capacity Gs:

$$Gc_t = Gc_{t-1} + Gd_{t-1} - Gs_{t-1}. \tag{4.57}$$

Generation capacity being comissioned Gs depends on investment decisions of past years:

$$Gs_t = Gd_{t-\tau} \tag{4.58}$$

where τ is the construction time, e.g. 4 years. Electricity market prices S depend on the ratio of demand L to installed capacity Ga as well as on variable generation costs Cv and full costs of generation Cf:

$$S_t = f_1 \left(\frac{L_t}{Ga_t}, Cv, Cf \right). \tag{4.59}$$

There is no correct function f_1. A plausible function has to be found that considers the following aspects:

- If the ratio of installed capacity to demand increases, electricity market prices can be expected to decrease.
- If the generation capacity is adequate in reference to the demand, electricity market prices can be expected to be close to full costs of new generation capacity.
- Market prices are expected to be above variable generation costs.

The function $f_1 = \max \left[Cf + 3 \cdot (\frac{L}{Ga} - 1) \cdot (Cf - Cv), Cv \right]$ was used for the following result example.

Investment decisions Gd_t are related to observed electricity market prices as well as to full costs of new generation capacity:

$$Gd_t = f_2(S_t, S_{t-1}, \ldots, S_{t-n}, Cf). \tag{4.60}$$

Once again there is no correct function f_2. A plausible function has to be chosen. In our example, $f_2 = \max \left[0.25 \cdot Ga_t \cdot \left(\frac{S_{t-1} + S_{t-2} S_{t-3}}{3 \cdot Cv_t} - 0.8 \right), 0 \right]$ was used for a model run with annual time resolution.

Variable generation costs Cv can be derived from the parameters fuel prices, CO_2 prices and power plant efficiency. Full costs of generation Cf consist of variable generation costs Cv plus specific operation and maintenance costs as well as capital costs for the investment.

Figure 4.26 shows the development of demand, installed generation capacity, capacity under construction, and electricity market prices for this small example model. Phases of high electricity market prices are followed by increased construction activity, which results in overcapacity and which reduces electricity prices. Owing to long lead times for new generation investments, the resulting length of the boom and bust cycles has a very long time period of more than 20 years.

A comprehensive review of system dynamics is provided in Sterman (2000). Examples of long-term electricity market models based on system dynamics are Grobbel (1999) and Sanchez and Centeno (2005).

4.3.4 Game Theory

Game theory is a discipline that is used to analyse strategic decision situations, which are characterised by:

- Economic returns of each individual decision maker depend on both their decisions and on the decisions of other decision makers.
- Each decision maker is aware of these interdependencies.
- Each decision maker takes these interdependencies into consideration for his individual decisions.

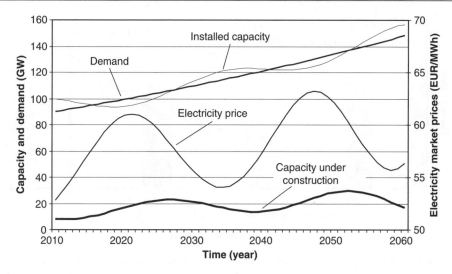

Figure 4.26   System dynamics result example

Game theory can be considered as a generalisation of decision theory which includes multiple decision makers and interdependencies. It is a formal framework for analysing strategic decision situations and provides methods for deriving optimal decisions within this framework. Similar to system dynamics models, fundamental market models based on game theory do not focus on forecasting, rather, they allow studying of market power and can assist market design and the development of regulatory measures.

The aim of this section is to describe strategic decisions in power markets, to provide a short introduction into game theory, and to explain with some examples how the concepts of game theory can be applied for analysing electricity markets.

Market Power in Electricity Markets

In section 4.3.1, we assumed independent players that offer their complete generation capacity at short run marginal costs (variable costs). In reality, generation companies can own more than one power plant and there are situations where it is possible to increase revenues by withholding generation capacity or offering it at prices above short-run marginal costs. In Figure 4.27, all generation capacity of company A is indicated. Under the assumption that company A sells all its capacity at the spot market, based on a merit order curve approach spot market profits M_A can be calculated as the difference between spot market price S and variable generation costs c_{i_A} multiplied with dispatched generation capacities P_{i_A} of all generation assets i_A as

$$M_A = d \cdot \sum P_{i_A} \cdot (S - c_{i_A}) \overset{!}{=} \max$$

$$\text{subject to} \qquad \sum_{i_A} P_{i_A} = Ptotal_A$$

$$P_{i_A} \le Pmax_{i_A} \tag{4.61}$$

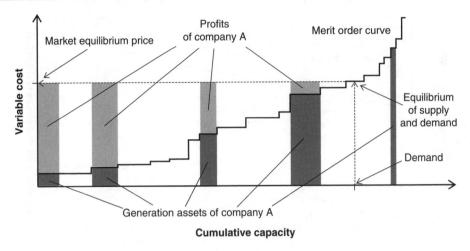

Figure 4.27   Spot market revenues achieved by offering all capacity at variable cost

where d is the duration of the time interval under consideration, $Ptotal_A$ is the total generation capacity sold by company A and $Pmax_{i_A}$ is the available generation capacity of power plant i_A.

Company A's aim is to optimise these revenues M_A. They depend on the chosen offer strategy $\mathcal{O}_A(M_A = f(\mathcal{O}_A))$. If company A assumes that its offers have no impact on market prices S, the optimal strategy is to offer all generation capacity at marginal cost. In this case, all power plants with variable generation costs c_{i_A} below the spot market price S will be dispatched.

In reality, market prices are not inelastic and do depend on strategy $\mathcal{O}_A$. If company A decides to withhold part of its capacity with variable costs below market prices, market prices will increase. As depicted in Figure 4.28, the right part of the merit order curve is shifted to the left-hand side. The new equilibrium of supply and demand moves towards higher prices. The change in revenues for company A is indicated in Figure 4.28: the losses incurred by withholding part of the capacity are outweighed by additional profits generated by plants further left in the merit order. For achieving this impact, it is not necessary to withhold capacity completely. Company A could also offer part of its capacity at prices above spot market so that this capacity moves to the right in the merit order above the intersection of supply and demand.

For analysing the potential for optimising company A's offer strategy $\mathcal{O}_A$, we can draw supply and demand curves from company A's perspective (Figure 4.29). The part of the supply side that can be influenced by company A is characterised by the merit order curve of its generation capacity. The rest of the market is characterised by the residual demand curve. This residual demand curve can be derived by subtracting the merit order curve of all other generation assets in the market from the demand. Company A's profits are the grey area. Its strategy $\mathcal{O}_A$ is expressed by the market offer curve. In a situation of complete information about the residual demand curve in the market, the shape of this offer curve does not play any role as long as it intersects at the same point with the residual demand curve, i.e. it could be also a vertical line (fixed capacity offer) or a horizontal line (fixed price offer). The optimal strategy $\mathcal{O}_A$ maximises company A's profits. In Figure 4.29, this optimisation

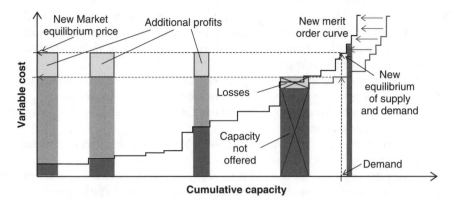

Figure 4.28   Increased spot market profits by withholding capacity

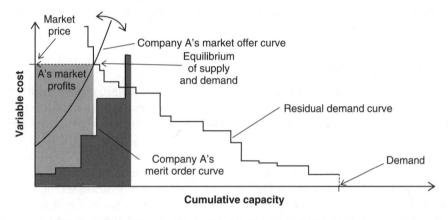

Figure 4.29   Market equilibrium derived from a residual demand curve

problem would be unconstrained as we have assumed inelastic demand and company A's generation capacity is required for meeting the assumed demand.

The potential for exerting market power depends on the shape of company A's merit order curve and on the shape of the residual demand curve. The steeper the slope of the residual demand curve at the intersection of supply and demand, the higher the potential for exerting market power. Also, the lower the slope of company A's merit order curve at the intersection of supply and demand, the higher the potential for exerting market power as well. In extreme peak load situations, the potential for increasing profits through exertion of market power is high.

In our example, it is possible for company A to exert market power independently of all other players. Price fixing or quantity fixing together with other companies as in a cartel is not required.

In real electricity markets, exertion of market power and deriving optimal offer strategies are not as easy as in this example because:

- Only incomplete information is available in the market. This transforms the optimisation of strategy O into a complex stochastic optimisation problem.

- Most generation companies do not sell all of their electricity generation in the spot market. Part of it is also sold in the forward market or futures to other market participants or is needed for satisfying final demand of direct customers. This reduces market power as shown in an example below.
- Spot market prices have additional impact on profits in the case of futures contracts or physical sales or purchase agreements that are indexed to the spot market.
- Spot market prices indirectly impact futures market prices, which impact the longer-term profits of a generation company.
- While electricity demand can be considered as inelastic in the short term, elasticities have to be considered in the longer term.
- Spot market prices above full costs of new generation capacity create investment incentives for new market participants. This reduces market power in the long run.

So far we have only considered strategic behaviour of one company. Game theory analyses optimal bidding strategies for all market participants. In the following, we will explain the basic concepts of game theory.

Representation of Games

Decision situations (games) studied by game theory are exactly defined mathematical objects. It consists of a set of players, a set of strategies available to these players and a specification of profits for each combination of strategies. There are two common ways for representing games:

- *Normal form*: The normal or strategic form usually represents a game by a matrix that shows players, strategies, and profits for each combination of strategies. In Table 4.4, we have two generation companies A and B. Each of them has one coal power plant with 100 MW capacity and variable generation costs of 30 EUR/MWh and one gas fired power plant with 50 MW capacity and variable generation costs of 50 EUR/MWh. For both companies, we consider three strategy options: to generate $P_1 = 50$ MW with the gas power plant, to generate $P_2 = 100$ MW with the coal power plant or to generate $P_3 = 150$ MW with the coal and the gas power plant. These strategies are represented by rows and columns in Table 4.4. The rest of the market consists of competitive players. Market prices $S = f(P_A + P_B)$ are characterised by the residual demand curve depicted in Figure 4.30. The resulting profits for one hour for company A and B are shown as pairs (M_A, M_B) inside the matrix. When a game is represented in nominal form, it is assumed that all players act simultaneously or without knowledge of the decisions of the others.
- *Extensive form*: If a game exists of several stages and players have information about decisions of other players, a game is usually represented in extensive form. The game is often represented as a tree. Figure 4.31 depicts an example with two stages and two decision options for each stage. Each node (or vertex) represents one point of a decision by one player. Lines out of a node represent possible decisions. Profits are represented at the right of the tree.

  The extensive form can also capture simultaneous decisions or games with incomplete information. A dotted line between two nodes indicates that they are part of the same information set, i.e. the players do not know at which of these linked nodes they are. In example Figure 4.31, this is the case for nodes N2 and N3.

Table 4.4 Normal form of profit-matrix for a two-player, three-strategy game: Profits (M_A, M_B) in 1000 EUR

		Strategy company B		
		50 MW	100 MW	150 MW
Strategy company A	50 MW	(10,10)	(5,12)	(3,11)
	100 MW	(12,5)	(8,8)	(4,5)
	150 MW	(11,3)	(5,4)	(2,2)

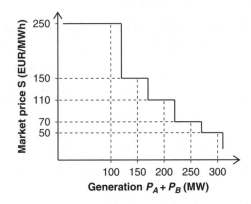

Figure 4.30 Residual demand function for deriving profit matrix

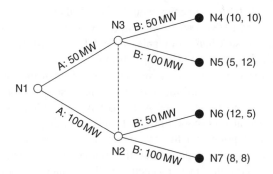

Figure 4.31 Extensive form for a two-player, three-strategy game

Nash Equilibrium

Game theory can be classified into two areas: *cooperative* and *non-cooperative*. A prerequisite for cooperative game theory is that it is possible for companies to make binding agreements about price fixing or quantity fixing and that these agreements can be enforced. As this is not the case in most real-world situations we only consider non-cooperative game theory here.

Non-cooperative games can be classified into *zero-sum games* and *non-zero-sum games*. In zero-sum games, the gains of one player are equivalent to the losses of the other players. In non-zero-sum games, the gains of one player are not equivalent to the losses of the other players. As this is the case in most economic situations, we will concentrate on non-zero-sum games. The solution for non-zero-sum games was first formulated by John Nash. The *Nash equilibrium* is the most common solution concept for non-zero-sum non-cooperative games.

In the example described above, the Nash equilibrium is reached when both companies offer 100 MW (see Table 4.5). In a cooperative game, both players would choose 50 MW as this leads to higher profits. But in a non-cooperative situation, this is not a stable situation as each company has an incentive to offer 100 MW regardless of what the other player chooses to offer. A Nash equilibrium is reached if, for a given set of chosen strategies by other players, each player's strategy is an optimal response to those strategies. At a Nash equilibrium it is not possible for one player to increase his profit by changing his strategy assuming that all other players' strategies remain the same.

Table 4.5 Nash equilibrium in a two-player, three-strategy game: Profits (M_A, M_B) in 1000 EUR

| | | | Strategy company B | |
		50 MW	100 MW	150 MW
Strategy company A	50 MW	(10,10)	(5,12)	(3,11)
	100 MW	(12,5)	(**8,8**)	(4,5)
	150 MW	(11,3)	(5,4)	(2,2)

Mitigation of Market Power through Futures Contracts

Table 4.6 shows the impact of company A and B's strategies on electricity market prices in our example above. If both companies would offer all their capacity at variable cost the market price would be 50 EUR/MWh, which is equivalent to the competitive equilibrium price. In the oligopoly case where companies A and B optimise their profits, the market price reaches 110 EUR/MWh at the Nash equilibrium.

In most electricity markets, generation companies sell part of their electricity production in advance on the futures or forward markets or to final customers for a fixed price. As an example, we assume that both companies A and B have sold 120 MW of futures contracts for 70 EUR/MWh settled at spot market prices. In this case, they have to pay the difference between the spot market price and the contract price to their counterparts (contract for difference). The resulting profits generated on the spot and on the futures market are shown in Table 4.7. The Nash equilibrium is reached if both companies produce 150 MW, which

Table 4.6 Electricity market prices depending on strategies: Market prices in EUR/MWh

| | | | Strategy company B | |
		50 MW	100 MW	150 MW
Strategy company A	50 MW	250	150	110
	100 MW	150	110	70
	150 MW	110	70	50

leads to the competitive market price of 50 EUR/MWh. Similar impacts are seen in the case of forward contracts or other physical sales at fixed prices.

Table 4.7   Nash equilibrium with 120 MW futures contracts: Profits (M_A, M_B) in 1000 EUR

		Strategy company B		
		50 MW	100 MW	150 MW
Strategy company A	50 MW	(−11.6, −11.6)	(−4.6, 0.4)	(1.8, 6.5)
	100 MW	(0.4, 4.6)	(3.2, 3.2)	(4, 5)
	150 MW	(6.8, −1.8)	(5, 4)	**(4.4, 4.4)**

The establishment of liquid futures markets is an effective measure for mitigating market power.

Duopolies

Many electricity markets have an oligopolistic structure with a small number of dominant players. Market strategies in oligopolies can be described as non-cooperative games. As a special case duopolies with only two strategic players are a common starting point for modelling. A *Bertrand model* describes a duopoly game in which each company chooses the price S for an identical product at which it is willing to produce. Neglecting output limits, we can assume that the company with lower prices will gain market share and that both companies will have equal output at equal price. If $L = L(S)$ describes how the demand L depends on the market price S and uniform production costs are c, market profits of company A can be calculated as

$$M_A(S_A, S_B) = \begin{cases} L_A \cdot (S_A - c_A) & \text{if } S_A < S_B \\ \frac{1}{2} \cdot L_A \cdot (S_A - c_A) & \text{if } S_A = S_B \\ 0 & \text{if } S_A > S_B. \end{cases} \tag{4.62}$$

A Bertrand game has a similar structure to our example in Table 4.4. If both companies decide to cooperate they are able to charge the monopoly price. But each company has an incentive to reduce the price slightly to gain market share and to increase his profit even though he knows that both companies will be worse off if both decide to reduce their price.

A *Cournot model* describes a duopoly game in which each company has to decide on the production quantity for an identical product without knowing the decision of the other player. We assume that P_A and P_B are the output decisions and that $S(P)$ is the inverse demand curve with S being the market price. The profit M_A of company A is

$$M_A(P_A, P_B) = P_A \cdot [S(P_A + P_B) - c_A]. \tag{4.63}$$

The strategy of each company is to choose its output P_A or P_B to maximise its profits without knowing the output decision of the other company. If both companies have no potential for increasing their profits by unilaterally adjusting their production the Nash equilibrium is reached.

Nash Equilibrium for Continuous Strategies

In the profit matrixes above, we have considered a discrete set of strategies. In economic analysis, it is often more realistic to consider a continuous set O of strategies like the decision as to how much to produce in the Cournot model above. As an example, we consider two generation companies $i \in \{A, B\}$. We approximate the merit order curves of both companies with the continuously differentiable function $C_i = P_i^2$ and neglect generation capacity limits. All other market participants are competitive. The residual demand function, which considers the supply and demand of all other market participants without companies A and B, can be described as $P = 180 - 0.5\,S$. The corresponding inverse demand function is $S = 360 - 2\,P$. The profit M_i for each company is described as $M_i = S(P_A + P_B) \cdot P_i - P_i^2$. In this equation, profits of one company depend on the output decision of the other company. Therefore, company A has to conjecture the output decisions P_B of company B in order to optimise its profits and vice versa. If company A takes the conjectured output decision P_B as given it optimises its profit $M_A(P_A, P_B)$ by adjusting output P_A to reach the first-order condition $\partial M_A(P_A, P_B)/\partial P_A = 0$. This behaviour is called *Cournot behaviour*.

How can company A derive a realistic forecast for P_B? For every output P_B, there is an optimal response $P_A = r_A(P_B)$ for company A and vice versa $P_B = r_B(P_A)$. An equilibrium $(P_A^\star, P_B^\star)$ is reached if $P_A^\star = r_A(P_B^\star)$ and $P_B^\star = r_B(P_A^\star)$. This equilibrium is a Nash equilibrium. It is also called *Cournot equilibrium* or *Cournot–Nash equilibrium*.

For our example, we first calculate the response functions r_A and r_B. The profit functions are

$$M_A = [360 - 2(P_A + P_B)] \cdot P_A - P_A{}^2$$
$$M_B = [360 - 2(P_A + P_B)] \cdot P_B - P_B{}^2. \tag{4.64}$$

The first-order conditions under which the profits M_A and M_B are maximised are

$$\frac{\partial M_A(P_A, P_B)}{\partial P_A} = 360 - 6P_A - 2P_B = 0$$
$$\frac{\partial M_B(P_A, P_B)}{\partial P_B} = 360 - 6P_B - 2P_A = 0. \tag{4.65}$$

We obtain as response functions r_A and r_B the following system of equations:

$$P_A = r_A(P_B) = 60 - \frac{1}{3}P_B$$
$$P_B = r_B(P_A) = 60 - \frac{1}{3}P_A. \tag{4.66}$$

These response functions r_A and r_B are plotted in Figure 4.32. The equilibrium $(P_A^\star, P_B^\star)$ can be derived by solving the system of equation (4.66). In Figure 4.32, it can be derived as the intersection of the two response functions. In our example, we obtain $P_A^\star = P_B^\star = 45$ and $S^\star = 180$. Profits are $M_A^\star = M_B^\star = S^\star \cdot P_i^\star - (P_i^\star)^2 = 180 \cdot 45 - 45^2 = 6075$.

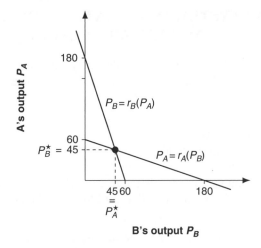

Figure 4.32   Cournot–Nash equilibrium in a duopoly

Implementation of Game Theory Models

Electricity market models based on game theory for studying oligopolies can be implemented as a *mixed complementary problem* (MCP). The supply side can be described by monotonically increasing polynomial costs functions $C_i(P_i)$ for every generation company i as an approximation of their merit order curves (equation (4.67)). Further, maximum output limits have to be respected (equation (4.68)).

$$C_i = c_{i,n} P_i^n + c_{i,n-1} P_i^{n-1} + \cdots + c_{i,2} P_i^2 + c_{i,1} P_i + c_{i,0} \tag{4.67}$$

$$P_i \leq Pmax_i. \tag{4.68}$$

The demand side can be modelled as an inverse linear demand function (4.69) or inverse constant elasticity demand function (4.70) where the dependence of the market price S on the total generation output P is described as

$$S = a - b \cdot P \tag{4.69}$$

or

$$S = \alpha \cdot P^{\frac{1}{\varepsilon}}, \tag{4.70}$$

respectively, where a and b are positive coefficients of the inverse linear demand function, α is a positive coefficient and ε is the demand elasticity, which is negative. As demand elasticities are difficult to derive from historical data, it is suggested to use the residual demand curve instead, which incorporates the supply of all market participants with competitive behaviour.

Based on these continuous supply and demand functions, it is possible to calculate Cournot equilibria with standard solvers for MCP optimisation problems. An example of the application of game theory for analysing electricity markets is presented by Ellersdorfer (2005). General introductions can be found in textbooks, e.g. Osborne (2003).

4.4   RELEVANT SYSTEM INFORMATION FOR ELECTRICITY MARKET MODELLING

Modelling results are never better than the input data they are based on. Practical modelling experience shows that finding adequate system information is often a crucial point. Key challenges are:

- Attainment of high quality data.
- Correct interpretation of information.
- Focus on relevant details.
- Good estimates and assumptions for missing or contradictory information.
- Building models with adequate detail with regard to available information.

In this section, we want to describe what type of data is needed for modelling and what additional information can be used for deriving unavailable details. Further, potential sources of information are listed.

4.4.1   Demand Side

Relevant for modelling of the demand side is the load for the whole modelling period with appropriate time resolution. In the case of game theory-based models, price elasticities of the demand are required.

TSOs, associations of grid operators like UCTE, and statistical offices publish load data as historical time series with high time resolutions and, in some cases, also load forecasts. This data, in general, does not describe final customer demand (since it is not metered for all customers in high time resolution); rather it is derived from generation data of central power stations and from measured transmission flows at the boundaries of transmission areas. Consequently, transmission and distribution losses are included and decentralised generation as well as industrial autogeneration are not included in published load data. Some data sources publish average values, e.g. hourly values, while other data sources publish real time data, e.g. for every full hour. Time stamps associated with metered data for a period can be the beginning or the end of this period. Many grid operators publish data with the end of a period as time stamp, e.g. an hourly value published for 07:00 is in this case the average value for the period from 06:00 to 07:00. Information about the precise content of published data should be taken into account.

It is important to have consistent model boundaries on the supply and demand side. For example, if load data does not include generation from industrial power plants, these plants must not be included on the supply side of the model either.

Load forecasting is required for deriving load values for future time periods. For short-term models, these forecasts can be based on weather forecasts (see section 5.4). For long-term models with low time resolution, historical load patterns can be used. As load strongly depends on weather conditions, especially in countries where electric heating or air-conditioning are common, scenarios for different weather conditions might be appropriate. One further input parameter is long-term load growth. It might be estimated based on an extrapolation of historical load growth rates or based on forecasts for economic growth and its correlation with load growth. Definition of several scenarios might be adequate.

Price elasticities of electricity demand needed for game theory-based models are very difficult to obtain. In most countries, real time pricing is not common and demand can be considered as very inelastic in the short term. In the longer term, elasticities certainly exist as the extent of energy efficiency measures implemented depends on electricity prices to a certain degree. But compared with other determinants of electricity demand, price elasticity certainly plays a minor role.

4.4.2 Supply Side

For modelling the supply side of an electricity market, it is necessary to estimate the generation capacity that is offered at a particular price by market participants. As explained in the following sections, different aspects have to be considered for different types of power plants.

In the case of market models based on game theory, it is also necessary to find out who is economically responsible for the dispatch of every power plant. This is not necessarily the owner or operator of a power plant, especially in the case of independent power producers (IPPs) or of plants with shared ownership. Based on tolling agreements or similar agreements, contract partners might be in charge of power plant dispatch and exposed to economic results of these decisions.

Conventional Thermal Power Plants

The main required parameters for conventional thermal power plants are available capacity $Pmax_g$ and variable generation costs c_g.

Available generation capacity $Pmax_g$ depends on the following parameters:

- *Nominal net generation capacity*: Unfortunately this figure is not clearly defined, but in most cases it is the maximum electric output of the plant that can be fed into the grid under optimal environmental conditions at the time of commissioning of the plant or after a plant retrofit. In many publications, gross capacity values can be found. This value is the maximum generator output and does not consider own use within the power plant, e.g. for coal mills or for flue gas cleaning.
- *Age of the power plant*: With increasing age of a power plant maximum generation output slightly decreases due to wear.
- *Environmental conditions*: Maximum generation output as well as plant efficiency depends on outside conditions, especially on air temperature and humidity, as well as on river temperatures. Maximum generation output increases at lower temperatures. Open cycle gas turbines (GTs) and combined cycle gas turbines (CCGTs) are very sensitive to air temperatures. In summer, their maximum generation output can be several percentage points less than in winter. Many thermal power plants rely on cooling water from rivers and have to respect water usage limits. In summer, flow rates of rivers might be low and river temperatures high. In this case, power plants often face restrictions regarding water withdrawal or heat discharge into rivers. Water withdrawal restrictions are relevant for power plants with cooling towers, which evaporate substantial amounts of water. Heat discharge restrictions are relevant for power plants with direct cooling. In hot and dry summers, maximum generation output can be restricted severely for days or weeks. In extreme conditions, some power plants cannot be operated at all.

- *Heat demand in combined heat and power plants*: Maximum electricity output of combined heat and power plants depends on the heat demand. Higher heat demand in winter reduces available electrical output and conversely in summer.
- *Power plant maintenance*: Power plants have to be shut down at regular intervals for maintenance. Maintenance intervals depend on plant type, age of the power plant and maintenance strategy of the plant operator. Often, maintenance periods are scheduled several months in advance. Preferred times for maintenance are periods of low demand. Peak demand periods are generally avoided for scheduled maintenance. Owing to a limited number of maintenance groups and incentives to adapt available capacity to system load, most plant operators avoid too many scheduled plant outages for maintenance at the same time. Commonly there are annual maintenance intervals with durations of three to six weeks.

  For market models, it is common to depict power plant maintenance with seasonal patterns unless more detailed information about maintenance schedules is available.
- *Unplanned outages*: Besides planned outages for maintenance, unplanned outages due to failures have to be considered. These outages occur stochastically during the whole year. For market models, it is common to reduce the generation capacity for the whole year by average values for unplanned outages.

Considering all of these aspects, the average available generation capacity of thermal power plants is often only between 80% and 85% of the nominal net generation capacity.

Variable generation costs c_g consist of several components. They can be calculated as

$$
c_g = \frac{(cfuel_f + ctx_f + ctransp_{f,g} + fCO_{2f} \cdot cCO_2) \cdot fc_f}{\eta_g} + cOM_g. \tag{4.71}
$$

The parameters of equation (4.71) are explained below:

- *Fuel prices $cfuel_f$*: In the case of gas and imported coal, fuel prices at trading hubs can be obtained for historical periods as well as for future periods covered by a futures market. In the case of fuels that are traded in other currencies, foreign exchange rates have to be considered. For other fuels like indigenous coal or lignite, it might be more difficult to obtain detailed information and estimates might be required.

  For gas fired power plants, long-term integrated contracts for fuel and transport are common. Significant deviations from market prices can occur. With further liberalisation of energy markets these differences are likely to disappear.
- *Fuel taxes ctx_f*: In some countries, taxes or other duties apply for fuels used in power stations.
- *Fuel transport costs $ctrans_{f,g}$*: Specific transport costs for fuels f to power station g depend on transport distance and means of transport. In the case of coal, the main means are transport by barge or rail. Additional harbour costs and handling costs might apply. In the case of barge transport, water levels on rivers might have an important impact on transport costs as low river levels reduce transport capacity of barges. In the case of gas, fuel transport costs might have fixed and variable components. Only variable components are relevant for calculating variable generation costs.
- *Calorific value fc_f*: As electric generation output is generally measured in other energy units than fuels, the calorific value of the fuel has to be considered as a conversion

factor. In the case of gas, it is important to notice that gas prices are generally related to the higher heating value while power plant efficiencies are sometimes related to the lower heating value. In this case, the difference of approximately 10% between higher and lower heating value has to be considered.

- *Specific CO_2 emissions fCO_{2f} per unit of fuel.*
- *CO_2 emission allowance price cCO_2.*
- *Power plant efficiency η_g*: Relevant for market modelling is the average net efficiency. It can be several percentage points lower than published nominal net efficiencies, which are only achieved by new power plants under optimal environmental conditions and do not reflect aging effects, real environmental conditions, and part-load efficiencies. Relevant average efficiencies are often 2 to 3% lower in absolute terms than nominal net efficiencies. If no detailed information on power plant efficiencies is available, values can be estimated based on power plant age, size, and technology.
- *Variable operation and maintenance costs cOM_g*: While labour costs are generally fixed costs, part of the maintenance cost can be allocated to plant operation, which causes wear. Which part of total operation and maintenance costs are considered as variable costs varies from plant operator to operator and can depend on maintenance contracts with external service companies. Auxiliary costs, e.g. for chemicals, ash disposal, water withdrawal, or emissions might apply and have to be considered as well. Transmission tariffs can have a variable component, which has to be considered as variable operation cost.

In the case of aggregated depiction of power plants, cumulative capacities and average cost values can be used.

Besides available generation capacity $Pmax_g$ and variable generation costs c_g, the following parameters can be relevant for more detailed market models:

- *Time-integral fuel or emission constraints*: For example, take-or-pay quantities in gas contracts.
- *Start-up costs*: Start-up costs consist of fuel costs and operation and maintenance costs allocated to start-ups. Fuel needed for one start-up depends on the idle time before the start-up. Required emission allowances related to fuel usage have to be considered as well. Start-up costs are significant and generally in the same order of magnitude as variable costs for one hour of full-load operation.
- *Minimum up- and downtimes*: These depend on power plant type and power plant size. Smaller plants and more flexible plants generally have lower minimum up- and downtimes. Often, no strict technical constraints exist, rather these constraints are introduced for reducing operational risks. Two to 8 hours are common values used for market models.
- *Minimum load constraints*: This parameter depends on power plant type and power plant size. Twenty to 40% of the maximum capacity are typical values.
- *Ramp rates*: For models with hourly or lower time resolution, ramp rates can be neglected.
- *Must-run constraints*. For the dispatch of some thermal power plants, must-run constraints due to grid requirements or heat requirements in case of combined heat and power plants have to be considered.

Nuclear Power Plants

The main parameter for nuclear power plants is the available capacity. For deriving this parameter, the same considerations as for conventional thermal power plants are valid. Maintenance periods for nuclear power plants are generally longer than for conventional thermal power plants.

Variable costs of nuclear power plants do not play an important role in most electricity markets as they are generally lower than variable costs of thermal power plants and as nuclear power plants are price setting in the market only for a few hours of the year. Depending on operation and maintenance strategy of plant operators, relevant variable costs range from zero in the case of fixed maintenance intervals with fixed exchange of fuel rods to consideration of opportunity costs in the case of limited remaining fuel quantities until the next scheduled maintenance period. In the latter case, operation patterns are similar to those of storage hydro power plant with limited reservoir content.

Hydro Power Plants

Data required for depicting hydro power plants in electricity market models depends on the modelling approach. In the case of depiction by typical production patterns, historical production patterns and forecasted production patterns are required. In some cases, the consideration of scenarios is adequate for depicting fluctuations.

For more detailed modelling approaches, installed pump and turbine capacities, hydrological interconnections of power plants and reservoirs, reservoir volumes, specific pump and turbine flow rates as well as inflows are required. Power plant availabilities have to be considered as expected values. For inflows, a scenario approach might be adequate. In some cases, variable transmission tariffs need to be considered for pumping.

As it is often not possible to depict all hydro power plants in detail they are commonly depicted as a small number of aggregated hydro power plants.

Renewables

The production of electricity from renewable energy sources plants except storage and pumped storage hydro power plants depends on resource availability. Therefore, historical production patterns as well as forecasts are required for renewable electricity generation. For short-term modelling, i.e. for time horizons of several days, generation forecasts based on weather forecasts can be used. For long-term market models, the main challenge is to estimate long-term development of installed capacities of different technologies. Scenarios might be adequate.

Waste to energy power plants is considered in some statistics as renewable power plants as well. Its generation pattern is generally a baseload pattern.

4.4.3 Transmission System

The transmission system has two main impacts on electricity markets: transmission capacities between different transmission regions are provided and create interdependencies between these regions, and reserve requirements impact power plant dispatch.

Transfer Capacities

In the case of single-region models, historical exchange patterns and forecasts for future time periods are required for describing exchanges with adjacent regions. For multi-regional market models, net transfer capacity (NTC) values between regions are relevant. NTC values depend on transmission system availability as well as on load flow conditions. Values published by grid operators generally do not include transmission capacity of independently owned and operated DC-links.[25]

Reserve Capacity Requirements

For depicting reserve capacity requirements adequately, values for the required capacity in positive and negative direction as well as information on typical means of reserve provision are required. Part of the required reserves may be provided by the supply side.

4.4.4   Historical Data for Backtesting

Backtesting is an important step for market model development. For identifying shortcomings of a market model, it is very useful to compare market modelling results for historical time periods with available historical data. Besides electricity market prices, generation by type of fuel as well as CO_2 emission figures are valuable data for this purpose.

4.4.5   Information Sources

Information sources and data availability vary strongly from country to country. Therefore, it is necessary to systematically search for available data. Common information sources are:

- *Transmission system operators*: Internet publications, annual reports, statistical year-books, press releases etc.
- *Associations of grid operators*: National associations as well as international associations of grid operators publish data in different ways. In Europe, for instance, ETSO, UCTE, and NORDEL publish relevant information in the Internet.
- *Generation companies*: Internet publications, annual reports, environmental reports, power plant brochures, press releases etc.
- *Energy regulators*: Internet publications and statistical reports.
- *Ministries for energy and environment*: Ministries often publish political programme for the future development of the electricity system. This information can be relevant for long-term models.
- *Statistical offices*: National and international statistical offices publish different relevant details regarding generation capacity and historical electricity production by fuel. Sometimes statistics on power plant availability, fuel and electricity prices, transport costs etc. are available.
- *Emissions registries*: National emissions registries or the Community Independent Transaction Log (CITL) publish historical emission data on installation level. This can be useful for backtesting.

---

[25] DC: direct current.

- *Energy exchanges*: Energy exchanges like the EEX or Nord Pool publish relevant system information e.g. on power plant availability as well as market results. Fuels and CO_2 emission allowances are traded at exchanges, which publish spot as well as futures market results (see sections 1.3.2, 1.1.2, 1.1.3, 1.2.2 and 1.5.4).
- *Energy brokers*: Besides price data for electricity fuels, and CO_2 emission allowances, brokers can provide other market information, e.g. in the form of newsletters or load and wind energy production forecasts.
- *Meteorological offices and private weather services*: Historical weather data as well as forecasts can be obtained by these institutions. In some cases, weather services provide special products like load forecasts and wind energy production forecasts as well.
- *Water authorities*: In some cases, these authorities publish relevant information not only in respect to hydro power generation but also in respect to production constraints of thermal power plants and transport restrictions on rivers.
- *Research institutes*: Many private and public research institutes analyse electricity markets or relevant aspects like renewable energy and can provide research results as well as data. But it is important to mention that many research institutes have a strong focus on methodological issues and do not necessarily pay attention to data accuracy.
- *Consulting companies*: Specialised consulting companies have detailed knowledge about electricity markets and can provide information, assist market model development, and sometimes even sell complete market models including data updates.
- *Financial institutions*: Many investment banks publish reports and other information regarding electricity markets and market participants.
- *Financial data providers*: Besides relevant financial information like exchange rates, these companies also provide market data of electricity and fuel markets.
- *Real time data providers*: Real time data about production of large power plants as well as on physical electricity flows at major interconnections can be obtained from specialised information providers.
- *Journals and newspapers*: Some relevant information, e.g. regarding power plant development, can be found in journals specialised in energy or in general newspapers.

A good overview on the European electricity system and relevant companies as well as institutions is provided in Meller *et al.* (2006).

As information content changes rapidly it is important to keep well informed about information availability so as to keep market models as up to date and precise as possible.

4.5   APPLICATION OF ELECTRICITY MARKET MODELS

Fundamental electricity market models are widely used in middle offices of energy trading companies, in strategy departments of utilities, in energy consulting companies, and at research institutes. Typical areas for the application of market models are:

- *Spot markets*: Fundamental market models can assist spot market trading decisions by quantifying price effects of exogeneous impacts. Many electricity trading companies use market models for short-term price forecasts up to seven days into the future. Based on these price forecasts it is possible to take short-term trading positions, e.g. to buy electricity for the next day OTC and sell it later at the auction of the electricity exchange if OTC prices are below the expected auction price. For deriving good short-term price forecasts, it is important to use all available information for the relevant time period. The main focus should be on load forecasts, forecasts for renewable energy production, especially wind energy production, and changes in power plant availability. Significant changes in spot market fuel prices and futures market electricity prices have to be considered as well. The latter impact influences opportunity costs for generation of storage hydro power plants. Rather than deriving absolute prices directly, it is more appropriate to derive price changes that are caused by changes of fundamental factors.

Figure 4.33 shows an illustrative example based on a merit order approach. If the market price for one hour was 50 EUR/MWh, then this value can be used as a starting point for forecasting the market price for the same hour of the following day. In the merit order diagram, we can backtrack the load associated to this price following arrows 1 and 2. This load is not necessarily identical to the load forecast for this hour due to model inaccuracies. We consider three changes in fundamental influencing factors from one day to the next:

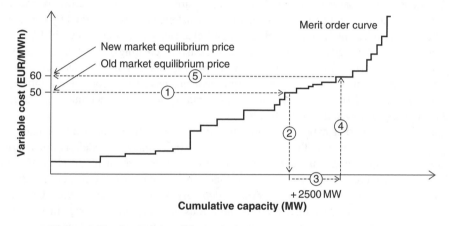

Figure 4.33   Spot market delta analysis based on a merit order approach

– Increase of system load by 2000 MW. The forecasts are relevant.
– Increase of wind energy generation by 1000 MW. Again forecasts are relevant.
– Unplanned outage of one nuclear power plant with 1500 MW capacity.

In total, we have a resulting change of +2500 MW (arrow 3). Finally, we can read the new price as forecast for the second day in the merit order diagram. Following arrows 4 and 5 we obtain the value 60 EUR/MWh.

For spot market trading, market models can be used for quantifying price risks. If it is possible to quantify uncertainties, e.g. if there is news that one specific large power plant in the market might be back to service after maintenance the next day or not, it is possible to analyse resulting price impacts. This kind of risk analysis is especially valuable in situations in which total demand comes close to available generation capacity and therefore high price peaks could occur.

- *Futures markets*: Electricity market models can provide price forecasts for the time horizon covered by futures markets for electricity and fuels. These forecasts can be used as a basis for the development of trading strategies. While for the spot market fuel and

CO_2 prices can be considered as constant from one day to the next, over several months or years significant changes occur. Fundamental market models can be used for quantifying the impact of fuel and CO_2 price changes. This consideration leads to the development of multi-commodity trading strategies. If, for instance, market model results indicate that present electricity forward market prices are too high considering present forward market prices for fuels and CO_2, a multi-commodity trading strategy might consist of buying electricity futures or forwards and selling appropriate amounts of coal, gas, oil, and CO_2 for the same period. The required estimation of these *appropriate* amounts can be based on a sensitivity analysis using market models for quantifying the impact of fuel and CO_2 price changes on electricity market prices. If different commodities are traded in different currencies, foreign exchange contracts should be included in the multi-commodity trading strategy to exclude currency risks.

- *Long-term scenarios*: For long-term decisions, e.g. the construction of a new power plant, long-term scenarios are required for project evaluation. For long-term scenarios, the focus is not on correct scenarios as there are no correct scenarios as such, but rather on plausible and consistent scenarios. Consistency can be achieved by considering fundamental relations between fuel, CO_2, and electricity prices as shown in Figure 4.2. Fundamental electricity market models can assist in creating consistent scenarios for long-term scenarios. Besides fuel and CO_2 prices, changes in the electricity system, e.g. the expansion of renewable generation capacity have to be considered. Often, it is important to build several consistent sets of scenarios to reflect uncertainty in the future development of key influencing factors.

    If historical market data is available this information should be used for calibrating market models. However, the application of electricity market models is not restricted to established electricity markets. For emerging markets without liquid electricity markets, market models can be especially valuable in simulating a future market. But it is important to note that electricity market models rely on implicit assumptions with regard to electricity market design. If these assumptions are not adequate, e.g. in the case of regulated electricity prices or oligopolistic market structures, additional approaches might be required for scenario generation.

Electricity market models can provide decision support for the development of trading strategies and for strategic long-term decisions. But it is important to check the plausibility of market modelling results carefully as inadequate assumptions regarding input data or market design might lead to inadequate results.

4.6   GAS MARKET MODELS

Fundamental gas market models are used for natural gas market analysis with short- to long-term perspectives. While the basic modelling approaches are similar to electricity market models, there are significant differences on the demand as well as on the supply side. Furthermore, transmission and storage of gas play an important role. A clear separation into different market regions, e.g. on a country by country basis, which can then be modelled independently from adjacent regions, is more difficult than in electricity markets. Many market regions cannot be modelled separately, as gas import capacities are very significant compared to domestic production capacities. With increasing LNG (liquefied natural gas) capacities, even a global gas marked is emerging (see section 1.2.4). Another difference between gas and electricity markets is the impact of regulation. Especially regarding transmission and storage, regulations have significant market impacts and differ strongly from country to country. It is necessary to adapt modelling approaches accordingly.

The optimisation of a gas portfolio consisting of delivery contracts, supply contracts, transmission capacities, and storage facilities is a task comparable to economic power plant dispatch in the electricity sector. Understanding gas portfolio optimisation is a prerequisite for understanding gas markets. Furthermore, it provides a good starting point for developing gas market models. In the following sections, we describe how these portfolio components can be described for both portfolio optimisation and gas market modelling.

While balancing periods of 15 or 30 minutes are common in electricity markets, balancing periods of one day are common in gas markets.[26] Load fluctuations within one day are compensated by the network operators, which can modulate pipeline pressures within certain ranges (line packing). This flexibility can be used for balancing intra-day fluctuations. The delivery period of spot market trades is generally also one day. Therefore, portfolio optimisation is conducted with daily time resolution.

The unit for gas flow is either volume per time or energy per time. For modelling purposes, the use of energy units is recommended, as heat rates of gas vary between different parts of the system.

4.6.1 Demand Side

In Europe, natural gas demand has a strong seasonal pattern and is very temperature sensitive in winter. Figure 4.34 shows the cumulative gas demand of most regions in France. Winter peak demand is more than five times the demand of an average summer day. A regular weekly pattern can be observed in summer. In winter, demand is negatively correlated with outside temperatures as gas is used predominantly for heating. The weekly demand pattern also exists in winter, but is much less obvious due to the strong temperature sensitivity. This temperature sensitivity results in significant differences in cumulative winter demand between years. Forecast uncertainty, e.g. on a monthly basis, is much higher for gas demand than for electricity demand. For capturing this uncertainty, scenario approaches can be applied.

The gas demand $L_{n,t}$ in region n during time interval t can be modelled as a function of outside temperature τ_t and day type D_t:

$$L_{n,t} = f(\tau_t, D_t). \tag{4.72}$$

Gas supply contracts with large industrial customers often contain interruption clauses. The gas supplier can interrupt the supply with prior notice (e.g. one day in advance). Contracts specifying temperatures below which the supply can be interrupted or specifying a maximum number of days with interruption during the winter period are common. Short-term price elasticity of gas demand has to be considered for portfolio optimisation as well. In industrial sectors, fuel oil can be used for substituting natural gas in many applications. In the electricity sector, gas demand depends on the price differential between variable generation costs of

---

[26] In Germany, hourly balancing periods are common. While in some markets the balancing periods are calendar days, in other markets, daily periods start at 6 am and last until 6 am the following day.

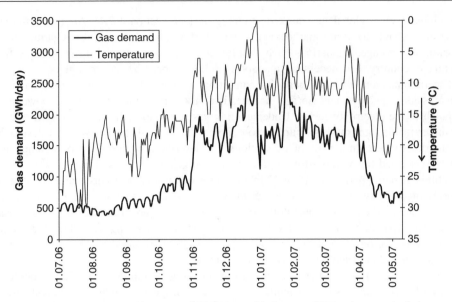

Figure 4.34   Gas demand in France (GDF Network). Source: GDF and own calculations

coal and of gas power plants. The extent of this fuel switching potential in the power sector depends on installed coal and gas generation capacities. In the United Kingdom, this potential is very significant, for example. Final customer gas demand with or without interruptibility and with or without price elasticity can be part of a gas portfolio. For simplicity reasons, we assume that gas demand $L_{n,t}$ is given.

4.6.2   Supply Side

There are three main sources for natural gas supply:

- *Domestic gas supply*: In Europe, domestic gas sources are mainly located in the North Sea (United Kingdom and Norway) and in the Netherlands. Production rates have been declining in recent years with declining remaining resources in the gas fields.
- *Pipeline gas*: Long distance pipelines are used for the delivery of gas to Europe from Russia and from Algeria.
- *LNG*: Pipeline transport is only economically efficient for large quantities and moderate distances. Pipeline construction off-shore is much more cost intensive than on-shore. LNG is transported by ship on routes that would not be economically efficient for pipeline transport. LNG terminals with regasification facilities exist in Europe in several countries including Belgium, France, Italy, Spain, and the United Kingdom. With declining domestic gas production and technological progress reducing LNG transport costs, LNG is gaining market share.

Natural gas is not a uniform commodity as gas qualities differ from source to source. Domestic gas in the Netherlands and in Germany has a lower calorific value than gas from Norway or Russia. For different gas distribution networks, different gas specifications apply.

Most common are L-gas with a calorific value of approximately $10\,kWh/m^3$ and H-gas with approximately $12\,kWh/m^3$. The conversion of H-gas to L-gas is possible, but not vice versa. For portfolio optimisation, regions with different gas qualities can be considered as separate portfolios unless conversion capacities from H-gas to L-gas are part of the portfolio. Accordingly for simplicity, we consider a gas portfolio or gas supply system with only one gas quality.

Economically, gas supply is characterised by high investment costs and negligible variable production costs. The same holds for long distance gas transport. Variable costs occur only in the form of gas used for transport. For pipeline transport, gas is needed for the operation of compressors. For LNG transport, gas is needed for the liquefication process and for the regasification process. Furthermore, during sea transport, part of the LNG evaporises (boil off) and is partly used as fuel for the ship's engine. In total, approximately 20% losses occur throughout the LNG chain.

While in many electricity markets wholesale market prices are based on short run marginal system costs, this cannot be the case in gas markets as short run marginal production costs are negligible. Instead of variable production costs, gas import conditions have to be considered for understanding market prices. Gas imports are predominantly based on long-term contracts with oil-indexation. Oil-indexation was introduced to ensure economic viability of gas in comparison with gasoil or fuel oil. Final customer gas prices are calculated to ensure that the use of gas is slightly cheaper than oil for the same application. In some cases, coal indexed prices are also found. With this direct or indirect indexation on the supply and demand side, gas import companies remain without any major price or volume risks. Gas producers bear the price risk but no major volume risk. For more deatils on indexed gas contracts see section 1.2.3.

Import contracts c are characterised by the following parameters:

- *Contract price*: The contract price $p_{c,t}$ is generally variable and indexed to different oil product or other commodity prices $p_{i,t}$. Often, a time lag Δt and the averaging of price indices over several months applies (see section 1.2.3). The indexed price can be expressed as

$$p_{c,t} = p_{oc} + \sum_i \left(a_{i,c} \cdot (p_{i,t-\Delta t} - p_{i,t_o}) \right), \tag{4.73}$$

where t_o is the reference time, p_{oc} is the reference price at time t_o, and $a_{i,c}$ are weights for different price indices $p_{i,t}$.
- *Contract duration*: In Europe, contract durations between 10 and 40 years are common for long-term import contracts.
- *Contract volume*: The contract volume Q_c is generally defined as annual maximum quantity.
- *Take-or-pay volume*: Many import contracts are flexible with regard to the annual volume. The take-or-pay volume $Qmin_c$ is the minimum volume that has to be payed for, e.g. 80% of the contract volume. In addition, some contracts define take-or-pay volumes for the summer period. Carry forward clauses are also common. They allow the importer to shift a limited volume of gas to be used to the following year if he falls below the take-or-pay limit in one year.
- *Swing*: Within one year, the importer can be flexible within certain ranges. This flexibility is called *swing*. The maximum daily volume $Qmaxd_c$ is generally limited. For example, a swing of 20% would allow the importing company to receive up to $Qmaxd_c = 1.20 \cdot Q_c/365$ of gas per day.

We introduce the positive flow variable $QC_{c,t}$ for long-term contracts. Assuming daily time resolution and an annual modelling period we can formulate the following constraints for imports:

The daily flow $QC_{c,t}$ is limited by the maximum swing to

$$QC_{c,t} \leq Qmaxd_c \quad \forall (c, t).^{27} \tag{4.74}$$

The annual volume is constrained to the contract volume Q_c. We obtain

$$\sum_t QC_{c,t} \leq Q_c \quad \forall c. \tag{4.75}$$

The lower limit for the annual volume is given by the take-or-pay volume $Qmin_c$. We obtain

$$\sum_t QC_{c,t} \geq Qmin_c \quad \forall c, \tag{4.76}$$

assuming that no carry forward is possible.[28]

Long-term gas supply is delivered to a delivery point n specified in the contract. We denote by the index $c(n)$ all long-term contracts c that have node n as their delivery point.

As an additional supply option we assume a liquid spot market in some regions or at some trading hubs or balancing points n. Relevant for modelling is the spot market price $S_{n,t}$. For future time periods, it can be derived from a price forward curve or scenario. The volume traded at the spot market is described by variable $QSp_{n,t}$. In the case of spot market purchases, $QSp_{n,t}$ is positive; in the case of sales it is negative. For reflecting limited market liquidity in some regions, the parameter $QSpmax_{n,t}$ is introduced as an upper limit for sales and purchases. As constraints we obtain

$$QSp_{n,t} \leq QSpmax_{n,t} \quad \forall (n, t) \tag{4.77}$$

and

$$QSp_{n,t} \geq -QSpmax_{n,t} \quad \forall (n, t). \tag{4.78}$$

In most cases, the import of LNG is also based on long-term contracts, but in some cases, LNG imports are more flexible and transport can be diverted to regions with higher gas prices. With increasing LNG volumes and sufficient flexibility in the LNG chain, regional gas markets will become more and more linked to each other. LNG imports can be either modelled as long-term contracts c or, in the case of flexible destinations, as sources with variable volume and prices. These prices can be derived from the price forward curve at alternative destinations under consideration of differences in transport costs.

4.6.3 Transport

Transmission is regulated in different ways in different countries. Most relevant for portfolio optimisation and market model development are the rules for capacity allocation to market

---

[27] $\forall (c, t)$: for all long-term contracts c is the gas portfolio and for all time intervals t is the optimisation period.
[28] It would also be possible to take less volume than the take-or-pay volume and still pay for this minimum volume. To reflect this theoretical possibility, we formulate the node balance equation (4.86) as a lower bound for gas arriving at a node.

participants. Most common are entry/exit systems. Different entry and exit points are defined for every market area. Entry capacity is required for gas flows entering a market region and exit capacity is required for gas flows exiting a market region. Within the region, gas can be transported freely. Physical bottlenecks within a region, which might occur, are resolved by the system operator, e.g. by purchasing load flow commitments. There are two predominant means for allocating entry and exit capacities to market participants: auctions and allocations based on a first come first served basis with fixed, published tariffs. Capacity allocation is possible for different time frames. Part of the capacity allocation can be long term, i.e. for several years, part of it on an annual, quarterly, or monthly basis, and part of it day-ahead. Use-it-or-lose-it rules may apply. They allow system operators to offer capacity not nominated the day ahead once again to the market. In some markets, a secondary transport capacity market starts to develop. Capacity can be allocated as firm or as interruptible capacity. Generally, different tariffs apply to firm and to interruptible capacity. In the case of interruptible tariffs, a priority order is established on a first-come-first-served basis. Modelling interruptible capacity in portfolio optimisation or in a risk control context requires the estimation of the probability of interruptions, which proves difficult.

We use a nodal model structure for depicting the gas supply system's topology. Figure 4.35 shows an example of the representation of a gas transport network. Every market area contains one node. Trading hubs that are adjacent to several market areas have to be considered as separate nodes.

We introduce the flow variable $QF_{n,m,t}$ for flows from node n to node m during time interval t. $QF_{n,m,t}$ is a positive variable.

As an example, we assume that firm transport capacity (exit and entry capacity) from node n to node m is available on an annual basis. The combined entry and exit tariffs are $TC_{n,m}$. The flow $QF_{n,m,t}$ is constrained by the capacity variable $CF_{n,m}$ by

$$QF_{n,m,t} \leq CF_{n,m} \quad \forall (n, m, t). \tag{4.79}$$

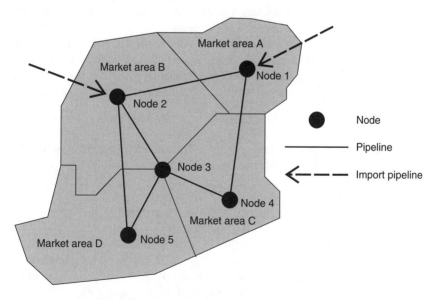

Figure 4.35 Nodal gas transport system topology

4.6.4 Storage

As the flexibility provided by the swing of import contracts is limited, gas storage facilities are used for compensating changes in gas demand. There are four main types of gas storage facilities:

- *Depleted gas or oil fields or aquifers*: These storage facilities have small injection and withdrawal rates in relation to the storage volume. They are mainly used for seasonal storage.
- *Underground caverns*: They are predominantly constructed in underground salt domes by washing out part of the salt for creating the cavern. Specific injection and withdrawal rates are higher than for depleted oil or gas fields or aquifers. Underground caverns are used for weekly or monthly storage rather than for seasonal storage.
- *LNG storage facilities*: Liquefied natural gas can be stored in tanks. LNG storage facilities are predominantly located at LNG terminals.
- *Pipeline storage facilities*: The pipeline system itself can be used as a storage facility to a certain degree by pressure variation (line packing). Additional flexibility can be created by increasing pipeline diameters or by additional pipelines, often arranged in a square pattern. Pipeline storage is predominantly used in the distribution system for intra-day balancing.

Access to storage facilities is regulated in some markets. Tariffs and conditions differ significantly. Besides using physical storage facilities, virtual storage products can be obtained in the gas market. A virtual gas storage is a complex product that allows the buyer to inject gas into and withdraw gas from a virtual gas account. He delivers gas to the seller or receives gas from the seller, respectively, based on daily nominations. For physical storage facilities, many constraints have to be considered, including volume dependency of injection and withdrawal rates, gas required for operation of the compressor, maintenance, and unplanned outages. Virtual storage products have fewer constraints.

Physical storage facilities have many non-linear constraints. Here we consider constraints relevant for underground gas storage facilities (depleted oil or gas fields, aquifers, or caverns). For reducing complexity, we describe a linear approximation to these constraints and neglect maintenance and other causes of unavailability. We introduce the following parameters and variables:

- $Vmax_s$: Maximum gas content of the storage s. The minimum content is assumed to be 0.
- $V_{s,t}$: Storage content at the end of time interval t (positive variable).
- $QImax_s$: Maximum injection rate.
- $QWmax_s$: Maximum withdrawal rate.
- $QI_{s,t}$: Injection rate during time interval t (positive variable).
- $QW_{s,t}$: Withdrawal rate during time interval t (positive variable).
- fI_s: Specific compressor gas consumption in relation to the injection rate. For keeping the model linear, we assume a constant parameter. In practice, this parameter depends on the pressure difference between the storage and the connecting pipeline. Besides gas fuelled compressors, electric compressors are used. In these cases, electricity prices have to be taken into account.

Gas storage facilities are linked to a specific node n of the system. In the following equations, we will use the index $s(n)$ for storage facilities connected to node n.

Possible injection and withdrawal rates depend on the storage content $V_{s,t}$. Possible injection rates decrease with increasing storage content and possible withdrawal rates increase. These constraints are depicted schematically in Figure 4.36. The non-linear part of these curves can be approximated by lines $\mathbf{f_1}$ and $\mathbf{f_2}$ that are defined by parameters a, b, c, and d where $-b$ and d are the slope of the lines $\mathbf{f_1}$ and $\mathbf{f_2}$, respectively.

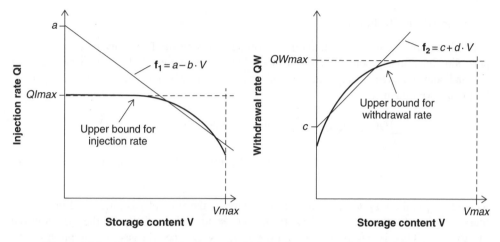

Figure 4.36   Gas storage injection and withdrawal rates depending on storage content

Injection rates $QI_{s,t}$ are constrained by the maximum injection rate $QImax_s$ and by line $\mathbf{f_1}$. We obtain

$$QI_{s,t} \leq QImax_s \qquad \forall(s, t) \tag{4.80}$$

and

$$QI_{s,t} \leq a - b \cdot V_{s,t} \qquad \forall(s, t). \tag{4.81}$$

Withdrawal rates $QW_{s,t}$ are constrained by

$$QW_{s,t} \leq QWmax_s \qquad \forall(s, t) \tag{4.82}$$

and

$$QW_{s,t} \leq c + d \cdot V_{s,t} \qquad \forall(s, t). \tag{4.83}$$

The storage content $V_{s,t}$ is limited by the maximum content $Vmax_s$:

$$V_{s,t} \leq Vmax_s \qquad \forall(s, t). \tag{4.84}$$

The storage content $V_{s,t}$ at the end of time interval t is equivalent to the storage content $V_{s,t\leftarrow 1}$ at the end of the previous time interval $t^{\leftarrow 1}$ plus injections $QI_{s,t}$ and minus withdrawals $QW_{s,t}$ during time interval t. This is expressed by the storage balance equation

$$V_{s,t} = V_{s,t\leftarrow 1} + QI_{s,t} - QW_{s,t} \qquad \forall (s,t). \tag{4.85}$$

Additional constraints are required for defining start and end values for the storage content. For simplicity, they are neglected here.

4.6.5 Portfolio Optimisation

Portfolio optimisation aims to maximise revenues utilising the flexibility inherent in a gas portfolio. Its primary constraint is the node balance equation (4.86), which ensures that demand does not exceed supply at any node n at any time t. Considering all flows from and to a node, we obtain

$$\sum_{c(n)} QC_{c,t} + QSp_{n,t} + \sum_{m} (QF_{m,n,t} - QF_{n,m,t})$$
$$+ \sum_{s(n)} (QW_{s,t} - (1 + fI_s) \cdot QI_{s,t}) \geq L_{n,t} \qquad \forall (n,t), \tag{4.86}$$

where $QC_{c,t}$ is the long-term contract flow, $QSp_{n,t}$ is the flow of gas purchased in the spot market, $QF_{m,n,t}$ is the transport flow from node m to node n, $QW_{s,t}$ is the gas flow out of storage s, $QI_{s,t}$ is gas flow into storage s, fI_s is the specific gas consumption of the compressor for the storage, and $L_{n,t}$ is the customer demand.

The objective of portfolio optimisation is to maximise revenues or to minimise costs. We choose to use a cost minimising formulation, as we have defined all prices on the cost side. Revenues from spot market sales $QSp_{n,t} < 0$ result in negative costs $QSp_{n,t} \cdot S_{n,t}$. We have to consider costs for long-term gas contracts $QC_{c,t} \cdot p_{c,t}$, costs for spot market purchases $QSp_{n,t} \cdot S_{n,t}$, and transmission capacity costs $CF_{n,m} \cdot TC_{n,m}$ for obtaining the total cost C for the whole optimisation period:

$$C = \sum_{c,t} (QC_{c,t} \cdot p_{c,t}) + \sum_{n,t} (QSp_{n,t} \cdot S_{n,t}) + \sum_{n,m} (CF_{n,m} \cdot TC_{n,m}) \overset{!}{=} \min. \tag{4.87}$$

Equation (4.87) is the objective function of the portfolio optimisation problem. It is a linear programming (LP) problem, which can be solved with standard solvers. If final customer demand is a significant part of the gas portfolio, scenario approaches are required for reflecting demand uncertainty. In this case, a decomposition approach might be required for solving the resulting stochastic programming problem. Different optimisation approaches are discussed in more detail in section 4.2.3.

4.6.6 Formulation of the Market Model

In contrast to gas portfolio optimisation, gas market models have to consider the whole market consisting of the sum of the portfolios of all market participants. There are significant differences between models for short-term and long-term market models. As short-term market models are closer to gas portfolio optimisation and as they are more suitable for explaining observed market prices, we will concentrate first on short-term models with a modelling horizon of one to five years.

Short-Term Market Models

We assume that none of the market participants exerts market power. In this case, a short-term gas market model can be considered as a portfolio optimisation problem for the whole system under consideration. While the main approach is identical to the mathematical description of the portfolio optimisation problem above, some differences apply:

- *Scope of the market model*: It is necessary to carefully define the scope of the market model. In addition to market areas for which model results are required, all connected market areas might have to be considered as well. It is possible to exclude market areas from the scope of the model, if the gas flows between the modelled system and these external areas can be considered as inelastic with respect to market prices.
- *Demand*: As elevant demand $L_{n,t}$, we have to consider the complete demand in all market areas n. Besides final customer demand, the demand required for the operation of the gas transport and distribution system (gas demand for compressors) has to be included.
- *Supply*: Besides supply based on long-term import contracts described in section 4.6.2, we have to consider domestic supply and flexible imports on a short-term basis via pipeline or LNG. In many cases, domestic supply can be considered exogenous with predefined flows $QD_{n,t}$ following typical seasonal production patterns. Alternatively, they can be described similarly to long-term contracts with minimum and maximum daily and annual volumes.

  Imports on a short-term basis can be considered as spot market purchases $QSp_{n,t}$ at defined prices $S_{n,t}$ and with maximum volumes $QSpmax_{n,t}$, entering the system from external areas. Assuming that spot market exports are not relevant, $QSp_{n,t}$ has to be defined as a positive variable. Spot market trades within the scope of the market model need not be considered, as the complementary deals are also within the scope of the model.
- *Transport*: The gas transport system can be modelled with a nodal topology as explained in section 4.6.3. Maximum transport capacities $QFmax_{n,m,t}$ have to be introduced to limit pipeline flows $QF_{n,m,t}$. As a constraint we obtain

$$QF_{n,m,t} \leq QFmax_{n,m,t} \qquad \forall (n, m, t). \tag{4.88}$$

In the case of auction-based capacity allocation for entry and exit capacities, transport prices can be assumed to be equal to 0 in the model. In the case of transport bottlenecks, price differences between nodes in the modelling results can be interpreted as expected values for capacity prices. In the case of tariff-based capacity allocation, these tariffs will have to be reflected in the model. If they are entered into a linear programming (LP) model as capacity prices for longer time periods, they will be reflected in the modelling results as market price differences between nodes only in time intervals t with maximum capacity utilisation. For avoiding these unrealistic results, capacity tariffs can be broken down to daily tariffs based on estimates for capacity utilisation factors. We assume that daily specific transport costs $TC_{n,m,t}$ can be estimated for this purpose.

In addition, exogenous gas flows $QFx_{n,t}$ from and to external regions have to be considered. In the case of positive flows to node n, $QFx_{n,t}$ is positive.

- *Storage*: In addition to underground storage facilities s described in section 4.6.4, LNG storage might have to be considered separately. The dependency of injection and withdrawal rates on storage content (equations (4.81) and (4.83)) can be neglected in many cases. In markets with regulated access to storage facilities, storage tariffs need also to be included in the model.

The gas market model can be formulated as an LP problem with constraints (4.74), (4.75), and (4.76) on long-term contract flows $QC_{c,t}$, with constraint (4.77) on spot market import flows $QSp_{n,t}$, with constraint (4.85) on pipeline flows $QF_{n,m,t}$, and with constraints (4.80), (4.82), (4.84), and (4.85) on storage injection flows $QI_{s,t}$ and storage withdrawal flows $QW_{s,t}$. We have to add exogenous domestic production $QD_{n,t}$ and exogenous transmission flows $QFx_{n,t}$ to equation (4.86) to obtain the node balance equation of the market model:

$$\sum_{c(n)} QC_{c,t} + QSp_{n,t} + \sum_m (QF_{m,n,t} - QF_{n,m,t}) + \sum_{s(n)} \left(QW_{s,t} - (1 + fI_s) \cdot QI_{s,t}\right)$$

$$+ QD_{n,t} + QFx_{n,t} \geq L_{n,t} \qquad \forall(n, t). \tag{4.89}$$

In the objective function (4.87), the representation of transport tariffs has to be modified accordingly to receive the objective function of the market model

$$C = \sum_{c,t} (QC_{c,t} \cdot p_{c,t}) + \sum_{n,t} (QSp_{n,t} \cdot S_{n,t}) + \sum_{n,m,t} (QF_{n,m,t} \cdot TC_{n,m,t}) \overset{!}{=} \min. \tag{4.90}$$

Market prices can be derived as marginal costs of the node balance equation (4.89). In addition, especially pipeline flows $QF_{m,n,t}$ can be modelling results relevant for market analysis. Pipeline flow results help to identify bottlenecks which can lead to significant price differences between nodes.

Long-Term Market Models

Long-term gas market models include the whole supply chain from gas production to final customer demand. The following system expansion options have to be considered and described by discrete expansion variables:

- Production capacity expansion
- Construction of new pipelines
- Construction of new LNG regasification terminals
- LNG transport capacity expansion
- Construction of new LNG liquefaction terminals
- Storage capacity expansion

For all of these system expansion options, lead times, capital investment costs, economic lifetimes, and annual operation and maintenance costs have to be considered.

The scope of long-term market models is generally a whole world region, e.g. Europe together with Northern Africa and Russia as supply regions. With increasing importance of LNG, global models might be required for reflecting the interdependency of different regional markets. Monthly time resolution is adequate if storage is considered, otherwise, annual time resolution is sufficient.

An example of a European long-term gas market model is explained by Perner (2002). A worldwide model with specific focus on the emerging LNG market is described by Seeliger (2006).

Methodological Modelling Approaches

The application of linear programming (LP) or mixed integer programming (MIP) is most common for simulating competitive gas markets. If market power is relevant, approaches based on system dynamics or on game theory can be applied (see sections 4.3.3 and 4.3.4).

4.6.7 Application of Gas Market Models

Short-term gas market models can be used for supporting the gas market analysis of an energy trading company. In comparison to electricity market models, it is more difficult to use gas market models for deriving actual market prices, as gas market prices are not based on short-term marginal production costs. However, gas market models can be used for identifying bottlenecks in the transport system and for deriving price differences between trading hubs. Furthermore, they can be used for analysing the impact of system modifications, such as the expansion of pipeline capacities or the commissioning of new pipelines or new LNG terminals. Gas market models can be used for the development of trading strategies.

Another application for short-term market models is analysing the impact of regulatory changes. One example is the application of a regional gas market model by Scheib *et al.* (2006) for analysing the impact of different numbers of market areas in Germany.

Long-term gas market models are more common than short-term models. Long-term market models can be used for system expansion planning in general or for decision support in more specific areas, including:

- Gas supply infrastructure projects
- Gas storage projects
- Gas fired power plant projects
- Long-term gas contracts
- National energy security considerations

The level of detail, the time resolution and the geographical coverage of long-term market models might have to be adapted for different applications.

4.7 MARKET MODELS FOR OIL, COAL, AND CO_2 MARKETS

Fundamental market models are not restricted to electricity and gas markets. Similar modelling approaches can also be applied to other fuel markets and to emissions markets. For these markets, it is also possible to derive cost-based supply and demand curves and market clearing prices.

Oil market models can be developed for crude oil or for oil products. For crude oil, worldwide supply and demand has to be considered. A multi-regional model is generally not required, as transport costs are small in comparison to oil prices. Compared to electricity markets oil markets are less transparent and purely cost-based approaches might not be adequate. Oil prices cannot be explained directly by short- or long-term marginal production costs. Therefore, price mechanisms have to be analysed in detail. Modelling approaches based on game theory can be applied for reflecting market power of OPEC. Even if it is not possible to use fundamental oil market models for price forecasting, they can assist market analysis in a structured way. They can be used for identifying key influencing factors on the supply and demand side and for supporting risk analysis.

Market models for oil products focus on oil refining capacities as supply side and on demand for different oil products. Transport costs might have to be considered.

Market models for coal can either depict regional markets or the global coal market. Steam coal and coking coal are different products in the world coal market. But as some steam coal qualities can also be used as coking coal, it might be appropriate to consider the interdependence of these markets. Transport costs are significant in comparison to coal prices. Therefore, a multi-regional nodal model structure similar to the structure of multi-regional electricity market models discussed in section 4.3.2 can be applied. Besides transport restrictions, transport costs have to be considered.

Fundamental market models for CO_2 certificates are widely used to describe the European Emissions Trading Scheme (EU ETS). On the supply side, national allocation plans (NAPs) as well as international supply by Certified Emission Reductions (CERs) and Emission Reduction Units (ERUs) are relevant. On the demand side, all emissions within the trading scheme have to be depicted. The most important sector is the electricity generation sector, which may be covered by electricity market models. The electricity sector is also the sector with the highest potential for short-term CO_2 price driven emission reductions. In many countries, electricity generation from coal as well as gas power plants is possible. As variable fuel costs in gas power plants are generally higher than in coal power plants, the utilisation factors of gas fired power plants are lower. Specific CO_2 emissions from gas power plants are lower than from coal power plants. With increasing CO_2 prices utilisation factors of gas power plants increase and the ones of coal power plants decrease. This fuel switching potential is the main mechanism that creates short-term price elasticity in the CO_2 market. But overall, the total price elasticity on the demand side is very low. For all other sectors in the EU emissions trading scheme, production quantities, and technological improvements are the key drivers for the development of CO_2 emissions. The development of production quantities and decisions about technical improvements can currently be considered as almost independent from CO_2 prices.

CO_2 market models will not be able to forecast CO_2 prices reliably. The main reasons are the price-inelastic demand in combination with fixed supply by the NAPs and many exogeneous impacts like economic development, weather impacts (which influence electricity demand as well as hydro power generation), and politics. Nevertheless, fundamental CO_2 market models can be used as decision support tools for trading decisions as well as for long-term investment decisions.

5

Electricity Retail Products

5.1 INTERACTION OF WHOLESALE AND RETAIL MARKETS

For utilities, pricing of retail contracts was a requirement long before the markets became liberalised, and long before the existence of a wholesale market. Therefore, the question of the way in which wholesale and retail markets are connected is reasonable. In most markets lower prices are expected in the wholesale market than in the retail market, otherwise there would be no profit margin for resellers and no incentive for entry into the retail market. In electricity markets retail prices are sometimes found to be below those in the wholesale market. This can occur at the establishment of a wholesale market, when the market is dominated by strategic considerations of the participants. But if the market is already in place and works effectively, each utility has the opportunity to push the energy onto the wholesale market instead of selling it to individual retail customers. This possibility is only restricted by market liquidity. Even if trading activities are rather low, this opportunity exists at least in a marginal consideration. This means, instead of selling power to a specific customer, there is always the alternative of pushing this incremental energy to the wholesale market. Hence, for this specific customer the retail price deduces from the wholesale price. Because this argument is also true for the next retail offer, prices for trading products will determine prices for end customers. There are analogue mechanisms in other markets. Acquisition costs are often based on actual stock prices. This is the case even though the trading volume is often significantly less than the volume of the acquisition.

To deduce retail prices from the prices of traded products, consider the situation of a utility which has power distribution but no self-generation. The utility sells electricity to end customers and has to arrange sourcing with respect to the price risk. There is minimal price risk if the utility covers its short position immediately after selling the energy to an end customer. If the sold energy corresponds to a traded product, the utility is able to assure a safe margin. Figure 5.1 shows this idealised situation.

The risk management process concerning price risk is as follows. First, the market price F of the corresponding trading product is determined. Subsequently, a price quotation to the end customer with the selected margin M can be made, which is $F + M$. If the customer accepts the quotation, the short position in the portfolio can be covered with the corresponding trading product. This risk management process is not very exciting and does not differ from other markets.

The next step takes into account the difference between retail and traded products. Initially a retail contract is regarded as an individual schedule resulting from the load forecast. Supplementary costs resulting from an uncertain load or from the demand of balancing power are subsequently considered in section 5.5.

As discussed in section 1.4, predominantly *baseload* and *peakload* products are traded. For these products the power is constant over all delivery hours, in contrast to the continuously

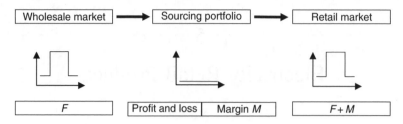

Figure 5.1   Portfolio of a utility with distribution only, idealised

varying true load of a customer. In principle, sourcing can also be done by purchasing a compatible power schedule leading to the same situation described above. But because of the limited liquidity of the market for power schedules covering the short position with a standard forward or a standard futures contract may be more economical. In this case the first task is to identify standard trading products that may minimise the remaining price risk. There are several approaches for solving this problem. The major differences between them concerns the quantity to minimise. Against a more technical background the remaining energetic position can be minimised which is what most utilities do. Other approaches, such as hedging a *delta position* or minimising the variance of the profit and loss function will be discussed in section 6.1. All these approaches share the fact that the position in the portfolio is not perfectly balanced and therefore a price risk still remains. The portfolio contains the difference between the purchased baseload and peakload contracts and the expected hourly load profile of the end customer. The remaining position can be interpreted as a non-standard forward or a power schedule and can be covered at the spot market for a presently unknown price S. Even if the retail customer will be charged with $F + \hat{S}$, where $\hat{S}$ denotes the presently expected value of S, there remains a price risk. This gives the situation shown in Figure 5.2 in contrast to the idealised situation in Figure 5.1, and the final margin is not fixed until the time of delivery.

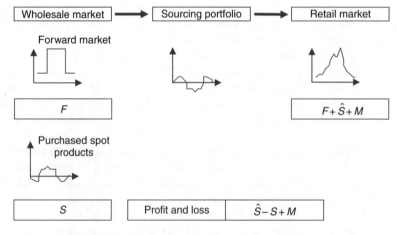

Figure 5.2   Portfolio of a utility with distribution only

The last consideration is the situation of a utility which also owns generation assets. There is always the opportunity of selling some or all of the electricity generated by its own plants to the wholesale market. This would require that some or all of the energy needed for supplying end customers has to be purchased. If there is a separate generation portfolio all profit created by the assets can be separated. The transaction price between the generation and the sourcing portfolio should be the price which can be obtained at the trading market. Hedging of the generation portfolio is then a process that can be handled separately. Managing the position in the generation portfolio then follows from the risk management strategy of the utility and is independent of the retail activity. In most cases it will be adequate to purchase the required primary fuels (e.g. coal, gas, or oil) simultaneously with power transfer from the generation to the sourcing portfolio. The disposition process is shown in Figure 5.3 where an additional risk premium R is introduced to cover the remaining risks from the retail sales. This risk premium will be discussed in section 5.5.

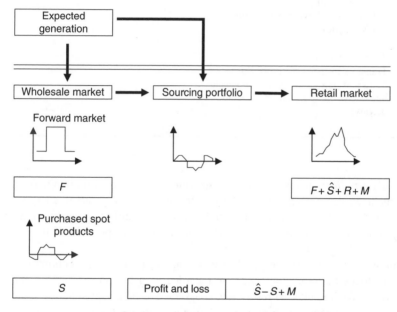

Figure 5.3 Portfolio of a utility with own generation

Concerning the retail pricing process, there is no significant difference between utilities owning generation assets and those without. Subtle differences do, however, occur when risk premiums are considered. The position in the sourcing portfolio is a power schedule which can be covered by an internal transaction from the generation portfolio. The transfer price is the actual market price for this power schedule. The problem of high bid–offer spreads for individual power schedules is solved. The lower remaining price risk in the retail portfolio requires a smaller retail risk premium and the *price profile risk* in the generation portfolio is reduced. The transaction is a profit for both portfolios and an advantage for integrated utilities.

This section concludes with a portfolio concept that supports the described processes. The profit of the generation unit and the profit of the sales and distribution activity are shown separately as two essential portfolios, one for generation and one for retail activities. Transfer prices are always deduced from the wholesale price. Table 5.1 shows this portfolio concept.

Table 5.1 Portfolio Concept

Generation portfolio	Retail portfolio

• Expected power generation and the resultant
 	
  – Coal position
  – Gas position
  – Oil position
  – Nuclear fuel position
  – Emission allowances position
  – FX position
 	
• Asset related contracts
• Transfers to the retail portfolio
• Sales and purchases on the wholesale market for hedging and optimisation purposes
	• Retail sales
	• Transfers from the generation portfolio
	• Purchases from the wholesale market

The *retail portfolio* contains all sales activities and the associated sourcing. The *generation portfolio* includes all transfers at market prices for retail sourcing and all energy sold on the wholesale market. The separate retail portfolio allows the utility to verify the adequacy of the risk premiums. The target value for the profit in the retail portfolio is the retail margin and the additional aspired price for taking the risk.

The following conventions are used in this chapter. There are no continuous stochastic processes in focus therefore the time t is regarded as a discrete variable. Granularity of traded products, or time interval resolution, is assumed as hourly granularity. Summing over t with $t \in [T_1, T_2]$ means summing over all single hours between date T_1 and T_2. $F(t_0, t)$ denotes the price of a forward valid at t_0 with delivery at the hour t. $\hat{L}(t_0, t)$ denotes the load forecast for the load at t forecasted at t_0. If t_0 is fixed, the notation $F(t)$ and $\hat{L}(t)$ are used.

5.2   RETAIL PRODUCTS

5.2.1   Common Full Service Contracts

Historically almost all delivery contracts were *full service contracts* where the customer purchased all of their power consumption from one provider. Usually these were fixed price contracts with an energy price $P + M + R$, and a fixed delivery period $[T_1, T_2]$ where P denotes the basic price, M the retail margin and R the risk premium. The power consumer could use the energy at any time. The basic pricing process requires the load of the customer $L(t), t \in [T_1, T_2]$ to be forecasted. Then the price P per MWh for the expected load $\hat{L}(t)$ is

$$P = \frac{\sum_{t=T_1}^{T_2} \hat{L}(t)F(t)}{\sum_{t=T_1}^{T_2} \hat{L}(t)}. \tag{5.1}$$

While the fixed price P is calculated with a load forecast the billing is based on the real load. There is a *load profile risk*, that the actual load differs from the forecasted profile and causes higher costs. An alternative which reduces this risk is to introduce time dependent tariffs. For example, the energy price can be composed of a *high tariff price* P_{HT} and a *low tariff price* P_{LT}. The validity of the tariffs can be based on the date where peak and off-peak contracts are delivered. Another possibility to reduce the load profile risk is splitting P into a price for the energy P_L and a *demand charge* P_C for the capacity. This assumes that there exists a means of recording the capacity. From a technical point of view, since the energy in a time slice is metered the average capacity in the time slice can be determined. The maximum average capacity determines the demand charge P_C. If transmission costs and energy costs are strictly separated there is no reason that a price difference will occur with a demand charge. This means that the sum

$$P = P_{\hat{L}} + P_{\hat{C}} \frac{\hat{C}}{\hat{L}}$$

has to fulfil equation (5.1), where $\hat{L}$ denotes the accumulated expected load in $[T_1, T_2]$ and $\hat{C}$ is the expected maximal capacity. The advantage of a demand charge for the capacity is that the risk of higher sourcing prices caused by a changing demand is reduced. If a retail customer purchases a new machine which operates only in times of high power prices and increases the required capacity, the supplier receives a higher price that may compensate his additional costs. In return the supplier can reduce his risk premium as an advantage for the retail customer.

5.2.2 Indexed Contracts

With the acceptance of wholesale prices as a basis for the retail price, more and more *indexed contracts* are being concluded. The main advantage of these contracts for the purchaser is a diversification as the energy price is not fixed all at once. The risk of buying the energy at the wrong moment when prices are near a local maximum is reduced. This is important when power prices are relevant for the purchaser's business competition. Index-linked contracts are also interesting for resellers (e.g. municipalities) if the price can be fixed in parts. Then the reseller can cover its own sales by fixing the sourcing price, and can organise the risk management process as shown in Figure 5.1. Let $I(t)$ denote the value of the index at t, T_0 the closing date of the contract, P the basic price determined in equation (5.1), R the risk premium, M the retail margin, and n the number of possible fixings, then an established form of an indexed price P_x is described by

$$P_x = (P + R + M)\frac{\sum_{k=1}^{n} I(t_k)}{nI(T_0)}, t_k \in [T_0, T_1]. \tag{5.2}$$

The buyer has the possibility of fixing their energy price n-times for $1/n$ of the total quantity each. An example with four fixings is displayed in Figure 5.4.

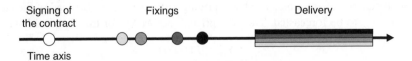

Figure 5.4   Fixing of indexed contracts

If the purchaser does not fix their energy price there is usually an automatic fixing at a specified date prior to delivery. The index can be a convex combination of two or more forwards or futures contracts. If baseload and peakload contracts with the prices F_B, F_P are traded liquidly, then the price index is usually

$$I(t) = (1 - a)F_B(t, T_1, T_2) + aF_P(t, T_1, T_2), a \in [0, 1].$$

The peakload ratio a can be determined from the energetic peakload contingent.

Sometimes the index is not a power price, but a primary energy index such as the coal TFS API#2 index. The buyer then has a virtual power plant and the involved chances and risks. Consider a Euro-based coal price indexed power supply contract with a monthly adapted power price P_m valid for delivery month m. Let the positive number c be the coal price ratio, C_m the monthly average of the coal index for the month m, C_0 the initial value of the coal index, X_m the average value of one Dollar in Euros for the month m, and $m = 0$ the initial month, when the contract and P are fixed. Then the power price P_m is given by

$$P_m = (P + M + R)\left(1 + c\left(\frac{X_m}{X_0}\frac{C_m}{C_0} - 1\right)\right)$$

and the coal price ratio c determines the influence of coal prices to the power supply price. If one tonne of coal is needed for generating three MWh electricity, a value for the ratio $c = 33\%$ can be calculated. The contract may not consider emission prices as would be required with a self-owned coal fired plants however, the formula can be extended accordingly.

5.2.3   Partial Delivery Contracts

Since retail customers can change their supplier, *partial delivery contracts* have appeared to allow energy consumers to manage energy price risk. These contracts provide the possibility of having more than one supplier. A customer with partial delivery contracts can manage their energy portfolio without setting up a trading department. According to the rules of the transmission system operator (TSO) and avoiding the risk of high prices for balancing power there is a specified supplier who owns the remaining *open contract*. This supplier must know the quantities of energy purchased by the customer and agrees to deliver the remaining quantity. The supplier's risk in relation to the sold energy is higher compared to a full service contract, yielding a higher risk premium R. Figure 5.5 shows the functionality of partial delivery contracts.

The sourcing process of the supplier owning the open contract starts with calculation of a load forecast. Next the partial delivery is defined, usually as a combination of standardised baseload and peakload contract quantities. Then the price for the open contract and the risk premium can be determined. The purchase of the partial delivery is the responsibility of the retail customer. If the customer fails there needs to be a fall-back arrangement such as an automatic price fixing by the supplier holding the open contract.

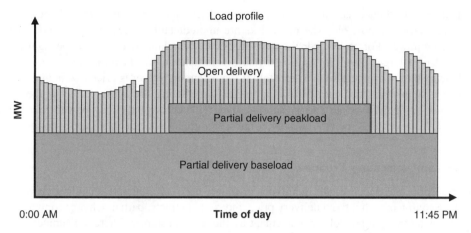

Figure 5.5   Partial delivery contract

5.2.4   Portfolio Management

For a retail customer it is important to determine the energy price risk they are prepared to take. With the described partial delivery contracts they have some of these possibilities, similar to a utility with its own trading department. These possibilities can be expanded if the customer has a delivery contract which allows portfolio management by the customer's order. The supplying utility acts more like a broker than a supplier. With this type of contract, the retail customer can determine exactly the points of time $k, k \in 1 \ldots n$, when they want to buy standardised wholesale products $F(t_k, \cdot, \cdot)$. Load forecast and portfolio management are the responsibility of the retail customer. Energy not covered by the purchased wholesale products $F(t_k, \cdot, \cdot)$ will be complemented by purchasing spot products, normally for single hours. Balancing power is needed in addition for the deviations of the true load from the load forecast, and must be accounted for by the retail customer directly. The principle of these contracts is displayed in Figure 5.6.

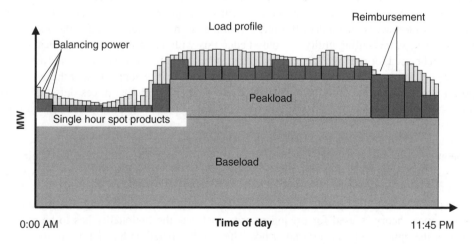

Figure 5.6   Portfolio management by the customer's order

If a retail customer has such a portfolio-style delivery contract, they must forecast their load as exactly as possible. The main risks are unpredictable prices for spot products and balancing power. For an individual customer, prices for balancing power can be significant. As part of a larger portfolio there is a risk diversification and therefore the premium for balancing power can be lower. Alternately if the balancing power is priced without a spread between supply and demand, there is a chance of reducing the energy price. If the retail customer has purchased an energy surplus, they will receive balancing power prices. We assume, however, that the retail customer has a significant uncertainty in their supply price.

5.2.5 Supplementary Products

This section introduced established types of power delivery contracts including classic full service contracts with a fixed delivery price, indexed contracts, partial delivery contracts and contracts allowing a portfolio management by the retail customer. There are supplementary products which can be combined with all of these delivery contracts and are discussed below.

Reserve Contracts

If a customer with generation capabilities cannot or does not want to manage their energy demand, they need an additional supply contract. With this contract they can transfer the risk of default of their own plants to the supplier. They can also order additional energy for times of maintenance of plants. These *reserve contracts* include some optionality for the customer, and are a challenge for the pricing department of the supplier. First, the quantity of reserve energy has to be determined. This can be done by fixing a maximum capacity for the regular supply. In the case of maintenance or default of the customer's generation units, the maximal capacity may be exceeded. The consumption of reserve energy can be determined as the energy exceeding the maximal capacity and information about the customer's power plant dispatching is not necessarily used. For pricing purposes, a differentiation between announced and unexpected demand of reserve energy is reasonable. The announced demand of reserve energy can be priced at the time of announcement as described in equation (5.1). The disadvantage for the retail customer is the reserve energy prices uncertainty. The prices are fixed when the times of maintenance are defined and announced and not necessarily when the supply contract is concluded. If a retail customer wants a fixed price for the announced reserve energy, the selling utility can only hedge this with an option. The theoretical option price can be used for pricing. The problem remains that an option price is calculated assuming that the option can be exercised, market price depending. This is not the case if the additional power is needed for the times of maintenance. Thus an approach that prices only the risk of a reserve contract, like the RAROC approach discussed further in equation (5.9), is a good alternative.

Hedging of an unexpected demand such as that caused by a default of a retail customer's generation unit is also a challenge for the supplying utility. The utility can use their own plants or balancing power if this is consistent with the rules of the TSO. An unexpected demand can be regarded as an option on balancing power and can be priced that way. There is the problem that this option cannot be exercised market price depending. Furthermore, if option price theory is used for pricing reserve contracts the optionality has to be charged whether the option will be exercised or not. This can be solved with a charge for the supply of the capacity.

Interruptible Contracts

Because of the volatile spot market prices for power, options on spot products are particularly valuable. The previous section discussed reserve contracts, where the utility sells some additional optionality to a retail customer. Consider the contrary situation, where a retail customer accepts a market price dependent switch-off of his power supply, effectively selling an option to his supplier. In practice, the switch-off can be announced one day in advance and the option premium can be included in a reduced energy price. As a retail customer-oriented alternative, each individual switch-off requires the customer's acceptance and instead of a reduced energy price the customer receives a premium for the accepted interruption.

Right of Cancellation

Selling a right of cancellation of the supply contract is another alternative for a retail customer to receive a reduced energy price. The option premium is used to reduce the energy price for the period of the supply contract where no cancellation is possible. Instead of a contract cancellation the retail customer can sell the right, not the obligation, of a price adjustment. As an example, a retail customer signs a full service contract in 2007 for delivery in the years 2008 and 2009. The calculated energy price for the year 2008 is 60 EUR/MWh and for 2009 it is 62 EUR/MWh. The retail customer can reduce the energy price in 2008 by the option premium (e.g. 2 EUR/MWh), if they sell the supplier the right of a price alignment at the end of the year 2008 and for the energy to be delivered in 2009. A retail customer who signs such a contract has to take into account that their energy price will follow the wholesale price according to equation (5.2) if, and only if, wholesale prices are increasing. The price reduction in 2008 would cause a risk in 2009 which has to be managed.

5.3 SOURCING

A key factor in the sourcing process for a utility with end customers is to minimise the price risk. The impact of the price risk on the operating profit of a utility cannot be overrated. In recent years the price volatility in electricity markets on an annual basis was a multiple of the retail margin. To avoid a random operating profit and to secure the survival of a utility, effective risk management is required. Prompt sourcing is an important requirement as the short position in the portfolio has to be covered. This section describes the short position which arises from sales activity. In this context the short position is interpreted as an energetic position, meaning that the sold energy will be purchased. There are, however, better performing hedge ratios such as the delta position or minimising the variance of the profit and loss function. These hedge ratios will be discussed in section 6.1. Hedging the energetic position is the basis for the more sophisticated methods and is discussed first. For this purpose the retail customers are classified into:

- *Business-to-business (B2B)*: These are business customers with power measurement so that an individual load forecast is possible.
- *Business-to-consumer (B2C)*: These are end customers without power measurement with delivery by standardised load profiles.
- *Small accounts*: Business customers that are too small for an individual load forecast.

- *Municipalities and resellers*: Full service contracts with a potential option on the delivered energy amount, allowing the reseller to acquire new customers or lose current customers. Load forecasting with these customers may be challenging.

5.3.1   Business-to-Business (B2B)

For B2B customers the short position resulting from a fixed price full service contract is simply the load forecast. It must be contained in the risk-management system used for determining the energetic position and can be hedged with existing trading products. As illustrated in Figure 5.7, the energy needed can be divided into off-peak and peak contingents in a granularity conforming to existing trading products (e.g. monthly contracts).

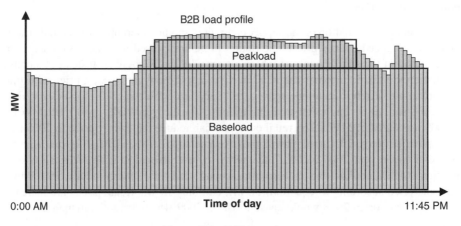

Figure 5.7   B2B sourcing

For determining the short position of an indexed full service contract, we analyse equation (5.2). For simplification, let $I(t) = F(t, T_1, T_2)$. This means that the index is the price of a traded forward or futures contract with a delivery starting at T_1 and ending at T_2. The following consideration is also true if $I(t)$ is a combination of two or more forwards or futures contracts prices. If T_0 denotes the time when the contract is concluded, the sold indexed contract can be decomposed by:

- Selling a full service contract with a fixed price P at T_0.
- Buying the forward respectively futures contract with the price $F(T_0, T_1, T_2)$ at T_0. If $\hat{L}$ denotes the accumulated expected customers load, the energy amount of the forward respectively futures contract is

$$\frac{(P + R + M)\hat{L}}{F(T_0, T_1, T_2)}.$$

- Selling the forward respectively futures contract with the price $F(t_k, T_1, T_2)$ in the quantity

$$\frac{1}{n} \frac{(P + R + M)\hat{L}}{F(T_0, T_1, T_2)},$$

which each fixing at $t_k, k \in \{1, \ldots, n\}$.

The decomposition reflects the energetic leg of selling a fixed price contract and the financial leg of purchasing the forward or futures contract. If the indexed supply contract is decomposed it can be easily hedged by the supplying utility. The purchasing customer has the inverse position. If they are a reseller, they can use the decomposition above to represent the energetic position in their risk management system. For the purchasing customer there is no need to hedge the indexed contract immediately. Otherwise they will obtain a fixed price contract which can be purchased directly.

5.3.2   Business-to-Consumer (B2C)

As a main difference between the B2B and the B2C segment there is no individual power measurement for B2C customers. Because of the large number of B2C customers with a low consumption they are normally not represented separately in the risk management system. Individual start and end dates of the contracts are not often used. In markets like Germany and France where B2C customers rarely change their supplier, this simplification is justified. In the UK changing the supplier for B2C customers is more common. We assume that the market environment does not demand an individual representation of B2C customers, and therefore no risk management process as for B2B customers is needed. We further assume that the B2C customers have fixed price full service contracts. In principle, the supplying utility can purchase the energy needed for delivery periods $[T_1, T_2]$ in n parts at $t_1, t_2, \ldots, t_n$. If the number of B2C customers with different contract periods is large enough, then with an adequate n and $t_1, t_2, \ldots, t_n$ the effectiveness of this hedging strategy should be sufficient. For determining sourcing dates some considerations about the B2C market are necessary. Normally, price alignments in the B2C segment are delayed and the price volatility is small compared with both the wholesale market and the B2B retail segment. If the delay is significant then sourcing at t_1 can start long before delivery begins at T_1. A large number of sourcing parts n increases the averaging effect. Consider the example where delivery period is the entire year 2009 and the sourcing can be done in four parts $n = 4$ at the beginning of each quarter in the year 2008 (Figure 5.8).

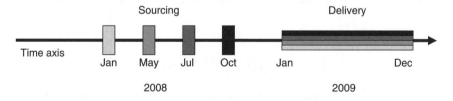

Figure 5.8   B2C sourcing

If the price alignment for B2C customers is in the fourth quarter then the retail price can follow the sourcing price. The short position in the risk management system can be represented analogously. At the beginning of each quarter in 2008 the short position for the delivery in 2009 will increase by a quarter of the expected energy amount needed by the B2C customers.

5.3.3   Small Accounts

Some B2B customers are too small for individual power measurement or individual load forecasts. In these cases the supplying utility can hedge the sold energy in the same way as for B2C customers. As described above the problem is to determine an adequate number of sourcing parts n and sourcing dates $t_1, t_2, \ldots, t_n$. Small accounts are more price sensitive than B2C customers, therefore, t_1 is near to the delivery start date T_1. For example, if the delivery period is year 2009, sourcing can be done in three parts, $n = 3$, at the beginning of October, November and December in the year 2008.

5.3.4 Municipalities and Reseller

If a utility is supplying a reseller the utility has the additional problem that the reseller's load may vary with the number of customers of the reseller. With a fixed price the reseller can easily acquire new customers in times of increasing prices and vice versa in times of decreasing prices they may lose some customers. Both of these changes in load will cause a loss for the supplying utility if the reseller has a common full service contract. A full service contract with a fixed price concluded with a reseller implies a call option. The reseller can use the option to acquire new customers in times of increasing prices. If the quantity the option refers to is defined, option price theory can be used for pricing this option because the reseller can use the optionality market price depending. If the utility fixes the price for the full service contract for a longer period the reseller also has a put option. If the reseller fixes their resale prices for a shorter period they will lose customers in times of decreasing prices. The supplying utility then has an energy surplus in comparison to the forecasted load. Limiting this optionality is in the interest of both the supplying utility and the reseller. If the value of the implied option is too high the reseller will be charged with an option premium and this will raise his sourcing costs. The supplying utility has to manage this optionality, and hedging with options in the wholesale market is not always possible. The reseller has to determine their potential for new customers and then boundaries for the quantity the option refers to can be defined. If the boundaries are narrow the option premium can be kept small. The option premium is not usually paid in advance, but there is a cost allocation on the forecasted energy amount which increases the supply price. This brings the risk that the option premium is not charged exactly. The short position for the supplying utility can be composed of the forecasted load and the delta position (see section 6.1.1) of the determined option.

5.4 LOAD FORECASTING

Load forecasting plays an important role in electricity system operation. For integrated utilities the main focus is forecasting of grid loads in their transmission or distribution areas.

In terms of forecasting horizon, load forecasting applications can be divided into four categories:

- *Long-term forecasting* with horizons of several years or decades: The main focus is on annual peak loads and annual average load as input for system expansion planning. Main influencing factors are population and economic growth rates.
- *Medium-term forecasting* with horizons up to one or two years: For most applications hourly time resolution is required. Forecasts for these time horizons are used for maintenance scheduling and operation planning for hydro storage power plants. Main characteristics are daily, weekly and seasonal patterns.

- *Short-term load forecasting* with horizons up to one week: Hourly or quarter-hourly time resolution is common. Applications are power plant and transmission system operation planning. Besides characteristic daily, weekly and seasonal patterns, weather forecasts are used as influencing factors.
- *Ultra-short-term load forecasting* with horizons up to several hours: Quarter-hourly or higher time resolution is common. Load forecasts for these time horizons are used for power plant dispatch and grid operation. Forecasts are based on short-term historical load data as well as on historical load curves of similar days.

There are many well-established techniques for grid load forecasting. Common are end-use and econometric approaches for long-term forecasts. For short- and ultra-short-term forecasts so-called similar-day approaches, regression models, time series models, artificial neuronal networks (ANN), expert systems and statistic learning algorithms are used. For medium term forecasts all of these approaches can be found. Often a combination of different approaches or of different forecasting systems gives the best results.

For integrated utilities forming regional monopolies grid loads are identical with the cumulative load of their customers. In liberalised energy markets one additional aspect is load forecasting for single customers. Medium-term single customer load forecasts are required for pricing full service contracts or partial delivery contracts (see section 5.2) and for portfolio management. Short-term forecasts are required for scheduling. For portfolio management and for scheduling, load forecasts for aggregates of customers are required. If the composition of these aggregates changes significantly over time, as it is generally the case in liberalised markets, forecasts for these aggregates have to be based on forecasts for individual customers.

Forecasting algorithms always use historical metering values as an input. For grid loads generally, long historical time series are available. Stochastic behaviour of individual customers has only a minor impact on grid loads representing a large number of individual customers. Therefore high forecasting accuracy can be achieved. Load forecasts for individual customers are more difficult as often less historical data is available, stochastic impacts are not compensated and significant changes in consumption patterns occur, e.g., in the case a change from two shift to three shift production. Therefore, robustness and flexibility are important characteristics of individual customers' load forecasting algorithms.

The following similar-day approach is suitable for medium-term load forecasts for individual customers: the basic principle of a similar-day approach is to select historical days for which metering data is available and which are similar to the day for which the forecast has to be made and use the average of these days as forecast. It is also possible to use a weighted average where the weight of historical days depends on the similarity. Similarity can be defined by the following criteria:

- *Season*: Load patterns show typical seasonal behaviour. Similarity can be defined as seasonal distance between days. For example, historical days which have a seasonal distance of plus or minus three weeks to the day the forecast is made for might be considered as similar. But also days in spring might be similar to days in autumn and vice versa.
- *Day of the week*: While Tuesdays, Wednesdays and Thursdays have similar load patterns in most countries, all other weekdays are distinct.

- *Irregular sectoral non-work or limited activity days*: These include public holidays, school holidays, days between public holidays and weekends. These days are most difficult to forecast as there is often only a small number of similar historical days. Similarity between these days and normal days has to be considered, e.g. load patterns on public holidays can be similar to the ones on Sundays.
- *Historical distance*: Historical load data which is several years old might not be as suitable as more recent data.
- *Structural change*: Often structural changes in load patterns can be observed. It is important to realise these structural changes and not to use historical load profiles for similar days without adjustments for compensating structural changes. General trends, e.g. average load growth, can be considered as well by scaling historical load profiles.
- *Exceptional load patterns*: If a significant number of similar days, e.g. 10 days, with historical data have been identified, the load patterns for these days can be compared. If load patterns of single days deviate strongly from the load patterns of all other days, these days should not be considered in the weighted average. Reasons can be exceptional events like strikes or data errors.

A similar-day approach typically contains many parameters which can be modified. Intensive back-testing with many historical time series is required for deriving appropriate values for all parameters. It is also important to repeat this back-testing regularly, e.g. annually, to adjust the forecasting algorithm to systematic changes and trends, e.g. faster availability of historical metering data or changes in customer groups.

Short-term forecasts for individual customers required for scheduling can be based on the same similar-day approach as medium-term forecasts. Weather forecasts can be considered either by giving more weight to historical days with similar weather conditions or by a linear regression approach. It might be appropriate to assign higher weights to more recent historical values than in medium-term forecasts to capture shorter-term structural changes.

5.5 RISK PREMIUM

While selling energy on the retail market margins can be obtained, but this also bears additional risks. Determining an adequate risk premium for retail customers is an important task for a utility. First of all, retail activities involve some costs which are not obvious. The expected value of costs, in a mathematical sense, can be determined and has to be considered while pricing retail contracts. Second, the additional risk while entering the retail market requires the allocation of capital that is expensive. The return of these activities has to be adequate in view of the financial policy of the utility. Therefore the different parts of the risk premium can be divided in two categories. The first are these additional hidden costs which are not covered by the basic price defined in equation (5.1). They will be referred to as *expected additional costs*. The second category includes the risk premiums in a strict sense and these are referred to as *strict risk premiums*. On average there is no profit and no loss but there is the possibility of a loss. The strict risk premiums can be regarded as the required return for taking these corporate risks. Because of the dependence on the company's financial policy there is no standard for the determination of strict risk premiums.

In this section we describe how to quantify these risk premiums. The risk map must be adapted to the specific market and contract types. This quantification is interesting for suppliers and also for retail customers with large energy costs who should understand how their energy costs are composed. If a customer purchases a structured contract there may be a risk transfer from the supplier to the customer. These risks have to be managed and some additional costs may need to be taken into account.

The following risk premium types are discussed in more detail:

- *Price validity period*: An obliging price quotation valid for a determined period can be considered as an option free of charge for the retail customer. The supplying utility will have hidden costs from this granted option.
- *Balancing power*: The basic price defined in equation (5.1) does not include the costs of balancing power.
- *Credit risk*: Selling energy to a retail customer will cause a credit risk. In the case of insolvency of the customer the supplying utility will suffer a loss if the delivered energy cannot be paid for. Additionally, further energy is no longer required and there is the risk that it cannot be sold for the same price if market prices are decreasing.
- *Price–volume correlation*: The calculation of the basic price is based on a load forecast. Because of the correlation between the total grid load and power spot prices, there are additional costs for the supplying utility. In times of high spot prices the probability that the required energy exceeds the forecast is high. If in contrast the spot prices are low, the probability that the required energy is less than the forecast is also high.
- *Hourly price profile risk*: For the calculation of the basic price the price forward curve $P(\cdot)$ in the finest available granularity (e.g hourly) was used. Because of the absence of a forward market in an hourly granularity, $P(\cdot)$ has to be partly estimated from historical data (see section 3.4.1 for details). The estimated hourly price profile can change until delivery. On average, there should be no additional costs but for the additional risk a strict risk premium can be calculated.
- *Volume risk*: While the price–volume correlation are expected costs, there is the additional risk of an unsystematic change of the load of the retail customer. For the volume risk there are no expected additional costs (they are covered by the price–volume correlation), but for the additional risk a strict risk premium can be calculated.
- *Operational risk*: There are further risks which are not considered in the categories above. These include the duration of the sourcing process described in section 5.1, bid–offer spreads (which increase the basic price, calculated on a mid-market basis), or a low quality load and volume forecast. If these risks can be kept small this can be an important competitive advantage for the supplying utility.

5.5.1 Price Validity Period

Suppose a customer in need of a supply contract asks for a price quote. Assume that the customer receives an offer at time t_0 and at a fixed price P valid for a limited period of time, say until time t_1. The date t_1 results from the time the customer needs for his purchase decision. As the quotation is an obligation only for the supplier the retail customer gets at t_0 a call option with the strike price P and maturity t_1. If market prices decrease before the offer expires or before the offer is accepted the customer can request a new quote at a reduced price, possibly from another supplier. Vice versa, if market prices increase, the customer probably will close the contracts at the quoted, lower prices. Theoretically the risk can be covered by asking an up-front option premium for the obliging offer. Since this is unusual and hardly accepted by a retail customer the most promising way of lowering this risk for the supplier is to shorten the time period $t_1 - t_0$ as far as possible. The remaining risk can be covered partly by a risk premium which increases the price for the energy. Because this is not an up-front premium and only payed if the contract is concluded the risk premium cannot avoid a loss to the supplying utility. It only increases the strike price and makes the option less valuable, although the option is still free of charge. Furthermore, a high risk premium may threaten the success of the retail acquisition.

Asking for a risk premium is therefore a compromise between market conditions and the theoretical valuation. The option premium for a call with strike price P and maturity t_1 can be calculated with the Black–Scholes formula. This option premium can be used as an indication of the risk premium and added to the energy price even though a payment of an up-front premium cannot be achieved. The implicit volatility of traded options can be used for the calculation.

As an example, Table 5.2 shows the size of the risk premium for different option maturities. We assume that the peakload price is 75 EUR/MWh, the off-peak price is 40 EUR/MWh and the estimated annualised volatility is 20%.

Table 5.2 Premium for the price validity period

Maturity	Premium for off-peakload (EUR/MWh)	Premium for peakload (EUR/MWh)
1 day	0.20	0.38
1 week	0.44	0.83
2 weeks	0.62	1.17
1 month	0.91	1.71

For bigger retail customers a validity period of one day should be sufficient. If a utility offers supply contracts with different validity periods and matching risk premiums many retail customers will prefer the offer with the lowest rate. The supplying utility should avoid switching between offers with different validity periods.

5.5.2 Balancing Power

The costs for balancing power are market dependent because they are levied by the TSO and are subject to the conditions of grid access. Therefore the following considerations have to adapt to the specific market conditions.

The major component of costs for balancing power is usually included in the TSO's charges for using the grid. Costs for capacity which has to be reserved is typically a part of grid costs. Because it is assumed that the retail customer is charged with the grid usage costs separately, only the additional cost for the balancing energy has to be considered. We also assume that there is no price spread for this energy. This means that the costs for a utility which delivers insufficient energy for their customers in a specified grid correspond to the refund for delivering the same amount of surplus energy at the same point of time. More technically, the TSO will charge each supplier delivering less energy than their customer's consumption at a point in time t with the costs $B(t)$ per MWh for the balancing power. Here, the time t denotes a time interval defined by the TSO for the power schedule (e.g. 15 minutes). If the supplier delivers a surplus of energy, they will receive payment $B(t)$ per MWh. The TSO needs additional energy at short notice if there is not enough energy in total for their grid. $B(t)$ is high in this case and results from the costs of this balancing power. If, however, there is an energy surplus, $B(t)$ will be low and they will receive only a small amount for the energy, because of its poor ability to be resold at short notice. To calculate the expected costs for balancing power one has to take into account the influence a utility has on the total state of the control area.

If a utility supplies the majority of retail customers in the specified grid there is a high probability that delivering insufficient energy will cause a shortage in the control area with high costs. Delivering an energy surplus and causing a surplus in the control area would only bring small revenues. A small utility, which does not determine the grid shortage or energy surplus, can benefit from delivering an energy surplus if there is a shortage in the control area. It may also be able to purchase cheap energy when there is an energy surplus in the control area.

Thus the determination of a premium for balancing power is a difficult task. A utility that grows to supply an increasing number of retail customers may end up with noticeable balancing power costs. To determine a premium for balancing power costs previous payments are often used although there are analytical approaches. The following consideration aims to determine balancing power costs if additional customers are acquired into an existing retail portfolio.

Let $L(t)$ denote the total load at time t of the grid and control area respectively and $\hat{L}(t)$ the according forecast. $L_i(t)$ is the load for an individual customer i, and $\hat{L}_i(t)$ the corresponding forecast. It is assumed that each supplier delivers the forecasted energy for his customers so that $\hat{L}(t)$ is delivered in total. In this section load forecast means a short-term load forecast, i.e. forecast one day before delivery. The balancing power price risk can be minimised if the load is forecast shortly before the power schedule has to be announced to the TSO. The purchased balancing power for customer i at time t is

$$\Delta L_i(t) = L_i(t) - \hat{L}_i(t).$$

For customer i, the costs for balancing power $C_i(t)$ additional to the spot market price $S(t)$ are determined by

$$C_i(t) = \Delta L_i(t) \left(B(t) - S(t) \right),$$

where $B(t)$ is the price for balancing power.

The expected costs are

$$\hat{C}_i(t) = E\left[C_i(t)\right]$$
$$= E\left[\Delta L_i(t)\right] E\left[B(t) - S(t)\right] + \mathrm{Cov}\left[\Delta L_i(t), B(t) - S(t)\right]. \tag{5.3}$$

For further calculation we assume:

1. The required balancing power $\Delta L_i(t)$ and the spot price $S(t)$ are uncorrelated. This is justified because the spot price $S(t)$ and the short-term forecast are fixed one trading day before delivery and because all weather information at this time is used for the forecast as well as for the pricing. There should be no impact from the spot price $S(t)$ on the divergence between the forecast and the effective consumption.

2. There is a high balancing power price B^- in the case of a shortage and a low balancing power price B^+ in the case of an energy surplus in the control area. With

$$\theta(x) = \begin{cases} 1, & x > 0 \\ 0, & x \le 0 \end{cases}$$

we have

$$B(t) = B^- \theta(\Delta L(t)) + B^+ \theta(-\Delta L(t)).$$

3. The differences $\Delta L_i(t)$ between consumption and forecast of all consumers i are independent normally distributed random variables with expectation 0 and standard deviation $\sigma_i(t)$.

This is justified because the short-term load forecast considers the weather forecast and the weather dependent correlation between $\Delta L_i(t)$ and $\Delta L_j(t)$ of two retail customers can be neglected.

From assumptions 1 and 3 and equation (5.3) we derive

$$\hat{C}_i(t) = \text{Cov}\left[\Delta L_i(t), B(t)\right]. \tag{5.4}$$

This equation shows that the costs of balancing power for customers depends on their impact on the state of the control area. Let I denote the set of all customers in a control area, i an individual customer with $i \in I$, and N_1 and N_2 independent standard normally distributed random variables. We can now decompose $\Delta L(t)$ into $\Delta L_i(t)$ with standard deviation $\sigma_i(t)$ and $\sum_{k \in I, k \ne i} \Delta L_k(t)$ with standard deviation $\tilde{\sigma}_i(t)$. We have $\sigma_i^2(t) + \tilde{\sigma}_i^2(t) = \sigma^2(t)$.

From equation (5.4) and assumption 3 we derive the additional costs of balancing power

$$\begin{aligned} \hat{C}_i(t) &= \text{Cov}\left[\sigma_i(t)N_1, B^- \theta(\sigma_i(t)N_1 + \tilde{\sigma}_i(t)N_2) + B^+ \theta(\sigma_i(t)N_1 + \tilde{\sigma}_i(t)N_2)\right] \\ &= \sigma(t)\beta_i(t)\text{Cov}\left[N_1, B^-(X) + B^+(X)\right], \end{aligned} \tag{5.5}$$

with the random variable

$$X(t) = \beta_i(t)N_1 + \sqrt{1 - \beta_i^2(t)}N_2$$

and the notation

$$\beta_i(t) = \frac{\sigma_i(t)}{\sigma(t)}.$$

Note that $\sigma_i(t)$ and $\sigma(t)$ are volatilities belonging to the difference between load and load forecast. For initial calculation the dependence on t can be ignored. In a second step t can then be categorised with a similar-day approach (see equation (5.4)).

The additional costs for balancing power can be calculated by using equation (5.5) and a Monte Carlo simulation. The premium for balancing power per MWh for a contract with the delivery period $[T_1, T_2]$ and the additional customer i is

$$c_i = \frac{\sum_{t \in [T_1, T_2]} \hat{C}_i(t)}{\sum_{t \in [T_1, T_2]} \hat{L}_i(t)}.$$

In some countries (e.g. Germany) the quantity of balancing power and the balancing power prices are published on the web pages of TSOs. With this data B^- and B^+ can be calculated as the average of the balancing power prices in the particular state of the control area. With this published data σ can be estimated. The value of σ_i depends on each retail customer but for initial calculation setting $\sigma_i = \sigma$ can be used.

5.5.3   Credit Risk

For their sales activities all utilities have established a management of receivables. Additionally the sourcing discussed in section 5.3 requires that the delivery contracts will be fulfilled. If a retail customer becomes insolvent there will be not only a potential loss caused by the delivered energy not being paid for. The energy sold forward will not be taken and must be sold again on the market, probably for a lower price. This is the case in times of decreasing wholesale prices.

The expected loss for the retail portfolio has to be determined. For a large number of small retail customers most utilities have historical data and the expected loss can be calculated on a stable statistical foundation. For larger retail customers data from rating companies can be used. The method for determination of an expected loss is discussed further in section 6.3.3. To complete the consideration with the determination of an additional strict risk premium for the credit risk, it is possible to use RAROC methodology (discussed later in this chapter).

5.5.4   Price–Volume Correlation

The basic price P is calculated by using a load forecast for the retail customer. This forecast $\hat{L}(t)$ is the expected value $E[L(t)]$ of the load at t, and t_0 is the date when the retail contract is calculated. The date t_0 is fixed, therefore for a conditional expectation the short notation is used. Under the risk-neutral measure (see section 3.1.5) we derive

$$E_{t_0}[S(t)] = F(t_0, t) \quad \text{or short} \quad E[S(t)] = F(t).$$

Because of the positive correlation between the total grid load and wholesale prices in the spot market, the expected costs per MWh

$$\frac{E[L(t)S(t)]}{E[L(t)]}$$

are higher than the basic price

$$\frac{\hat{L}(t)F(t)}{\hat{L}(t)} = \frac{E[L(t)]E[S(t)]}{E[L(t)]}.$$

This is true for a well-diversified portfolio of retail customers. The price–volume correlation premium R_c results from these expected additional costs per MWh in the delivery period. Consider the example in Table 5.3 for the expected additional costs of a retail customer whose load depends on the outside temperature and is correlated with the spot price.

Since for an individual customer the existing load data is often not sufficient, the price–volume correlation premium is calculated using the total grid load and every retail customer is charged with the same average risk premium.

Table 5.3   Costs for the price–volume correlation

Temperature	Load (MWh)	Average price (EUR/MWh)	Total costs (EUR)
Mean temperature	100	50	5000
Cold day	120	60	7200
Warm day	80	40	3200
Total costs for two days with a mean temperature			10000
Total costs for a warm and a cold day			10400

The price–volume correlation premium R_c per MWh is given by the difference of the expected costs and the basic price

$$R_c = \frac{\sum_{t=T_1}^{T_2} E[L(t)S(t)] - \sum_{t=T_1}^{T_2} E[L(t)]E[S(t)]}{\sum_{t=T_1}^{T_2} E[L(t)]}$$

$$= E\left[\frac{\sum_{t=T_1}^{T_2} \left(L(t) - \hat{L}(t)\right) S(t)}{\sum_{t=T_1}^{T_2} \hat{L}(t)}\right]. \tag{5.6}$$

Using historical data for a calculation of R_c the grid load for a year is forecasted. For example, the known grid load for year 2006 is forecast in retrospect using historical load data from year 2005 or earlier. The usual forecasting algorithms should be applied. If the effective spot prices and the effective load in 2006 are known, R_c can be determined. For this purpose the expected value is approximated by evaluating the expression with historical data. This approximation is justified for a long time period $[T_1, T_2]$, usually a year or longer.

As an example, the grid load in Germany was estimated and the prices from the EEX were used. Table 5.4 shows that the correlation varies from year to year.

Table 5.4   Price–volume correlation premium calculated with historical data

Year	Price–volume risk premium (EUR/MWh)
2001	0.10
2002	0.21
2003	0.09
2004	0.10
2005	0.32
2006	0.39

A more sophisticated methodology for a calculation of the price–volume correlation premium R_c is to use the SMaPS model described in section 3.4.2. For a calculation of R_c with equation (5.6) simulated price paths and the corresponding load paths can be used. There is also the possibility for an analytic determination of R_c without using a Monte Carlo simulation, described below.

Using the notation of section 3.4.2 the stochastic spot price in the SMaPS model is given by

$$S(t) = \exp(f(t, L(t)/v(t)) \exp(X(t)) \exp(Y(t)),$$

with the average relative availability of power plants $v(t)$ (a deterministic variable), and the time series $X(t)$ and $Y(t)$ producing the short- and long-term variation.

The correlation between grid load and spot price is completely reflected by the function f. The remaining normally distributed load noise

$$l(t) := L(t) - \hat{L}(t)$$

and the remaining price noises $X(t)$ and $Y(t)$ are independent.

Calculating R_c by using equation (5.6) requires for each fixed $t \in [T_1, T_2]$ the evaluation of

$$
\begin{aligned}
E&\left[\left(L(t) - \hat{L}(t)\right) S(t)\right] \\
&= E\left[l(t) \exp\left(f\left(\frac{\hat{L}(t) + l(t)}{v(t)}\right)\right)\right] E\left[\exp(X(t))\right] E\left[\exp(Y(t))\right] \\
&= E\left[l(t) \exp\left(f\left(\frac{\hat{L}(t) + l(t)}{v(t)}\right)\right)\right] \exp\left(\frac{\mathrm{Var}[X(t)]}{2}\right) \exp\left(\frac{\mathrm{Var}[Y(t)]}{2}\right). \quad (5.7)
\end{aligned}
$$

Because $l(t)$ is normally distributed, the term

$$E\left[l(t) \exp\left(f\left(\frac{\hat{L}(t) + l(t)}{v(t)}\right)\right)\right]$$

can be calculated as an integral over the density of a normal distribution. Thus the equations (5.6) and (5.7) determine the price–volume correlation premium R_c.

5.5.5 Strict Risk Premiums

Supplying a retail customer bears risks, i.e. the possibility of a negative development of the profit, which cause no expectational loss on a long-term average. A strict risk premium covers this risk. Before discussing individual risks the general approach of determining strict risk premiums is considered.

Quantifying the risk with an adequate risk measure and using it directly or as a defined ratio is the simplest approach for determining a strict risk premium. This assures that taking a higher risk means receiving higher risk premiums. The standard deviation is often used as a risk measure where it specifies the typical variation of the financial result in the considered period, i.e. the time until delivery. The management of the utility can define a ratio (e.g. 50%) of the standard deviation as the required risk premium. If the considered financial result follows a normal distribution, requiring half a standard deviation as a risk premium means that there will be no loss in 69% of cases. This approach can be improved by using probabilities of ruin which are common in the insurance sector.

Another applicable concept is the *Risk Adjusted Return on Capital* (RAROC) approach originally developed for banks. RAROC was applied to the power market by Prokopczuk *et al.* (2007). The basic idea is a virtual deposit of economic capital to cover a possible loss. Because of the limitation of economic capital, business dealings are only realised if the return exceeds a specified hurdle rate. The possible loss, i.e. the required economic capital, can be determined via a standard risk measure such as Value-at-Risk (VaR) or Profit-at-Risk (PaR). The VaR is the loss corresponding to the specified quantile of change in the value of a given portfolio over a specified holding period. If $X(t)$ is the random variable of the market value of a given portfolio at time t with the probability distribution P, $t_1 - t_0$ the specified holding period and α the confidence level, then VaR can be calculated from the formula

$$P\left(X(t_1) - X(t_0) < -\text{VaR}(\alpha, t_1 - t_0)\right) = 1 - \alpha. \qquad (5.8)$$

The PaR is also a quantile of the change of market value for a given confidence level α. In distinction to the VaR the change of the market value is considered between t_0 and the time of delivery. Using VaR as a risk measure considers the risk for the time period $[t_0, t_1]$ only. This is sufficient if the (energetic) position can be closed until t_1. In markets with a restricted liquidity the PaR is adequate. More details about VaR and PaR can be found in section 6.2.

Now we define RAROC as:

$$RAROC = \frac{Expected\ Return}{Economic\ Capital}. \qquad (5.9)$$

The economic capital is the capital needed to cover heavy shocks of the value of a trade or a portfolio. RAROC can be used as an indicator of the profitability of a business activity in the sense of the capital policy of the utility. For this an internal hurdle rate μ will be specified which reflects the costs of equity capital. If this hurdle rate is reached the investment or the transaction can be carried out.

If the PaR is used as risk measure, the expected return must fulfil

$$RAROC = \frac{Expected\ Return}{\text{PaR}(\alpha)} = \mu. \qquad (5.10)$$

Using risk neutrality so that

$$E[Return] = X(t_0),$$

and defining $q_{1-\alpha}[\cdot]$ as the $1 - \alpha$ quantile, equation (5.10) can be written as

$$RAROC = \frac{E[Return]}{E[Return] - q_{1-\alpha}[Return]} = \mu. \qquad (5.11)$$

For calculating a strict risk premium R of a fixed price contract with delivery period $[T_1, T_2]$ and the basic price P concluded at t_0, the return of this contract has to be determined. Assume that the hurdle rate μ corresponds to the delivery period. In simple terms, at first no sourcing or hedging of the sold contract at the forward market will be considered.

If $L(\cdot)$ denotes the load in an hourly granularity and $S(\cdot)$ the spot price, the return of the contract is given by

$$Return = \sum_{t=T_1}^{T_2} (P + R - S(t))L(t). \tag{5.12}$$

Next, we take energetic hedging described in section 5.3 into account. $F_B(\cdot, T_1, T_2)$, $F_P(\cdot, T_1, T_2)$ denotes the price of baseload and peakload futures contracts with delivery period $[T_1, T_2]$ which are used for hedging purposes. γ_B, γ_P denotes the baseload and peakload hedge ratios respectively, which are needed for an energetic hedging, based on the load forecast $\hat{L}(t)$. It is assumed that the baseload and peakload futures contracts are standardised with a capacity of 1 MW. Finally $1_{Peak}(t)$ denotes the peak indicator function so that:

$$1_{Peak}(t) = \begin{cases} 1, & \text{if } t \text{ is a peakload hour} \\ 0, & \text{else.} \end{cases}$$

The return of the contract is then given by

$$Return = \sum_{t=T_1}^{T_2} \left(\left(P + R - S(t) \right) L(t) - \gamma_B F_B(t_0, T_1, T_2) \right.$$

$$\left. - \gamma_P F_P(t_0, T_1, T_2) 1_{Peak}(t) + (\gamma_B + \gamma_P 1_{Peak}(t)) S(t) \right). \tag{5.13}$$

An adequate risk premium can now be calculated using equations (5.11) and (5.13). Note that the $1 - \alpha$ quantile of the distribution of the return is used, which is composed of the correlated random variables $S(t)$ and $L(t)$. For a calculation of the $1 - \alpha$ quantile a stochastic spot price model is required which also models the load (e.g. the SMaPS model). With the SMaPS model a Monte Carlo simulation of $S(t)$ and $L(t)$ can be made simultaneously. Simulated price and load paths are used for the determination of the $1 - \alpha$ quantile of the return. If $P + R$ is the fixed price such that equation (5.11) holds, R is the strict risk premium to be calculated; however, the covered risks cannot be interpreted easily. The strict risk premium covers price risks caused from hedge inefficiencies as well as volume risks or correlation risks. Because different types of retail contracts imply different risks, dividing the strict risk premium depending on the type of covered risk is useful. In this way a modular system of risk premiums is developed. With such a modular system the applicable premiums for each type of retail contract can be determined. For this purpose, we divide the risk premium R into a premium R_c for the already calculated *price–volume correlation risk*, a premium R_p for the *hourly price profile risk* and a premium R_v for the *volume risk*:

$$R = R_c + R_p + R_v. \tag{5.14}$$

5.5.6 Hourly Price Profile Risk

A retail contract cannot be hedged perfectly with wholesale products. Since hourly products are not traded at the forward market there remains a price risk which can only be closed at the spot market. As *hourly price profile risk* we will denote the risk that the return of a portfolio which contains a sold fixed power schedule and standardised baseload and peakload contracts for an (energetic) hedging is uncertain. This means that even with a deterministic load $L(t)$ the return in equation (5.13) is a random variable. If we assume that the forward prices are expected spot prices and if $\hat{L}(t)$ denotes the load forecast (or the deterministic load), R_p denotes the risk premium for the hourly price profile risk, the expected return deduced from equation (5.13) is

$$E[Return] = \sum_{t=T_1}^{T_2} (P + R_p - E[S(t)])\hat{L}(t). \qquad (5.15)$$

Note that the price–volume correlation premium R_c is not considered because the load was assumed as deterministic and the calculation of the volume risk premium as the additional risk for the varying load is considered later.

We have

$$q_{1-\alpha}[Return] = q_{1-\alpha}\left[\sum_{t=T_1}^{T_2} \left((P + R_p - S(t))\,\hat{L}(t) - \gamma_B F_B(t_0, T_1, T_2)\right.\right.$$

$$\left.\left. - \gamma_P F_P(t_0, T_1, T_2)1_{Peak} + (\gamma_B + \gamma_P 1_{Peak})S(t)\right)\right]. \qquad (5.16)$$

The strict risk premium R_p is then determined by equations (5.11), (5.15) and (5.16). Because the $1 - \alpha$ quantile of a distribution is used, which is determined by the random variable $S(t)$, a spot price model for power prices is required. A stochastic model for the load is not necessary.

5.5.7 Volume Risk

If a utility sells a full service contract to a retail customer it takes the risk of an uncertain load. If there is a price–load correlation then the utility will have expected additional costs which are covered by the risk premium R_c for the price–volume correlation. But there will also be an unsystematic part of the load variation which is referred to as *volume risk*. On average there are no costs and the risk premium R_v for the volume risk is therefore a strict risk premium. For calculating the risk premium for the volume risk we use equation (5.13) and stochastic load curves. The risk premiums for the hourly price profile risk R_p and the price–volume correlation R_c can be used to reach the target of decomposing the risk premium R. The process for the calculation of the risk premium requires that first the risk premiums R, R_c and R_p are calculated. R_v is then determined by difference, assuring that the risk premiums build an additive modular system. For the calculation of R and so R_v a stochastic price model which also models the load is required (e.g. the SMaPS model).

5.5.8 Operational Risk

The sourcing process described in section 5.3 is complex for a large number of customers and there are many details which have to be considered. With increasing complexity the sensitivity to errors increases. The operational risk appears to be the most significant risk which can cause a high potential loss. A general quantification of the operational risk is impossible. Key tasks are sensitive with respect to the risk management process. These are

1. Determination of load profiles and load volumes
2. Time-critical sourcing
3. Settlement of the grid access

Delayed sourcing is a risk to be noted. This risk can be quantified if it is assumed that the forward prices follow a geometric Brownian motion. As a risk measure the VaR can be used and with a RAROC approach a strict risk premium can be calculated.

If a retail contract is concluded at t_0 and there is a delay of the sourcing of N trading days and there are T trading days a year, the volatility for the time period N of the log-normally distributed forward price $F(t_0 + N, T_1, T_2)$ with the annualised volatility σ is $\sigma\sqrt{N/T}$.

The risk, measured as VaR with a confidence level α, is

$$\mathrm{VaR}(\alpha, N) = q_\alpha \left[F(t_0 + N, T_1, T_2) - F(t_0, T_1, T_2) \right],$$

where q_α denotes the α quantile.

Based on a period of one year the risk is lower. As an example assume that there are T/N consecutive, non-overlapping process delays a year (assumed to be an integer), then the risk for T/N delays with a confidence level α can be calculated as

$$q_\alpha \left[\sum_{i=1}^{T/N} (F(t_0 + iN, T_1, T_2) - F(t_0 + (i-1)N, T_1, T_2)) \right]$$

$$= q_\alpha \left[F(t_0 + T, T_1, T_2) \right] - F(t_0, T_1, T_2).$$

Consider an example with $\sigma = 25\%$, using a normal distribution as an approximation, and a current forward price $F(t_0, T_1, T_2) = 50$ EUR/MWh, the risk of a single sourcing delay of $N = 5$ trading days, measured as VaR with a 98% confidence level, is

$$\mathrm{VaR}(98\%, 5 \text{ days}) = q_{0.98} \left[F(t_0 + 5, T_1, T_2) \right] - F(t_0, T_1, T_2) = 3.63 \,\mathrm{EUR/MWh}.$$

The apparent risk seems high, but as a yearly average with the assumptions above the risk is smaller and in this example it results in:

$$\frac{1}{50} q_{0.98} \left[F(t_0 + 50N, T_1, T_2) \right] - F(t_0, T_1, T_2) = 0.51 \,\mathrm{EUR/MWh}.$$

Using a hurdle rate of 20%, for example, a risk premium of 0.1 EUR/MWh is adequate.

5.5.9 Risk Premium Summary

Delivering energy to retail customers holds hidden costs and additional risks. A utility can cover these risks with an adequate risk premium. Understanding these hidden costs and risks is as important for the customer as for the supplier. A retail customer purchasing a structured product must be aware that depending on the type of structured product, a part of these additional costs may be transferred to him. These additional costs should be included

Table 5.5   Risk components by retail contract type

Type of risk	Full service contract	Indexed contract	Schedule delivery	B2C (standard load profile)
Price validity period	Supplier	None	None	None
Balancing power	Supplier	Supplier	Customer	TSO
Credit risk	Supplier	Supplier	Supplier	Supplier
Price–volume correlation	Supplier	Supplier	Customer	TSO
Hourly price profile	Supplier	Supplier	Supplier	Supplier
Volume risk	Supplier	Supplier	Customer	Supplier

in the customer's calculation and the purchased structured product must still be competitive compared to a full service contract. This is not always the case and sometimes a full service contract is the most economical choice for a retail customer. Purchasing a structured product requires awareness about the involved risk. This is particularly the case for contracts with embedded options such as a right of cancellation.

Table 5.5 shows the types of risk for some types of retail contracts and identifies the party who is likely to bear the costs. The costs accepted by the TSO are market dependent and the table must be adapted to each specific market.

6

Risk Management

In this chapter the main features of a risk management process in the energy industry will be described in a practice-oriented fashion. The risk management process starts with a risk map.

This risk map should contain the main risks of the considered company. Figure 6.1 illustrates such a risk map.

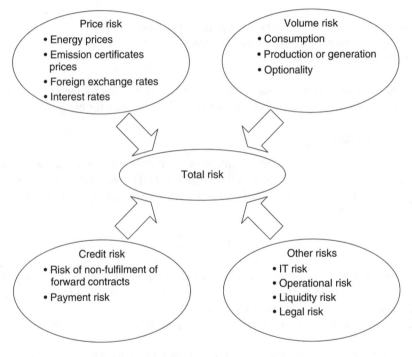

Figure 6.1 Risk map

Among the quantifiable risks, the price risk seems to be the most significant risk. Therefore the price risk will be considered first.

6.1 MARKET PRICE EXPOSURE

A key feature of the risk management process is the transparentising of market price exposures. First, the position of the entire portfolio has to be determined. There are several ways to definite the position of an energy portfolio, which are illustrated in Figure 6.2.

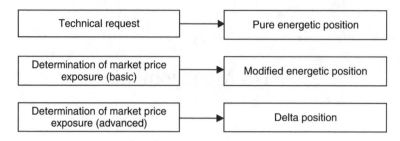

Figure 6.2   Determination of the position of an energy portfolio

Market participants with assets such as exploration fields, pipelines, or power plants must know their energetic position for technical reasons.

Using this energetic position for explaining market price exposures is possible, if some corrections are made. The most important adjustments are:

- Including futures contracts, even if there is no physical delivery.
- Including the financial leg of indexed contracts.
- Including the option delta.

A modified energetic position in this vein was used in section 5.3 for the explanation of the retail sourcing process. But there is a better performing measure for the position.

6.1.1   Delta Position

We define the delta position as the sensitivity of the portfolio value against a market price change of a tradable product. More technically, if $V(t, F(t))$ denotes the value of a portfolio at t depending on the market prices $F(t)$ of some traded product, the delta position $\Delta(F)$ is defined as (for fixed t)

$$\Delta(F) = \frac{\partial V(F)}{\partial F}.$$

Many risk management systems can compute these sensitivities numerically. They simulate the value of the portfolio, if the price F increases by one monetary unit. The change of the portfolio value is the delta position with respect to F.

Some elementary properties of the delta position are (see section 2.2.4 for a derivation):

1. As a derivative, the delta position is linear with respect to the quantity of the trading product.
2. If F is the price of a futures contract with physical delivery, the delta position and the energetic position are the same.
3. If F is the price of a forward contract the delta position can be considered as a discounted energetic position.
4. The delta position is the sensitivity of the portfolio against market price changes of F.
5. The unit of the delta position is equal to the unit of the quantity of the trading product. Particularly if F belongs to an energy product with the unit MWh, then the delta position $\Delta(F)$ also has the unit MWh.
6. The delta position of an option is the common option delta defined in section 2.2.4.

Example for the Delta Position: Oil Price Indexed Gas Price Formula

As a practical example consider the purchase of a 100 MW natural gas baseload contract, which is oil price indexed. The delivery period are the gas years 2008/2009 and 2009/2010, this means the delivery starts at 1 October 2008 and ends on 30 September 2010. The price formula for the natural gas price $P(t_0)$ (per MWh) for delivery at month t_0 is

$$P(t_0) = P_0 + bGO_a(t_0) + cFO_a(t_0),$$

where P_0 denotes a fixed basic price (with no impact on the delta position), $GO_a(t_0)$ the average gasoil price, and $FO_a(t_0)$ the average fuel oil price per tonne. $b = 0.035$ MWh/t and $c = 0.0175$ MWh/t are constants. The recalculation date of GO is at the beginning of each quarter, the recalculation date of FO at the beginning of each month. The average gasoil price $GO_a(t_0)$, i.e. the average fuel oil price, is given by

$$GO_a(t_0) = \frac{1}{8}\sum_{k=1}^{8} GO(t_0 - k - 1),\ FO_a(t_0) = \frac{1}{3}\sum_{k=1}^{3} FO(t_0 - k),$$

where $GO(t_0 - k - 1), FO(t_0 - k)$ denotes the price for gasoil at $(k+1)$-months and fuel oil at k-months before the month t_0. The pricing scheme for gasoil is illustrated in Figure 6.3 and for fuel oil in Figure 6.4. Now, the sensitivities against a change of market prices shall be analysed. At first the relevant trading products have to be determined.

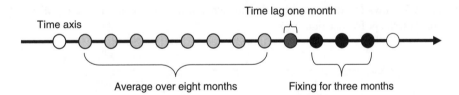

Figure 6.3   Gasoil price component

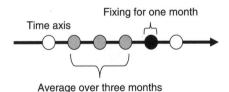

Figure 6.4   Fuel oil price component

In our example $P(t_0), P(t_0 + 1), \ldots, P(t_0 + 23)$ are the forward prices for natural gas for the 24 delivery months. $GO(t_0 - 9), GO(t_0 - 8), \ldots, GO(t_0 + 18), GO(t_0 + 19)$ denote the relevant forward gasoil prices for delivery at the months January 2008 until May 2010, and $FO(t_0 - 3), FO(t_0 - 2), \ldots, FO(t_0 + 21), FO(t_0 + 22)$ denote the relevant forward fuel oil prices for delivery at the months July 2008 until August 2010.

If the price for a natural gas forward with delivery in October 2008 rises about 1 USD/MWh, our profit will rise by the discounted value of

$$1 \times 100\,\text{MW} \times 31 \times 24\text{h} \times 1 \text{ USD/MWh} = 74\,400 \text{ USD}.$$

This means that the delta position of natural gas in October 2008 is, except for discounting, equal to the energetic position of 74 400 MWh (see property 3 of the delta position).

Consider if the price for a gasoil forward with delivery in January 2008 rises about 1 USD/t. This price has an impact on the expected price for natural gas with delivery in the third quarter 2008 and the monthly payment dates t_1, t_2, t_3. Our profit will change by

$$-\frac{1}{8} \times b \times 100\,\text{MW} \times (31e^{-r(t_1-t)} + 30e^{-r(t_2-t)} + 31e^{-r(t_3-t)}) \text{ d} \times 24\,\text{h/d} \times 1 \text{ USD/t}.$$

Except for the discounting, the delta position of gasoil with delivery in January 2008 is therefore -966 tonnes. Note that the energetic gasoil position is zero and we have only a financial sensitivity against a change of gasoil prices. Finally the delta position of fuel oil with delivery in July 2008 will be determined. If the fuel oil price rises about 1 USD/t our profit will change by the discounted value of

$$-\frac{1}{3} \times c \times 100\,\text{MW} \times 31\,\text{d} \times 24\,\text{h/d} \times 1 \text{ USD/t} = -434 \text{ USD}.$$

Except for the discounting, the delta position of fuel oil with delivery in July 2008 is -434 tonnes, while the energetic fuel oil position is zero.

Figure 6.5 shows the delta position for all relevant monthly natural gas, gasoil and fuel oil products (except for discounting).

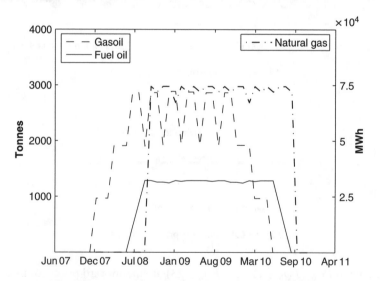

Figure 6.5   Delta position gasoil, fuel oil and natural gas

Analysing figure 6.5 we can see that the delta position for gasoil varies strongly. Taking an average gasoil price for eight months and fixing the price component for a quarter means that the monthly gasoil forward prices have an impact on the natural gas price for two or for three months. This generates an inefficiency if the contract is hedged with a yearly gasoil swap instead of monthly products.

The Delta Position of Power Schedules

There is a significant difference between the energetic and the delta position of power schedules. Because the delta position is a better performing hedge ratio than the energetic position, the difference will be explained in more detail using an example which consists of different steps.

The power schedule is denoted by $L(T_i)$, where $T_i, i = 1, \ldots, T_N$ denote the delivery hours and the value $V(t)$ of the power schedule is given by

$$V(t) = \sum_{i=1}^{N} e^{-r(T_i-t)} L(T_i) F(t, T_i),$$

with the hourly forward curve $F(t, \cdot)$. The hourly forward curve is determined so that it is consistent with the prices of the traded forward contracts. If F denotes the price of such a forward at t the delta position of L with respect to F is given by

$$\Delta(F) = \sum_{i=1}^{N} e^{-r(T_i-t)} L(T_i) \left(\bar{F}(t, T_i) - F(t, T_i) \right), \tag{6.1}$$

where $\bar{F}(t, \cdot)$ denotes the simulated forward curve consistent with a forward price increased by one monetary unit, i.e. consistent with $\bar{F} = F + 1$.

This means that the impact of the price of the traded forward F on the hourly forward curve $F(t, T_i)$ is determining the delta position of L. For a calculation of the hourly forward curve we refer to section 3.4.1. Using the notation of this chapter the process for determining the delta position of L with respect to a forward with price F is as follows: F and other traded forwards give a linear system of $N_b + N_p$ equations (3.38) and (3.39). Solving this linear system determines α_k and β_k and therefore $F(t, T_i)$. In a second step F is substituted by $\bar{F}$ and the associated $\bar{\alpha}_k$ and $\bar{\beta}_k$ are determining $\bar{F}(t, T_i)$. Finally the delta position of the power schedule L can be calculated from equation (6.1).

The decision for a system of relevant risk factors is also an important task. A set of sensitivities has to be determined, which describes the market price exposure. Baseload and peakload contracts are tradable products, but the difficulty is that a baseload contract includes a delivery of peakload. Shifting the price of the baseload contract by one monetary unit for a calculation of the baseload contract sensitivity implies that the other risk factors are kept constant. If the peakload contract price is also a risk factor the delta position with respect to the baseload contract of any schedule with delivery only during peakload hours is zero. Therefore a system of risk factors which contains off-peak and peakload forwards is more convenient, even if baseload is the most established trading product.

In the next step this calculation shall be done for the simplest case where only one baseload forward with price F^b and one peakload forward with price F^p are used for determining the scaling factors α and β. The risk factors are the peakload forwards with price F^p and the off-peak forwards with price F^{op}. The delivery period of all considered forwards is identical to the delivery period of L (i.e. $J^B = \{T_1, T_2, \ldots, T_N\}$). Furthermore, the delta position of

L will be calculated with respect to the peakload forward with price F^p. Assume that the second risk factor F^{op} is constant.

From the linear system of equations (3.38) and (3.39) we deduce:

$$\alpha = \frac{F^b|J^b| - F^p|J^p|}{\sum\limits_{j\in J^b} s_j - \sum\limits_{j\in J^p} s_j} \quad \text{and} \quad \beta = \frac{F^p|J^p|}{\sum\limits_{j\in J^p} s_j} - \alpha.$$

Substituting F^p by the simulated forward price $\bar{F}^p = F^p + 1$ gives

$$\bar{F}^b = F^b + \frac{|J^p|}{|J^b|}$$

and the new scaling factors:

$$\bar{\alpha} = \frac{(F^b + \frac{|J^p|}{|J^b|})|J^b| - (F^p + 1)|J^p|}{\sum\limits_{j\in J^b} s_j - \sum\limits_{j\in J^p} s_j} = \alpha$$

$$\bar{\beta} = \frac{(F^p + 1)|J^p|}{\sum\limits_{j\in J^p} s_j} - \bar{\alpha} = \beta + \frac{|J^p|}{\sum\limits_{j\in J^p} s_j}.$$

Equation (6.1) gives

$$\Delta(F) = \sum_{i\in J^b} e^{-r(T_i - t)} L(T_i) s_i \left(\bar{\alpha} - \alpha + 1_{peak}(i)(\bar{\beta} - \beta)\right)$$

$$= \frac{|J^p|}{\sum\limits_{j\in J^p} s_j} \sum_{i\in J^p} e^{-r(T_i - t)} L(T_i) s_i. \tag{6.2}$$

In the simplest case, that the power schedule is constant during the peakload hours, i.e. $L(T_i) = c, \forall T_i \in J^p$ we get as an approximation:

$$\Delta(F) = c|J^p|.$$

As expected, the delta position is then equal to the energetic position beside some discounting effects.

In the interesting case of an hourly varying schedule $L(T_i)$ the energetic position of the power schedule is $\sum_{i=1}^{N} L(T_i)$, while the delta position is a discounted and value weighted sum of the $L(T_i)$. The principle differences between the delta position and the energetic position are:

- The energy of the power schedule at T_i is weighted with the price scaling factor s_i. Power delivered at times of high prices affects the delta position more than the same energy amount delivered at times of low prices.
- As a financial sensitivity, the delta position is discounted. As a consequence the delta position of comparable futures and forward contracts is different.

In a last step assume that the delivery hours of the power schedule L are the expensive noontime hours $M \in J^B$ on weekdays 11 am–12 pm and the energy price at these noon hours is twice the average peakload price,

$$L(T_i) = \begin{cases} 1, & i \in M \\ 0, & \text{elsewhere,} \end{cases}$$

$$s_i = \begin{cases} 2, & i \in M \\ 1 - \frac{|M|}{|J^P| - |M|}, & \text{elsewhere.} \end{cases}$$

Ignoring the discounting effect equation (6.2) gives

$$\Delta(F) = 2|M|,$$

which is twice the energetic position.

This example shows that the difference between the delta and the energetic position can be remarkable. If such a purchased power schedule should be hedged with the peakload contract F^P, twice the energy should be sold. Using an hourly forward curve with scaling factors like those introduced in section 3.4.1 implies that a price change of the baseload or peakload contracts changes the hourly prices proportional to their value. Using the delta position as a hedge ratio is consistent with this fact. The performance of the energetic position as a hedge ratio would be only comparable with the delta position if a price change of the baseload or peakload contracts changes the hourly prices with the same absolute value, which cannot be observed.

6.1.2 Variance Minimising Hedging

In this section a hedge ratio will be introduced which considers the stochastic behaviour of prices and volume. The problem is determining optimal quantities of standard trading products for hedging a portfolio containing non-standard products. Using a stochastic model for the price and perhaps volume risk for the portfolio, the hedge ratios are determined by minimising the variance of the stochastic portfolio value.

This will be exemplified for a portfolio P containing a load with delivery at T_i, $i = 1, 2, \ldots, N$ and the expected (forecasted at t) delivery $L(t, T_i)$. If for hedging purposes standard baseload and peakload contracts F_k^b, F_k^P with the quantity μ_k, ν_k are added (assuming $J_k^b \subset \{T_1, T_2, \ldots, T_N\}$, $J_k^P \subset \{T_1, T_2, \ldots, T_N\}$ without any interferences), the present value of the portfolio is

$$V_{P,t} = \sum_{i=1}^{N} e^{-r(T_i - t)} \left(L(t, T_i) - \sum_k (\mu_k e_{ki} + \nu_k f_{mi}) \right) F(t, T_i), \qquad (6.3)$$

where

$$e_{ki} = \begin{cases} 1 & \text{for } T_i \in J_k^b \\ 0 & \text{otherwise} \end{cases}, \qquad f_{ki} = \begin{cases} 1 & \text{for } T_i \in J_k^P \\ 0 & \text{otherwise.} \end{cases}$$

If there is also a volume risk for P, i.e. the load $L(t, T_i)$ is a random variable, a stochastic model for price and load is needed to calculate the variance of $V_{P,t}$. If the price risk is measured until delivery, i.e. if in equation (6.3) $F(t, T_i)$ is replaced by the stochastic spot price $S(T_i)$, the SMaPS model can be used for minimising this variance. As an initial value of the optimisation problem the energetic hedge ratios can be used.

In the example illustrated in Figure 6.6, P contains a deterministic load and a baseload, and a peakload forward with the optimal hedge ratios μ, ν. In contrast to an energetic hedging the variance minimising hedging demands purchasing more standard products (typically between 3% and 6%) for a sold power schedule. The standard deviation of $V_{P,t}$ can then be reduced by 10% to 40%.

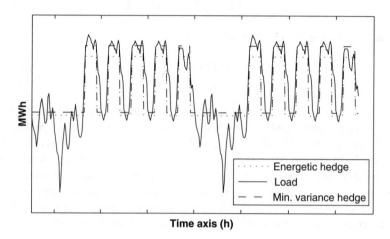

Figure 6.6   Variance minimising hedging

6.2   VALUE-AT-RISK AND FURTHER RISK MEASURES

Determining adequate risk measures for a company's business activities is an important, ongoing process. There are well-known general concepts like Value-at-Risk (VaR) or Profit-at-Risk (PaR) but the transfer to their own activities is at least as critical as the choice of the concept itself. At first a definition of risk is helpful to clarify the usage of the chosen risk measure. A common definition of risk is a possible negative divergence in relation to corporate planning. This definition is useful to guarantee the shareholders the promised returns. Another benchmark for financial assets is their actual value. This is a benchmark with a closer relation to the trading activities. Risk can be defined as a possible negative divergence in relation to the actual value of these assets. Both values can be converted into each other and the following considerations are restricted to the second definition.

6.2.1   Definition of Value-at-Risk

Value-at-Risk (VaR) is a risk measure widely used by financial institutions just as well as by fund managers or corporate treasures. The acceptance is shown by the fact that even central bank regulators use VaR for determining the capital required by a bank to reflect the market risk it is bearing. The popularity of VaR increased dramatically with the publication of JP Morgan's RiskMetrics Technical Document (cf. Guldimann 1995).

There are comprehensive publications concerning VaR so we will restrict our considerations to the principal methods and their practical usage in the energy business. For further reading we refer to Jorion (2001) or Holton (2003). A more application-oriented introduction to the Value-at-Risk concept can be also found in Hull (2005).

VaR, as illustrated in Figure 6.7, is the loss corresponding to the specified quantile of the change in the value of a given portfolio over a specified holding period. If $X(t)$ is the random variable of the market value of a given portfolio at time t with the probability distribution P, the specified holding period $t_1 - t_0$ and the confidence level α, VaR is defined by

$$P\left(X(t_1) - X(t_0) < -\mathrm{VaR}(\alpha, t_1 - t_0) \right) = 1 - \alpha. \tag{6.4}$$

VaR is one number expressing the total market price risk of a portfolio. Its advantage is that VaR is easy to understand and it answers the fundamental question of management: "How bad can things get?" Because VaR responds to this question only within the given confidence level its main disadvantage is that VaR gives no idea what happens beyond this level. A portfolio with the distribution of the change of the market value as shown in Figure 6.8 is more risky, but has the same VaR, as a portfolio with the distribution shown in Figure 6.7.

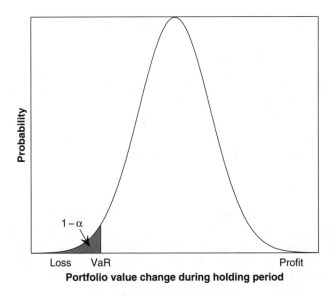

Figure 6.7   Value-at-Risk

For solving this problem VaR can be substituted or complemented by *Conditional VaR*. Conditional VaR is defined as the expectation of loss during the holding period conditional on being in the left tail of the distribution not belonging to the confidence level α.

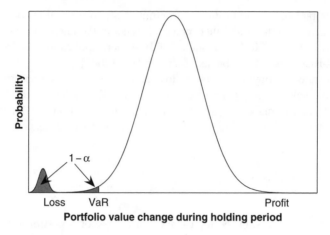

Figure 6.8 Portfolio with a low VaR compared to its risk

6.2.2   Parameters of the Value-at-Risk Measure

The two parameters of VaR are time horizon (or holding period) and confidence level. Assume that the changes in the value of the portfolio on successive days have independent identical normally distributions with mean zero, we have:

$$\text{VaR}(\alpha, N) = \sqrt{N}\text{VaR}(\alpha, 1).\qquad(6.5)$$

Therefore a VaR with a given time horizon can be easily converted, if another time horizon is requested. In practice equation (6.5) is used as an approximation, even if the assumption above is not true. VaR is calculated with a time horizon of one day and is afterwards converted into a VaR with the requested time horizon. For products with delivery during the time horizon this is not precise. Large energy portfolios usually contain products which have to be split up into those with no delivery during the time horizon and the risk of the remaining fraction has to be calculated, e.g. with a Profit-at-Risk approach.

How to Choose the Time Horizon

In the Basel Committee on Banking Supervision 1996 BIS Amendment and the associated 2005 update (cf. Basel Committee on Banking Supervision 2005) the calculation of capital is given for the trading book using the VaR measure with a time horizon $N = 10$ and a confidence level $\alpha = 99\%$. A criteria for the selected time horizon is the liquidity of the market. In a liquid market a time horizon of 10 days gives the trader the chance for balancing their position, so that after the holding period the market risk is eliminated.

Confidence level

Usually a confidence level between 95% and 99% is chosen. If the change of the portfolio is normally distributed, the VaR for a given confidence level can be easily converted using a factor if another confidence level is requested. Table 6.1 shows the conversion factors for some common confidence levels.

Table 6.1 Quantiles of a centred normal distribution quoted as multiples of the standard deviation

Confidence level	99%	98%	95%	90%	84%
Probability	1%	2%	5%	10%	16%
Quantile as multiples of the std deviation	−2.33	−2.05	−1.64	−1.28	−1.00

For example, the VaR belonging to a 99% confidence level is $2.33/1.64 = 1.4$ times the VaR of a 95% level in the normally distributed case. As a worst case scenario, the confidence level of the VaR should be high; however, all methods for calculating the VaR and the implied distribution assumptions have inaccuracies. In practice a confidence level above 99% is just a parameter but cannot be used as a value for the confidence level of the real distribution. A back-testing shows that for commodity portfolios there are usually more outliers.

6.2.3 Computation Methods

For a calculation of VaR of a portfolio there are several approaches. They all share the first step of identifying the market variables affecting the value of the portfolio. In a large energy portfolio there are numerous risk factors. For all energy contracts there are diverse traded contracts with daily, weekly, monthly, quarterly and yearly delivery periods and further risk factors like foreign exchange, interest rates or implied volatilities. All approaches for a VaR calculation require a sufficient database for these prices.

- *Historical simulation method*: The historical data is used in a direct way for the determination of the risk scenarios. If the settlement prices for the last k days are used, each day of observation generates a scenario for tomorrow's market prices based on the prices today. The percentage change of the market prices between the observation days i and $i+1$ with $i \in 1, 2, \ldots, k-1$ give the percentage change of the scenarios for tomorrow. The price scenarios include the observed correlations of different trading products. For each scenario the modified value of the portfolio will be determined and the $(1 - \alpha)$ quantile of the distribution of the changes in the portfolio value gives the VaR. For $k = 1000$ and $\alpha = 0.98$ the VaR(0.98,1 day) is the 20th highest loss in the portfolio value. To this point the historical simulation method does not require any assumption about the distribution of the change of the portfolio value. However, if equation (6.5) is used for calculating the VaR with a longer holding period the corresponding assumption must be fulfilled. Applying the historical simulation method to any time series of market data requires that the observation grid matches the holding period. If the holding period is 10 days, the percentage change in market prices after 10 days gives the scenario for the market prices 10 days in the future.

  The advantage of the historical simulation method is that it is robust, and easy to understand and implement. The disadvantages are that it is computationally slow and that incidents (as percentage changes in the market prices) not seen in the past are not considered.
- *Analytical method*: The analytical method is fast and the most common method for calculating VaR. Assuming a distribution for the market prices, i.e. their yield, the resulting changes of the portfolio value are calculated using the market price sensitivities of the portfolio. The most common assumption is that market prices are log-normally

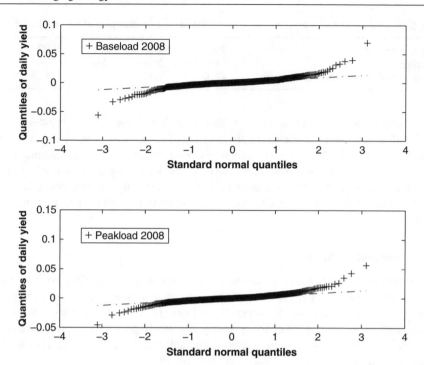

Figure 6.9   QQ-plot of the yield base-/peakload 2008 versus standard normal

distributed, implying that the returns of the trading products are normally distributed. In practice this assumption is critical. The qq-plot for the power products baseload and peakload 2008 in Figure 6.9 shows the typical problems of these assumption. If the returns were normally distributed the qq-plot of the returns would be linear, but the fat tails are clearly visible. Nevertheless, calculating the VaR with the log-normal assumption for a large diversified portfolio performs better than expected by looking only at Figure 6.9. This observed property can be motivated by the central limit theorem. The analytical method can be differentiated in the way the portfolio value is calculated while there is a shift in market prices.

– *Delta-normal method*: The delta-normal method uses only the delta position of a portfolio for determining its value change. Therefore there are inaccuracies if the portfolio contains non-linear products like options.
– *Delta-gamma method*: If the change of the portfolio value is written as a Taylor series (equation (6.6) shows this explicitly) depending on the market prices, additional to the linear term the quadratic term is also used. The method is then also adequate for options, because their gamma is also considered.

• *Structured Monte Carlo method*: The structured Monte Carlo method requires a stochastic model for the risk factors which generate price samples. With these price samples the possible changes of the portfolio value can be simulated and the VaR can be determined as a quantile of the associated probability distribution.

Analytical Method

For practical use the analytical method as the most common method is discussed in more detail. In a first step the market sensitivities (i.e. the risk factors) have to be determined. If a portfolio P has the market prices $F_1, F_2, \ldots, F_n$ as risk factors, then the VaR$(\alpha, \Delta t)$ is the $(1 - \alpha)$ quantile of the change of the market value V of P in the holding period Δt. Using the Taylor series expansion $V(F_1, F_2, \ldots, F_n)$ can be written as

$$\Delta V(F_1, F_2, \ldots, F_n) = \sum_{i=1}^{n} \frac{\partial V}{\partial F_i} \Delta F_i$$

$$+ \frac{1}{2} \sum_{i=1}^{n} \sum_{j=1}^{n} \frac{\partial^2 V}{\partial F_i \partial F_j} \Delta F_i \Delta F_j$$

$$+ R(\Delta(F_1, F_2, \ldots, F_n)), \tag{6.6}$$

where $R(\cdot)$ denotes the small remainder term.

Delta-Normal Approach

The impact of a change of market prices on the change of the portfolio value is not always linear. If a portfolio contains options the interrelation described in section 2.2.4 is complex. The delta-normal method is a linear approximation of the change of the portfolio value which is adequate if the portfolio contains basically linear instruments like forward or futures contracts.

Determining the VaR with the delta–normal method means a linear approximation of the change of the portfolio value ΔV, i.e.

$$\Delta V(F_1, F_2, \ldots, F_n) = \sum_{i=1}^{n} \frac{\partial V}{\partial F_i} \Delta F_i.$$

The partial derivative $\frac{\partial V}{\partial F_i}$ is the delta position of F_i. To avoid confusion between the delta position $\Delta(F_i)$ and the change ΔF_i we denote the delta position of F_i (interpreted as quantity) as q_i.

If the portfolio contains only one futures contract F as risk factor (i.e. one tradable product) the VaR calculation can be straightforward. Analogous to option price theory (see, e.g. Black's Futures Price Model described in 2.2.2) we assume that market prices follow a geometric Brownian motion. The change of the logarithms of the futures prices is normally distributed and can be written as

$$\log(F(t)) - \log(F(t_0)) = -\frac{\sigma^2}{2}(t - t_0) + \sigma \sqrt{t - t_0} X,$$

where X denotes a standard normally distributed random variable and σ the annualised volatility of F. With the requested confidence level α and the belonging multiplier m_α (see Table 6.1) we have with a probability of α

$$F(t) - F(t_0) \geq F(t_0) \left(\exp\left(-\frac{\sigma^2}{2}(t - t_0) - m_\alpha \sigma \sqrt{t - t_0} \right) - 1 \right).$$

The VaR with the confidence level α and the holding period $t - t_0$ is therefore

$$\text{VaR}(\alpha, t - t_0) = F(t_0) \left(\exp\left(-\frac{\sigma^2}{2}(t - t_0) - m_\alpha \sigma \sqrt{t - t_0} \right) - 1 \right).$$

Considering a portfolio of different trading products, the change of the portfolio value is the sum of log-normally distributed random variables. Because this sum is not log-normally distributed itself, determining the VaR (i.e. a specified quantile) is more complex. One possibility is using a Monte Carlo simulation for the log-normally distributed prices F_i for calculating the requested quantile of the change of the portfolio value. An alternative is to use approximations for the distributions, which will be elaborated now.

The normally distributed continuous compounding return is denoted as

$$\bar{r}_i[t_0, t] = \ln\left(\frac{F_i(t)}{F_i(t_0)} \right).$$

As a difference to option price theory the focus of VaR calculations is usually short time periods (change in the portfolio over a short time period), while in option theory longer periods (maturities up to a year or longer) are regarded as well. For a small discrete return (i.e. a small $\Delta t = t - t_0$)

$$r_i[t_0, t] = \frac{F_i(t) - F_i(t_0)}{F_i(t_0)}$$

the linear approximation

$$\ln(1 + r_i[t_0, t]) \approx r_i[t_0, t]$$

gives

$$\bar{r}_i[t_0, t] = \ln\left(1 + \frac{F_i(t) - F_i(t_0)}{F_i(t_0)} \right) \approx r_i[t_0, t].$$

Even though this is a deterministic consideration only, it is an indication that with a normally distributed continuous compounding return $\bar{r}_i[t_0, t]$ the discrete return $r_i[t_0, t]$ is approximately normally distributed, for a small time interval $[t_0, t]$. Figure 6.10 shows the small difference of the distribution functions of a log-normal and a normal distribution with the same standard deviation of annualised 20% and converted for a holding period of 10 days.

The procedure for calculating the VaR is as follows. With the common assumption of option price theory, that the market prices follow a geometric Brownian motion, the VaR is calculated for a one day period and is scaled to the requested holding period by equation (6.5), which is an approximation. The discrete return $r_i[t_0, t_0 + 1]$ of F_i for a small holding period of one day is approximately normally distributed and additionally it is assumed that the mean of the discrete return is zero. Therefore the change of the portfolio value

$$\Delta V(F_1, F_2, \ldots, F_n) = \sum_{i=1}^{n} q_i F_i(t_0) \frac{F_i(t_0 + 1) - F_i(t_0)}{F_i(t_0)} = \sum_{i=1}^{n} q_i F_i(t_0) r_i[t_0, t_0 + 1],$$

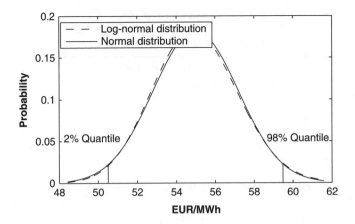

Figure 6.10   Comparison of the density of a log-normal and a normal distribution with 20% volatility (annualised) converted for a holding period of 10 days

is approximately normally distributed with a mean of zero and only the standard deviation $\sigma_{\Delta V}$ has to determined. If σ_i denotes the standard deviation of $r_i[t_0, t_0 + 1]$ (approximately the daily volatility), $(\mathbf{C}_{i,j})$ the correlation matrix of the r_i, and $\mathbf{v}$ the column vector

$$\mathbf{v} = (q_1 F_1(t_0)\sigma_1, \ldots, q_n F_n(t_0)\sigma_n),$$

we have

$$\sigma_{\Delta V} = \sqrt{\mathbf{v}^T (\mathbf{C}_{i,j}) \mathbf{v}}. \tag{6.7}$$

If the standard deviation $\sigma_{\Delta V}$ is determined, the $\text{VaR}(\alpha, \Delta t)$ can be easily calculated using the multiplier m_α belonging to the confidence level α indicated in Table 6.1:

$$\text{VaR}(\alpha, \Delta t) = \sigma_{\Delta V} m_\alpha \sqrt{\Delta t} \tag{6.8}$$

Example for a Value-at-Risk Calculation Using the Delta-Normal Method

As a practical example the VaR(98%,10 d) of an assumed energy portfolio described in Table 6.2 will be calculated by using the delta-normal method.

Table 6.2   Assumed energy portfolio

Product	Delta position	Market price	Volatility 1 d
Power: baseload 2009	10 000 000 MWh	55 EUR/MWh	1%
Power: peakload 2009	5 000 000 MWh	80 EUR/MWh	0.8%
Coal	−1 000 000 tonnes	85 EUR/t	0.8%
USD	−85 000 000 USD	0.75 EUR/USD	0.6%
CO_2-emission allowances	−1 000 000 tonnes	20 EUR/t	3.5%

The assumed correlation matrix is shown in Table 6.3.

Table 6.3   Market price correlations

	Baseload 2009	Peakload 2009	Coal	USD	CO_2
Baseload 2009	1.0	0.9	0.2	0.0	0.5
Peakload 2009	0.9	1.0	0.2	0.0	0.4
Coal	0.2	0.2	1.0	0.0	0.1
USD	0.0	0.0	0.0	1.0	0.0
CO_2	0.5	0.4	0.1	0.0	1.0

Following equation (6.7) the standard deviation of the change of the portfolio value is determined by

$$
\sigma_{\Delta V}^2 =
\begin{pmatrix} 5\,500\,000 \\ 3\,200\,000 \\ -680\,000 \\ -381\,982 \\ -700\,000 \end{pmatrix}^T
\begin{pmatrix} 1.0 & 0.9 & 0.2 & 0.0 & 0.5 \\ 0.9 & 1.0 & 0.2 & 0.0 & 0.4 \\ 0.2 & 0.2 & 1.0 & 0.0 & 0.1 \\ 0.0 & 0.0 & 0.0 & 1.0 & 0.0 \\ 0.5 & 0.4 & 0.1 & 0.0 & 1.0 \end{pmatrix}
\begin{pmatrix} 5\,500\,000 \\ 3\,200\,000 \\ -680\,000 \\ -381\,982 \\ -700\,000 \end{pmatrix},
$$

which means

$$
\sigma_{\Delta V} = 8\,084\,251.
$$

From equation (6.8) the VaR with the holding period of 10 days and confidence level 98% is:

$$
\text{VaR}(98\%, 10\,\text{d}) = \sigma_{\Delta V} \times 2.05 \times \sqrt{10} = 52\,407\,524\,\text{EUR}.
$$

Delta-Gamma Approach

When a portfolio includes options a change of the market prices involves a change of the delta position of the portfolio. The discussed delta-normal method ignores this effect. A more appropriate approximation can be obtained if the quadratic term of the Taylor series expansion given in equation (6.6) is also used. In a first step the moments of ΔV can be calculated and subsequently the Cornish–Fisher expansion (see, e.g. Holton 2003) can be used to estimate quantiles of the probability distribution from these moments.

Qualitatively a portfolio with a positive gamma (e.g. it includes a long call option) reduces its market price sensitivity (i.e. its delta position) in the case of decreasing market prices. If market prices are increasing there is a positive effect from an increasing delta. A VaR calculated with the delta-normal method is therefore too high. Vice versa, the calculated VaR will be too low if the portfolio has a negative gamma.

6.2.4   Liquidity-Adjusted Value-at-Risk

The aim of Value-at-Risk is giving an answer to the question "How bad can things get?" There may be companies using VaR only as a relative risk measure to compare today's price risk with yesterday's price risk. If this is not sufficient and the absolute risk value is used for management decisions, the holding period must be chosen in a meaningful way so that the portfolio can be liquidated within that time period. For trading portfolios in liquid markets a holding period of only a few trading days is typical.

The price risk calculation for an energy company with a substantial asset book containing its primary activities, such as production, generation or sales, is exceptionally complex because it is often too large for closing the open position in a time horizon of a few days. On the other hand the price risk of the asset portfolio is an important indicator for the management of energy companies to anticipate possible negative divergences from the corporate plan. In such a situation the standard VaR with a fixed and relatively short holding period has only a limited significance. Simply extending the holding period is not adequate, because it ignores the successive reduction of the position over time or at least the possibility of such a reduction.

One possibility for solving this problem is to calculate a *liquidity-adjusted VaR* (LVaR) where instead of a single holding period a successive closing of the open position is assumed. This implies that there is an explicit management of the market risk of the considered asset book and that selling the generation or production is not driven by an unpredictable demand.

At first the portfolio is approximated by tradable standard contracts $F_1, \ldots, F_n$ with the quantities (delta positions) $q_1, \ldots, q_n$. Then for each trading product the number β_i of contracts which can be sold respectively purchased in a given short time period Δt (e.g. one trading day) without any significant impact on the market prices is determined. Therefore the open position q_i can be reduced to $q_i - k\beta_i$ after the period $k\Delta t$. We define $p := \max \{q_i/\beta_i : i \in \{1, \ldots, n\}\}$ (p can be assumed to be an integer) and a_{ik} as an indication if the total number of contracts has been reached:

$$a_{ik} = \begin{cases} 1, & \text{if } k\beta_i \leq q_i \\ 0, & \text{else} \end{cases}, i \in \{1, \ldots, n\}, k \in \{1, \ldots, p\}.$$

Thus the assumed portfolio at period k consists of the trading products $F_i, i \in \{1, \ldots, n\}$ with quantities $a_{ik}(q_i - k\beta_i)$ and the standard deviation of their changes σ_i. At period p all positions have been closed. The variance $\sigma^2(k)$ of the change of market value for the portfolio at period k over the period Δt is

$$\sigma^2(k) = \Delta t \mathbf{v_k}^T (\mathbf{C}_{i,j}) \mathbf{v_k}, k \in \{1, \ldots, p\}, \tag{6.9}$$

where $(\mathbf{C}_{i,j})$ denotes the correlation matrix of the daily returns r_i and $\mathbf{v_k}$ denotes the column vector

$$\mathbf{v_k} = (a_{1k}(q_1 - k\beta_1)F_1(t_0)\sigma_1, \ldots, a_{nk}(q_n - k\beta_n)F_n(t_0)\sigma_n).$$

Assuming that the changes of market prices over the successive time periods are independent and by approximation normally distributed with mean zero and variance σ_i^2, the change of the total asset portfolio as a sum of independent normally distributed random variables is also normally distributed with mean zero and variance

$$\sigma^2 = \sum_{k=1}^{p} \sigma^2(k) = \sum_{k=1}^{p} \Delta t \mathbf{v_k}^T (\mathbf{C}_{i,j}) \mathbf{v_k}. \tag{6.10}$$

Using the multiplier m_α belonging to the requested confidence level α indicated in Table 6.1 the LVaR(α) for the portfolio is

$$\text{LVaR}(\alpha) = m_\alpha \sigma.$$

The usual simplification is the uniform reduction of an asset portfolio. Most producers close their long position (producing or generation side) in the same degree that they close their short position of the source material (e.g. fuel).

With p as defined above, the quantity β_i is replaced by the smaller quantity $\bar{\beta}_i = q_i/p$ forcing a uniform closing of all positions without violating any liquidity restrictions. Then we have $a_{ik} = 1$ for all $i = 1, \ldots, n$, $k = 1, \ldots, p$ and

$$q_i - k\bar{\beta}_i = (p - k)\bar{\beta}_i.$$

Equation (6.10) gives

$$\sigma^2 = \Delta t \mathbf{v}^T (\mathbf{C}_{i,j}) \mathbf{v} \sum_{k=1}^{p} (p - k)^2, \tag{6.11}$$

where $\mathbf{v}$ denotes the column vector

$$\mathbf{v} = \left(\bar{\beta}_1 F_1(t_0)\sigma_1, \ldots, \bar{\beta}_n F_n(t_0)\sigma_n \right).$$

The sum can be reduced to

$$\sum_{k=1}^{p} (p - k)^2 = \sum_{k=1}^{p-1} k^2 = \frac{(p-1)p(2p-1)}{6}.$$

As an example the portfolio described in Table 6.2 is reconsidered.

We assume that the closing of the position requires 100 trading days because of the limited market liquidity so that $\Delta t = 1$ and $p = 100$. It is assumed that all trading products will always be reduced uniformly as described above. The position that can be closed during one trading day contains one hundredth of the initial portfolio and equation (6.11) gives

$$\sigma^2 = \frac{99 \times 100 \times 199}{6} \begin{pmatrix} 55\,000 \\ 32\,000 \\ -6800 \\ -3819 \\ -7000 \end{pmatrix}^T \begin{pmatrix} 1.0 & 0.9 & 0.2 & 0.0 & 0.5 \\ 0.9 & 1.0 & 0.2 & 0.0 & 0.4 \\ 0.2 & 0.2 & 1.0 & 0.0 & 0.1 \\ 0.0 & 0.0 & 0.0 & 1.0 & 0.0 \\ 0.5 & 0.4 & 0.1 & 0.0 & 1.0 \end{pmatrix} \begin{pmatrix} 55\,000 \\ 32\,000 \\ -6800 \\ -3819 \\ -7000 \end{pmatrix}$$

$$= 2\,145\,935\,054\,909\,250.$$

The liquidity-adjusted VaR with a confidence level of 98% is therefore

$$\text{LVaR}(98\%) = 2.05\,\sigma = 2.05 \times 46\,324\,238 = 94\,964\,689\,\text{EUR}.$$

How can this quantification of the market risk be interpreted? A utility that owns generation capacities may have a portfolio described in Table 6.2. For the future (the year 2009) they have a long position in power (they can generate power) and they need fuel and emission allowances for their plants. If the utility has a risk management strategy allowing the reduction of the open position restricted only by the market liquidity, the risk against the actual portfolio value is 95 million Euros.

6.2.5   Estimating Volatilities and Correlations

If the analytical method is used for calculating VaR, the volatilities σ_i for the daily returns $r_i[t, t+1]$ of the trading products are required. In the following discussion the trading product is fixed and the associated subscript i is omitted.

On the day t_{n-1} the most recent m observations of the (discrete) return are denoted by

$$r(t_{n-j}) = r[t_{n-j-1}, t_{n-j}] = \ln \left(\frac{F(t_{n-j})}{F(t_{n-j-1})} \right), j \in \{1, 2, \ldots, m\}.$$

If the volatility σ would be constant, then it could be estimated using these oberservations:

$$\sigma^2 = \frac{1}{m-1} \sum_{j=1}^{m} \left(r(t_{n-j}) - \bar{r} \right)^2,$$

where

$$\bar{r} = \frac{1}{m} \sum_{j=1}^{m} r(t_{n-j})$$

denotes the mean of the $r(t_{n-j})$. Because of the assumption that the mean of the returns is zero, we have approximately

$$\sigma^2 = \frac{1}{m} \sum_{j=1}^{m} r^2(t_{n-j}). \tag{6.12}$$

Using equation (6.12) is the simplest method for estimating the volatility σ.

Noting that in reality σ is not constant but a function of time, a forecasting method for these time dependent standard deviations $\sigma(t_n)$ of $r(t_n)$ is required. The following are the most common methods for an improvement of equation (6.12).

The Exponentially Weighted Moving Average Model (EWMA)

The basic idea is weighting recent data higher than older observations. Introducing weights in equation (6.12) gives

$$\sigma^2(t_n) = \sum_{j=1}^{m} \alpha_j r^2(t_{n-j}), \tag{6.13}$$

with

$$\sum_{j=1}^{m} \alpha_j = 1.$$

If the weights decrease exponentially, depending on the trading days since the observation of the returns, these weights can be written as

$$\exp(a(t_n - t_{n-j})) = \exp(a \times j) = \exp^j(a).$$

With $\lambda := \exp(a)$ the equation for an estimation of $\sigma(t_n)$ is

$$\sigma^2(t_n) = (1 - \lambda) \sum_{j=1}^{m} \lambda^{j-1} r^2(t_{n-j}) + \lambda^m \sigma^2(t_{n-m}). \qquad (6.14)$$

For the sum of the weights we have

$$(1 - \lambda) \sum_{j=1}^{m} \lambda^{j-1} + \lambda^m = 1.$$

If m is large the term λ^m is small so that equation (6.14) can be regarded as a special case of equation (6.13) with $\alpha_j = (1 - \lambda)\lambda^{j-1}$.

The procedure for calculating the time dependent volatility is:

- Calculate an initial value for the volatility using equation (6.14) and ignoring the term $\lambda^m \sigma_{n-m}^2$.
- The volatility can be actualised with low computational effort using the recursion

$$\sigma^2(t_n) = (1 - \lambda) r^2(t_{n-1}) + \lambda \sigma^2(t_{n-1}), \qquad (6.15)$$

which follows from equation (6.14) if $m = 1$.

If the EWMA approach is used for estimating the volatility the parameter $\lambda \in (0, 1)$ has to be specified. If λ is close to 1 a long history is used for estimating $\sigma(t_n)$. The estimation is stable but new market information is slowly integrated. Such a λ is adequate if the VaR for a large asset portfolio has to be calculated. If λ is lower the volatility itself is very volatile. For a proprietary trading portfolio a fast adaptation to the actual volatility is useful. One way to specify λ is defining a half period, i.e. a date, where the observation of the return is weighted half as much as the most recent observation. Equation (6.14) shows that the weight of an observation made j trading days ago is reduced to half if λ fulfils: $\lambda^{j-1} = 1/2$. J.P. Morgan (see J.P. Morgan 1995) uses a parameter $\lambda = 0.94$ for their RiskMetrics database. This corresponds to a half period of approximately 10 days and is found to be convenient in the energy market as well.

GARCH Models

Another useful method for estimating volatilities are the GARCH models proposed by Bollerslev (1986). With the GARCH(1,1) model the volatility can be estimated with a recursion formula similar to equation (6.15):

$$\sigma^2(t_n) = \lambda_1 \bar{\sigma} + \lambda_2 r^2(t_{n-1}) + \lambda_3 \sigma^2(t_{n-1}),$$

where the non-negative weights λ_i sum to one and $\bar{\sigma}$ is a long-run average volatility. The GARCH(1,1) model tends to get pulled back to the long-run average volatility $\bar{\sigma}$. GARCH(1,1) allows modelling of a wide range of behaviour of the volatility, in particular heavy changes. In energy markets, volatilities can change very fast so GARCH models seem to be adequate. However, in reaction to strong market movements GARCH models can produce extreme scenarios which seem unrealistic and are not as robust as the EWMA model. A careful estimation of the parameters and a permanent backtesting are therefore essential.

Estimating Correlations

The methods for estimating the volatilities can be adapted for estimating the correlations. If F_1, F_2 are trading products with the daily returns r_1, r_2 and the daily volatilities σ_1, σ_2 the correlation between the returns is

$$\mathrm{Corr}(r_1, r_2) = \frac{\mathrm{Cov}(r_1, r_2)}{\sigma_1 \sigma_2} = \frac{\mathbb{E}[r_1 - \mathbb{E}[r_1]]\mathbb{E}[r_2 - \mathbb{E}[r_2]]}{\sigma_1 \sigma_2}. \tag{6.16}$$

Analogous to equation (6.12) the covariance and therefore the correlation at t_n can be estimated by:

$$\mathrm{Cov}_{t_n}(r_1, r_2) = \frac{1}{m} \sum_{j=1}^{m} r_1(t_{n-j}) r_2(t_{n-j}).$$

The EWMA approach can also be used for estimating the covariance. The recursion formula analogue to (6.15) is

$$\mathrm{Cov}_{t_n}(r_1, r_2) = (1 - \lambda) r_1(t_{n-1}) r_2(t_{n-1}) + \lambda \mathrm{Cov}_{t_{n-1}}(r_1, r_2).$$

6.2.6   Backtesting

Backtesting is an important, ongoing task because VaR and other risk measures require extensive assumptions on the stochastic process representing market prices. There are many influencing factors that are critical to the VaR calculation. If the backtesting rejects the appointed VaR model, the reason is often inadequate model parameters and this does not always mean that the VaR concept itself is not adequate for the specific problem. Critical factors concerning VaR are:

- Choosing the risk drivers for the VaR calculation. All risk factors must be identified and often some assumptions are necessary. One usual assumption is that delivery periods are considered in relation to today, e.g. month ahead, year ahead etc., and that there is a rollover in the time series. Possible seasonal patterns for volatilities and correlations are ignored and it must be decided if this is adequate.
- The risk for non-standard products (e.g. power schedules) must be considered in an adequate way. The price of standard contracts is often the basis for the valuation of the other contracts and shifting standard contract prices should reflect the risk of non-standard products.

- If the estimation of volatilities and correlations is not stable, large market shifts can cause unrealistic parameters and therefore an unrealistic VaR.

Figure 6.11 shows the daily change of a substantial energy portfolio versus the calculated 98% confidence interval. There are 2% outliers expected. If the probability distribution of the daily value change is symmetric (e.g. normally distributed) outliers belonging to a positive value change also provide information concerning the adequateness of the implied VaR method. Because the holding period is 1 day and the backtesting involves 200 trading days, there are 8 expected outliers (4 higher and 4 lower values). In the backtested portfolio are fewer outliers (but not too few) and the backtesting supports the selected model.

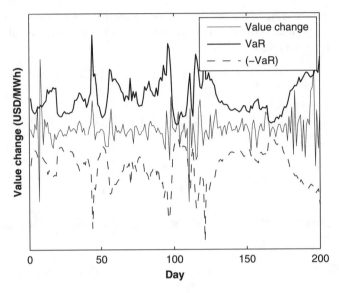

Figure 6.11   Backtesting: VaR(98%, 1 day) versus daily change of an energy portfolio's value

6.2.7   Further Risk Measures

Value-at-Risk is by far the most popular risk measure. However, there are disadvantages, most of which have been discussed. Recapitulating the results, VaR is a risk measure which is adequate for short holding periods and for price risks concerning the future market. For voluminous portfolios where market risks cannot be eliminated in a short holding period a liquidity-adjusted VaR is useful.

In energy markets there are products that cannot be traded on the future market and therefore a market risk exists until delivery. As an example hourly profiles in the power market can be traded on the spot market, but there is no future market for power delivered for one hour only. Spot prices are found to be much more volatile than future prices, especially for commodities that can hardly be stored. Because the distribution of spot prices is often heavy-tailed the assumption of a log-normal distribution is not adequate. There are risk measures like Profit-at-Risk, Earnings-at-Risk or Cashflow-at-Risk, which integrate spot market risks and give a separate view on the market risk.

- *Cashflow-at-Risk*: The considered random variable is the cashflow of a company until a specified date. The Cashflow-at-Risk is the difference between the expected cashflow and the cashflow corresponding to the given confidence level α, i.e. the $(1 - \alpha)$ quantile of the distribution of the cashflow. CFaR reflects whether a company has adequate cash reserves and can be used to help companies assess their capital structure and creditworthiness.
- *Earnings-at-Risk*: The considered random variable is the earnings of a company until a specified date. For energy companies this includes spot price revenues generated by the assets less all production costs among all payoffs of the trading and hedging transactions. Earnings-at-Risk is the difference between the expected earnings and the earnings corresponding to the given confidence level.
- *Profit-at-Risk*: PaR is related to Earnings-at-Risk and was designed for the energy markets to include volatile spot prices in the market risk consideration. With a given confidence level α, PaR is the $(1 - \alpha)$ quantile of the change in the value of a given portfolio until delivery. Using PaR requires an effective spot market model such as the SMaPS model or the regime-switching model introduced in section 3.4.2 and section 3.4.3, respectively.

Among these standard risk measures a scenario analysis is useful and can help to get an impression of the market risks without requiring a market model. The historical simulation method described in the VaR context (section 6.2.3) can be easily extended to spot prices. Also some extreme market scenarios of the past can be used for evaluating the market price risk of the actual portfolio.

6.3   CREDIT RISK

Before the markets became liberalised credit risk was only considered as the risk that customers cannot pay for the energy obtained. Contracts between utilities were not regarded because the risk of a default of a utility seemed to be negligible. What the collapse of Barings Bank was for financial institutions, Enron was for the energy industry. Additionally there was the insolvency of US American energy merchants such as Dynegy, Mirant and El Paso and other US American energy companies leaving Europe as a marketplace.

Nowadays credit risk is one of the major risks monitored and managed. But also a growing wholesale market requires instruments for limiting credit risk. Hedging a utility's asset position should not result in a credit risk that compares to the primary market risk.

Credit risk is the risk that a counterparty cannot fulfil his contractual obligations. His main obligations are the payment, the agreed physical delivery or acceptance. Credit risk can be classified as follows.

- *Settlement risk*: Settlement risk is defined as the possibility that a counterparty cannot pay the obtained benefits, e.g. the delivered energy amount.
- *Replacement risk*: Replacement risk is defined as the possibility that a counterparty will be unable to meet the terms of a contract even for the future and thus a new replacement contract will have to be entered into. The new replacement contract can only be concluded under the actual market conditions and prices may differ in a negative way since the original contract was created.

For example, a utility buys 30 000 tonnes of coal for 60 USD/t in January 2008 for delivery in January 2009 and the continuously compounding interest rate for USD is 4% p.a. At end of June 2008 the price for coal is 70 USD/t and the settlement risk is

$$30\,000\,\text{tonnes} \times 10 \text{ USD/t} \times \exp(-0.04 \times 0.5) = 294\,060 \text{ USD}.$$

When entering a fixed price contract the settlement risk is predictable even for the future. The cashflow dates and amounts are fixed. However, the replacement risk depends on the development of market prices. Strict credit risk limitations can only hold if there is a margin agreement with the counterparty. The *credit risk exposure* is the sum of the settlement and the replacement risk.

As displayed in Figure 6.12, managing credit risk has many components. It begins with the selection of the counterparties and with the design of the master agreement. The next step is the quantifying and limitation of credit risk.

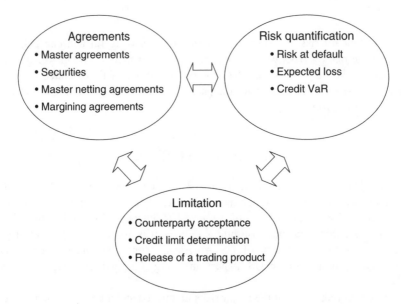

Figure 6.12   Credit risk components

6.3.1   Legal Risk

The management of credit risk starts with the contractual basis. To enable an efficient trading, all trading contracts are subject to the master agreement concluded with the counterparty. Each individual trade refers to this master agreement and there is only a brief individual trade confirmation necessary. Master agreements are developed from different organisations with the intention to set a standard. To allow individual specifications the master agreement includes an election sheet where possible versions of a clause can be selected. Some important organisations in Europe with published master agreements are:

- *EFET – European Federation of Energy Traders*
  EFET is a group of more than 60 European energy trading companies and is designed to improve conditions for energy trading in Europe. The following master agreements are published:

  - EFET Power: Master agreement for power with physical delivery.
  - EFET Gas: Master agreement for gas with physical delivery.
  - EFET Allowance Appendix: Appendix for CO_2 emission trading with physical delivery of the allowances.

- *IETA – International Emissions Trading Association*
  IETA is an organisation dedicated to the establishment of effective systems for trading in greenhouse gas emissions. The IETA master agreement is therefore designed for CO_2 emission trading with physical delivery of the allowances.
- *ISDA – International Swaps and Derivatives Association*
  ISDA is a large global trade association and has over 750 member institutions. The ISDA master agreement is widely used for products with a financial settlement, e.g. swaps.
- *EBF – European Banking Federation*
  EBF has published the European Master Agreement (EMA). There are also national master agreements such as the Deutsche Rahmenvertrag published from the Association of German Banks (Bundesverband deutscher Banken) and the incentive particularly from German and French Banks while developing the EMA is to establish a European standard.

The advantage of a uniform contractual basis is the reduction of back-to-back risks. For example, a force majeure clause can pose a high risk if the sourcing contract contains a far-ranging force majeure clause and the belonging supply contract does not.

6.3.2 Quantifying Credit Risk

There are several risk numbers describing credit risk and their usage depends on the particular application.

- *Risk-at-Default*: The Risk-at-Default figure is how much the company will lose as a result of the default of a specified counterparty. The loss is contingent upon the amount to which the firm was exposed at the time of default. A recovery rate may be assumed (the amount that a creditor would receive in final satisfaction of his claims).
- *Expected Loss*: The Expected Loss is the product of the calculated credit exposure and the estimated probability of default.
- *Potential Exposure*: Analogous to the market risk metric of VaR the Potential Exposure is the maximal likely credit exposure with a given confidence level (e.g. 98%). For this purpose market price scenarios are used for generating scenarios for the credit risk exposure. For fixed price contracts the settlement risk is predictable and the scenarios concern the replacement risk only, but for indexed contracts scenarios for the settlement risk must be generated as well.

  The Potential Exposure answers the question: "What is the most I could lose to this counterparty with some degree of confidence?" and is useful for limit setting and stress testing.

- *Credit VaR*: Credit VaR can be defined similarly to the way VaR is defined for market risk. With a given confidence level α and a holding period according to the duration of the contracts, the credit VaR is the $(1 - \alpha)$ quantile of the loss as a consequence of a default. For banks, where credit risk is the main risk, the confidence level is often deduced from the own target rating. The probability of default of this target rating can be used as a confidence level. In this case, events beyond this confidence level are as seldom as the insolvency of a company with the target rating. The probability of default of the own company is therefore equal or higher than the loss caused by events beyond the confidence level. The credit risk calculated in this way can be compared, for example, with the equity. An approach for obtaining the joint distribution function of the risk caused by a default of one or more counterparties is the Gaussian copula model of time to default. For banks, models for credit rating changes are also necessary, because of their influence on bond prices. If credit risk is only used for managing the default risk of trading counterparties, modelling the credit rating changes is less important.

Credit Risk Reducing Activities

Reducing credit risk is a key problem of credit risk management. While market risk can be reduced easily by closing an open position, reducing credit risk is not straightforward. If utility A buys a forward from a counterparty B and the price for this forward increases, the credit risk increases as well. If there is no other agreement A has no possibility of controlling the credit risk without cooperation from B. The credit risk is market price driven only. For an effective credit risk management most risk reducing arrangements must be made before concluding contracts.

Common credit risk reducing agreements are listed below:

- *Margining agreement*: The most powerful instruments for limiting credit risk are margining agreements. There is a credit support annex published by the European Federation of Energy Traders (EFET), for example. Both parties fix a credit limit (normally a bilateral limit) and if the credit risk exceeds the limit there are margin payments directly to the party on the upside of the transactions or into a margining account. This implies that the values of all derivatives between each of the parties are periodically (often daily) marked-to-market which excludes illiquid products from the margining process.
- *Exchange futures for physical*: If counterparties have done an OTC transaction there are exchanges (e.g. European Energy Exchange) which offer to transfer the transaction in a regular futures contracts position. Because of margining, credit risk can be reduced immediately. As a disadvantage there are exchange fees, modified cashflows and perhaps implications on accounting.
- *Additional collateralisation*: The party on the downside of the transactions may collateralise their transactions additionally. Depending on the structure of credit risk management this can be taken into account while calculating credit risk and then this reduces the credit risk immediately, or this can be considered while determining the credit limit and increasing it.
- *Countertrade*: If there is a netting agreement, the conclusion of a countertrade with the same counterparty reduces the settlement risk of sold forward contracts and locks the actual replacement risk. Since the countertrade is concluded at the actual market price the replacement risk cannot be reduced.

- *Price adjustment*: The price of transactions with a high replacement risk can be adjusted on the actual market price. The present value of the price adjustment will be paid directly. The modified cashflow may have implications for accounting.

6.3.3   Credit Rating

No capital is required for entering forward contracts. However, if the contract is not covered there is a high market price risk. Therefore forward contracts should only be closed with counterparties with sufficient financial strength. Before a counterparty is accepted their credit rating is checked. This credit rating is then used as a basis for assigning a credit limit with this counterparty.

Credit ratings can be external ratings from international ratings agencies such as Moody's, Standard & Poor's or Fitch or internal ratings based, for example, on a scoring system. For such an internal rating publicly available information such as annual reports or information from credit information providers like Dun and Bradstreet or Creditreform can be used.

There are comprehensive publications concerning credit analysis and we will restrict the following considerations to some main features.

External Ratings

Many companies use external ratings if they are available for the counterparty. International rating agencies have a broad database and a wide experience and can deliver ratings of a high quality which are adjusted continuously. The relevant counterparties can be observed with little effort using a watchlist. Actual rating-relevant information about the counterparties marked in the watchlist will then be sent to the rating agencies' customers.

The definitions for long-term ratings of the international rating agencies are similar, and as an example Moody's rating definitions are listed in Table 6.4.

Table 6.4   Moody's long-term ratings definitions

Rating	Definition
Aaa	Highest quality, minimal credit risk
Aa	High quality, subject to very low credit risk
A	Upper-medium grade, subject to low credit risk
Baa	Medium grade, subject to moderate credit risk
Ba	Speculative elements, subject to substantial credit risk
B	Speculative, subject to high credit risk
Caa	Poor standing, subject to very high credit risk
Ca	Highly speculative and likely in, or very near, default
C	Lowest rated class and typically in default

Note: Moody's appends numerical modifiers 1, 2, and 3 to each generic rating classification from Aa to Caa. Modifier 1 indicates that the rank is in the higher end of its generic rating category; modifier 2 indicates a mid-range ranking; and modifier 3 indicates a ranking in the lower end of that generic rating category.

The rating categories of other rating agencies are similar and Table 6.5 compares the long-term ratings of some international rating agencies.

Table 6.5   Long-term rating scales comparison

Moody's	Aaa	Aa1	Aa2	Aa3	A1	A2	A3
S&P	AAA	AA+	AA	AA−	A+	A	A−
Fitch	AAA	AA+	AA	AA−	A+	A	A−

Baa1	Baa2	Baa3	Ba1	Ba2	Ba3	B1	B1	B3
BBB+	BBB	BBB−	BB+	BB	BB−	B+	B	B−
BBB+	BBB	BBB−	BB+	BB	BB−	B+	B	B−

Caa1	Caa2	Caa3	Ca	C	
CCC+	CCC	CCC−	CC	C	D
CCC+	CCC	CCC−	CC	C	D

A rating can be considered as an estimated classification of probabilities of default for the future. If the rating and the credit exposure is known, an expected loss or the credit VaR can be determined. The rating agencies and some banks have a broad database and offer probabilities of default for the different rating categories. These probabilities are estimated from statistical data. For the highest ranking categories there are only a few events of default, which makes an estimate of the probability of default difficult. A empirically determined default probability table may not have the desired properties of an increasing probability of default for lower rating categories or longer time horizons. Therefore rating agencies like Moody's offer idealised default probability tables which are smoothed and have the desired properties. Table 6.6 shows idealised default probabilities published by Moody's Investors Service.

Table 6.6   Moody's idealised default probability table (in %)

Moody's rating	Year					
	1	2	3	4	5	10
Aaa	0.0001	0.0002	0.0007	0.0018	0.0029	0.0100
Aa1	0.0006	0.0030	0.0100	0.0210	0.0310	0.1000
Aa2	0.0014	0.0080	0.0260	0.0470	0.0680	0.2000
Aa3	0.0030	0.0190	0.0590	0.1010	0.1420	0.4000
A1	0.0058	0.0370	0.1170	0.1890	0.2610	0.7000
A2	0.0109	0.0700	0.2220	0.3450	0.4670	1.2000
A3	0.0389	0.1500	0.3600	0.5400	0.7300	1.8000
Baa1	0.0900	0.2800	0.5600	0.8300	1.1000	2.6000
Baa2	0.1700	0.4700	0.8300	1.2000	1.5800	3.6000
Baa3	0.4200	1.0500	1.7100	2.3800	3.0500	6.1000
Ba1	0.8700	2.0200	3.1300	4.2000	5.2800	9.4000
Ba2	1.5600	3.4700	5.1800	6.8000	8.4100	13.5000
Ba3	2.8100	5.5100	7.8700	9.7900	11.8600	17.6600
B1	4.6800	8.3800	11.5800	13.8500	16.1200	22.2000
B2	7.1600	11.6700	15.5500	18.1300	20.7100	27.2000
B3	11.6200	16.6100	21.0300	24.0400	27.0500	34.9000
Caa1	17.3816	23.2341	28.6386	32.4788	36.3137	47.7000
Caa2	26.0000	32.5000	39.0000	43.8800	48.7500	65.0000
Caa3	50.9902	57.0088	62.4500	66.2420	69.8212	80.7000

In the event of a default, there is a fraction of the exposure which may be recovered through bankruptcy proceedings or some other form of settlement, the recovery rate. Estimating the recovery rate is difficult, but there are also published rates from the rating agencies depending on the rating categories and the time horizon since the rating was given. The recovery rate multiplied with the default probability gives the expected loss, which is shown in Table 6.7.[1]

Table 6.7   Moody's idealised expected loss table (in %)

Moody's Rating	Year					
	1	2	3	4	5	10
Aaa	0.0000	0.0001	0.0004	0.0010	0.0016	0.0055
Aa1	0.0003	0.0017	0.0055	0.0116	0.0171	0.0550
Aa2	0.0007	0.0044	0.0143	0.0259	0.0374	0.1100
Aa3	0.0017	0.0105	0.0325	0.0556	0.0781	0.2200
A1	0.0032	0.0204	0.0644	0.1040	0.1436	0.3850
A2	0.0060	0.0385	0.1221	0.1898	0.2569	0.6600
A3	0.0214	0.0825	0.1980	0.2970	0.4015	0.9900
Baa1	0.0495	0.1540	0.3080	0.4565	0.6050	1.4300
Baa2	0.0935	0.2585	0.4565	0.6600	0.8690	1.9800
Baa3	0.2310	0.5775	0.9405	1.3090	1.6775	3.3550
Ba1	0.4785	1.1110	1.7215	2.3100	2.9040	5.1700
Ba2	0.8580	1.9085	2.8490	3.7400	4.6255	7.4250
Ba3	1.5455	3.0305	4.3285	5.3845	6.5230	9.7130
B1	2.5740	4.6090	6.3690	7.6175	8.8660	12.2100
B2	3.9380	6.4185	8.5525	9.9715	11.3905	14.9600
B3	6.3910	9.1355	11.5665	13.2220	14.8775	19.1950
Caa1	9.5599	12.7788	15.7512	17.8634	19.9726	26.2350
Caa2	14.3000	17.8750	21.4500	24.1340	26.8125	35.7500
Caa3	28.0446	31.3548	34.3475	36.4331	38.4017	44.3850

Internal Ratings

Even if only internal ratings are used, the structure should be matchable to those of the rating agencies. If there is a mapping from an internal rating to a rating category of a rating agency, default probabilities and recovery rates can be used which are otherwise difficult to obtain.

An internal rating is usually based on specified criteria which will be evaluated in a scoring approach. There are evaluation categories for each of the rating criteria. The number of these evaluation categories should be sufficient to avoid volatile results.

The factors for the determination of an internal rating can be differentiated into quantitative and qualitative criteria. The quantitative criteria can be obtained from business reports, financial statements etc. and refer to the past. Qualitative criteria are appraisals referring to the future of a company. Usually the qualitative factors have a weighting of 40–60%. If the internal rating is used only in the context of the credit risk of the trading activities,

---

[1] Source: *Moody's Approach to Rating Synthetic Resecuritizations*, published 2003 by Moody's Investors Service.

the fraction of the qualitative factors can be lower. The reason for this is that the business sector of the counterparties is similar and rating criteria based on the sector do not result in a differentiation of the rating. The applied factors and their weights are the decision of the responsible rating unit and cannot be generalised, but some frequently used criteria are listed below.

Common quantitative factors for an internal rating:

- *Size of the company*: The size of the company measured by its balance sheet total.
- *Company's owners*: The structure and the financial strength of the company's owners.
- *Tangible net worth*: The tangible net worth is a measure of the physical worth of a company. Tangible net worth is calculated by taking a firm's total assets and subtracting the value of all liabilities and the value of all intangible assets (e.g. copyrights, patents and intellectual property).
- *Revenue reserves*: Trends of increase or decrease in revenue reserves.
- Criteria based on debts and repayment:

  - *Funds from operations to total debts*: The amount of cash generated or employed by the company in its operating activities in proportion to its total debts.
  - *Funds from operations to interests*: The amount of cash generated or employed by the company in its operating activities in proportion to its interests.
  - *Total debts to total capitalisation*: Total debts in proportion to equity and long-term debts.
  - *EBIT to interests*: Earnings before interest and taxes in proportion to the paid interests.

- Criteria concerning maturity matching:

  - *Current assets*: Current assets in proportion to current liabilities.
  - *Equity/assets ratio*: Equity and long-term debts in proportion to the asset capital.

- *Return on equity*: The return on equity (ROE) is a measure of a company's profitability that reveals how much profit it generates with the money shareholders have invested.
- Criteria concerning the development of the business ratios:

  - *Development of sales*: Annual percentage change of sales.
  - *Development of the operative margin*: Annual percentage change of the operative margin.

The quantitative factors must be adapted to the applied accounting standard (IFRS, US-GAAP etc.). While the quantitative factors can be analysed more or less mechanically, most qualitative factors require an estimation by an analyst, with good knowledge of the business sector.

Common qualitative factors for an internal rating:

- *Market position of a company*: Is the company among the leading companies in its sector?
- *Sector characteristics*: Are there high market entry barriers? Are there substitute products?
- *Economic situation of the sector*: Is there a boom, a stable cycle or a recession?
- *Duration of the business connection*: How long has the business connection existed with the counterparty?
- *Payment history*: Did the company exceed the terms of payment in the history of the relationship?

- *Seasonality of cashflow*: Are there substantial seasonal fluctuations of the cashflow?
- *Place of business*: Where is the registered office of the company?

A calibration of an internal rating method with external ratings is useful. For these purposes some companies with an external rating are chosen and after applying the internal rating method the result is compared with the external rating. For substantial differences there should be an obvious reason, otherwise the weights or the rating criteria should be reevaluated.

Appendices

Appendix A: Mathematical background

This appendix reviews some important mathematical concepts that are used throughout the book. However, it does not give mathematically exact formulations or proofs. For these we refer to specialised books on econometrics, stochastic analysis or financial mathematics.

A.1 ECONOMETRIC METHODS

A.1.1 Linear Regression

A *linear regression* models a linear relationship between a dependent variable y and a number of independent variables (*regressors*) $x_1, \ldots, x_n$ of the form

$$y = \beta_1 x_1 + \beta_2 x_2 + \cdots + \beta_n x_n + \epsilon, \qquad (A.1)$$

where ϵ is an error term. Setting $x_1 = 1$ a constant term can be included in the model. The linear regression is used to find the coefficients of such a relationship based on a number of observations on y and x_i. If those observations are made at different times t, the given data is y_t and x_{ti} for $i = 1, \ldots, n$ and $t = 1, \ldots, N$ and the linear relation becomes

$$y_t = \beta_1 x_{t1} + \beta_2 x_{t2} + \cdots + \beta_n x_{tn} + \epsilon_t.$$

In vector notation, using $\mathbf{y} = (y_1, \ldots, y_N)^T$, $\beta = (\beta_1, \ldots, \beta_n)^T$, $\epsilon = (\epsilon_1, \ldots, \epsilon_N)^T$ and $\mathbf{X}$ for the $N \times n$-matrix (x_{ti}), this is written as

$$\mathbf{y} = \mathbf{X}\beta + \epsilon.$$

The *ordinary least squares* (OLS) estimator for β minimises the quadratic error

$$\min_{\beta} \|\mathbf{y} - \mathbf{X}\beta\|^2.$$

The solution to this problem is given by

$$\hat{\beta} = (\mathbf{X}^T\mathbf{X})^{-1} \mathbf{X}^T\mathbf{y}. \qquad (A.2)$$

In many numerical libraries or statistical software packages there are methods available to solve this least-squares problem efficiently.

We now make the following general assumptions

1. The regressors x_{ti} are non-stochastic.
2. The error terms ϵ_t are independent and normally distributed with mean zero and standard deviation σ. The covariance matrix of ϵ is then given by

$$\text{Cov}[\epsilon] = \mathbb{E}[\epsilon\epsilon^T] = \sigma^2 I_{N \times N}.$$

The standard error σ can be estimated from the residual sum of squares (RSS) as

$$\hat{\sigma}^2 = s^2 = \frac{RSS}{N-n},$$

where

$$RSS = \left(\mathbf{y} - \mathbf{X}\hat{\beta}\right)^T \left(\mathbf{y} - \mathbf{X}\hat{\beta}\right) = \mathbf{y}^T\mathbf{y} - \hat{\beta}^T\mathbf{X}^T\mathbf{y}.$$

One typical measure of the goodness of fit of the model is the squared correlation coefficient

$$R^2 = \frac{\hat{\beta}^T\mathbf{X}^T\mathbf{X}\hat{\beta}}{\mathbf{y}^T\mathbf{y}} = \frac{\sum_{t=1}^N \left(\sum_{i=1}^n \hat{\beta}_i x_{ti}\right)^2}{\sum_{t=1}^N y_t^2}.$$

Even if the true value of the model parameter β has a fixed (non-stochastic) value, the OLS estimator $\hat{\beta}$ is a random variable due to the randomness of y. Estimating β from a different sample with different values of ϵ will give a different estimation of $\hat{\beta}$. It can be shown that the covariance matrix for $\hat{\beta}$ is

$$\text{Cov}\left[\hat{\beta}\right] = \sigma^2 \left(\mathbf{X}^T\mathbf{X}\right)^{-1}$$

with estimator

$$\hat{\mathbf{v}}^\beta = s^2 \left(\mathbf{X}^T\mathbf{X}\right)^{-1}.$$

The estimated standard error of β_i is denoted by $\hat{\sigma}_i^\beta = \sqrt{\hat{v}_{ii}^\beta}$. To get confidence bounds for β, one can build the t-ratio

$$t = \frac{\hat{\beta}_i - \beta_i}{\hat{\sigma}_i^\beta} \tag{A.3}$$

which is t-distributed with $\nu = N - n$ degrees of freedom. A 95% confidence interval for β_i is given by

$$\hat{\beta}_i - t_{\nu,0.025}\hat{\sigma}_i^\beta < \beta_i < \hat{\beta}_i + t_{\nu,0.025}\hat{\sigma}_i^\beta,$$

where $t_{\nu,0.025}$ denotes the 2.5% percentile for the t-distribution with ν degrees of freedom.

When testing a regressor for significance one can set $\beta = 0$ in (A.3) and compare the t-ratio $t = \hat{\beta}_i/\hat{\sigma}_i^\beta$ to the critical value $t_{\nu,\alpha}$. If the t-ratio exceeds the critical value, the regressor is significant for the given confidence level.

More details on regression methods can be found in Alexander (2001) or Hamilton (1994).

A.1.2   Stationary Time Series and Unit Root Tests

Stochastic models for time series often have a deterministic component, such as a trend or a periodicity, and a stochastic component. In simple cases, the stochastic properties of the stochastic component do not change over time in which case the component is called *stationary*. The more exact definition is:

Definition A.1 *A stochastic process $X(t)$ is covariance-stationary or simply stationary if*

1. *Expectation $\mathbb{E}[X(t)]$ and variance $\mathrm{Var}[X(t)]$ are finite and constant over time.*
2. *The autocovariance $\mathrm{Cov}[X(t), X(t-s)]$ depends only on the lag s.*

The process $X(t)$ is called strict stationary if the whole joint distribution of $X(t)$ and $X(t-s)$ depends only on s.

A time series with trend $x_t = at + \epsilon_t$ where ϵ_t are independent normally distributed random numbers is not stationary since $\mathbb{E}[x_t] = at$ depends on t. A random walk model $x_t = x_{t-1} + \epsilon_t$ is also not stationary since the variance $\mathrm{Var}[x_t] = t$ increases with time t.

The following classes of time series models give examples of stationary processes:

AR(p) models: The *autoregressive* model is given by

$$x_t = \mu + \alpha_1 x_{t-1} + \alpha_2 x_{t-2} + \cdots + \alpha_p x_{t-p} + \epsilon_t,$$

where $\epsilon_t \sim N(0, \sigma)$ are independent normally distributed random numbers with variance σ^2. The expectation value of x_t is

$$\mathbb{E}[x_t] = \mu \left(1 - \alpha_1 - \alpha_2 - \cdots - \alpha_p\right)^{-1}.$$

It can be shown that the time series is stationary if all roots of the polynomial

$$1 - \alpha_1 x - \alpha_2 x^2 - \cdots - \alpha_p x^p$$

lie outside the unit circle.

MA(q) models: The *moving average* model is given by

$$x_t = \mu + \epsilon_t + \beta_1 \epsilon_{t-1} + \beta_2 \epsilon_{t-2} + \cdots + \beta_q \epsilon_{t-q},$$

where $\epsilon_t \sim N(0, \sigma)$ are independent normally distributed random numbers with variance σ^2. The expectation value of x_t is $\mathbb{E}[x_t] = \mu$ and the process is always stationary.

ARMA(p, q) models: The *autoregressive moving average* model is given by

$$x_t = \mu + \alpha_1 x_{t-1} + \cdots + \alpha_p x_{t-p} + \epsilon_t + \beta_1 \epsilon_{t-1} + \cdots + \beta_q \epsilon_{t-q}.$$

The ARMA(p,q) model is stationary under the same conditions as the AR(p) model.

To indentify which model is appropriate for a given time series the following two indicators are useful:

1. **Correlograms:** The empirical autocorrelation function

$$\rho(s) = \frac{\text{Cov}[x_t, x_{t-s}]}{\text{Var}[x_t]}$$

should match the theoretical one, which can be calculated for any ARMA process. If a model specification is appropriate, the autocorrelation function of the (empirical) residuals ϵ_t should be near zero. There are also statistical tests available for the autocorrelation (see, e.g., Alexander (2001) or Hamilton (1994)).

2. **Significance test:** Using a regression approach for the model parameters of an AR(p,q) process, the t-ratio shows whether all of the parameters are significant. In this way the model can be reduced to lower parameters.

Financial time series are often not stationary, but have trends or increasing variance. From a non-stationary process one can build the differentiated process

$$\Delta x_t = x_t - x_{t-1}.$$

If the process Δx_t is stationary the process is called an *integrated process* of order 1, denoted by $I(1)$. A stationary process is also denoted as $I(0)$. As an example, the random walk

$$x_t = x_{t-1} + \epsilon_t$$

is not stationary because of increasing variance. Applying the difference operator yields

$$\Delta x_t = \epsilon_t,$$

which is a stationary white noise process, so the random walk is $I(1)$.

If a time series exhibits a trend, but the deviates from the fitted trend is a stationary process, then it is also called a *trend-stationary process*.

A statistical test for stationarity is the *Dickey–Fuller (DF) test*. The idea is to take first differences and regress them on the first lag:

$$\Delta x_t = c + \alpha x_{t-1} + \epsilon_t.$$

The equation is an equivalent reformulation of $x_t = c + (1 + \alpha)x_{t-1} + \epsilon_t$. If α is significantly less than zero the time series is stationary. For this purpose one can use the t-ratio described in section A.1.1. The critical values for the t-ratio in the Dickey–Fuller test differ from the standard t-test of the OLS because of a bias in the estimator. As an extension to the DF test, the *augmented Dickey–Fuller (ADF) test* takes into account more time lags of x_t. The DF and ADF tests are available in most statistical software packages.

A.1.3   Principal Component Analysis

Let $\mathbf{x}_t = (x_{t1}, \ldots, x_{tn}) \in \mathbb{R}^n$, $t = 1, \ldots, N$ be a stationary vector process. Then in general the ith and jth component series $(x_{ti})_t$ and $(x_{tj})_t$ are correlated. The aim of the *principal component analysis* (PCA) is to decompose $\mathbf{x}_t$ into independent factors

$$\mathbf{x}_t = w_{t1}\mathbf{p}_1 + \cdots + w_{tn}\mathbf{p}_n, \tag{A.4}$$

where $\mathbf{p}_i$ are the principal component factors ordered by their significance to explain the variance of $\mathbf{x}_t$ and w_{ti} are the *factor loads*.

To carry out the PCA the vector series $\mathbf{x}_t$ is written as a matrix

$$X = (x_{ti}) \in \mathbb{R}^{N \times n}.$$

As a first step, X is assumed to be normalised, such that all columns have mean zero and standard deviation 1. This is achieved by replacing x_{ti} with $(x_{ti} - \bar{x}_i)/\sigma_i$, where $\bar{x}_i$ and σ_i are mean and standard deviation of the ith column of X. In the following it is assumed that X already is normalised.

Let $V = X^T X/N$ be the covariance matrix of $\mathbf{x}_t$ and P the $n \times n$-matrix of eigenvectors of V, i.e.

$$VP = P\Lambda,$$

where $\Lambda = \mathrm{diag}(\lambda_1, \ldots, \lambda_n)$ is the diagonal matrix of eigenvalues. The factor $\mathbf{p}_i$ in (A.4) is now defined as the columns of P.

The matrix notation of (A.4) is

$$X = WP^T.$$

Since P as a matrix of eigenvectors is orthogonal $(P^T = P^{-1})$, the matrix W of factor loads are calculated as

$$W = XP.$$

The factor loads are indeed uncorrelated, since their covariance matrix is

$$W^T W = P^T X^T XP = NP^T VP = NP^T P\Lambda = N\Lambda$$

and the variance of the ith factor load is the ith eigenvalue λ_i.

A.1.4   Kalman Filtering Method

The Kalman filter (Kalman 1960) is a flexible algorithm to forecast and calibrate stochastic dynamical systems. It can be used in those cases where not all stochatic processes (states) can directly be observed. Details on the Kalman filtering method can be found in Hamilton (1994) or Harvey (1991).

The state-space representation

The state-space representation of a dynamic model for $y_t \in \mathbb{R}^n$ is given by the following system of equations:

$$\mathbf{a}_{t+1} = \mathbf{T}_t \mathbf{a}_t + \mathbf{c}_t + \mathbf{v}_{t+1} \quad \text{(state equation)}$$

$$\mathbf{y}_t = \mathbf{H}_t \mathbf{a}_t + \mathbf{d}_t + \mathbf{w}_t \quad \text{(measurement equation)},$$

(A.5)

where $\mathbf{a}_t \in \mathbb{R}^r$ is the (possibly) unobservable state vector, $\mathbf{c}_t \in \mathbb{R}^r$, $\mathbf{d}_t \in \mathbb{R}^n$ are displacement vectors and $\mathbf{T}_t \in \mathbb{R}^{r \times r}$, $\mathbf{H}_t \in \mathbb{R}^{n \times r}$ are matrices. The vectors $\mathbf{v}_t$ and $\mathbf{w}_t$ are uncorrelated white noise processes with covariance matrices

$$\text{Cov}[\mathbf{v}_t] = \mathbf{Q}_t, \quad \text{Cov}[\mathbf{w}_t] = \mathbf{R}_t. \tag{A.6}$$

Example: Every ARMA process can be written in state-space form. This state-space representation, however, is not unique. Consider an ARMA(p,q) process of the form

$$y_t - \mu = \phi_1(y_{t-1} - \mu) + \cdots + \phi_r(y_{t-r} - \mu) \tag{A.7}$$

$$+ \epsilon_t + \theta_1 \epsilon_{t-1} + \cdots + \theta_{r-1} \epsilon_{t-r+1} \tag{A.8}$$

with $r = \max(p, q+1)$. In this equation the additional coefficients not needed for the ARMA(p,q) process are understood to be zero, i.e. $\phi_{p+1} = \cdots = \phi_r = 0$ and $\theta_{q+1} = \cdots = \theta_{r-1} = 0$. State equation and observation equation are given by

$$\mathbf{a}_{t+1} = \begin{bmatrix} \phi_1 & \phi_2 & \cdots & \phi_{r-1} & \phi_r \\ 1 & 0 & \cdots & 0 & 0 \\ 0 & 1 & \cdots & 0 & 0 \\ \vdots & \vdots & \cdots & \vdots & \vdots \\ 0 & 0 & \cdots & 1 & 0 \end{bmatrix} \mathbf{a}_t + \begin{bmatrix} \epsilon_{t+1} \\ 0 \\ \vdots \\ 0 \end{bmatrix}$$

$$y_t = \mu + \begin{bmatrix} 1 & \theta_1 & \theta_2 & \cdots & \theta_{r-1} \end{bmatrix} \mathbf{a}_t.$$

The Kalman iterations

Given observations $\mathbf{x}_0, \ldots, \mathbf{x}_T$ and $\mathbf{y}_0, \ldots, \mathbf{y}_T$ the Kalman filtering algorithm iteratively calculates forecasts $\hat{\mathbf{a}}_{t+1|t}$ of the unobservable state $\mathbf{a}_{t+1}$ based on all observations up to time t and the associated mean square error

$$\mathbf{P}_{t+1|t} = \mathbb{E}\left[(\mathbf{a}_{t+1} - \hat{\mathbf{a}}_{t+1|t})^T (\mathbf{a}_{t+1} - \hat{\mathbf{a}}_{t+1|t})\right].$$

Furthermore, it yields a maximum likelihood function for the observations. The results can be used to calibrate unknown parameters in (A.5) and forecast values $\mathbf{y}_{T+1}, \mathbf{y}_{T+2}, \ldots$. The iteration steps are the following:

1. **Iteration start:** The iteration is started with

$$\hat{\mathbf{a}}_{1|0} = \mathbb{E}[\mathbf{a}_1]$$

$$\mathbf{P}_{1|0} = \mathbb{E}\left[(\mathbf{a}_1 - \mathbb{E}[\mathbf{a}_1])^T (\mathbf{a}_1 - \mathbb{E}[\mathbf{a}_1])\right].$$

In many cases the initial values can be calculated as $\hat{\mathbf{a}}_{1|0} = 0$ (for $\mathbf{c}_t = 0$) and $\text{vec}(\mathbf{P}_{1|0}) = (\mathbf{I}_{r^2} - \mathbf{T} \otimes \mathbf{T})^{-1} \cdot \text{vec}(\mathbf{Q})$, where $\mathbf{T} \otimes \mathbf{T}$ is the $r^2 \times r^2$ Kronecker product matrix consisting of the submatrices $F_{ij}\mathbf{T}$ and $\text{vec}(\mathbf{Q}) \in \mathbb{R}^{r^2}$ (similarly $\text{vec}(\mathbf{P}_{1|0})$) is the vector of stacked columns of $\mathbf{Q}$, i.e. $\text{vec}(\mathbf{Q}) = (Q_{11}, \ldots, Q_{r1}, Q_{21}, \ldots, Q_{rr})^T$. In this way $\mathbf{P}_{1|0}$ solves the matrix equation $\mathbf{P}_{1|0} = \mathbf{T}\mathbf{P}_{1|0}\mathbf{T}^T + \mathbf{Q}$.

2. **Updating a:** Given $\hat{\mathbf{a}}_{t|t-1}$ and $\mathbf{P}_{t|t-1}$ the next forecast for $\mathbf{a}$ is calculated as

$$\hat{\mathbf{a}}_{t+1|t} = \mathbf{T}_{t+1}\hat{\mathbf{a}}_{t|t-1} + \mathbf{c}_t + \mathbf{K}_t(\mathbf{y}_t - \mathbf{d}_t - \mathbf{H}_t\hat{\mathbf{a}}_{t|t-1}), \tag{A.9}$$

where

$$\mathbf{K}_t = \mathbf{T}_{t+1}\mathbf{P}_{t|t-1}\mathbf{H}_t^T (\mathbf{H}_t\mathbf{P}_{t|t-1}\mathbf{H}_t^T + \mathbf{R}_t)^{-1}.$$

3. **Updating P:** Given $\mathbf{P}_{t|t-1}$ the next forecast for $\mathbf{P}$ is calculated as

$$\mathbf{P}_{t+1|t} = (\mathbf{T}_{t+1}\mathbf{P}_{t|t-1} - \mathbf{K}_t\mathbf{H}_t\mathbf{P}_{t|t-1})\mathbf{T}_{t+1}^T + \mathbf{Q}_{t+1}. \tag{A.10}$$

A.1.5   Regime-Switching Models

For many financial markets it can be observed that longer time series of prices or interest rates exhibit structural breaks at certain times. Those breaks can be caused by changes in the general market conditions such as changes in government policies, wars or by the behaviour of market participants. Regime-switching models can also be used to model price spikes occurring, for example, in electricity markets.

To model regime-dependent time series one can introduce a *regime* or *state* process $s_t \in \{1, \ldots, N\}$ and make the parameters in the time series equation depend on the current state. One further needs a law for s_t that governs the stochastic regime changes. Regime-switching models and calibration methods are described in detail by Hamilton (1994), pp. 677–703 and we follow his notation describing the basic methods.

Markov Chains

The simplest model for the integer-valued regime variable s_t is a Markov chain, where the probabilities to switch to a certain different regime depend only on the current regime and not on its history. We define

$$p_{ij} = P(s_t = j|s_{t-1} = i) = P(s_t = j|s_{t-1} = i, s_{t-2} = \cdots).$$

All transition probabilities put together define the *transition matrix* of the Markov chain

$$\mathbf{P} = \begin{pmatrix} p_{11} & p_{21} & \cdots & p_{N1} \\ p_{12} & p_{22} & \cdots & p_{N2} \\ \vdots & \vdots & \vdots & \vdots \\ p_{1N} & p_{2N} & \cdots & p_{NN} \end{pmatrix}.$$

We must have $\sum_{j=1}^{N} p_{ij} = 1$, since the entries in one column represent all possibilities to change to the next time step.

A convenient way to represent a Markov chain is to use a vector-valued process $\xi_t = \mathbf{e}_{s_t}$, where $\mathbf{e}_i$ is the ith unit vector $(0, \ldots, 1, \ldots, 0)$. In other words, we have $\xi_t = (1, 0, \ldots, 0)$ when $s_t = 1$, $\xi_t = (0, 1, 0, \ldots, 0)$, when $s_t = 2$ and so on. We have $\mathbb{E}\left[\xi_{t+1}|\xi_t\right] = \mathbf{P}\xi_t$ and, by iteration, $\mathbb{E}\left[\xi_{t+m}|\xi_t\right] = \mathbf{P}^m\xi_t$. The jth entry of the left-hand side can be interpreted as the probability that $s_{t+m} = j$ conditional on ξ_t. Thus, we get

$$\mathbf{P}^m\mathbf{e}_i = \begin{pmatrix} \mathbf{P}(s_{t+m} = 1|s_t = i) \\ \vdots \\ \mathbf{P}(s_{t+m} = N|s_t = i) \end{pmatrix}.$$

A Markov chain is called *reducible* if the states can be relabelled (i.e. we set $\tilde{s}_t = \sigma(s_t)$ for a permutation σ) in such a way that the new transition matrix $\tilde{P}$ (given by $\tilde{p}_{ij} = p_{\sigma(i)\sigma(j)}$) has a block structure

$$\tilde{\mathbf{P}} = \left(\begin{array}{c|c} \mathbf{B} & \mathbf{C} \\ \hline \mathbf{0} & \mathbf{D} \end{array}\right).$$

Once one of the first states $\tilde{s}$ corresponding to the matrix $\mathbf{B}$ is attained, the process will never again leave those states and the dynamic is reduced to a lower number of states with transition matrix $\mathbf{B}$. If a Markov chain is not reducible it is called *irreducible*.

We have seen that using $\mathbf{P}^m\mathbf{e}_i$, we can calculate the conditional probabilities that s_{t+m} is at a certain state j. For a certain class of Markov chains, the *ergodic* Markov chains, $\mathbf{P}^m\mathbf{e}_i$ converges to a vector π for $m \to \infty$. This limit vector π, called the *ergodic probability vector*, is independent of the state i at time t and gives the unconditional probabilities that the system is in a certain state.

Mathematically, a Markov chain is called *ergodic* if the transition matrix $\mathbf{P}$ has one eigenvalue of 1 and all other eigenvalues within the unit circle. We note from the property of transition matrices that the column elements add up to 1, we have $\mathbf{P}^T\mathbf{1} = \mathbf{1}$, where $\mathbf{1} = (1, \ldots, 1)^T \in \mathbb{R}^N$. This implies that 1 is always an eigenvalue of $\mathbf{P}$. The vector π of ergodic probabilities must satisfy $\mathbf{P}\pi = \pi$ and $\mathbf{1}^T\pi = 1$. In practice, π can be calculated from the linear system

$$\mathbf{A}^T\mathbf{A}\pi = \mathbf{e}_{N+1}$$

where $\mathbf{e}_{N+1}$ is the $(N+1)$th unit vector and

$$\mathbf{A} = \begin{pmatrix} \mathbf{I}_N - \mathbf{P} \\ \mathbf{1}^T \end{pmatrix} \in \mathbb{R}^{(N+1) \times N}.$$

The Hamilton Filter Algorithm

We assume that we are given an observable time series $(\mathbf{y}_t)_{t=0,1,2,\ldots}$ of vectors $\mathbf{y}_t \in \mathbb{R}^n$. If $(\mathbf{y}_t)$ is goverened by a regime-switching model we have transition probabilities

$$f(\mathbf{y}_t|s_t = j, \mathbf{y}_{t-1}, \mathbf{y}_{t-2}, \ldots).$$

To calibrate such a regime-switching model knowing only the observables $(\mathbf{y}_t)$ we cannot immediately use a maximum likelihood optimisation since we do not know the regime state (s_t) at each time.

To overcome this problem, the Hamilton filter can be used since it generates estimates for the probabilities that the system is in a certain regime j at a given time t using only information from the observable process $(\mathbf{y}_t)$. More specifically, it generates estimates $\hat{\xi}_{t|t}$ (*optimal inference*) for the vector of conditional probabilities

$$P(s_t = j | \mathbf{y}_t, \mathbf{y}_{t-1}, \ldots), \quad j = 1, \ldots, N$$

and estimates $\hat{\xi}_{t+1|t}$ (*forecast*) for the vector of conditional probabilities

$$P(s_{t+1} = j | \mathbf{y}_t, \mathbf{y}_{t-1}, \ldots), \quad j = 1, \ldots, N.$$

The optimal inference and forecast can be calculated iteratively from the equations

$$\hat{\xi}_{t|t} = \frac{\left(\xi_{t|t-1} \odot \eta_t\right)}{\mathbf{1}^T \left(\xi_{t|t-1} \odot \eta_t\right)} \tag{A.11}$$

$$\hat{\xi}_{t+1|t} = \mathbf{P} \cdot \hat{\xi}_{t|t}. \tag{A.12}$$

Here, the $\odot$ denotes the element-by-element multiplication and

$$\eta_t = \begin{pmatrix} f(\mathbf{y}_t | s_t = 1, \mathbf{y}_{t-1}, \mathbf{y}_{t-2}, \ldots) \\ \vdots \\ f(\mathbf{y}_t | s_t = N, \mathbf{y}_{t-1}, \mathbf{y}_{t-2}, \ldots) \end{pmatrix}$$

denotes the vector of conditional probability densities. If no further information is given, the iteration can be started with $\hat{\xi}_{1|0} = \pi$, where π is the ergodic probability vector.

From the calculations done within the Hamilton filter, one can immediately infer the value of the log likelihood function

$$\mathcal{L} = \sum_{t=1}^{T} \ln f\left(\mathbf{y}_t | \mathbf{y}_{t-1}, \mathbf{y}_{t-2}, \ldots\right)$$

using

$$f\left(\mathbf{y}_t | \mathbf{y}_{t-1}, \mathbf{y}_{t-2}, \ldots\right) = \mathbf{1}^T \left(\xi_{t|t-1} \odot \eta_t\right).$$

A.2   STOCHASTIC PROCESSES

A *stochastic process* $(X(t))_{t \in I}$ is a family of random variables, where I usually represents some time interval or a discrete set of times. One of the main examples is a price process $S(t)$, which represents the market price of some asset. Other examples are the temperature at a given place or the total load in a power grid. A stochastic process is *discrete* if I is a discrete set, usually a set of integer numbers (e.g. $t = 0, 1, \ldots, T$) representing days or hours. If I is a subinterval of the real line $\mathbb{R}$, the process is said to be *continuous* (e.g. $I = [0, \infty)$).

A.2.1   Conditional Expectation and Martingales

A typical task in financial mathematics is to calculate the expected value of a stochastic process at a future time T given all information up to today's time $t < T$. This quantity is denoted by the *conditional expectation* $\mathbb{E}_t[X(T)]$. Viewed as a function of t, the conditional expectation $Y(t) = \mathbb{E}_t[X(T)]$ is itself a stochastic process, since with increasing time t, the randomly incoming information is changing the expectation of $X(T)$.

Formally, conditional expectations can be defined by means of the *Radon–Nikodým theorem*, which we do not discuss here. For doing calculations with conditional expectations we have the following rules:

1. $\mathbb{E}_s[X(s)Y(t)] = X(s)\mathbb{E}_s[Y(t)]$ for $s \le t$
2. $\mathbb{E}_s[\mathbb{E}_t[X(T)]] = \mathbb{E}_s[X(T)]$ for $s \le t \le T$
3. $\mathbb{E}_t[\mathbb{E}_s[X(T)]] = \mathbb{E}_s[X(T)]$ for $s \le t \le T$

The first identity follows from the fact that, knowing all information up to time s, the value $X(s)$ is not stochastic anymore and can be pulled out of the expectation operator. The second identity says that the expectation at time s about the expectation at a later time t of $X(T)$ is just the expectation at time s of $X(T)$. The third identity is due to the fact that $\mathbb{E}_s[X(T)]$ is a deterministic quantity at a later time t, since it uses only information up to time s. Therefore it is equal to its expectation at time s.

An important class of stochastic processes is defined by the property that their future expected value equals today's value. If a process is known to have this property, it is easy to state analytical results about their expectations. The formal definition is:

Definition A.2   *A stochastic process $M(t)$ is called a martingale, if*

$$M(s) = \mathbb{E}_s[M(t)] \quad for\ s \le t.$$

Example: By the second rule above, the stochastic process $M(t) = \mathbb{E}_t[X(T)]$ is a martingale. This fact is extensively used in option pricing theory. For example, if we model a futures price as $F(t, T) = \mathbb{E}_t[S(T)]$ then we know that the futures price is a martingale. For other examples see section 3.1.5 and the following paragraphs of this section.

A.2.2   Brownian Motion

Since the work of Bachelier (1900), Brownian motion has been utilised as a main ingredient for modelling security prices. It is defined as follows:

Definition A.3   *A stochastic process $W = (W(t))_{t \ge 0}$ is a (standard) Brownian motion, if*

1. *$W(0) = 0$.*
2. *$W(t)$ has continuous paths.*
3. *$W(t)$ has independent, stationary, normally distributed increments, i.e. for $0 = t_0 < t_1 < \ldots < t_n$ the increments $Y_1 = W(t_1) - W(t_0), \ldots, Y_n = W(t_n) - W(t_{n-1})$ are independent and normally distributed with mean zero and variance $\mathrm{Var}[Y_j] = t_j - t_{j-1}$ for all $j = 1, \ldots, n$.*

The last property means that the increment from t to $t + u$ does not depend on the history of the process up to time t, but only on the time interval u. In particular, the process is therefore *Markovian* meaning that the process after time t depends only on the value at time t and not on the history before t. Since all increments have a mean of zero, another immediate conclusion is that $W(s) = \mathbb{E}_s[W(t)]$ for $s < t$, thus $W(t)$ is a martingale.

In practice, Brownian motion can be simulated numerically using normal random variables. If one is only interested in $W(T)$ for some time T the simulated values are just normally distributed random numbers with mean zero ($= W(0)$) and standard deviation $\sqrt{T}$. If one needs a whole simulation path $W(t_1), \ldots, W(t_n)$, the iterative scheme is

- $W(0) = 0$.
- $W(t_i) = W(t_{i-1}) + \sqrt{\Delta t_i}\epsilon_i$, where $\epsilon_1, \ldots, \epsilon_n$ are independent normally distributed random numbers.

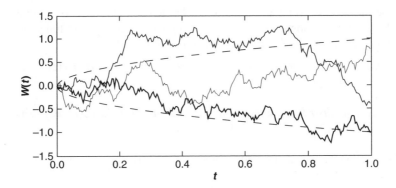

Figure A.1   Brownian motion sample paths

A.2.3   Stochastic Integration and Itô's Lemma

To give some motivation for stochastic integration we start with an example. Assume that a Brownian motion $W(t)$ models the price of a security and, at time t_0, we hold a number ξ_0 of that security. Then our profit or loss up to time t_1 is given by $\xi_0(W(t_1) - W(t_0))$. If we rebalance the portfolio at each time t_i, such that we hold a number ξ_i of the security at time t_i, then our profit or loss up to time t_n is given by the sum $\sum_{i=0}^{n-1} \xi_i(W(t_{i+1}) - W(t_i))$. If we make the time intervals between the portfolio rebalancings shorter and shorter, such that in the limit $X(t)$ denotes the number of securities we hold in our portfolio at time t, then the sum we had before representing the profit or loss of the portfolio becomes an integral $\int_0^t X(s)\, dW(s)$.

However, the usual integral (Lebesgue–Stieltjes integral) $\int X\, dW(t)$ with Brownian motion $W(t)$ as integrator does not exist, since the paths of $W(t)$ are not of bounded variation. A special integration theory, initiated by Itô (*Itô calculus*), can be used to give a mathematical meaning to expressions such as

$$\int_0^t X(s)\, dW(s),$$

where $X(t)$ may be another stochastic process. First, the integral is defined for the special case where $X(t)$ is a piecewise constant function that takes the value ξ_i on the interval $[t_i, t_{i+1})$, i.e.

$$X(t) = \sum_{i=0}^{n-1} \xi_i \mathbf{1}_{[t_i, t_{i+1})}(t)$$

with $0 = t_0 < t_1 < \cdots < t_n = t$. In this case the integral is defined by

$$\int_0^t X(s)\,dW(s) = \sum_{i=0}^{n-1} \xi_i \left(W(t_{i+1}) - W(t_i)\right).$$

Note that in the sum on the right-hand side, the integrand is evaluated at the left boundary of each interval $[t_i, t_{i+1})$. For financial applications this is consistent with the fact that decisions for the next period have to be made at the beginning of each period using information up to that point in time. A formal definition of stochastic integrals for more general integrands $X(t)$ can be given using approximations of $X(t)$ by piecewise constant functions.

The following properties of stochastic integrals will often be used:

Theorem A.1 *Let a stochastic process be given by $Z(t) = \int_0^t b(t)\,dW(t)$, where $b(t)$ is a deterministic function. Then*

1. *$Z(t)$ is normally distributed with mean zero and variance $\mathrm{Var}[Z(t)] = \int_0^t b^2(s)\,ds$.*
2. *$Z(t)$ is a martingale.*

In this theorem the martingale property is even true if $b(t)$ is a stochastic process instead of a deterministic function.

Many stochastic processes used to model financial data are constructed via stochastic integrals. Those processes, also called Itô processes, are defined as follows:

Definition A.4 *A process $X(t)$ is called an Itô process, if it is of the form*

$$X(t) = X_0 + \int_0^t a(s)\,ds + \int_0^t b(s)\,dW(s), \tag{A.13}$$

where $a(t)$ and $b(t)$ are functions or, more generally, stochastic processes. A shorthand notation for such an Itô process is

$$dX(t) = a(t)\,dt + b(t)\,dW(t). \tag{A.14}$$

The last expression is also called the stochastic differential equation describing $X(t)$.

For stochastic processes we have the following generalization of the chain rule:

Theorem A.2 ((Itô's lemma)) *Let $X(t)$ be an Itô process given by (A.14) and $f(t, X)$ a smooth function. Then $f(t, X(t))$ has the differential*

$$df(t, X(t)) = \frac{\partial f(t, X(t))}{\partial t}\,dt + a\frac{\partial f(t, X(t))}{\partial X}\,dX(t) + \frac{1}{2}\frac{\partial^2 f(t, X(t))}{\partial X^2}\,b^2(t)\,dt \tag{A.15}$$

$$= \left(\frac{\partial f}{\partial t} + a\frac{\partial f}{\partial X} + \frac{1}{2}b^2\frac{\partial^2 f}{\partial X^2}\right)dt + b\frac{\partial f}{\partial X}\,dW(t).$$

Example: In many financial applications we model a price $S(t)$ as the exponential $S(t) = \exp(X(t))$, where $X(t)$ is a Brownian motion with drift given by the Itô process

$$dX(t) = \tilde{\mu}dt + \sigma dW(t).$$

Now we can use Itô's lemma to find the stochastic differential equation describing $S(t)$:

$$dS(t) = de^{X(t)} = e^{X(t)}dX(t) + \frac{1}{2}\sigma^2 e^{X(t)}dt = \left(\tilde{\mu} + \frac{1}{2}\sigma^2\right)S(t)dt + \sigma S(t)dW(t).$$

Thus, writing $\mu = \tilde{\mu} + \frac{1}{2}\sigma^2$ we find the well-known Black–Scholes model

$$\frac{dS(t)}{S(t)} = \mu dt + \sigma dW(t).$$

Itô's lemma can be generalised to multiple dimensions.

A.2.4 The Feynman–Kac Theorem

By general option pricing theory, the fair value of an option is given as the conditional expectation of the discounted payoff $h(S(T))$, which often is a function of the stock price at the option's maturity date T (see section 3.1.5):

$$U = e^{-r(T-t)}\mathbb{E}_t\left[h(S(T))\right].$$

Therefore, a typical task is to evaluate such a conditional expectation either analytically or numerically. An important tool for this purpose is the following theorem:

Theorem A.3 (Feynman–Kac) *Let $u(t, x)$ be defined as the conditional expectation*

$$u(t, x) = \mathbb{E}_t\left[h(X(T))|X(t) = x\right],$$

where $X(t)$ is an Itô process of the form

$$dX(t) = a(X(t))dt + b(X(t))dW(t)$$

with $X(t) = x$. Then $u(t, x)$ satisfies the partial differential equation

$$\frac{\partial u(t, x)}{\partial t} + a\frac{\partial u(t, x)}{\partial x} + \frac{1}{2}b^2\frac{\partial^2 u(t, x)}{\partial x^2} = 0$$

with terminal value

$$u(T, x) = h(x) \quad \text{for all } x.$$

The terminal value problem given in theorem A.3 can be solved numerically using standard finite-differences methods (explicit, implicit, Crank–Nicolson) for parabolic partial differential equations.

Example: An example of the Feynman–Kac theorem is the Black–Scholes equation, where the spot price with risk-neutral drift is given by the stochastic model

$$dS(t) = rS(t)dt + \sigma S(t)dW(t).$$

The price of a European option is given by the conditional expectation

$$u(t, S) = e^{-r(T-t)}\mathbb{E}_t\left[h(S(T))\right].$$

By the Feynman theorem, the conditional expectation $v(t, S) = \mathbb{E}_t[h(S(T))]$ satisfies the partial differential equation

$$\frac{\partial v(t, S)}{\partial t} + rS\frac{\partial v(t, S)}{\partial S} + \frac{1}{2}\sigma^2 S^2\frac{\partial^2 v(t, S)}{\partial S^2} = 0$$

with terminal value $v(T, S) = h(S)$. Now we use the relation $v(t, S) = e^{r(T-t)}u(t, S)$, to make the substitutions

$$\frac{\partial v(t, S)}{\partial t} = -re^{r(T-t)}u(t, S) + e^{r(T-t)}\frac{\partial u(t, S)}{\partial t}$$

$$\frac{\partial v(t, S)}{\partial S} = e^{r(T-t)}\frac{\partial u(t, S)}{\partial S}$$

$$\frac{\partial^2 v(t, S)}{\partial S^2} = e^{r(T-t)}\frac{\partial^2 u(t, S)}{\partial S^2}$$

and arrive at the Black–Scholes equation

$$\frac{\partial u(t, S)}{\partial t} + rS\frac{\partial u(t, S)}{\partial S} + \frac{1}{2}\sigma^2 S^2\frac{\partial^2 u(t, S)}{\partial S^2} - ru(t, S) = 0$$

with terminal value $u(T, S) = h(S)$.

A.2.5   Monte Carlo Simulation

The Monte Carlo method can be used to calculate numerical approximations of an expectation value $\mathbb{E}[X]$. Since the fair value U of an option is given as the conditional expectation of the discounted payoff H (see section 3.1.5):

$$U = e^{-r(T-t)}\mathbb{E}_t[H],$$

the Monte Carlo method has an immediate application to option pricing problems. Monte Carlo methods in their basic form are easy to implement and are mainly used in the following situations:

- The stochastic model for the underlying is complex such that analytical or other numerical methods (tree, PDE) are not available or not efficient.
- The payoff H depends on underlying prices at different times. Examples for such path-dependent options are Asian options.

- The option has multiple underlyings $S_1(t), \ldots, S_n(t)$. For $n > 3$ other numerical methods, such as tree or PDE methods, become inefficient.

To use a Monte Carlo approach for options with early exercise rights (American options) one needs extensions to the classical Monte Carlo method. One example of such an extension is given in Longstaff and Schwartz (2001).

The basic Monte Carlo method for an option with maturity T and payoff function H depending on the underlying price at different times,

$$H = H(S(T_1), \ldots, S(T_n)),$$

consists of the following steps:

1. Compute N sample paths $S^{(1)}(t), \ldots, S^{(N)}(t)$ evaluated at times $T_1, \ldots, T_n$ for evaluating the option payoff. For the ith path, we have the values $S^{(i)}(T_1), \ldots, S^{(i)}(T_n)$. In total, these are $N \times n$ values.
2. Compute the sample option payoffs discounted to time t:

$$U^{(i)} = e^{-r(T-t)} H(S^{(i)}(T_1), \ldots, S^{(i)}(T_n)).$$

3. The Monte Carlo estimate of the option price at time t is the average

$$\hat{U} = \frac{1}{N} \sum_{i=1}^{N} U^{(i)}.$$

The standard estimation error can be calculated as follows: Let

$$s_U^2 = \frac{1}{N-1} \sum_{i=1}^{N} \left(U^{(i)} - \hat{U} \right)^2$$

be the variance estimator of the sample option values. Then the standard pricing error of the Monte Carlo approximation is

$$\epsilon_U = \frac{s_U}{\sqrt{N}}. \tag{A.16}$$

Asymptotically, the error is of order $1/\sqrt{N}$ meaning that to reduce the error by a factor $1/2$, the number of sample paths has to increase by a factor 4. Compared to other numerical methods (e.g. PDE solvers) the convergence with $1/\sqrt{N}$ is rather slow and achieving a good accuracy may require a large number of sample paths. An approach to reduce the number of samples needed and thereby to reduce the computing time is to reduce the variance of the sample option values s_U^2. The following two *variance reduction* methods are frequently used:

- *Antithetic paths*: Let the sample value $U_+^{(i)}$ be generated by the normally distributed random numbers $\epsilon_1^{(i)}, \ldots, \epsilon_n^{(i)}$. Then $-\epsilon_1^{(i)}, \ldots, -\epsilon_n^{(i)}$ give rise to a different sample path (the *antithetic path*) with sample value $U_-^{(i)}$. Using $U_+^{(i)}$ and $U_-^{(i)}$ as sample paths doubles the number of sample paths without having to generate new random numbers.

Additionally, the use of antithetic paths often decreases the variance s_U^2 of the sample option values. By equation (A.16) this reduces the approximation error for a given number of sample paths.

- *Control variates*: A very efficient way to reduce the variance s_U^2 in equation (A.16) is to use the Monte Carlo method not for the option itself but for the difference between the option and a similar option (the *control variate*) for which an exact analytical solution is known. Let V be such a control variate and $Z = U - V$ be the difference for which the Monte Carlo method yields an estimate $\hat{Z}$. Then the option price approximation is given by

$$\hat{U} = V + \hat{Z}.$$

A typical example is to use a geometric average Asian option, for which an analytical solution is known, as a control variate to the arithmetic average Asian option (see section 2.3.2).

Bibliography

Alexander, C. (2001) *Market Models: A Guide to Financial Data Analysis*. John Wiley & Sons Ltd.

Bachelier, L. (1900) Théorie de la spéculation. *Ann. Sci. Ecole Norm. Sup.*, 17:21–86.

Basel Committee on Banking Supervision. Amendment to the capital accord to incorporate market risks, 2005 http://www.bis.org.

Baxter, M. and Rennie, A. (1996) *Financial Calculus*. Cambridge University Press.

Bessembinder, H. and Lemmon, M. L. (2002) Equilibrium pricing and optimal hedging in electricity forward markets. *Journal of Finance*, 57(3):1347–1382.

Bhattacharya, K., Bollen, M. H., and Daalder, J. E. (2001) *Operation of Restructured Power Systems*. Kluwer, Boston.

Bingham, N. H. and Kiesel, R. (2004) *Risk-Neutral Valuation. Pricing and Hedging of Financial Derivatives*. Springer Finance. Springer, Berlin, 2nd edition.

Black, F. (1976) The pricing of commodity contracts. *Journal of Financial Economics*, 3.

Black, F. and Scholes, M. (1973) The pricing of options and corporate liabilities. *Journal of Political Economy*, 81:637–659.

Boerger, R. H. Cartea, A., Kiesel, R., and Schindlmayr, G. (2007) A multivariate commodity analysis and applications to risk management. *SSRN eLibrary* Working Paper.

Bollerslev, T. (1986) Generalized autoregressive conditional heteroskedasticity. *Journal of Econometrics*, 31:307–327.

Bompard, E., Correia, P., Gross, G., and Amelin, M. (2003) Congestion-management schemes: a comparative analysis under a unified framework. *IEE Transactions on Power Systems*, 18:346–352.

Boogert, A. and de Jong, C. (2006) Gas storage valuation using a Monte Carlo method Birkbeck Working Papers in Economics & Finance.

Boogert, A. and Dupont, D. (2005) On the effectiveness of the anti-gaming policy between the day-ahead and real-time electricity markets in The Netherlands. *Energy Economics*, 27:752–770.

BP. (2006) *Statistical Review of World Energy*.

Brockwell, P. J. and Davis, R. A. (2002) *Introduction to Time Series and Forecasting*. Springer Series in Statistics. Springer, Berlin, 2nd edition.

Burger, M., Klar, B., Müller, A., and Schindlmayr, G. (2004) A spot market model for pricing derivatives in electricity markets. *Quantitative Finance*, 4:109–122.

Bye, T. (2003) A Nordic energy market under stress. *Economic Survey from Statistics Norway*, (4):26–37, 2003. http://www.ssb.no/english/subjects/08/05/10/es/200304/bye.pdf.

Carr, P., Geman, H., and Madan, D. (2001) Pricing and hedging in incomplete markets. *Journal of Financial Economics*, 62:131–169.

Chong, E. K. P. and Zak, S. H. (2001) *An Introduction to Optimization*. John Wiley & Sons, 2nd edition.

Clewlow, L. and Strickland, C. (2000) *Energy Derivatives*. Lacima Publications.

Cox, J. C., Ingersoll, J. E., and Ross, S. A. (1985) A theory of the term structure of interest rates. *Econometrica*, 385–407.

Crotogino, F., Mohmeyer, K.-U., and Scharf, R. (2001) Huntorf CAES: more than 20 years of successful operation. In *SMRI Spring Meeting 2001, Orlando, 23–24.04.2001*, 351–357. http://www.kbbnet.de.

Deng, S. (2000) Stochastic models of energy commodity prices and their applications: mean-reversion with jumps and spikes. Working Paper.

Ellersdorfer, I. (August 2005) A multi-regional two-stage Cournot model for analyzing competition in the German electricity market. In *Proceedings of the 7th IAEE European Energy Conference, Bergen, 28–30*. http://elib.uni-stuttgart. de/opus/volltexte/2005/2450/.

Energy Information Administration. International Energy Outlook 2006. Technical report, US Department of Energy, 2006. http://www.eia.doe.gov/oiaf/ieo/index.html.

Eni S.p.A. (2006) World oil and gas review. http://www.eni.it.

ETSO. *Comparison on Transmission Pricing in Europe: Synthesis 2004*. ETSO Tariffs Task Force, Brussels, 2005. http://www.etso-net.org/activities/ tariff_benchmarking/e_default.asp.

European Commission. *Environmental Fact Sheet: Climate Change*. Brussels, 2005a. http://ec.europa. eu/environment/climat/pdf/cc_factsheet_aug2005.pdf.

European Commission. *The Support of Electricity from Renewable Energy Sources*. Commission of the European Communities, Brussels, 2005b. http://europa.eu.int/comm/energy/res/biomass_ action_plan/doc/2005_12_07_comm_biomass_electricity_en.pdf.

European Environment Agency. *Greenhouse Gas Emission Trends and Projections in Europe 2006*. Copenhagen, 2006.

European Parliament and the Council. Directive 2001/77/ec of the European Parliament and of the Council of 27 September 2001 on the promotion of electricity produced from renewable energy sources in the internal electricity market. *Official Journal of the European Communities L*, 283:33–40, 2001.

Eydeland, A. and Wolyniec, K. (2003) *Energy and Power Risk Management*. John Wiley & Sons.

Geman, H. (2005) *Commodities and Commodity Derivatives*. John Wiley & Sons.

Geman, H. and Vasicek, O. (2001) Forwards and futures on non storable commodities: the case of electricity. *RISK*, 14.

Graeber, B. (2002) *Grenzübergreifende integrierte Elektrizitätsplanung im südlichen Afrika (PhD thesis)*. Universität Stuttgart, Stuttgart, http://elib.uni-stuttgart.de/opus/volltexte/ 2002/1132/.

Graeber, B., Spalding-Fecher, R., and Gonah, B. (2005) Optimising trans-national power generation and transmission investments: a Southern African example. *Energy Policy*, 33: 2337–2349.

Grobbel, C. (1999) *Competition in Electricity Generation in Germany and Neighboring Countries form a System Dynamics Perspective. Outlook until 2012*. Peter Lang, Frankfurt.

Guldimann, T. M. (1995) RiskMetrics – Technical Document. *Morgan Guaranty*.

Hamilton, J. D. (1994) *Time Series Analysis*. Princeton University Press, Princeton, New Jersey.

Harvey, A. C. (1991) *Forecasting, Structural Time Series Models and the Kalman Filter*. Cambridge University Press.

Heath, D. and Jara, D. (2000) Term structure models based on futures prices, Working Paper.

Heath, D., Jarrow, R. A., and Morton, A. (1992) Bond pricing and the term structure of interest rates: a new methodology. *Econometrica*, 60(1):77–105.

Heitsch, H. and Römisch, W. (2003) Scenario reduction algorithms in stochastic programming. *Computational Optimization and Applications*, 24:187–206.

Heston, S. L. (1993) A closed form solution for options with stochastic volatility with applications to bond and currency options. *Review of Financial Studies*, 6:327–343.

Hillier, F. S. and Lieberman, G. J. (2004) *Introduction to Operations Research*. McGraw-Hill.

Holton, G. A. (2003) *Value-at-Risk, Theory and Practice*. Academic Press.

Hull, J. C. (2005) *Options, Futures and Other Derivatives*. Prentice Hall, 6th edition.

International Energy Agency. *Power to Choose – Demand Response in Liberalised Electricity Markets*. Paris, 2003.

International Energy Agency. *Energy Statistics Manual*. Paris, 2004.

International Panel on Climate Change. *Climate Change 1995, the Science of Climate Change: Summary for Policymakers and Technical Summary of the Working Group I Report*. Geneva, 2005.

Johnson, B. and Barz, G. (1999) Selecting stochastic processes for modelling electricity prices. In *Energy Modelling and the Management of Uncertainty*, 3–22. Risk Books, London.

Jorion, P. (2001) *Value-at-Risk, the New Benchmark for Managing Financial Risk*. McGraw-Hill, 2nd edition.

J.P. Morgan. (1995) *RiskMetrics Monitor*.

Kalman, R. E. (1960) A new approach to linear filtering and prediction problems. *Journal of Basic Engineering, Transactions of the ASME Series D*, 82:35–45.

Kiesel, R., Schindlmayr, G. and Börger, R. (2006) A two-factor model for the electricity forward market, *SSRN eLibrary*, 2007, Working paper.

Lamberton, D., and Lapeyre, B. (1996) *Introduction to Stochastic Calculus Applied to Finance*. Chapman & Hall.

Longstaff, F. A. and Schwartz, E. S. (2001) Valuing American options by simulation: a simple least-squares approach. *The Review of Financial Studies*, 14(1):113–147.

Margrabe, W. (1978) The value of an option to exchange one asset for another. *Journal of Finance*, 33:177–186.

Meadows, D. H., Meadows, D. L., Randers, J., and Behrens, W. W. (1972) *The Limits of Growth: A Report for the Club of Rome's Project on the Predicament of Mankind*. Universe Books, New York.

Meller, E., Milojcic, G., Wodopia, F.-J., and Schöning, G., eds. (2006) *Jahrbuch der europäischen Energie- und Rohstoffwirtschaft 2007*. VGE Verlag, Essen, 114th edition.

Merton, R. C. (1976) Option pricing when underlying stock returns are discontinuous. *Journal of Financial Economics*, 3:125–144.

Musiela, M. and Rutkowski, M. (2004) *Martingale Methods in Financial Modelling*. Stochastic Modelling and Applied Probability. Springer, Berlin.

Osborne, M. J. (2003) *An Introduction to Game Theory*. Oxford University Press, New York.

Pearson, N. D. (1995) An efficient approach for pricing spread options. *Journal of Derivatives*, 3:76–91.

Perner, J. (2002) *Die langfristige Erdgasversorgung Europas: Analysen und Simulationen mit dem Angebotsmodell EUGAS (PhD thesis)*, volume 60 of *Schriften des Energiewirtschaftlichen Instituts*. Oldenbourg Industrieverlag, München.

Pilipovic, D. (1997) *Energy Risk: Valuing and Managing Energy Derivatives*. McGraw-Hill.

Pindyck, R. S. (2001) The dynamics of commodity spot and futures markets: a primer. Working Paper.

Pindyck, R. S. (2002) Volatility and commodity price dynamics, Working Paper.

Press, W. H., Teukolsky, S. A., Vetterling, W. T., and Flannery, B. P. (1992) *Numerical Recipes in C*. Cambridge University Press, 2nd edition.

Prokopczuk, M., Rachev, S., Schindlmayr, G., and Trück, S. (2007) Quantifying risk in the electricity business: a RAROC-based approach. *Energy Economics*, 29:1033–1049.

Sanchez, J. J. and Centeno, E. (August 2005) System dynamics for electricity generation expansion analysis. In *15th PSCC, Liege, 22–26*.

Scheib, P., Kalisch, F., and Graeber, B. (2006) *Analysis of a Liberalised German Gas Market. CNI Working Paper 2006–11*. Center for Network Industries and Infrastructure, Technische Universität Berlin.

Schiffer, H.-W. (2005) *Energiemarkt Deutschland*. TÜV-Verlag, Köln, 9th edition.

Schindlmayr, G. (2005) A regime-switching model for electricity spot prices. 10th Symposium on Banking, Finance and Insurance, University of Karlsruhe.

Schwartz, E. and Smith, J. E. (2000) Short-term variations and long-term dynamics in commodity prices. *Management Science*, 46:893–911.

Schwartz, E. S. (1997) The stochastic behavior of commodity prices: implications for valuation and hedging. *Journal of Finance*, 52(3):923–973.

Seeliger, A. (2006) *Entwicklung des weltweiten Erdgasangebots bis 2030 (PhD thesis)*, volume 61 of *Schriften des Energiewirtschaftlichen Instituts*. Oldenbourg Industrieverlag, München.

Sen, S. and Kothari, D. P. (1998) Optimal thermal generation unit commitment – a review. *Electric Power & Energy Systems*, 20:443–451.

Sheble, G. and Fahd, G. (1994) Unit commitment literature synopsis. *IEE Transactions on Power Systems*, 9:128–135.

Skantze, P., Gubina, A., and Ilic, M. (2000) Bid-based stochastic model for electricity prices: the impact of fundamental drivers on market dynamics, 2000. Report, MIT Energy Laboratory.

Sterman, J. D. (2000) *Business Dynamics: System Thinking and Modeling for a Complex World*. McGraw-Hill, Boston.

Stoft, S. (2002) *Power System Economics*. John Wiley & Sons, New York.

UNFCCC. *National Greenhouse Gas Inventory Data for the Period 1990–2004 and Status of Reporting*. UNFCCC Subsidiary Body for Implementation, Bonn, 2006.

United Nations Conference on Trade and Development. A survey of commodity risk management instruments, 1998. UNCTAD/COM/15/Rev.2.

von der Fehr, N.-H. M., Amundsen, E. S., and Bergman, L. (2005) The Nordic market: signs of stress? *The Energy Journal*, 26 (Special Issue):71–98.

Vorst, T. (1992) Prices and hedge ratios of average exchange rate options. *International Review of Financial Analysis*, 1(3):179–194.

Weber, C. (2005) *Uncertainty in the Electric Power Industry: Methods and Models for Decision Support*. Springer, New York.

Wilmott, P. (1998) *Derivatives*. John Wiley & Sons.

Winston, W. L. (2003) *Operations Research. Applications and Algorithms*. Duxbury Press.

Index